Struts 2 Design and Programming

A Tutorial

Budi Kurniawan

Struts Design and Programming: A Tutorial
Copyright © 2008 by Budi Kurniawan
First Edition: March 2008

ISBN: 978-0-9803316-0-8

Book and Cover Designer: Mona Setiadi

Technical Reviewer: Paul Deck
Indexer: Chris Mayle

Warning and Disclaimer
Every effort has been made to make this book as accurate as possible. The
author and the publisher shall have neither liability nor responsibility to any
person or entity with respect to any loss or damages arising from the
information in this book

Table of Contents

Introduction

Welcome to *Struts 2 Design and Programming: A Tutorial.*

Servlet technology and JavaServer Pages (JSP) are the main technologies for developing Java web applications. When introduced by Sun Microsystems in 1996, Servlet technology was considered superior to the reigning Common Gateway Interface (CGI) because servlets stay in memory after responding to the first requests. Subsequent requests for the same servlet do not require re-instantiation of the servlet's class, thus enabling better response time.

The problem with servlets is it is very cumbersome and error-prone to send HTML tags to the browser because HTML output must be enclosed in **String**s, like in the following code.

```
PrintWriter out = response.getWriter();
out.println("<html><head><title>Testing</title></head>");
out.println("<body style=\"background:#ffdddd\">");
...
```

This is hard to program. Even small changes in the presentation, such as a change to the background color, will require the servlet to be recompiled.

Sun recognized this problem and came up with JSP, which allows Java code and HTML tags to intertwine in easy to edit pages. Changes in HTML output require no recompilation. Automatic compilation occurs the first time a page is called and after it is modified. A Java code fragment in a JSP is called a scriptlet.

Even though mixing scriptlets and HTML seems practical at first thought, it is actually a bad idea for the following reasons:

- Interweaving scriptlets and HTML results in hard to read and hard to maintain applications.
- Writing code in JSPs diminishes the opportunity to reuse the code. Of course, you can put all Java methods in a JSP and include this page from

other JSPs that need to use the methods. However, by doing so you're moving away from the object-oriented paradigm. For one thing, you will lose the power of inheritance.

- It is harder to write Java code in a JSP than to do it in a Java class. Let's face it, your IDE is designed to analyze Java code in Java classes, not in JSPs.
- It is easier to debug code if it is in a Java class.
- It is easier to test business logic that is encapsulated in a Java class.
- Java code in Java classes is easier to refactor.

In fact, separation of business logic (Java code) and presentation (HTML tags) is such an important issue that the designers of JSP have tried to encourage this practice right from the first version of JSP.

JSP 1.0 allowed JavaBeans to be used for encapsulating code, thereby supported code and presentation separation. In JSP you use **<jsp:useBean>** and **<jsp:setProperty>** to create a JavaBean and set its properties, respectively.

Unfortunately, JavaBeans are not the perfect solution. With JavaBeans, method names must follow certain naming convention, resulting in occasionally clumsy names. On top of that, there's no way you can pass arguments to methods without resorting to scriptlets.

To make code and HTML tags separation easier to accomplish, JSP 1.1 defines custom tag libraries, which are more flexible than JavaBeans. The problem is, custom tags are hard to write and JSP 1.1 custom tags have a very complex life cycle.

Later an effort was initiated to provide tags with specific common functionality. These tags are compiled in a set of libraries named JavaServer Pages Standard Tag Libraries (JSTL). There are tags for manipulating scoped objects, iterating over a collection, performing conditional tests, parsing and formatting data, etc.

Despite JavaBeans, custom tags, and JSTL, many people are still using scriptlets in their JSPs for the following reasons.

- Convenience. It is very convenient to put everything in JSPs. This is okay if your application is a very simple application consisting of only one or two pages and will never grow in complexity.

- Shortsightedness. Writing code and HTML in JSPs seems to be a more rapid way of development. However, in the long run, there is a hefty price to pay for building your application this way. Maintenance and code readability are two main problems.
- Lack of knowledge.

In a project involving programmers with different skill levels, it is difficult to make sure all Java code goes to Java classes. To make scriptlet-free JSPs more achievable, JSP 2.0 added a feature that allows software architects to disable scriptlets in JSPs, thus enforcing the separation of code and HTML. In addition, JSP 2.0 provides a simpler custom tag life cycle and allows tags to be built in tag files, if effect making writing custom tags easier.

Why Servlets Are Not Dead

The advent of JSP was first thought to be the end of the day for servlets. It turned out this was not the case. JSP did not displace servlets. In fact, today real-world applications employ both servlets and JSPs. To understand why servlets did not become obsolete after the arrival of JSP, you need to understand two design models upon which you can build Java web applications.

The first design model, simply called Model 1, was born right after the JSP was made available. Servlets are not normally used in this model. Navigating from one JSP to another is done by clicking a link on the page. The second design model is named Model 2. You will learn shortly why Model 1 is not recommended and why Model 2 is the way to go.

The Problems with Model 1

The Model 1 design model is page-centric. Model 1 applications have a series of JSPs where the user navigates from one page to another. This is the model you employ when you first learn JSP because it is simple and easy. The main trouble with Model 1 applications is that they are hard to maintain and inflexible. On top of that, this architecture does not promote the division of labor between the page designer and the web developer because the developer is involved in both page authoring and business logic coding.

To summarize, Model 1 is not recommended for these reasons:

- Navigation problem. If you change the name of a JSP that is referenced by other pages, you must change the name in many locations.
- There is more temptation to use scriptlets in JSPs because JavaBeans are limited and custom tags are hard to write. However, as explained above, mixing Java code and HTML in JSPs is a bad thing.
- If you can discipline yourself to not write Java code in JSPs, you'll end up spending more time developing your application because you have to write custom tags for most of your business logic. It's faster to write Java code in Java classes.

Model 2

The second design model is simply called Model 2. This is the recommended architecture to base your Java web applications on. Model 2 is another name for the Model-View-Controller (MVC) design pattern. In Model 2, there are three main components in an application: the model, the view, and the controller. This pattern is explained in detail in Chapter 1, "Model 2 Applications."

Note
The term Model 2 was first used in the JavaServer Pages Specification version 0.92.

In Model 2, you have one entry point for all pages and usually a servlet or a filter acts as the main controller and JSPs are used as presentation. Compared to Model 1 applications, Model 2 applications enjoy the following benefits.

- more rapid to build
- easier to test
- easier to maintain
- easier to extend

Struts Overview

Now that you understand why Model 2 is the recommended design model for Java web applications, the next question you'll ask is, "How do I increase productivity?"

This was also the question that came to servlet expert Craig R. McClanahan's mind before he decided to develop the Struts framework. After some preliminary work that worked, McClanahan donated his brainchild to the Apache Software Foundation in May 2000 and Struts 1.0 was released in June 2001. It soon became, and still is, the most popular framework for developing Java web applications. Its web site is http://struts.apache.org.

In the meantime, on the same planet, some people had been working on another Java open source framework called WebWork. Similar to Struts 1, WebWork never neared the popularity of its competitor but was architecturally superior to Struts 1. For example, in Struts 1 translating request parameters to a Java object requires an "intermediary" object called the form bean, whereas in WebWork no intermediary object is necessary. The implication is clear, a developer is more productive when using WebWork because fewer classes are needed. As another example, an object called interceptor can be plugged in easily in WebWork to add more processing to the framework, something that is not that easy to achieve in Struts 1.

Another important feature that WebWork has but Struts 1 lacks is testability. This has a huge impact on productivity. Testing business logic is much easier in WebWork than in Struts 1. This is so because with Struts 1 you generally need a web browser to test the business logic to retrieve inputs from HTTP request parameters. WebWork does not have this problem because business classes can be tested without a browser.

A superior product (WebWork) and a pop-star status (Struts 1) naturally pressured both camps to merge. According to Don Brown in his blog (www.oreillynet.com/onjava/blog/2006/10/my_history_of_struts_2.html), it all started at JavaOne 2005 when some Struts developers and users discussed the future of Struts and came up with a proposal for Struts Ti (for Titanium), a code name for Struts 2. Had the Struts team proceeded with the original proposal, Struts 2 would have included coveted features missing in version 1, including extensibility and AJAX. On WebWork developer Jason Carreira's suggestion, however, the proposal was amended to include a merger with

Introduction

WebWork. This made sense since WebWork had most of the features of the proposed Struts Ti. Rather than reinventing the wheel, 'acquisition' of WebWork could save a lot of time.

As a result, internally Struts 2 is not an extension of Struts 1. Rather, it is a re-branding of WebWork version 2.2. WebWork itself is based on XWork, an open source command-pattern framework from Open Symphony (http://www.opensymphony.com/xwork). Therefore, don't be alarmed if you encounter Java types that belong to package **com.opensymphony.xwork2** throughout this book.

Note

In this book, Struts is used to refer to Struts 2, unless otherwise stated.

So, what does Struts offer? Struts is a framework for developing Model 2 applications. It makes development more rapid because it solves many common problems in web application development by providing these features:

- page navigation management
- user input validation
- consistent layout
- extensibility
- internationalization and localization
- support for AJAX

Because Struts is a Model 2 framework, when using Struts you should stick to the following unwritten rules:

- No Java code in JSPs, all business logic should reside in Java classes called action classes.
- Use the Expression Language (OGNL) to access model objects from JSPs.
- Little or no writing of custom tags (because they are relatively hard to code).

Upgrading to Struts 2

If you have programmed with Struts 1, this section provides a brief introduction of what to expect in Struts 2. If you haven't, feel free to skip this section.

- Instead of a servlet controller like the **ActionServlet** class in Struts 1, Struts 2 uses a filter to perform the same task.
- There are no action forms in Struts 2. In Struts 1, an HTML form maps to an **ActionForm** instance. You can then access this action form from your action class and use it to populate a data transfer object. In Struts 2, an HTML form maps directly to a POJO. You don't need to create a data transfer object and, since there are no action forms, maintenance is easier and you deal with fewer classes.
- Now, if you don't have action forms, how do you programmatically validate user input in Struts 2? By writing the validation logic in the action class.
- Struts 1 comes with several tag libraries that provides custom tags to be used in JSPs. The most prominent of these are the HTML tag library, the Bean tag library, and the Logic tag library. JSTL and the Expression Language (EL) in Servlet 2.4 are often used to replace the Bean and Logic tag libraries. Struts 2 comes with a tag library that covers all. You don't need JSTL either, even though in some cases you may still need the EL.
- In Struts 1 you used Struts configuration files, the main of which is called **struts-config.xml** (by default) and located in the **WEB-INF** directory of the application. In Struts 2 you use multiple configuration files too, however they must reside in or a subdirectory of **WEB-INF/classes**.
- Java 5 and Servlet 2.4 are the prerequisites for Struts 2. Java 5 is needed because annotations, added to Java 5, play an important role in Struts 2. Considering that Java 6 has been released and Java 7 is on the way at the time of writing, you're probably already using Java 5 or Java 6.
- Struts 1 action classes must extend **org.apache.struts.action.Action**. In Struts 2 any POJO can be an action class. However, for reasons that will be explained in Chapter 3, "Actions and Results" it is convenient to

extend the **ActionSupport** class in Struts 2. On top of that, an action class can be used to service related actions.

- Instead of the JSP Expression Language and JSTL, you use OGNL to display object models in JSPs.
- Tiles, which started life as a subcomponent of Struts 1, has graduated to an independent Apache project. It is still available in Struts 2 as a plug-in.

Overview of the Chapters

This book is for those wanting to learn to develop Struts 2 applications. However, this book does not stop short here. It takes the extra mile to teach how to design effective Struts applications. As the title suggests, this book is designed as a tutorial, to be read from cover to cover, written with clarity and readability in mind.

The following is the overview of the chapters.

Chapter 1, "Model 2 Applications" explains the Model 2 architecture and provides two Model 2 applications, one using a servlet controller and one utilizing a filter dispatcher.

Chapter 2, "Starting with Struts" is a brief introduction to Struts. In this chapter you learn the main components of Struts and how to configure Struts applications.

Struts solves many common problems in web development such as page navigation, input validation, and so on. As a result, you can concentrate on the most important task in development: writing business logic in action classes. **Chapter 3, "Actions and Results"** explains how to write effective action classes as well as related topics such as the default result types, global exception mapping, wildcard mapping, and dynamic method invocation.

Chapter 4, "OGNL" discusses the expression language that can be used to access the action and context objects. OGNL is a powerful language that is easy to use. In addition to accessing objects, OGNL can also be used to create lists and maps.

Struts ships with a tag library that provides User Interface (UI) tags and non-UI tags (generic tags). **Chapter 5, "Form Tags"** deals with form tags, the

UI tags for entering form data. You will learn that the benefits of using these tags and how each tag can be used.

Chapter 6, "Generic Tags" explains non-UI tags. There are two types of non-UI tags, control tags and data tags.

HTTP is type-agnostic, which means values sent in HTTP requests are all strings. Struts automatically converts these values when mapping form fields to non-**String** action properties. **Chapter 7, "Type Conversion"** explains how Struts does this and how to write your own converters for more complex cases where built-in converters are not able to help.

Chapter 8, "Input Validation" discusses input validation in detail.

Chapter 9, "Message Handling" covers message handling, which is also one of the most important tasks in application development. Today it is often a requirement that applications be able to display internationalized and localized messages. Struts has been designed with internationalization and localization from the outset.

Chapter 10, "Model Driven and Prepare Interceptors" discusses two important interceptors for separating the action and the model. You'll find out that many actions will need these interceptors.

Chapter 11, "The Persistence Layer" addresses the need of a persistence layer to store objects. The persistence layer hides the complexity of accessing the database from its clients, notably the Struts action objects. The persistence layer can be implemented as entity beans, the Data Access Object (DAO) pattern, by using Hibernate, etc. This chapter shows you in detail how to implement the DAO pattern. There are many variants of this pattern and which one you should choose depends on the project specification.

Chapter 12, "File Upload" discusses an important topic that often does not get enough attention in web programming books. Struts supports file upload by seamlessly incorporating the Jakarta Commons FileUpload library. This chapter discusses how to achieve this programming task in Struts.

Chapter 13, "File Download" deals with file download and demonstrates how you can send binary streams to the browser.

In **Chapter 14, "Security"** you learn how to configure the deployment descriptor to restrict access to some or all of the resources in your applications. What is meant by "configuration" is that you need only modify your deployment descriptor file—no programming is necessary. In addition, you learn how to use the **roles** attribute in the **action** element in your Struts configuration file. Writing Java code to secure web applications is also discussed.

Chapter 15, "Preventing Double Submits" explains how to use Struts' built-in features to prevent double submits, which could happen by accident or by the user's not knowing what to do when it is taking a long time to process a form.

Debugging is easy with Struts. **Chapter 16, "Debugging and Profiling"** discusses how you can capitalize on this feature.

Chapter 17, "Progress Meters" features the Execute and Wait interceptor, which can emulate progress meters for long-running tasks.

Chapter 18, "Custom Interceptors" shows you how to write your own interceptors.

Struts supports various result types and you can even write new ones. **Chapter 19, "Custom Result Types"** shows how you can achieve this.

Chapter 20, "Velocity" provides a brief tutorial on Velocity, a popular templating language and how you can use it as an alternative to JSP.

Chapter 21, "FreeMarker" is a tutorial on FreeMarker, the default templating language used in Struts.

Chapter 22, "XSLT" discusses the XSLT result type and how you can convert XML to another XML, XHTML, or other formats.

Chapter 23, "Plug-ins" discusses how you can distribute Struts modules easily as plug-ins.

Chapter 24, "The Tiles Plug-in" provides a brief introduction to Tiles 2, an open source project for laying out web pages.

Chapter 25, "JFreeChart Plug-ins" discusses how you can easily create web charts that are based on the popular JFreeChart project.

Chapter 26, "Zero Configuration" explains how to develop a Struts application that does not need configuration and how the CodeBehind plug-in makes this feature even more powerful.

AJAX is the essence of Web 2.0 and it is becoming more popular as time goes by. **Chapter 27, "AJAX"** shows Struts' support for AJAX and explains how to use AJAX custom tags to build AJAX components.

Appendix A, **"Struts Configuration"** is a guide to writing Struts configuration files.

Appendix B, "The JSP Expression Language" introduces the language that may help when OGNL and the Struts custom tags do not offer the best solution.

Appendix C, "Annotations" discusses the new feature in Java 5 that is used extensively in Struts.

Prerequisites and Software Download

Struts 2 is based on Java 5, Servlet 2.4 and JSP 2.0. All examples in this book are based on Servlet 2.5, the latest version of Servlet. (As of writing, Servlet 3.0 is being drafted.) You need Tomcat 5.5 or later or other Java EE container that supports Servlet version 2.4 or later.

The source code and binary distribution of Struts can be downloaded from here:

```
http://struts.apache.org/downloads.html
```

There are different ZIP files available. The **struts-*VERSION*-all.zip** file, where ***VERSION*** is the Struts version, includes all libraries, source code, and sample applications. Its size is about 86MB and you should download this if you have the bandwidth. If not, try **struts-*VERSION*-lib.zip** (very compact at 4MB), which contains the necessary libraries only.

Once you download a ZIP, extract it. You'll find dozens of JARs in the **lib** directory. The names of the JARs that are native to Struts 2 start with **struts2**. The name of each Struts JAR contains version information. For instance, the core library is packaged in the **struts2-core-*VERSION*.jar** file, where ***VERSION*** indicates the major and minor version numbers. For Struts 2.1.0, the core library name is struts2-core-2.1.0.jar.

There are also dependencies that come from other projects. The commons JAR files are from the Apache Jakarta Commons project. You must include these commons JARs. The **ognl-*VERSION*.jar** contains the OGNL engine, an important dependency. The **freemarker-*VERSION*.jar** contains the FreeMarker template engine. It is needed even if you use JSP as your view technology because FreeMarker is the template language for Struts custom tags. The **xwork-*VERSION*.jar** contains XWork, the framework Struts 2 depends on. Always include this JAR.

The only JARs you can exclude are the plug-in files. Their names have this format:

```
struts2-xxx-plugin-VERSION.jar
```

Here, *xxx* is the plug-in name. For example, the Tiles plug-in is packaged in the **struts2-tiles-plugin-*VERSION*.jar** file.

You do not need the Tiles JARs either unless you use Tiles in your application.

Sample Applications

The examples used in this book can be downloaded from this site.

```
http://jtute.com
```

The naming of these applications in each chapter follows this format:

```
appXXy
```

where *XX* is the two digit chapter number and *y* is a letter that represents the application order in the chapter. Therefore, the second application in Chapter 1 is **app01b**.

Tomcat 6 was used to test all applications. All of them were run on the author's machine on port 8080. Therefore, the URLs for all applications start with **http://localhost:8080**, followed by the application name and the servlet path.

Chapter 1
Model 2 Applications

As explained in Introduction, Model 2 is the recommended architecture for all but the simplest Java web applications. This chapter discusses Model 2 in minute detail and provides two Model 2 sample applications. A sound understanding of this design model is crucial to understanding Struts and building effective Struts applications.

Model 2 Overview

Model 2 is based on the Model-View-Controller (MVC) design pattern, the central concept behind the Smalltalk-80 user interface. As the term "design pattern" had not been coined yet at that time, it was called the MVC paradigm.

An application implementing the MVC pattern consists of three modules: model, view, and controller. The view takes care of the display of the application. The model encapsulates the application data and business logic. The controller receives user input and commands the model and/or the view to change accordingly.

Note
The paper entitled *Applications Programming in Smalltalk-80(TM): How to use Model-View-Controller (MVC)* by Steve Burbeck, Ph.D. talks about the MVC pattern. You can find it at http://st-www.cs.uiuc.edu/users/smarch/st-docs/mvc.html.

In Model 2, you have a servlet or a filter acting as the controller of the MVC pattern. Struts 1 employs a servlet controller whereas Struts 2 uses a filter. Generally JavaServer Pages (JSPs) are employed as the views of the application, even though other view technologies are supported. As the models, you use POJOs (POJO is an acronym for Plain Old Java Object).

POJOs are ordinary objects, as opposed to Enterprise Java Beans or other special objects. Figure 1.1 shows the diagram of a Model 2 application.

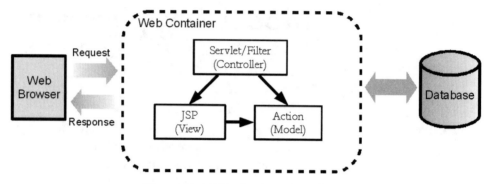

Figure 1.1: Model 2 architecture

In a Model 2 application, every HTTP request must be directed to the controller. The request's Uniform Request Identifier (URI) tells the controller what action to invoke. The term "action" refers to an operation that the application is able to perform. The POJO associated with an action is called an action object. In Struts 2, as you'll find out later, an action class may be used to serve different actions. By contrast, Struts 1 dictates that you create an action class for each individual action.

A seemingly trivial function may take more than one action. For instance, adding a product would require two actions:

1. Display the "Add Product" form to enter product information.
2. Save the data to the database.

As mentioned above, you use the URI to tell the controller which action to invoke. For instance, to get the application to send the "Add Product" form, you would use the following URI:

```
http://domain/appName/Product_input.action
```

To get the application to save a product, the URI would be:

```
http://domain/appName/Product_save.action
```

The controller examines every URI to decide what action to invoke. It also stores the action object in a place that can be accessed from the view, so that server-side values can be displayed on the browser. Finally, the controller uses a **RequestDispatcher** object to forward the request to the view (JSP). In the JSP, you use custom tags to display the content of the action object.

In the next two sections I present two simple Model 2 applications. The first one uses a servlet as the controller and the second one employs a filter.

Model 2 with A Servlet Controller

This section presents a simple Model 2 application to give you a general idea of what a Model 2 application looks like. In real life, Model 2 applications are far more complex than this.

The application can be used to enter product information and is named **app01a**. The user will fill in a form like the one in Figure 1.2 and submit it. The application will then send a confirmation page to the user and display the details of the saved product. (See Figure 1.3)

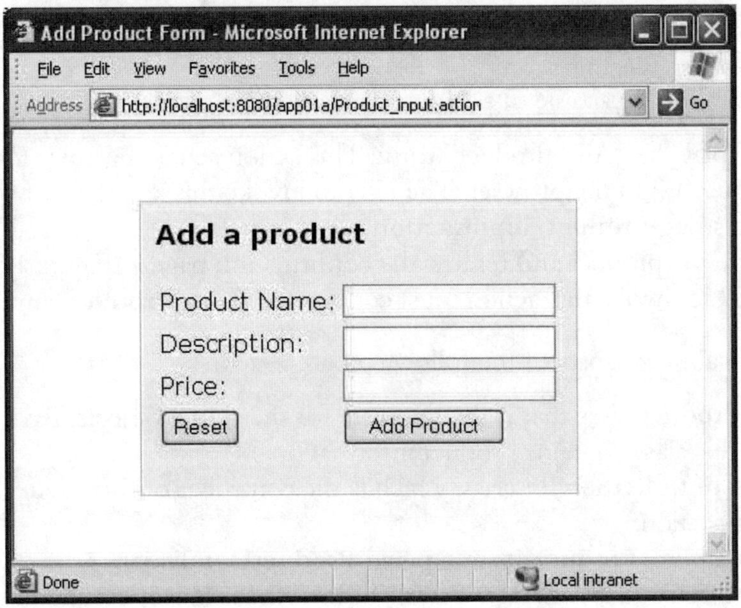

Figure 1.2: The Product form

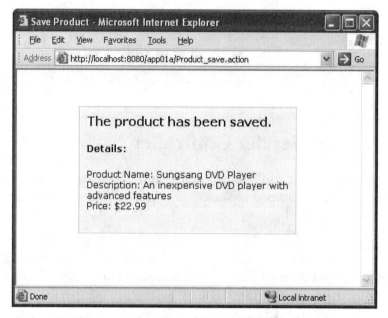

Figure 1.3: The product details page

The application is capable of performing these two actions:

1. Display the "Add Product" form. This action sends the entry form in Figure 1.2 to the browser. The URI to invoke this action must contain the string **Product_input.action**.
2. Save the product and returns the confirmation page in Figure 1.3. The URI to invoke this action must contain the string **Product_save.action**.

The application consists of the following components:

1. A **Product** class that is the template for the action objects. An instance of this class contains product information.
2. A **ControllerServlet** class, which is the controller of this Model 2 application.
3. Two JSPs (**ProductForm.jsp** and **ProductDetails.jsp**) as the views.
4. A CSS file that defines the styles of the views. This is a static resource.

The directory structure of this application is shown in Figure 1.4.

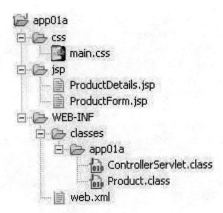

Figure 1.4: app01a directory structure

Let's take a closer look at each component in **app01a**.

The Product Action Class

A **Product** instance is a POJO that encapsulates product information. The **Product** class (shown in Listing 1.1) has three properties: **productName**, **description**, and **price**. It also has one method, **save**.

Listing 1.1: The Product class

```
package app01a;
import java.io.Serializable;

public class Product implements Serializable {
    private String productName;
    private String description;
    private String price;

    public String getProductName() {
        return productName;
    }
    public void setProductName(String productName) {
        this.productName = productName;
    }
    public String getDescription() {
        return description;
    }
    public void setDescription(String description) {
        this.description = description;
```

```
    }
    public String getPrice() {
        return price;
    }
    public void setPrice(String price) {
        this.price = price;
    }
    public String save() {
        // add here code to save the product to the database
        return "success";
    }
}
```

The ControllerServlet Class

The **ControllerServlet** class (presented in Listing 1.2) extends the **javax.servlet.http.HttpServlet** class. Both its **doGet** and **doPost** methods call the **process** method, which is the brain of the servlet controller. I know it's a bit weird that the class for a servlet controller should be called **ControllerServlet**, but I'm following the convention that says all servlet classes should end with **Servlet**.

Listing 1.2: The ControllerServlet Class

```
package app01a;
import java.io.IOException;
import javax.servlet.RequestDispatcher;
import javax.servlet.ServletException;
import javax.servlet.http.HttpServlet;
import javax.servlet.http.HttpServletRequest;
import javax.servlet.http.HttpServletResponse;

public class ControllerServlet extends HttpServlet {
    public void doGet(HttpServletRequest request,
            HttpServletResponse response)
            throws IOException, ServletException {
        process(request, response);
    }

    public void doPost(HttpServletRequest request,
            HttpServletResponse response)
            throws IOException, ServletException {
        process(request, response);
    }
```

```java
private void process(HttpServletRequest request,
        HttpServletResponse response)
        throws IOException, ServletException {

    String uri = request.getRequestURI();
    /*
     * uri is in this form: /contextName/resourceName,
     * for example: /app01a/Product_input.action.
     * However, in the case of a default context, the
     * context name is empty, and uri has this form
     * /resourceName, e.g.: /Product_input.action
     */
    int lastIndex = uri.lastIndexOf("/");
    String action = uri.substring(lastIndex + 1);
    // execute an action
    if (action.equals("Product_input.action")) {
        // there is nothing to be done
    } else if (action.equals("Product_save.action")) {
        // instantiate action class
        Product product = new Product();
        // populate action properties
        product.setProductName(
                request.getParameter("productName"));
        product.setDescription(
                request.getParameter("description"));
        product.setPrice(request.getParameter("price"));
        // execute action method
        product.save();
        // store action in a scope variable for the view
        request.setAttribute("product", product);
    }

    // forward to a view
    String dispatchUrl = null;
    if (action.equals("Product_input.action")) {
        dispatchUrl = "/jsp/ProductForm.jsp";
    } else if (action.equals("Product_save.action")) {
        dispatchUrl = "/jsp/ProductDetails.jsp";
    }
    if (dispatchUrl != null) {
        RequestDispatcher rd =
                request.getRequestDispatcher(dispatchUrl);
        rd.forward(request, response);
    }
}
```

```
}
```

The **process** method in the **ControllerServlet** class processes all incoming requests. It starts by obtaining the request URI and the action name.

```
String uri = request.getRequestURI();
int lastIndex = uri.lastIndexOf("/");
String action = uri.substring(lastIndex + 1);
```

The value of **action** in this application can be either **Product_input.action** or **Product_save.action**.

Note
The **.action** extension in every URI is the default extension used in Struts 2 and is therefore used here.

The **process** method then continues by performing these steps:

1. Instantiate the relevant action class, if any.
2. If an action object exists, populate the action's properties with request parameters. There are three properties in the **Product_save** action: **productName, description,** and **price**.
3. If an action object exists, call the action method. In this example, the **save** method on the **Product** object is the action method for the **Product_save** action.
4. Forward the request to a view (JSP).

The part of the **process** method that determines what action to perform is in the following **if** block:

```
// execute an action
if (action.equals("Product_input.action")) {
    // there is nothing to be done
} else if (action.equals("Product_save.action")) {
    // instantiate action class
    ...
}
```

There is no action class to instantiate for the action **Product_input**. For **Product_save**, the **process** method creates a **Product** object, populates its properties, and calls its **save** method.

```
Product product = new Product();
// populate action properties
```

```
product.setProductName(
        request.getParameter("productName"));
product.setDescription(
        request.getParameter("description"));
product.setPrice(request.getParameter("price"));
// execute action method
product.save();
// store action in a scope variable for the view
request.setAttribute("product", product);
}
```

The **Product** object is then stored in the **HttpServletRequest** object so that the view can access it.

The **process** method concludes by forwarding to a view. If **action** equals **Product_input.action**, control is forwarded to the **ProductForm.jsp** page. If **action** is **Product_save.action**, control is forwarded to the **ProductDetails.jsp** page.

```
// forward to a view
String dispatchUrl = null;
if (action.equals("Product_input.action")) {
    dispatchUrl = "/jsp/ProductForm.jsp";
} else if (action.equals("Product_save.action")) {
    dispatchUrl = "/jsp/ProductDetails.jsp";
}
if (dispatchUrl != null) {
    RequestDispatcher rd =
            request.getRequestDispatcher(dispatchUrl);
    rd.forward(request, response);
}
```

The Views

The application utilizes two JSPs for the views of the application. The first JSP, **ProductForm.jsp**, is displayed if the action is **Product_input.action**. The second page, **ProductDetails.jsp**, is shown for **Product_save.action**. **ProductForm.jsp** is given in Listing 1.3 and **ProductDetails.jsp** in Listing 1.4.

Chapter 1: Model 2 Applications

Listing 1.3: The ProductForm.jsp page

```
<html>
<head>
<title>Add Product Form</title>
<style type="text/css">@import url(css/main.css);</style>
</head>
<body>
<div id="global">
    <h3>Add a product</h3>
    <form method="post" action="Product_save.action">
    <table>
    <tr>
        <td>Product Name:</td>
        <td><input type="text" name="productName"/></td>
    </tr>
    <tr>
        <td>Description:</td>
        <td><input type="text" name="description"/></td>
    </tr>
    <tr>
        <td>Price:</td>
        <td><input type="text" name="price"/></td>
    </tr>
    <tr>
        <td><input type="reset"/></td>
        <td><input type="submit" value="Add Product"/></td>
    </tr>
    </table>
    </form>
</div>
</body>
</html>
```

Listing 1.4: The displaySavedProduct.jsp page

```
<html>
<head>
<title>Save Product</title>
<style type="text/css">@import url(css/main.css);</style>
</head>
<body>
<div id="global">
    <h4>The product has been saved.</h4>
    <p>
        <h5>Details:</h5>
        Product Name: ${product.productName}<br/>
```

```
        Description: ${product.description}<br/>
        Price: $${product.price}
    </p>
</div>
</body>
</html>
```

The **ProductForm.jsp** page contains an HTML form for entering a product's details. The **ProductDetails.jsp** page uses the JSP Expression Language (EL) to access the **product** scoped object in the **HttpServletRequest** object. Struts 2 does not depend on the EL to access action objects. Therefore, you can still follow the examples in this book even if you do not understand the EL.

The Deployment Descriptor

A servlet/JSP application, **app01a** needs a deployment descriptor (**web.xml** file). The one for this application is shown in Listing 1.5.

Listing 1.5: The deployment descriptor (web.xml) for app01a

```
<?xml version="1.0" encoding="ISO-8859-1"?>
<web-app xmlns="http://java.sun.com/xml/ns/javaee"
    xmlns:xsi="http://www.w3.org/2001/XMLSchema-instance"
    xsi:schemaLocation="http://java.sun.com/xml/ns/javaee
➡ http://java.sun.com/xml/ns/javaee/web-app_2_5.xsd"
    version="2.5">

    <servlet>
        <servlet-name>Controller</servlet-name>
        <servlet-class>app01a.ControllerServlet</servlet-class>
    </servlet>
    <servlet-mapping>
        <servlet-name>Controller</servlet-name>
        <url-pattern>*.action</url-pattern>
    </servlet-mapping>

    <!-- Restrict direct access to JSPs.
        For the security constraint to work, the auth-constraint
        and login-config elements must be present -->
    <security-constraint>
        <web-resource-collection>
            <web-resource-name>JSPs</web-resource-name>
            <url-pattern>/jsp/*</url-pattern>
        </web-resource-collection>
```

```
        <auth-constraint/>
    </security-constraint>

    <login-config>
        <auth-method>BASIC</auth-method>
    </login-config>
</web-app>
```

The deployment descriptor defines the **app01a.ControllerServlet** servlet and
names it **Controller**. The servlet can be invoked by any URL pattern that ends
with ***.action**. Requests for static resources, such as images and CSS files,
bypass the controller and are handled directly by the container.

In this application, as is the case for most Model 2 applications, you need
to prevent the JSPs from being accessed directly from the browser. There are a
number of ways to achieve this, including:

- Putting the JSPs under **WEB-INF**. Anything under **WEB-INF** or a
  subdirectory under **WEB-INF** is protected. If you put your JSPs under
  WEB-INF you cannot access them by using a browser, but the
  controller can still dispatch requests to those JSPs. However, this is not a
  recommended approach since not all containers implement this feature.
  BEA's WebLogic is an example that does not.
- Using a servlet filter and filter out requests for JSP pages.
- Using security restriction in your deployment descriptor. This is easier
  than using a filter since you do not have to write a filter class. This
  method is chosen for this application.

Using the Application

Assuming you are running the application on your local machine on port 8080,
you can invoke the application using the following URL:

```
http://localhost:8080/app01a/Product_input.action
```

You will see something similar to Figure 1.2 on your browser.

When you submit the form, the following URL will be sent to the server:

```
http://localhost:8080/app01a/Product_save.action
```

Model 2 with A Filter Dispatcher

While a servlet is the most common controller in a Model 2 application, a filter can act as a controller too. As a matter of fact, filters have life cycle methods similar to those of servlets. These are life cycle methods of a filter.

- **init**. Called once by the web container just before the filter is put into service.
- **doFilter**. Called by the web container each time it receives a request with a URL that matches the filter's URL pattern.
- **destroy**. Called by the web container before the filter is taken out of service, i.e. when the application is shut down.

There is one distinct advantage of using a filter over a servlet as a controller. With a filter you can conveniently choose to serve all the resources in your application, including static ones. With a servlet, your controller only handles access to the dynamic part of the application. Note that the **url-pattern** element in the **web.xml** file in the previous application is

```
<servlet>
    <servlet-name>Controller</servlet-name>
    <servlet-class>...</servlet-class>
</servlet>
<servlet-mapping>
    <servlet-name>Controller</servlet-name>
    <url-pattern>*.action</url-pattern>
</servlet-mapping>
```

With such a setting, requests for static resources are not handled by the servlet controller, but by the container. You wouldn't want to handle static resources in your servlet controller because that would mean extra work.

A filter is different. A filter can opt to let through requests for static contents. To pass on a request, call the **filterChain.doFilter** method in the filter's **doFilter** method. You'll learn how to do this in the application to come.

Consequently, employing a filter as the controller allows you to block all requests to the application, including request for static contents. You will then have the following setting in your deployment descriptor:

```
<filter>
```

```
    <filter-name>filterDispatcher</filter-name>
    <filter-class>...</filter-class>
</filter>
<filter-mapping>
    <filter-name>filterDispatcher</filter-name>
    <url-pattern>/*</url-pattern>
</filter-mapping>
```

What is the advantage of being able to block static requests? One thing for sure, you can easily protect your static files from curious eyes. The following code will send an error message if a user tries to view a JavaScript file:

```
public void doFilter(ServletRequest request, ServletResponse
        response, FilterChain filterChain) throws IOException,
        ServletException {
    HttpServletRequest req = (HttpServletRequest) request;
    HttpServletResponse res = (HttpServletResponse) response;
    String uri = req.getRequestURI();
    if (uri.indexOf("/css/") != -1
            && req.getHeader("referer") == null) {
        res.sendError(HttpServletResponse.SC_FORBIDDEN);
    } else {
        // handle this request
    }
}
```

It will not protect your code from the most determined people, but users can no longer type in the URL of your static file to view it. By the same token, you can protect your images so that no one can link to them at your expense.

On the other hand, using a servlet as the controller allows you to use the servlet as a welcome page. This is an important feature since you can then configure your application so that the servlet controller will be invoked simply by the user typing your domain name (such as http://example.com) in the browser's address box. A filter does not have the privilege to act as a welcome page. Simply typing the domain name won't invoke a filter dispatcher. In this case, you will have to create a welcome page (that can be an HTML, a JSP, or a servlet) that redirects to the default action.

The following example (**app01b**) is a Model 2 application that uses a filter dispatcher.

The directory structure of **app01b** is shown in Figure 1.5.

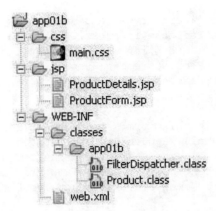

Figure 1.5: app01b directory structure

The JSPs and the **Product** class are the same as the ones in **app01a**. However, instead of a servlet as the controller, we have a filter called **FilterDispatcher** (given in Listing 1.6).

Listing 1.6: The FilterDispatcher class

```
package app01b;
import java.io.IOException;
import javax.servlet.Filter;
import javax.servlet.FilterChain;
import javax.servlet.FilterConfig;
import javax.servlet.RequestDispatcher;
import javax.servlet.ServletException;
import javax.servlet.ServletRequest;
import javax.servlet.ServletResponse;
import javax.servlet.http.HttpServletRequest;
import javax.servlet.http.HttpServletResponse;

public class FilterDispatcher implements Filter {
    private FilterConfig filterConfig;

    public void init(FilterConfig filterConfig) throws
        ServletException {
        this.filterConfig = filterConfig;
    }

    public void destroy() {
        this.filterConfig = null;
    }
```

```java
public void doFilter(ServletRequest request,
        ServletResponse response, FilterChain filterChain)
        throws IOException, ServletException {
    HttpServletRequest req = (HttpServletRequest) request;
    HttpServletResponse res = (HttpServletResponse) response;
    String uri = req.getRequestURI();
    /*
     * uri is in this form: /contextName/resourceName,
     * for example /app01b/Product_input.action
     * However, in the case of a default context,
     * the context name is empty, and uri has this form
     * /resourceName, e.g.: /Product_input.action
     */
    if (uri.endsWith(".action")) {
        // action processing
        int lastIndex = uri.lastIndexOf("/");
        String action = uri.substring(lastIndex + 1);
        if (action.equals("Product_input.action")) {
            // do nothing
        } else if (action.equals("Product_save.action")) {
            // instantiate action class
            Product product = new Product();
            // populate action properties
            product.setProductName(
                    request.getParameter("productName"));
            product.setDescription(
                    request.getParameter("description"));
            product.setPrice(request.getParameter("price"));
            // execute action method
            product.save();
            // store action in a scope variable for the view
            request.setAttribute("product", product);
        }

        // forward to a view
        String dispatchUrl = null;
        if (action.equals("Product_input.action")) {
            dispatchUrl = "/jsp/ProductForm.jsp";
        } else if (action.equals("Product_save.action")) {
            dispatchUrl = "/jsp/ProductDetails.jsp";
        }
        if (dispatchUrl != null) {
            RequestDispatcher rd = request
                    .getRequestDispatcher(dispatchUrl);
            rd.forward(request, response);
        }
```

```
    } else if (uri.indexOf("/css/") != -1
            && req.getHeader("referer") == null) {
        res.sendError(HttpServletResponse.SC_FORBIDDEN);
    } else {
        // other static resources, let it through
        filterChain.doFilter(request, response);
    }
  }
}
```

The **doFilter** method performs what the **process** method in **app01a** did,
namely

1. Instantiate the relevant action class, if any.
2. If an action object exists, populate the action's properties with request
   parameters.
3. If an action object exists, call the action method. In this example, the
   save method on the **Product** object is the action method for the
   Product_save action.
4. Forward the request to a view (JSP).

Note that since the filter captures all requests, including those for static
requests, we can easily add extra processing for CSS files. By checking the
referer header for requests for CSS files, a user will see an error message if he
or she types in the URL to the CSS file:

```
http://localhost:8080/app01b/css/main.css
```

The deployment descriptor is given in Listing 1.7.

Listing 1.7: The deployment descriptor for app01b

```xml
<?xml version="1.0" encoding="ISO-8859-1"?>
<web-app xmlns="http://java.sun.com/xml/ns/javaee"
    xmlns:xsi="http://www.w3.org/2001/XMLSchema-instance"
    xsi:schemaLocation="http://java.sun.com/xml/ns/javaee
➥ http://java.sun.com/xml/ns/javaee/web-app_2_5.xsd"
    version="2.5">

    <filter>
        <filter-name>filterDispatcher</filter-name>
        <filter-class>app01b.FilterDispatcher</filter-class>
    </filter>
    <filter-mapping>
        <filter-name>filterDispatcher</filter-name>
```

```
        <url-pattern>/*</url-pattern>
    </filter-mapping>

    <!-- Restrict direct access to JSPs.
        For the security constraint to work, the auth-constraint
        and login-config elements must be present -->
    <security-constraint>
        <web-resource-collection>
            <web-resource-name>JSPs</web-resource-name>
            <url-pattern>/jsp/*</url-pattern>
        </web-resource-collection>
        <auth-constraint/>
    </security-constraint>

    <login-config>
        <auth-method>BASIC</auth-method>
    </login-config>
</web-app>
```

To test the application, direct your browser to this URL:

```
http://localhost:8080/app01b/Product_input.action
```

Summary

In this chapter you learned the Model 2 architecture and how to write Model 2 applications, using either a servlet controller or a filter dispatcher. These two types of Model 2 applications were demonstrated in **app01a** and **app01b**, respectively.

Practically the filter dispatcher in **app01b** illustrates the main function of the Struts 2 framework. However, what you've seen does not cover even 0.1% of what Struts can do. You'll write your first Struts application in the next chapter and learn more features in subsequent chapters.

Chapter 2
Starting with Struts

In Chapter 1, "Model 2 Applications" you learned the advantages of the Model 2 architecture and how to build Model 2 applications. This chapter introduces Struts as a framework for rapid Model 2 application development. It starts with a discussion of the benefits of Struts and how it expedites Model 2 application development. It also discusses the basic components of Struts: the filter dispatcher, actions, results, and interceptors.

Introducing Struts configuration is another objective of this chapter. Most Struts application will have a **struts.xml** file and a **struts.properties** file. The former is the more important as it is where you configure your actions. The latter is optional as there exists a **default.properties** file that contains standard settings that work for most applications.

Note
Appendix A, "Struts Configuration" explains Struts configuration in detail.

The Benefits of Struts

Struts is an MVC framework that employs a filter dispatcher as the controller. When writing a Model 2 application, it is your responsibility to provide a controller as well as write action classes. Your controller must be able to do these:

1. Determine from the URI what action to invoke.
2. Instantiate the action class.
3. If an action object exists, populate the action's properties with request parameters.
4. If an action object exists, call the action method.
5. Forward the request to a view (JSP).

The first benefit of using Struts is that you don't have to write a controller and can concentrate on writing business logic in action classes. Here is the list of features that Struts is equipped with to make development more rapid:

- Struts provides a filter dispatcher, saving you writing one.
- Struts employs an XML-based configuration file to match URIs with actions. Since XML documents are text files, many changes can be made to the application without recompilation.
- Struts instantiates the action class and populates action properties with user inputs. If you don't specify an action class, a default action class will be instantiated.
- Struts validates user input and redirects user back to the input form if validation failed. Input validation is optional and can be done programmatically or declaratively. On top of that, Struts provides built-in validators for most of the tasks you may encounter when building a web application.
- Struts invokes the action method and you can change the method for an action through the configuration file.
- Struts examines the action result and executes the result. The most common result type, Dispatcher, forwards control to a JSP. However, Struts comes with various result types that allow you to do things differently, such as generate a PDF, redirect to an external resource, send an error message, etc.

The list shows how Struts can help you with the tasks you did when developing the Model 2 applications in Chapter 1, "Model 2 Applications." There is much more. Custom tags for displaying data, data conversion, support for AJAX, support for internationalization and localization, and extension through plug-ins are some of them.

How Struts Works

Struts has a filter dispatcher similar to that in **app01b**. Its fully qualified name is **org.apache.struts2.dispatcher.FilterDispatcher**. To use it, register it in the deployment descriptor (**web.xml** file) using this **filter** and **filter-mapping** elements.

```
<filter>
    <filter-name>struts2</filter-name>
    <filter-class>
        org.apache.struts2.dispatcher.FilterDispatcher
    </filter-class>
</filter>
<filter-mapping>
    <filter-name>struts2</filter-name>
    <url-pattern>/*</url-pattern>
</filter-mapping>
```

There's a lot that a filter dispatcher in a Model 2 application has to do and Struts' filter dispatcher is by no means an exception. Since Struts has more, actually much more, features to support, its filter dispatcher could grow infinitely in complexity. However, Struts approaches this by splitting task processing in its filter dispatcher into subcomponents called interceptors. The first interceptor you'll notice is the one that populates the action object with request parameters. You'll learn more about interceptors in the section "Interceptors" later in this chapter.

In a Struts application the action method is executed after the action's properties are populated. An action method can have any name as long as it is a valid Java method name.

An action method returns a **String** value. This value indicates to Struts where control should be forwarded to. A successful action method execution will forward to a different view than a failed one. For instance, the **String** "success" indicates a successful action method execution and "error" indicates that there's been an error during processing and an error message should be displayed. Most of the time a **RequestDispatcher** will be used to forward to a JSP, however JSPs are not the only allowed destination. A result that returns a file for download does not need a JSP. Neither does a result that simply sends a redirection command or sends a chart to be rendered. Even if an action needs to be forwarded to a view, the view may not necessarily be a JSP. A Velocity template or a FreeMarker template can also be used. Chapter 20, "Velocity" explains the Velocity templating language and Chapter 20, "FreeMarker" discusses FreeMarker.

Now that you know all the basic components in Struts, I'll continue by explaining how Struts works. Since Struts uses a filter dispatcher as its controller, all activities start from this object.

The Case for Velocity and FreeMarker

JSP programmers would probably mumble, "Why introduce new view technologies and not stick with JSP?" Good question. The answer is, while you can get away with just JSP, there's a compelling reason to learn Velocity and/or FreeMarker. Velocity and FreeMarker templates can be packaged in a JAR, which is how Struts plug-ins are distributed (Plug-ins are discussed in Chapter 23, "Plug-ins"). You cannot distribute JSPs in a JAR, at least not easily, although you'll find a way to do so if you're determined enough. For example, check out this thread in Sun's developer forum:

```
http://forum.java.sun.com/thread.jspa?threadID=5132356
```

Therefore, it makes sense to invest in Velocity or FreeMarker. FreeMarker is more advanced than Velocity, so if you can only afford to learn one new template language, go with FreeMarker. In fact, WebWork developers switched from Velocity to FreeMarker starting from WebWork version 2.2.

The first things that a filter dispatcher does is verify the request URI and determine what action to invoke and which Java action class to instantiate. The filter dispatcher in **app01b** did this by using a string manipulation method. However, this is impractical since during development the URI may change several times and you will have to recompile the filter each time the URI or something else changes.

For matching URIs with action classes, Struts uses a configuration file named **struts.xml**. Basically, you need to create a **struts.xml** file and place it under **WEB-INF/classes**. You define all actions in the application in this file. Each action has a name that directly corresponds to the URI used to invoke the action. Each action declaration may specify the fully qualified name of an action class, if any. You may also specify the action method name unless its name is **execute**, the default method name Struts will assume in the absence of an explicit one.

An action class must have at least one result to tell Struts what to do after it executes the action method. There may be multiple results if the action method may return different results depending on, say, user inputs.

The **struts.xml** file is read when Struts starts. In development mode, Struts checks the timestamp of this file every time it processes a request and will reload it if it has changed since the last time it was loaded. As a result, if you are in development mode and you change the **struts.xml** file, you don't need to restart your web container. Saving you time.

Configuration file loading will fail if you don't comply with the rules that govern the **struts.xml** file. If, or should I say when, this happens, Struts will fail to start and you must restart your container. Sometimes it's hard to decipher what you've done wrong due to unclear error messages. If this happens, try commenting out actions that you suspect are causing it, until you isolate and fix the one that is impending development.

Note
I'll discuss Struts development mode when discussing the Struts configuration files in the section "Configuration Files" later in this chapter.

Figure 2.1 shows how Struts processes action invocation. It does not include the reading of the configuration file, that only happens once during application launch.

For every action invocation the filter dispatcher does the following:

1. Consult the Configuration Manager to determine what action to invoke based on the request URI.
2. Run each of the interceptors registered for this action. One of the interceptors will populate the action's properties.
3. Execute the action method.
4. Execute the result.

Note that some interceptors run again after action method execution, before the result is executed.

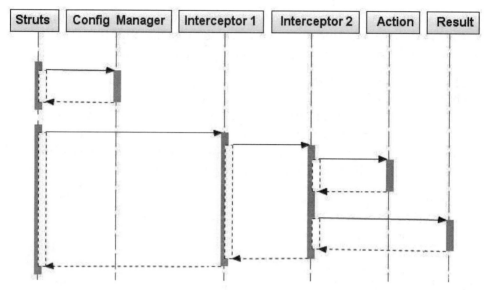

Figure 2.1: How Struts works

Interceptors

As mentioned earlier, there are a lot of things a filter dispatcher must do. Code that would otherwise reside in the filter dispatcher class is modularized into interceptors. The beauty of interceptors is they can be plugged in and out by editing the Struts' configuration file. Struts achieves a high degree of modularity using this strategy. New code for action processing can be added without recompiling the main framework.

Table 2.1 lists Struts default interceptors. The words in brackets in the Interceptor column are names used to register the interceptors in the configuration file. Yes, as you will see shortly, you need to register an interceptor in the configuration file before you can use it. For example, the registered name for the Alias interceptor is **alias**.

There are quite a number of interceptors, and this can be confusing to a beginner. The thing is you don't have to know about interceptors intimately before you can write a Struts application. Just know that interceptors play a vital role in Struts and we will revisit them one at a time in subsequent chapters.

Most of the time the default interceptors are good enough. However, if you need non-standard action processing, you can write your own interceptor. Writing custom interceptors is discussed in Chapter 18, "Custom Interceptors."

Interceptor	Description
Alias (alias)	Converts similar parameters that may have different names between requests.
Chaining (chain)	When used with the Chain result type, this interceptor makes the previous action's properties available to the current action. See Chapter 3, "Actions and Results" for details.
Checkbox (checkbox)	Handles check boxes in a form so that unchecked check boxes can be detected. For more information, see the discussion of the **checkbox** tag in Chapter 5, "Form Tags."
Cookie (cookie)	Adds a cookie to the current action.
Conversion Error (conversionError)	Adds conversion errors to the action's field errors. See Chapter 7, "Type conversion" for more details.
Create Session (createSession)	Creates an **HttpSession** object if one does not yet exist for the current user.
Debugging (debugging)	Supports debugging. See Chapter 16, "Debugging and Profiling."
Execute and Wait (execAndWait)	Executes a long-processing action in the background and sends the user to an intermediate waiting page. This interceptor is explained in Chapter 17, "Progress Meters."
Exception (exception)	Maps exceptions to a result. See Chapter 3, "Actions and Results" for details.
File Upload (fileUpload)	Supports file upload. See Chapter 12, "File Upload" for details.
I18n (i18n)	Supports internationalization and localization. See Chapter 9, "Message Handling."
Logger (logger)	Outputs the action name.
Message Store (store)	Stores and retrieves action messages or action errors or field errors for action objects whose classes implement **ValidationAware**.
Model Driven (modelDriven)	Supports for the model driven pattern for action classes that implement **ModelDriven**. See Chapter 10, "The Model Driven Pattern" for details.
Scoped Model Driven (scopedModelDriven)	Similar to the Model Driven interceptor but works for classes that implement **ScopedModelDriven**.

Parameters (params)	Populates the action's properties with the request parameters.
Prepare (prepare)	Supports action classes that implement the **Preparable** interface. See Chapter 10, "The Model Driven Pattern" for more details.
Scope (scope)	Provides a mechanism for storing action state in the session or application scope.
Servlet Config (servletConfig)	Provides access to the **Maps** representing **HttpServletRequest** and **HttpServletResponse**.
Static Parameters (staticParams)	Maps static properties to action properties.
Roles (roles)	Supports role-based action. See Chapter 14, "Security" for details.
Timer (timer)	Outputs the time needed to execute an action.
Token (token)	Verifies that a valid token is present. See Chapter 15, "Preventing Double Submits" for details.
Token Session (tokenSession)	Verifies that a valid token is present. See Chapter 15, "Preventing Double Submits" for details.
Validation (validation)	Supports input validation. See Chapter 8, "Input Validation" for details.
Workflow (workflow)	Calls the **validate** method in the action class.
Parameter Filter (n/a)	Removes parameters from the list of those available to the action.
Profiling (profiling)	Supports action profiling. See Chapter 16, "Debugging and Profiling" for details.

Table 2.1: Struts default interceptors

Struts Configuration Files

A Struts application uses a number of configuration files. The primary two are **struts.xml** and **struts.properties**, but there can be other configuration files. For instance, a Struts plug-in comes with a **struts-plugin.xml** configuration file. And if you're using Velocity as your view technology, expect to have a **velocity.properties** file. This chapter briefly explains the **struts.xml** and **struts.properties** files. Details can be found in Appendix A, "Struts Configuration."

Note

It is possible to have no configuration file at all. The zero configuration feature, discussed in Chapter 26, "Zero Configuration," is for advanced developers who want to skip this mundane task.

In **struts.xml** you define all aspects of your application, including the actions, the interceptors that need to be called for each action, and the possible results for each action.

Interceptors and result types used in an action must be registered before they can be used. Happily, Struts configuration files support inheritance and default configuration files are included in the **struts2-core-*VERSION*.jar** file. The **struts-default.xml** file, one of such default configuration files, registers the default result types and interceptors. As such, you can use the default result types and interceptors without registering them in your own **struts.xml** file, making it cleaner and shorter.

The **default.properties** file, packaged in the same JAR, contains settings that apply to all Struts applications. As a result, unless you need to override the default values, you don't need to have a **struts.properties** file.

Let's now look at **struts.xml** and **struts.properties** in more detail.

The struts.xml File

The **struts.xml** file is an XML file with a **struts** root element. You define all the actions in your Struts application in this file. Here is the skeleton of a **struts.xml** file.

```
<?xml version="1.0" encoding="UTF-8" ?>
<!DOCTYPE struts PUBLIC
    "-//Apache Software Foundation//DTD Struts Configuration 2.0//EN"
    "http://struts.apache.org/dtds/struts-2.0.dtd">
<struts>

...

</struts>
```

The more important elements that can appear between **<struts>** and **</struts>** are discussed next.

The package Element

Since Struts has been designed with modularity in mind, actions are grouped into packages. Think packages as modules. A typical **struts.xml** file can have one or many packages:

```
<struts>
    <package name="package-1" namespace="namespace-1"
            extends="struts-default">
        <action name="..."/>
        <action name="..."/>
            ...
    </package>
    <package name="package-2" namespace="namespace-2">
            extends="struts-default">
        <action name="..."/>
        <action name="..."/>
            ...
    </package>

        ...

    <package name="package-n" namespace="namespace-n">
            extends="struts-default">
        <action name="..."/>
        <action name="..."/>
            ...
    </package>
</struts>
```

A **package** element must have a **name** attribute. The **namespace** attribute is optional and if it is not present, the default value "/" is assumed. If the **namespace** attribute has a non-default value, the namespace must be added to the URI that invokes the actions in the package. For example, the URI for invoking an action in a package with a default namespace is this:

```
/context/actionName.action
```

To invoke an action in a package with a non-default namespace, you need this URI:

```
/context/namespace/actionName.action
```

A **package** element almost always extends the **struts-default** package defined in **struts-default.xml**. By doing so, all actions in the package can use the result types and interceptors registered in **struts-default.xml**. Appendix A, "Struts Configuration" lists all the result types and interceptors in **struts-default**. Here is the skeleton of the **struts-default** package. The interceptors have been omitted to save space.

```
<?xml version="1.0" encoding="UTF-8" ?>
<!DOCTYPE struts PUBLIC
    "-//Apache Software Foundation//DTD Struts Configuration 2.0//EN"
    "http://struts.apache.org/dtds/struts-2.0.dtd">

<struts>
    <package name="struts-default">
        <result-types>
            <result-type name="chain" class="com.opensymphony.
                ➥xwork2.ActionChainResult"/>
            <result-type name="dispatcher" class="org.apache.
                ➥struts2.dispatcher.ServletDispatcherResult"
                default="true"/>
            <result-type name="freemarker" class="org.apache.
                ➥struts2.views.freemarker.FreemarkerResult"/>
            <result-type name="httpheader" class="org.apache.
                ➥struts2.dispatcher.HttpHeaderResult"/>
            <result-type name="redirect" class="org.apache.struts2.
                ➥dispatcher.ServletRedirectResult"/>
            <result-type name="redirect-action" class="org.apache.
                ➥struts2.dispatcher.ServletActionRedirectResult"/>
            <result-type name="stream" class="org.apache.struts2.
                ➥dispatcher.StreamResult"/>
            <result-type name="velocity" class="org.apache.struts2.
                ➥dispatcher.VelocityResult"/>
            <result-type name="xslt" class="org.apache.struts2.
                ➥views.xslt.XSLTResult"/>
            <result-type name="plaintext" class="org.apache.struts2.
                ➥dispatcher.PlainTextResult"/>
        </result-types>

        <interceptors>

            [all interceptors]

        </interceptors>
    </package>
</struts>
```

The include Element

A large application may have many packages. In order to make the **struts.xml** file easier to manage for a large application, it is advisable to divide it into smaller files and use **include** elements to reference the files. Each file would ideally include a package or related packages.

A **struts.xml** file with multiple **include** elements would look like this.

```
<?xml version="1.0" encoding="UTF-8" ?>
<!DOCTYPE struts PUBLIC
    "-//Apache Software Foundation//DTD Struts Configuration 2.0//EN"
    "http://struts.apache.org/dtds/struts-2.0.dtd">

<struts>

    <include file="module-1.xml" />
    <include file="module-2.xml" />
    ...
    <include file="module-n.xml" />

</struts>
```

Each **module.xml** file would have the same **DOCTYPE** element and a **struts** root element. Here is an example:

```
<?xml version="1.0" encoding="UTF-8"?>
<!DOCTYPE struts PUBLIC
    "-//Apache Software Foundation//DTD Struts Configuration 2.0//EN"
    "http://struts.apache.org/dtds/struts-2.0.dtd">

<!-- file module-n.xml -->
<struts>
    <package name="test" extends="struts-default">
        <action name="Test1" class="test.Test1Action">
            <result>/jsp/Result1.jsp</result>
        </action>
        <action name="Test2" class="test.Test2Action">
            <result>/ajax/Result2.jsp</result>
        </action>
    </package>
</struts>
```

Note
Most sample applications in this book only have one **struts.xml** file. The only sample application that splits the **struts.xml** file into smaller files can be found in Chapter 25, "The JFreeChart Plug-in."

The action Element

An **action** element is nested within a **package** element and represents an action. An action must have a name and you may choose any name for it. A good name reflects what the action does. For instance, an action that displays a form for entering a product's details may be called **displayAddProductForm**. By convention, you are encouraged to use the combination of a noun and a verb. For example, instead of calling an action **displayAddProductForm**, name it **Product_input**. However, it is totally up to you.

An action may or may not specify an action class. Therefore, an **action** element may be as simple as this.

```
<action name="MyAction">
```

An action that does not specify an action class will be given an instance of the default action class. The **ActionSupport** class is the default action class and is discussed in Chapter 3, "Actions and Results."

If an action has a non-default action class, however, you must specify the fully class name using the **class** attribute. In addition, you must also specify the name of the action method, which is the method in the action class that will be executed when the action is invoked. Here is an example.

```
<action name="Address_save" class="app.Address" method="save">
```

If the **class** attribute is present but the **method** attribute is not, **execute** is assumed for the method name. In other words, the following **action** elements mean the same thing.

```
<action name="Employee_save" class="app.Employee" method="execute">
<action name="Employee_save" class="app.Employee">
```

The result Element

<result> is a subelement of **<action>** and tells Struts where you want the action to be forwarded to. A **result** element corresponds to the return value of an action method. Because an action method may return different values for different situations, an **action** element may have several **result** elements, each of which corresponds to a possible return value of the action method. This is to say, if a method may return "success" and "input," you must have two **result** elements. The **name** attribute of the **result** element maps a result with a method return value.

Note

If a method returns a value without a matching **result** element, Struts will try to find a matching result under the **global-results** element (See the discussion of this element below). If no corresponding **result** element is found under **global-results**, an exception will be thrown.

For example, the following **action** element contains two **result** elements.

```
<action name="Product_save" class="app.Product" method="save">
    <result name="success" type="dispatcher">
        /jsp/Confirm.jsp
    </result>
    <result name="input" type="dispatcher">
        /jsp/Product.jsp
    </result>
</action>
```

The first result will be executed if the action method **save** returns "success," in which case the **Confirm.jsp** page will be displayed. The second result will be executed if the method returns "input," in which case the **Product.jsp** page will be sent to the browser.

By the way, the **type** attribute of a **result** element specifies the result type. The value of the **type** attribute must be a result type that is registered in the containing package or a parent package extended by the containing package. Assuming that the action **Product_save** is in a package that extends **struts-default**, it is safe to use a Dispatcher result for this action because the Dispatcher result type is defined in **struts-default**.

If you omit the **name** attribute in a **result** element, "success" is implied. In addition, if the **type** attribute is not present, the default result type **Dispatcher** is assumed. Therefore, these two **result** elements are the same.

```
<result name="success" type="dispatcher">/jsp/Confirm.jsp</result>

<result>/jsp/Confirm.jsp</result>
```

An alternative syntax that employs the **param** element exists for the Dispatcher **result** element. In this case, the parameter name to be used with the **param** element is **location**. In other words, this **result** element

```
<result>/test.jsp</result>
```

is the same as this:

```
<result>
    <param name="location">/test.jsp</param>
</result>
```

You'll learn more about the **param** element later in this section.

The global-results Element

A **package** element may contain a **global-results** element that contains results that act as general results. If an action cannot find a matching result under its action declaration, it will search the **global-results** element, if any.

Here is an example of the **global-results** element.

```
<global-results>
    <result name="error">/jsp/GenericErrorPage.jsp</result>
    <result name="login" type="redirect-action">Login</result>
</global-results>
```

The Interceptor-related Elements

There are five interceptor-related elements that may appear in a **struts.xml** file: **interceptors, interceptor, interceptor-ref, interceptor-stack,** and **default-interceptor-ref.** They are explained in this section.

An **action** element must contain a list of interceptors that will process the action object. Before you can use an interceptor, however, you have to register it using an **interceptor** element under **<interceptors>**. Interceptors defined in a package can be used by all actions in the package.

For example, the following **package** element registers two interceptors, **validation** and **logger**.

```
<package name="main" extends="struts-default">
    <interceptors>
        <interceptor name="validation" class="..."/>
        <interceptor name="logger" class="..."/>
```

```
        </interceptors>
</package>
```

To apply an interceptor to an action, use the **interceptor-ref** element under the **action** element of that action. For instance, the following configuration registers four interceptors and apply them to the **Product_delete** and **Product_save** actions.

```
<package name="main" extends="struts-default">
    <interceptors>
        <interceptor name="alias" class="..."/>
        <interceptor name="i18n" class="..."/>
        <interceptor name="validation" class="..."/>
        <interceptor name="logger" class="..."/>
    </interceptors>

    <action name="Product_delete" class="...">
        <interceptor-ref name="alias"/>
        <interceptor-ref name="i18n"/>
        <interceptor-ref name="validation"/>
        <interceptor-ref name="logger"/>
        <result>/jsp/main.jsp</result>
    </action>

    <action name="Product_save" class="...">
        <interceptor-ref name="alias"/>
        <interceptor-ref name="i18n"/>
        <interceptor-ref name="validation"/>
        <interceptor-ref name="logger"/>
        <result name="input">/jsp/Product.jsp</result>
        <result>/jsp/ProductDetails.jsp</result>
    </action>
</package>
```

With these settings every time the **Product_delete** or **Product_save** actions are invoked, the four interceptors will be given a chance to process the actions. Note that the order of appearance of the **interceptor-ref** element is important as it determines the order of invocation of registered interceptors for that action. In this example, the **alias** interceptor will be invoked first, followed by the **i18n** interceptor, the **validation** interceptor, and the **logger** interceptor.

With most Struts application having multiple **action** elements, repeating the list of interceptors for each action can be a daunting task. In order to alleviate this problem, Struts allows you to create interceptor stacks that group

required interceptors. Instead of referencing interceptors from within each
action element, you can reference the interceptor stack instead.

For instance, six interceptors are often used in the following orders:
exception, **servletConfig**, **prepare**, **checkbox**, **params**, and
conversionError. Rather than referencing them again and again in your action
declarations, you can create an interceptor stack like this:

```
<interceptor-stack name="basicStack">
    <interceptor-ref name="exception"/>
    <interceptor-ref name="servlet-config"/>
    <interceptor-ref name="prepare"/>
    <interceptor-ref name="checkbox"/>
    <interceptor-ref name="params"/>
    <interceptor-ref name="conversionError"/>
</interceptor-stack>
```

To use these interceptors, you just need to reference the stack:

```
<action name="..." class="...">
    <interceptor-ref name="basicStack"/>
    <result name="input">/jsp/Product.jsp</result>
    <result>/jsp/ProductDetails.jsp</result>
</action>
```

The **struts-default** package defines several stacks. In addition, it defines a
default-interceptor-ref element that specifies the default interceptor or
interceptor stack to use if no interceptor is defined for an action:

```
<default-interceptor-ref name="defaultStack"/>
```

If an action needs a combination of other interceptors and the default stack,
you must redefine the default stack as the **default-interceptor-ref** element will
be ignored if an **interceptor** element can be found within an **action** element.

The param Element

The **param** element can be nested within another element such as **action**,
result-type, and **interceptor** to pass a value to the enclosing object.

The **param** element has a **name** attribute that specifies the name of the
parameter. The format is as follows:

```
<param name="property">value</param>
```

Used within an **action** element, **param** can be used to set an action property. For example, the following **param** element sets the **siteId** property of the action.

```
<action name="customer" class="…">
    <param name="siteId">california01</param>
</action>
```

And the following **param** element sets the **excludeMethod** of the validation **interceptor-ref**:

```
<interceptor-ref name="validation">
    <param name="excludeMethods">input,back,cancel</param>
</interceptor-ref>
```

The **excludeMethods** parameter is used to exclude certain methods from invoking the enclosing interceptor.

The constant Element

In addition to the **struts.xml** file, you can have a **struts.properties** file. You create the latter if you need to override one or more key/value pairs defined in the **default.properties** file, which is included in the **struts2-core-VERSION.jar** file. Most of the time you won't need a **struts.properties** file as the **default.properties** file is good enough. Besides, you can override a setting in the **default.properties** file using the **constant** element in the **struts.xml** file.

The **constant** element has a **name** attribute and a **value** attribute. For example, the **struts.devMode** setting determines whether or not the Struts application is in development mode. By default, the value is **false**, meaning the application is not in development mode.

The following **constant** element sets **struts.devMode** to **true**.

```
<struts>
    <constant name="struts.devMode" value="true"/>

    ...
</struts>
```

The struts.properties File

You create a **struts.properties** file if you need to override settings in the **default.properties** file. For example, the following **struts.properties** file overrides the value of **struts.devMode** in **default.properties**.

```
struts.devMode = true
```

A **struts.properties** file must reside in the classpath or in **WEB-INF/classes**. Appendix A, "Struts Configuration" provides the complete list of key/value pairs that may appear in a **struts.properties** file.

To avoid creating a new file, you can use **constant** elements in the **struts.xml** file. Alternatively, you can use the **init-param** element in the filter declaration of the Struts filter dispatcher:

```
<filter>
    <filter-name>struts</filter-name>
    <filter-class>
        org.apache.struts2.dispatcher.FilterDispatcher
    </filter-class>
    <init-param>
        <param-name>struts.devMode</param-name>
        <param-value>true</param-value>
    </init-param>
</filter>
```

A Simple Struts Application

Let's now rewrite **app01b** using Struts and call the new application **app02a**. You will use similar JSPs and an action class called **Product**.

The directory structure of **app02a** is given in Figure 2.2.

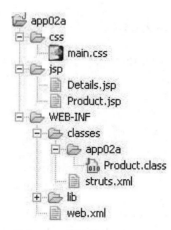

Figure 2.2: app02a directory structure

Each component of the application is discussed in the next sub-sections.

The Deployment Descriptor and the Struts Configuration File

The deployment descriptor is given in Listing 2.1 and the Struts configuration file in Listing 2.2.

Listing 2.1: The deployment descriptor (web.xml file)

```
<?xml version="1.0" encoding="ISO-8859-1"?>
<web-app xmlns="http://java.sun.com/xml/ns/javaee"
    xmlns:xsi="http://www.w3.org/2001/XMLSchema-instance"
    xsi:schemaLocation="http://java.sun.com/xml/ns/javaee
      ➥http://java.sun.com/xml/ns/javaee/web-app_2_5.xsd"
    version="2.5">

    <filter>
        <filter-name>struts2</filter-name>
        <filter-
    class>org.apache.struts2.dispatcher.FilterDispatcher</filter-
        class>
    </filter>
    <filter-mapping>
        <filter-name>struts2</filter-name>
        <url-pattern>/*</url-pattern>
    </filter-mapping>
```

```
<!-- Restrict direct access to JSPs.
     For the security constraint to work, the auth-constraint
     and login-config elements must be present -->
<security-constraint>
    <web-resource-collection>
        <web-resource-name>JSPs</web-resource-name>
        <url-pattern>/jsp/*</url-pattern>
    </web-resource-collection>
    <auth-constraint/>
</security-constraint>

<login-config>
    <auth-method>BASIC</auth-method>
</login-config>
</web-app>
```

Listing 2.2: The struts.xml

```
<?xml version="1.0" encoding="UTF-8" ?>
<!DOCTYPE struts PUBLIC
    "-//Apache Software Foundation//DTD Struts Configuration 2.0//EN"
    "http://struts.apache.org/dtds/struts-2.0.dtd">

<struts>
    <package name="app02a" namespace="/" extends="struts-default">
        <action name="Product_input">
            <result>/jsp/ProductForm.jsp</result>
        </action>

        <action name="Product_save" class="app02a.Product">
            <result>/jsp/ProductDetails.jsp</result>
        </action>
    </package>
</struts>
```

The **struts.xml** file defines a package (**app02a**) that has two actions,
Product_input and **Product_save**. The **Product_input** action does not have
an action class. Invoking **Product_input** simply forwards control to the
ProductForm.jsp page. This page contains an entry form for entering
product information.

The **Product_save** action has a non-default action class (**app02.Product**).
Since no **method** attribute is present in the action declaration, the **execute**
method in the **Product** class will be invoked.

Note

During development you can add these two constant elements on top of your package element.

```
<constant name="struts.enable.DynamicMethodInvocation"
        value="false" />
<constant name="struts.devMode" value="true" />
```

The first constant disables dynamic method invocation, explained in Chapter 3, "Actions and Results." The second **constant** element causes Struts to switch to development mode.

The Action Class

The **Product** class in Listing 2.3 is the action class for action **Product_save**. The class has three properties (**productName**, **description**, and **price**) and one action method, **execute**.

Listing 2.3: The Product action class

```
package app02a;
import java.io.Serializable;
public class Product implements Serializable {
    private String productName;
    private String description;
    private String price;

    public String getProductName() {
        return productName;
    }
    public void setProductName(String productName) {
        this.productName = productName;
    }
    public String getDescription() {
        return description;
    }
    public void setDescription(String description) {
        this.description = description;
    }
    public String getPrice() {
        return price;
    }
    public void setPrice(String price) {
        this.price = price;
```

```
    }
    public String execute() {
        return "success";
    }
}
```

Running the Application

This application is a Struts replica of the applications in Chapter 1. To invoke the first action, use the following URL (assuming Tomcat is used)

```
http://localhost:8080/app02a/Product_input.action
```

You will see something like Figure 1.2 in your browser. Enter values in the fields and submit the form. Your browser will display a confirmation message similar to Figure 1.3.

Congratulations. You've just seen Struts in action!

Dependency Injection

Before we continue, I'd like to introduce a popular design pattern that is used extensively in Struts: dependency injection. Martin Fowler wrote an excellent article on this pattern. His article can be found here:

```
http://martinfowler.com/articles/injection.html
```

Before Fowler coined the term "dependency injection," the phrase "inversion of control" was often used to mean the same thing. As Fowler notes in his article, the two are not exactly the same. This book therefore uses "dependency injection."

Overview

I'll explain dependency injection with an example.

If you have two components, **A** and **B**, and **A** depends on **B**, you can say **A** is dependent on **B** or **B** is a dependency of **A**. Suppose **A** has a method, **importantMethod**, that uses **B** as defined in the following code fragment:

```
public class A {
    public void importantMethod() {
        B b = ... // get an instance of B
        b.usefulMethod();
        ...
    }

    ...

}
```

A must obtain an instance of **B** before it can use **B**. While it is as straightforward as using the **new** keyword if **B** is a Java concrete class, it can be problematic if **B** is not and there are various implementations of **B**. You will have to choose an implementation of **B** and by doing so you reduce the reusability of A (you cannot use **A** with implementations of **B** that you did not choose).

As a more concrete example, consider the following **PersistenceManager** class that can be used to persist objects to a database.

```
public class PersistenceManager {
    public void store(Object object) {
        DataSource dataSource = ... // obtain DataSource
        try {
            Connection connection = dataSource.getConnection();

            ... // store object in the database

        } catch (SQLException e) {

        }

    }
}
```

PersistenceManager depends on **DataSource**. It has to obtain a **DataSource** before it can create a **Connection** object to insert data to the database. In a Java EE application, obtaining a data source often involves performing a JNDI lookup using the following boilerplate code:

```
DataSource dataSource = null;
try {
    context = new InitialContext();
    dataSource = (DataSource)
```

```
    context.lookup("java:/comp/env/jdbc/myDataSource");
} catch (NamingException e) {
}
```

Here is a problem. To perform a JNDI lookup you need a JNDI name.
However, there's no guarantee every application that uses
PersistenceManager will provide the same JNDI name. If you hard-code the
JNDI like I did in the code above, **PersistenceManager** will become less
reusable.

Dependency injection dictates that dependency should be injected to the
using component. In the context of the **PersistenceManager** example here, a
DataSource object should be passed to the **PersistenceManager** instead of
forcing **PersistenceManager** to create one.

One way to do it is by providing a constructor that accepts the
dependency, in this case a **DataSource**:

```
public class PersistenceManager {
    private DataSource dataSource;
    public PersistenceManager(DataSource dataSource) {
        this.dataSource = dataSource;
    }

    public void store(Object object) {
        try {
            Connection connection = dataSource.getConnection();

            ... // store object in the database

        } catch (SQLException e) {
        }
    }
}
```

Now, anyone who wants to use **PersistenceManager** must "inject" an
instance of **DataSource** through the **PersistenceManager** class's constructor.
PersistenceManager has now become decoupled from the **DataSource**
instance it is using, making **PersistenceManager** more reusable. The user of
PersistenceManager will likely be in a better position to provide a
DataSource than the author of **PersistenceManager** because the user will be
familiar with the environment **PersistenceManager** will be running on.

Forms of Dependency Injection

Injecting dependency through the constructor is not the only form of dependency injection. Dependency can also be injected through a setter method. Back to the **PersistenceManager** example, the class author may opt to provide this method:

```
public void setDataSource(DataSource dataSource) {
    this.dataSource = dataSource;
}
```

In addition, as explained in Fowler's article, you can also use an interface for dependency injection.

Struts uses setter methods for its dependency injection strategy. For example, the framework sets action properties by injecting HTTP request parameters' values. As a result, you can use an action's properties from within the action method, without having to worry about populating the properties.

Note

Java 5 EE supports dependency injection at various levels. Feel free to visit this site:

```
http://java.sun.com/developer/technicalArticles/J2EE/injection/
```

Summary

In this chapter you have learned what Struts offers to speed up Model 2 application development. You have also learned how to configure Struts applications and written your first Struts application.

Chapter 3
Actions and Results

As Struts ships with interceptors and other components that solve common problems in web application development, you can focus on writing business logic in the action class. This chapter discusses topics you need to know to write effective action classes, including the **ActionSupport** convenience class and how to access resources. In addition, it explains related subjects such as the standard result types, global exception mapping, wildcard mapping, and dynamic method invocation.

Action Classes

Every operation that an application can perform is referred to as an action. Displaying a Login form, for example, is an action. So is saving a product's details. Creating actions is the most important task in Struts application development. Some actions are as simple as forwarding to a JSP. Others perform logic that needs to be written in action classes.

An action class is an ordinary Java class. It may have properties and methods and must comply with these rules.

- A property must have a get and a set methods. Action property names follow the same rules as JavaBeans property names. A property can be of any type, not only **String**. Data conversion from String to non-String happens automatically.
- An action class must have a no-argument constructor. If you don't have a constructor in your action class, the Java compiler will create a no-argument constructor for you. However, if you have a constructor that takes one or more arguments, you must write a no-argument constructor. Or else, Struts will not be able to instantiate the class.

- An action class must have at least one method that will be invoked when the action is called.
- An action class may be associated with multiple actions. In this case, the action class may provide a different method for each action. For example, a **User** action class may have **login** and **logout** methods that are mapped to the **User_login** and **User_logout** actions, respectively.
- Since Struts 2, unlike Struts 1, creates a new action instance for every HTTP request, an action class does not have to be thread safe.
- Struts 2, unlike Struts 1, by default does not create an **HttpSession** object. However, a JSP does. Therefore, if you want a completely session free action, add this to the top of all your JSPs:

```
<%@page session="false"%>
```

The **Employee** class in Listing 3.1 is an action class. It has four properties (**firstName**, **lastName**, **birthDate**, and **emails**) and one method (**register**).

Listing 3.1: The Employee action class

```
package app03a;
import java.util.Collection;
import java.util.Date;

public class Employee {
    private String firstName;
    private String lastName;
    private Date birthDate;
    private Collection emails;

    public Date getBirthDate() {
        return birthDate;
    }
    public void setBirthDate(Date birthDate) {
        this.birthDate = birthDate;
    }
    public Collection getEmails() {
        return emails;
    }
    public void setEmails(Collection emails) {
        this.emails = emails;
    }
    public String getFirstName() {
        return firstName;
    }
```

```
public void setFirstName(String firstName) {
    this.firstName = firstName;
}
public String getLastName() {
    return lastName;
}
public void setLastName(String lastName) {
    this.lastName = lastName;
}

public String register() {

    // do something here
    return "success";
}
}
```

As you can see in Listing 3.1, an action class does not have to extend a certain parent class or implement an interface. Having said that, most of your action classes will implement the **com.opensymphony.xwork2.Action** interface indirectly by extending a convenience class named **ActionSupport**. I'll explain **ActionSupport** in the section "The ActionSupport Class" later in this chapter.

If you implement **Action**, you will inherit the following static fields:

- **SUCCESS**. Indicates that the action execution was successful and the result view should be shown to the user.
- **NONE**. Indicates that the action execution was successful but no result view should be shown to the user.
- **ERROR**. Indicates that that action execution failed and an error view should be sent to the user.
- **INPUT**. Indicates that input validation failed and the form that had been used to take user input should be shown again.
- **LOGIN**. Indicates that the action could not execute because the user was not logged in and the login view should be shown.

You need to know the values of these static fields as you will use the values when configuring results. Here they are.

```
public static final String SUCCESS = "success";
public static final String NONE = "none";
public static final String ERROR = "error";
public static final String INPUT = "input";
public static final String LOGIN = "login";
```

Note

One thing to note about the Struts action is you don't have to worry about how the view will access it. Unlike in the **app01a** and **app01b** applications where values had to be stored in scoped attributes so that the view could access them, Struts automatically pushes actions and other objects to the Value Stack, which is accessible to the view. The Value Stack is explained in Chapter 4, "OGNL."

Accessing Resources

From an action class, you can access resources such as the **ServletContext**, **HttpSession**, **HttpServletRequest**, and **HttpServletResponse** objects either through the **ServletActionContext** object or by implementing **Aware** interfaces. The latter is an implementation of dependency injection and is the recommended way as it will make your action classes easier to test.

This section discusses the techniques to access the resources.

The ServletActionContext Object

There are two classes that provide access to the aforementioned resources, **com.opensymphony.xwork2.ActionContext** and **org.apache.struts2.ServletActionContext**. The latter wraps the former and is the easier to use between the two. **ServletActionContext** provides the following static methods that you will often use in your career as a Struts developer. Here are some of them.

```
public static javax.servlet.http.HttpServletRequest getRequest()
```
Returns the current **HttpServletRequest**.

```
public static javax.servlet.http.HttpServletResponse getResponse()
```
Returns the current **HttpServletResponse** object.

```
public static javax.servlet.ServletContext getServletContext()
```
Returns the **ServletContext** object.

You can obtain the **HttpSession** object by calling one of the **getSession** methods on the **HttpServletRequest** object. The **HttpSession** object will be created automatically if you use the **basicStack** or **defaultStack** interceptor stack.

Note

You should not call the methods on the **ServletActionContext** from an action class's constructor because at this stage the underlying **ActionContext** object has not been passed to it. Calling **ServletActionContext.getServletContext** from an action's constructor will return null.

As an example, Listing 3.2 shows an action method that retrieves the **HttpServletRequest** and **HttpSession** objects through **ServletActionContext**.

Listing 3.2: Accessing resources through ServletActionContext

```
public String execute() {
    HttpServletRequest request = ServletActionContext.getRequest();
    HttpSession session = request.getSession();
    if (session.getAttribute("user") == null) {
        return LOGIN;
    } else {
        // do something
        return SUCCESS;
    }
}
```

Aware Interfaces

Struts provides four interfaces that you can implement to get access to the **ServletContext**, **HttpServletRequest**, **HttpServletResponse**, and **HttpSession** objects, respectively: The interfaces are

- org.apache.struts2.util.ServletContextAware
- org.apache.struts2.interceptor.ServletRequestAware
- org.apache.struts2.interceptor.ServletResponseAware
- org.apache.struts2.interceptor.SessionAware

I discuss these interfaces in the following subsections and provide an example of an action that implements these interfaces in the next section.

ServletContextAware

You implement the **ServletContextAware** interface if you need access to the **ServletContext** object from within your action class. The interface has one method, **setServletContext**, whose signature is as follows.

```
void setServletContext(javax.servlet.ServletContext servletContext)
```

When an action is invoked, Struts will examine if the associated action class implements **ServletContextAware**. If it does, Struts will call the action's **setServletContext** method and pass the **ServletContext** object prior to populating the action properties and executing the action method. In your **setServletContext** method you need to assign the **ServletContext** object to a class variable. Like this.

```
private ServletContext servletContext;
public void setServletContext(ServletContext servletContext) {
    this.servletContext = servletContext;
}
```

You can then access the **ServletContext** object from any point in your action class through the **servletContext** variable.

ServletRequestAware

This interface has a **setServletRequest** method whose signature is as follows.

```
void setServletRequest(javax.servlet.http.HttpServletRequest
    servletRequest)
```

Implementing **ServletRequestAware** allows you access to the **HttpServletRequest** object from within your action class. When an action is invoked, Struts checks to see if the action class implements this interface and, if it does, calls its **setServletRequest** method, passing the current **HttpServletRequest** object. Struts does this before it populates the action properties and before it executes the action method.

In the implementation of the **setServletRequest** method, you need to assign the passed **HttpServletRequest** object to a class variable:

```
private HttpServletRequest servletRequest;
public void setServletRequest(HttpServletRequest servletRequest) {
    this.servletRequest = servletRequest;
}
```

Now you can access the **HttpServletRequest** object via the **servletRequest** reference.

ServletResponseAware

The **setServletResponse** method is the only method defined in **ServletResponseAware**. Here is its signature.

```
void setServletResponse(javax.servlet.http.HttpServletResponse
        servletResponse)
```

Implement this interface if you need to access the **HttpServletResponse** object from your action class. When an action is invoked, Struts checks to see if the action class implements **ServletResponseAware**. If it does, Struts calls its **setServletResponse** method passing the current **HttpServletResponse** object. You need to assign the passed object to a class variable. Here is an example of how to do it.

```
private HttpServletResponse servletResponse;
public void setServletResponse(HttpServletResponse
        servletResponse) {
    this.servletResponse = servletResponse;
}
```

You can now access the **HttpServletResponse** object via the **servletResponse** variable.

SessionAware

If you need access to the **HttpSession** object from within your action class, implementing the **SessionAware** interface is the way to go. The **SessionAware** interface is a little different from its three other counterparts discussed earlier. Implementing **SessionAware** does not give you the current **HttpSession** instance but a **java.util.Map**. This may be confusing at first, but let's take a closer look at the **SessionAware** interface.

This interface only has one method, **setSession**, whose signature is this.

```
void setSession(java.util.Map map)
```

In an implementing **setSession** method you assign the **Map** to a class variable:

```
private Map session;
void setSession(Map map) {
```

```
        this.session = map;
}
```

Struts will call the **setSession** method of an implementing action class when the action is invoked. Upon doing so, Struts will pass an instance of **org.apache.struts2.dispatcher.SessionMap**, which extends **java.util.AbstractMap**, which in turn implements **java.util.Map**. **SessionMap** is a wrapper for the current **HttpSession** object and maintains a reference to the **HttpSession** object.

The reference to the **HttpSession** object inside **SessionMap** is protected, so you won't be able to access it directly from your action class. However, **SessionMap** provides methods that make accessing the **HttpSession** object directly no longer necessary. Here are the public methods defined in the **SessionMap** class.

```
public void invalidate()
```
Invalidates the current **HttpSession** object. If the **HttpSession** object has not been created, this method exits gracefully.

```
public void clear()
```
Removes all attributes in the **HttpSession** object. If the **HttpSession** object has not been created, this method does not throw an exception.

```
public java.util.Set entrySet() {
```
Returns a **Set** of attributes from the **HttpSession** object. If the **HttpSession** object is null, this method returns an empty set.

```
public java.lang.Object get(java.lang.Object key)
```
Returns the session attribute associated with the specified key. It returns null if the **HttpSession** object is null or if the key is not found.

```
public java.lang.Object put(java.lang.Object key,
        java.lang.Object value)
```
Stores a session attribute in the **HttpSession** object and returns the attribute value. If the **HttpSession** object is null, it will create a new **HttpSession** object.

```
public java.lang.Object remove(java.lang.Object key)
```
Removes the specified session attribute and returns the attribute value. If the **HttpSession** object is null, this method returns null.

For example, to invalidate the session object, call the **invalidate** method on the **SessionMap**:

```
if (session instanceof org.apache.struts2.dispatcher.SessionMap) {
    ((SessionMap) session).invalidate();
}
```

SessionMap.invalidate is better than **HttpSession.invalidate** because the former does not throw an exception if the underlying **HttpSession** object is null.

Note
Unfortunately, the **SessionMap** class does not provide access to the session identifier. In the rare cases where you need the identifier, use the **ServletActionContext** to obtain the **HttpSession** object.

Note
For this interface to work, the Servlet Config interceptor must be enabled. Since this interceptor is part of the default stack, by default it is already on.

Using Aware Interfaces to Access Resources

The **app03a** application shows how to use **Aware** interfaces to access resources. The application defines three actions as shown in Listing 3.3.

Listing 3.3: Action Declarations in app03a

```
<package name="app03a" extends="struts-default">
    <action name="User_input">
        <result>
            <param name="location">/jsp/Login.jsp</param>
        </result>
    </action>
    <action name="User_login" class="app03a.User" method="login">
        <result name="success">/jsp/Menu.jsp</result>
        <result name="input">/jsp/Login.jsp</result>
    </action>
    <action name="User_logout" class="app03a.User" method="logout">
        <result name="success">/jsp/Login.jsp</result>
    </action>
</package>
```

The **User_login** and **User_logout** actions are based on the **User** action class in Listing 3.4. This class has two properties (**userName** and **password**) and implements **ServletContextAware**, **ServletRequestAware**,

ServletResponseAware, and **SessionAware** to provide access to resources. Note that to save space the get and set methods for the properties are not shown.

Listing 3.4: The User class

```
package app03a;
import java.util.Map;
import javax.servlet.ServletContext;
import javax.servlet.http.HttpServletRequest;
import javax.servlet.http.HttpServletResponse;
import org.apache.struts2.dispatcher.SessionMap;
import org.apache.struts2.interceptor.ServletRequestAware;
import org.apache.struts2.interceptor.ServletResponseAware;
import org.apache.struts2.interceptor.SessionAware;
import org.apache.struts2.util.ServletContextAware;

public class User implements SessionAware, ServletRequestAware,
        ServletResponseAware, ServletContextAware {
    private String userName;
    private String password;
    private ServletContext servletContext;
    private HttpServletRequest servletRequest;
    private HttpServletResponse servletResponse;
    private Map sessionMap;

    // getters and setters not shown

    public void setServletRequest(
            HttpServletRequest servletRequest) {
        this.servletRequest = servletRequest;
    }
    public void setSession(Map map) {
        this.sessionMap = map;
    }
    public void setServletResponse(
            HttpServletResponse servletResponse) {
        this.servletResponse = servletResponse;
    }
    public void setServletContext(ServletContext servletContext) {
        this.servletContext = servletContext;
    }
    public String login() {
        String referrer = servletRequest.getHeader("referer");
        if (referrer != null && userName.length() > 0
                && password.length() > 0) {
```

```
        int onlineUserCount = 0;
        synchronized (servletContext) {
            try {
                onlineUserCount = (Integer) servletContext
                        .getAttribute("onlineUserCount");
            } catch (Exception e) {
            }
            servletContext.setAttribute("onlineUserCount",
                    onlineUserCount + 1);
        }
        return "success";
    } else {
        return "input";
    }
}

/*
 * The onlineUserCount is accurate only if we also
 * write a javax.servlet.http.HttpSessionListener
 * implementation and decrement the
 * onlineUserCount attribute value in its
 * sessionDestroyed method, which is called by the
 * container when a user session is inactive for
 * a certain period of time.
 */
public String logout() {
    if (sessionMap instanceof SessionMap) {
        ((SessionMap) sessionMap).invalidate();
    }
    int onlineUserCount = 0;
    synchronized (servletContext) {
        try {
            onlineUserCount = (Integer) servletContext
                    .getAttribute("onlineUserCount");
        } catch (Exception e) {
        }
        servletContext.setAttribute("onlineUserCount",
                onlineUserCount - 1);
    }
    return "success";
}

}
```

The **User** class can be used to manage user logins and maintain the number of users currently logged in. In this application a user can log in by typing in a non-empty user name and a non-empty password in a Login form.

You can access the **HttpServletRequest** object because the **User** class implements **ServletRequestAware**. As demonstrated in the **login** method, that gets invoked every time a user logs in, you retrieve the **referer** header by calling the **getHeader** method on the **servletRequest** object. Verifying that the **referer** header is not null makes sure that the action was invoked by submitting the Login form, not by typing the URL of the **User_input** action. Next, the **login** method increments the value of the application attribute **onlineUserCount**.

The **logout** method invalidates the **HttpSession** object and decrements **onlineUserCount**. Therefore, the value of **onlineUserCount** reflects the number of users currently logged in.

You can test this application by invoking the **User_input** action using this URL:

```
http://localhost:8080/app03a/User_input.action
```

You will see the Login form like the one in Figure 3.1. You can log in by entering a non-empty user name and a non-empty password. When you submit the form, the **User_login** action will be invoked. If login is successful, you'll see the second page that looks like the one in Figure 3.2. The number of users online is displayed here.

Finally, click the **log out** link to invoked **User_logout**.

Passing Static Parameters to An Action

Request parameters are mapped to action properties. However, there's another way of assigning values to action properties: by passing the values in the action declaration.

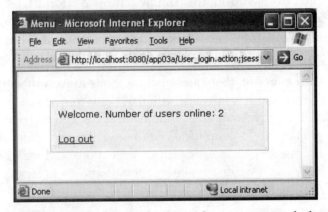

Figure 3.1: The Login form

Figure 3.2: Displaying the number of users currently logged in

An **action** element in a **struts.xml** file may contain **param** elements. Each **param** element corresponds to an action property. The Static Parameters (**staticParams**) interceptor is responsible for mapping static parameters to action properties.

Here is an example of how to pass static parameters to an action.

```
<action name="MyAction" class="...">
   <param name="siteId">california01</param>
   <param name="siteType">retail</param>
```

```
</action>
```

Every time the action **MyAction** is invoked, its **siteId** property will be set to "california01" and its **siteType** property to "retail."

The ActionSupport Class

The **com.opensymphony.xwork2.ActionSupport** class is the default action class. Struts will create an instance of this class if an action declaration does not specify an action class. You may also want to extend this class when writing action classes.

Since **ActionSupport** implements the **Action** interface, you can use the static fields **ERROR, INPUT, LOGIN, NONE,** and **SUCCESS** from a class that extends it. There's already an implementation of the **execute** method, inherited from **Action**, that simply returns **Action.SUCCESS**. If you implement the **Action** interface directly instead of extending **ActionSupport**, you have to provide an implementation of **execute** yourself. Therefore, it's more convenient to extend **ActionSupport** than to implement **Action**.

In addition to **execute**, there are other methods in **ActionSupport** that you can override or use. For instance, you may want to override **validate** if you're writing code for validating user input. And you can use one of the many overloads of **getText** to look up localized messages in properties files. Input validation is discussed in Chapter 8, "Input Validation" and we'll look at the **getText** methods when we discuss internationalization and localization in Chapter 9, "Message Handling."

For now bear in mind that extending **ActionSupport** helps.

Results

An action method returns a **String** that determines what result to execute. An action declaration must contain **result** elements that each corresponds to a possible return value of the action method. If, for example, an action method returns either **Action.SUCCESS** or **Action.INPUT**, the action declaration must have two **result** elements like these

```
<action ... >
    <result name="success"> ... </result>
    <result name="input"> ... </result>
</action>
```

A **result** element can have these attributes:

- **name**. The name of the result that matches the output of the action method. For example, if the value of the **name** attribute is "input," the result will be used if the action method returns "input." The **name** attribute is optional and its default value is "success."
- **type**. The result type. The default value is "dispatcher," a result type that forwards to a JSP.

The default values of both attributes help you write shorter configuration. For example, these **result** elements

```
<result name="success type="dispatcher">/Product.jsp</result>
<result name="input" type="dispatcher">/ProductForm.jsp</result>
```

are the same as these:

```
<result>/Product.jsp</result>
<result name="input">/ProductForm.jsp</result>
```

The first **result** element does not have to contain the **name** and **type** attributes as it uses the default values. The second **result** element needs the **name** attribute but does not need the **type** attribute.

Dispatcher is the most frequently used result type, but it's not the only type available. Table 3.1 shows all standard result types. The words in brackets in the Result Type column are names used to register the result types in the configuration file. That's right, you must register a result type before you can use it.

In addition to the ones in Table 3.1, many third party developers deploy plug-ins that encapsulate new result types. You too can write your own and Chapter 19, "Custom Result Types" teaches you how.

Result Type	Description
Chain (chain)	Used for action chaining
Dispatcher (dispatcher)	The default result type, used for JSP forwarding
FreeMarker (freemarker)	Used for FreeMarker integration
HttpHeader (httpheader)	Used to send HTTP headers back to the browser

Redirect (redirect)	Used to redirect to another URL
Redirect Action (redirect-action)	Used to redirect to another action
Stream (stream)	Used to stream an **InputStream** to the browser
Velocity (velocity)	Used for Velocity integration
XSLT (xslt)	Used for XML/XSLT integration
PlainText (plaintext)	Used to send plain text, normally to show a JSP's source.

Table 3.1: Bundled result types

Each of the result types is explained below.

Chain

The Chain result type is there to support action chaining, whereby an action is forwarded to another action and the state of the original action is retained in the target action. The Chaining interceptor makes action chaining possible and since this interceptor is part of **defaultStack**, you can use action chaining right away.

The following declarations show an example of action chaining.

```
<package name="package1" extends="struts-default">
    <action name="action1" class="...">
        <result type="chain">action2</result>
    </action>

    <action name="action2" class="...">
        <result type="chain">
            <param name="actionName">action3</param>
            <param name="namespace">/namespace2</param>
        </result>
    </action>
</package>

<package name="package2" namespace="/namespace2"
        extends="struts-default">
    <action name="action3" class="...">
        <result>/MyView.jsp</result>
    </action>
</package>
```

action1 in **package1** is chained to **action2**, which in turn is chained to **action3** in a different package. Chaining to an action in a different package is allowed as long as you specify the **namespace** parameter of the target action.

If **action-x** is chained to **action-y**, **action-x** will be pushed to the Value Stack, followed by **action-y**, making **action-y** the top object in the Object Stack. As a result, both actions can be accessed from the view. If **action-x** and **action-y** both have a property that shares the same name, you can access the property in **action-y** (the top object) using this OGNL expression:

```
[0].propertyName
```

or

```
propertyName
```

You can access the property in **action-x** using this expression:

```
[1].propertyName
```

Use action chaining with caution, though. Generally action chaining is not recommended as it may turn your actions into spaghetti code. If **action1** needs to be forwarded to **action2**, for example, you need to ask yourself if there's code in **action2** that needs to be pushed into a method in a utility class that can be called from both **action1** and **action2**.

Dispatcher

The Dispatcher result type is the most frequently used type and the default type. This result type has a **location** parameter that is the default parameter. Since it is the default parameter, you can either pass a value to it by using the **param** element like this:

```
<result name="...">
    <param name="location">resource</param>
</result>
```

or by passing the value to the **result** element.

```
<result name="...">resource</result>
```

Use this result type to forward to a resource, normally a JSP or an HTML file, in the same application. You cannot forward to an external resource and its

location parameter cannot be assigned an absolute URL. To direct to an external resource, use the Redirect result type.

As almost all accompanying applications in this book utilize this result type, a separate example is not given here.

FreeMarker

This result type forwards to a FreeMarker template. See Chapter 21, "FreeMarker" for details.

HttpHeader

This result type is used to send an HTTP status to the browser. For example, the **app03a** application has this action declaration:

```
<default-action-ref name="CatchAll"/>

<action name="CatchAll">
    <result type="httpheader">
        <param name="status">404</param>
    </result>
</action>
```

The **default-action-ref** element is used to specify the default action, which is the action that will be invoked if a URI does not have a matching action. In the example above, the **CatchAll** action is the default action. **CatchAll** uses a HttpHeader result to send a 404 status code to the browser. As a result, if there's no matching action, instead of getting Struts' error messages:

```
Struts Problem Report
Struts has detected an unhandled exception:
Messages: There is no Action mapped for namespace / and action name
blahblah
```

the user will get a 404 status report and will see a default page from the container.

Redirect

This result type redirects, instead of forward, to another resource. This result type accepts these parameters

- **location**. Specifies the redirection target.
- **parse**. Indicates whether or not the value of **location** should be parsed for OGNL expressions. The default value for **parse** is **true**.

The main reason to use a redirect, as opposed to a forward, is to direct the user to an external resource. A forward using Dispatcher is preferable when directing to an internal resource because a forward is faster. Redirection would require a round trip since the client browser would be forced to re-send a new HTTP request.

Having said that, there is a reason why you may want to redirect to an internal resource. You normally redirect if you don't want a page refresh invokes the previously invoked action. For instance, in a typical application, submitting a form invokes a **Product_save** action, that adds a new product to the database. If this action forwards to a JSP, the Address box of the browser will still be showing the URL that invoked **Product_save**. If the user for some reason presses the browser's Reload or Refresh button, the same action will be invoked again, potentially adding the same product to the database. Redirection removes the association with the previous action as the redirection target has a new URL.

Here is an example of redirecting to an external resource.

```
<action name="..." class="...">
    <result name="success" type="redirect">
        http://www.example.com/test.html
    </result>
</action>
```

And this to an internal resource:

```
<action name="..." class="...">
    <result name="success" type="redirect">
        /jsp/Product.jsp
    </result>
</action>
```

When redirecting to an internal resource, you specify a URI for the resource. The URI can point to an action. For instance,

```
<action name="..." class="...">
    <result name="success" type="redirect">
        User_input.action
    </result>
</action>
```

In the last two examples, the target object was a resource relative to the current URL. Redirect does not care if the target is a JSP or an action, it always treat it as if the target is another page. Contrast this with the Redirect Action result type explained in the next section.

The underlying class for the Redirect result type calls **HttpServletResponse.sendRedirect**. Consequently, the action that was just executed is lost and no longer available. If you need the state of the source action available in the target destination, you can pass data through the session or request parameters. The **RedirectTest** action below redirects to the **User_input** action and passes the value of the **userName** property of the **TestUser** action class as a **userName** request parameter. Note that the dynamic value is enclosed in **${** and **}**.

```
<action name="RedirectTest" class="app03a.TestUser">
    <result type="redirect">
        User_input.action?userName=${userName}
    </result>
</action>
```

Note also that you need to encode special characters such as & and + . For example, if the target is http://www.test.com?user=1&site=4, you must change the **&** to **&**.

```
<result name="login" type="redirect">
    http://www.test.com?user=1&amp;site=4
</result>
```

Redirect Action

This result type is similar to Redirect. Instead of redirecting to a different resource, however, Redirect Action redirects to another action. The Redirect Action result type can take these parameters:

- **actionName**. Specifies the name of the target action. This is the default attribute.
- **namespace**. The namespace of the target action. If no **namespace** parameter is present, it is assumed the target action resides in the same namespace as the enclosing action.

For example, the following Redirect Action result redirects to a **User_input** action.

```
<result type="redirect-action">
    <param name="actionName">User_input</param>
</result>
```

And since **actionName** is the default parameter, you can simply write:

```
<result type="redirect-action">User_input</result>
```

Note that the value of the redirection target is an action name. There is no **.action** suffix necessary as is the case with the Redirect result type.

In addition to the two parameters, you can pass other parameters as request parameters. For example, the following result type

```
<result type="redirect-action">
    <param name="actionName">User_input</param>
    <param name="userId">xyz</param>
    <param name="area">ga</param>
</result>
```

will be translated into this URI:

```
User_input.action?userId=xyz&area=ga
```

Stream

This result type does not forward to a JSP. Instead, it sends an output stream to the browser. See Chapter 13, "File Download" for examples.

Velocity

This result type forwards to a Velocity template. See Chapter 20, "Velocity" for details.

XSLT

This result type uses XML/XSLT as the view technology. This result type is explained further in Chapter 22, "XSLT."

PlainText

A PlainText result is normally used for sending a JSP's source. For example, the action **Source_show** below displays the source of the **Menu.jsp** page.

```
<action name="Source_show" class="...">
    <result name="success" type="plaintext">/jsp/Menu.jsp</result>
</action>
```

Exception Handling with Exception Mapping

In a perfect world, all computer programs would be bug-free. In the real world, however, this is not the case. No matter how you take care to handle your code, some bugs might still try to creep out. Sometimes it's not even your fault. Third-party components you use in your code may have bugs that are not known at the time you deploy your application. Any uncaught exception will result in an embarrassing HTTP 500 code (internal error).

Fortunately for Struts programmers, Struts lets you catch whatever you cannot catch in your action classes by using the **exception-mapping** element in the configuration file.

This **exception-mapping** element has two attributes, **exception** and **result**. The **exception** attribute specifies the exception type that will be caught. The **result** attribute specifies a result name, either in the same action or in the **global-results** declaration, that will be executed if an exception is caught. You can nest one or more **exception-mapping** elements under your action declaration. For example, the following **exception-mapping** element catches all exceptions thrown by the **User_save** action and executes the **error** result.

```
<action name="User_save" class="...">
    <exception-mapping exception="java.lang.Exception"
            result="error"/>
    <result name="error">/jsp/Error.jsp</result>
```

```
    <result>/jsp/Thanks.jsp</result>
</action>
```

You can also provide a global exception mapping through the use of the **global-exception-mappings** element. Any **exception-mapping** declared under the **global-exception-mappings** element must refer to a **result** in the **global-results** element. Here is an example of **global-exception-mappings**.

```
<global-results>
    <result name="error">/jsp/Error.jsp</result>
    <result name="sqlError">/jsp/SQLError.jsp</result>
</global-results>
<global-exception-mappings>
    <exception-mapping exception="java.sql.SQLException"
            result="sqlError"/>
    <exception-mapping exception="java.lang.Exception"
            result="error"/>
</global-exception-mappings>
```

Behind the scenes is the Exception interceptor that handles all exceptions caught. Part of the default stack, this exception adds two objects to the Value Stack (which you'll learn in Chapter 4, "OGNL"), for every exception caught by an **exception-mapping** element.

- **exception**, that represents the **Exception** object thrown
- **exceptionStack**, that contains the value from the stack trace.

This way, you can display the exception message or the stack trace in your view, if you so choose. The **property** tag that you will learn in Chapter 5, "Form Tags" can be used for this purpose:

```
<s:property value="exception.message"/>
<s:property value="exceptionStack"/>
```

Wildcard Mapping

A large application can have dozens or even a hundred action declarations. These declarations can clutter the configuration file and make it less readable. To ease this situation, you can use wildcard mapping to merge similar mappings to one mapping.

Consider these package and action declarations.

Chapter 3: Actions and Results

```
<package name="wildcardMappingTest" namespace="/wild"
        extends="struts-default">
    <action name="Book_add" class="app03a.Book" method="add">
        <result>/jsp/Book.jsp</result>
    </action>
</package>
```

You can invoke the **Book_add** action by using this URI that contains the combination of the package namespace and the action name:

```
/wild/Book_add.action
```

However, if there is no action with the name **Book_add**, Struts will match the URI with any action name that includes the wildcard character *****. For example, the same URI will invoke the action named ***_add** if **Book_add** does not exist.

Now consider this package declaration.

```
<package name="wildcardMappingTest" namespace="/wild"
        extends="struts-default">
    <action name="*_add" class="app03a.Book" method="add">
        <result>/jsp/Book.jsp</result>
    </action>
</package>
```

The action in the package above can be invoked using any URI that contains the correct namespace and **_add**, including

```
/wild/Book_add.action
/wild/Author_add.action
/wild/_add.action
/wild/Whatever_add.action
```

If more than one wildcard match was found, the last one found prevails. In the following example, the second action will always get invoked.

```
<package name="wildcardMappingTest" namespace="/wild"
        extends="struts-default">
    <action name="*_add" class="app03a.Book" method="add">
        <result>/jsp/Book.jsp</result>
    </action>
    <action name="*" class="app03a.Author" method="add">
        <result>/jsp/Author.jsp</result>
    </action>
</package>
```

If multiple matches were found, the pattern that does not use a wildcard character wins. Look at these action declarations again:

```
<package name="wildcardMappingTest" namespace="/wild"
        extends="struts-default">
    <action name="Book_add" class="app03a.Book" method="add">
        <result>/jsp/Book.jsp</result>
    </action>
    <action name="*_add" class="app03a.Author" method="add">
        <result>/jsp/Author.jsp</result>
    </action>
</package>
```

The URI **/wild/Book_add.action** matches both actions. However, since the first action declaration does not use a wildcard character, it will take precedence over the second.

There's more to it.

The part of the URI that was matched by the wildcard is available as **{1}**. What it means is if you use the URI **/wild/MyAction_add.action** and it matches an action whose name is ***_add**, **{1}** will contain **MyAction**. You can then use **{1}** to replace other parts of the configuration.

For instance, using both ***** and **{1}** the action declarations

```
<package name="wildcardMappingTest" namespace="/wild"
        extends="struts-default">
    <action name="Book_add" class="app03a.Book" method="add">
        <result>/jsp/Book.jsp</result>
    </action>
    <action name="Author_add" class="app03a.Author" method="add">
        <result>/jsp/Author.jsp</result>
    </action>
</package>
```

can be replaced by this one:

```
<package name="wildcardMappingTest" namespace="/wild"
        extends="struts-default">
    <action name="*_add" class="app03a.{1}" method="add">
        <result>/jsp/{1}.jsp</result>
    </action>
</package>
```

The URI **/wild/Book_add.action** will invoke the action ***_add**, where "Book" was matched by ***** . The class name will be **app03a.Book** and the JSP to forward to will be **Book.jsp**.

Using **/wild/Author_add.action**, on the other hand, will also invoke the action ***_add**, where "Author" was matched by *. The class name will be **app03a.Author** and the JSP to forward to will be **Author.jsp**.

If you try **/wild/Whatever_add.action**, it will still match the action ***_add**. However, it will throw an exception because there are no **Whatever** class and **Whatever.jsp** JSP.

Using multiple wildcards is possible. Consider the following:

```
<package name="wildcardMappingTest" namespace="/wild"
        extends="struts-default">
    <action name="Book_add" class="app03a.Book" method="add">
        <result>/jsp/Book.jsp</result>
    </action>
    <action name="Book_edit" class="app03a.Book" method="edit">
        <result>/jsp/Book.jsp</result>
    </action>
    <action name="Book_delete" class="app03a.Book" method="delete">
        <result>/jsp/Book.jsp</result>
    </action>

    <action name="Author_add" class="app03a.Author" method="add">
        <result>/jsp/Author.jsp</result>
    </action>
    <action name="Author_edit" class="app03a.Author" method="edit">
        <result>/jsp/Author.jsp</result>
    </action>
    <action name="Author_delete" class="app03a.Author"
            method="delete">
        <result>/jsp/Author.jsp</result>
    </action>
</package>
```

You've seen that **Book_add** and **Author_add** can be combined into ***_add**. By extension, **Book_edit** and **Author_edit** can also merge, and so can **Book_delete** and **Author_delete**. If you note that an action name contains the combination of the action class name and the action method name and realizing that **{1}** contains the first replacement and **{2}** the second replacement, you can shorten the six action declarations above into this.

```
<package name="wildcardMappingTest" namespace="/wild"
        extends="struts-default">
    <action name="*_*" class="app03a.{1}" method="{2}">
        <result>/jsp/{1}.jsp</result>
    </action>
</package>
```

For example, the URI **/wild/Book_edit.action** will match ***_***. The replacement for the first ***** is **Book** and the replacement for the second ***** is **edit**. Therefore, **{1}** will contain **Book** and **{2}** will contain **edit**. **/wild/Book_edit.action** consequently will invoke the **app03a.Book** class and execute its **edit** method.

Note
{0} contains the whole URI.

Note also that ***** matches zero or more characters excluding the slash ('/') character. To include the slash character, use ******. To escape a character, use the '\' character.

Dynamic Method Invocation

In Struts jargon the '!' character is called the bang notation. It is used to invoke a method dynamically. The method may be different from the one specified in the **action** element for that action.

For example, this action declaration does not have a **method** attribute.

```
<action name="Book" class="app03a.Book">
```

As a result, the **execute** method on **Book** will be invoked. However, using the bang notation you can invoke a different method in the same action. The URI **/Book!edit.action**, for example, will invoke the **edit** method on **Book**.

You are not recommended to use dynamic method invocation because of security concerns. You wouldn't want your users to be able to invoke methods that you do not expose.

By default, dynamic method invocation is enabled. The **default.properties** file specifies a value of **true** for **struts.enable.DynamicMethodInvocation**:

```
struts.enable.DynamicMethodInvocation = true
```

To disable this feature, set this key to false, either in a **struts.properties** file or in a **struts.xml** file using a **constant** element like this:

```
<constant name="struts.enable.DynamicMethodInvocation"
          value="false" />
```

Testing Action Classes

Since action classes are POJO classes, testing action classes is easy. All you need is instantiate the class, set its properties, and call its action method. Here is an example.

```
MyAction action = new MyAction();
action.setUserName("jon");
action.setPassword("secret");
String result = action.execute();
if ("success".equals(result)) {
    // action okay
} else
    // action not okay
}
```

Summary

Struts solves common problems in web application development such as page navigation, input validation, and so on. As a result, you can concentrate on the most important task in development: writing business logic in action classes. This chapter explained how to write effective action classes as well as related topics such as the default result types, global exception mapping, wildcard mapping, and dynamic method invocation.

Chapter 4
OGNL

The view in the Model-View-Controller (MVC) pattern is responsible for displaying the model and other objects. To access these objects from a JSP, you use OGNL (Object-Graph Navigation Language), the expression language Struts inherits from WebWork.

OGNL can help you do the following.

- Bind GUI elements (text fields, check boxes, etc) to model objects and converts values from one type to another.
- Bind generic tags with model objects.
- Create lists and maps on the fly, to be used with GUI elements.
- Invoke methods. You can invoke any method, not only getters and setters.

OGNL is powerful, but only part of its power is relevant to Struts developers. This chapter discusses OGNL features that you will need for Struts projects. If you're interested in learning other features of OGNL, visit these websites.

```
http://www.opensymphony.com/ognl
http://www.ognl.org
```

Note

After reading this chapter the first time, do not worry if you don't get a firm understanding of OGNL. Just skip to the next chapter and see how OGNL is used in form tags and generic tags. Once you've started using it, you can revisit this chapter for reference.

The Value Stack

For each action invocation, an object called the Value Stack is created prior to action method execution. The Value Stack is used to store the action and other objects. The Value Stack is accessed during processing (by interceptors) and by the view to display the action and other information. In order for a JSP to access the Value Stack, the Struts framework stores it as a request attribute named **struts.valueStack**.

There are two logical units inside the Value Stack, the Object Stack and the Context Map, as illustrated in Figure 4.1. Struts pushes the action and related objects to the Object Stack and pushes various maps to the Context Map.

Note
The term Value Stack is often used to refer to the Object Stack in the Value Stack.

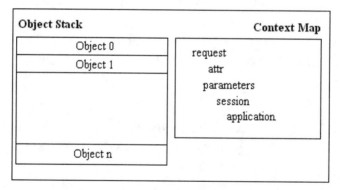

Figure 4.1: The Value Stack

The following are the maps that are pushed to the Context Map.

- **parameters**. A **Map** that contains the request parameters for the current request.
- **request**. A **Map** containing all the request attributes for the current request.
- **session**. A **Map** containing the session attributes for the current user.
- **application**. A **Map** containing the **ServletContext** attributes for the current application.

- **attr**. A **Map** that searches for attributes in this order: **request**, **session**, and **application**.

You can use OGNL to access objects in the Object Stack and the Context Map. To tell the OGNL engine where to search, prefix your OGNL expression with a **#** if you intend to access the Context Map. Without a **#**, search will be conducted against the Object Stack.

Note

A request parameter always returns an array of **String**s, not a **String**. Therefore, to access the number of request parameters, use this

```
#parameters.count[0]
```

and not

```
#parameters.count
```

Now let's look at the OGNL in more depth.

Reading Object Stack Object Properties

To access the property of an object in the Object Stack, use one of the following forms:

```
object.propertyName
object['propertyName']
object["propertyName"]
```

Object stack objects can be referred to using a zero-based index. For example, the top object in the Object Stack is referred to simply as [0] and the object right below it as [1]. For example, the following expression returns the value of the **message** property of the object on top:

```
[0].message
```

Of course, this can also be written as **[0]["message"]** or **[0]['message']**.

To read the **time** property of the second object in the stack, you can use **[1].time** or **[1]["time"]** or **[1]['time']**.

For example, the **property** tag, one of the many tags you'll learn in Chapter 5, "Form Tags," is used to print a value. Using the **property** tag to print the **time** property of the first stack object, you can write any of the following:

```
<s:property value="[0].time"/>
<s:property value="[0]['time']"/>
<s:property value='[0]["time"]'/>
```

An important characteristic of the OGNL implementation in Struts is that if the specified property is not found in the specified object, search will continue to the objects next to the specified object. For example, if the top object does not have a **name** property, the following expression will search the subsequent objects in the Object Stack until the property is found or until there's no more object in the stack:

```
[0].name
```

The index [*n*] specifies the starting position for searching, rather than the object to search. The following expression searches from the third object in the stack for the property **user**.

```
[2]["user"]
```

If you want a search to start from the top object, you can remove the index entirely. Therefore,

```
[0].password
```

is the same as

```
password
```

Note also that if the returned value has properties, you can use the same syntax to access the properties. For instance, if a Struts action has an **address** property that is returns an instance of **Address**, you can use the following expression to access the **streetNumber** property of the **address** property of the action.

```
[0].address.streetNumber
```

Reading Context Map Object Properties

To access the property of an object in the Context Map, use one of these forms.

```
#object.propertyName
```

```
#object['propertyName']
```

```
#object["propertyName"]
```

For example, the following expression returns the value of the session attribute **code**.

```
#session.code
```

This expression returns the **contactName** property of the request attribute **customer**.

```
#request["customer"]["contactName"]
```

The following expression tries to find the **lastAccessDate** attribute in the request object. If no attribute is found, the search will continue to the session and application objects.

```
#attr['lastAccessDate']
```

Invoking Fields and Methods

You can invoke static fields and methods in any Java class, not necessarily on objects that are loaded to the Value Stack. In addition, you can call public fields and methods (static or otherwise) on any object in the Value Stack. In both cases, you can pass arguments to a method.

To call a static field or method, use this syntax:

```
@fullyQualifiedClassName@fieldName
```

```
@fullyQualifiedClassName@methodName(argumentList)
```

As an example, this expression accesses the static field **DECEMBER** in **java.util.Calendar**:

```
@java.util.Calendar@DECEMBER
```

To call the static method **now** in the **app04.Util** class (shown in Listing 4.1), use this:

```
@app04a.Util@now()
```

Listing 4.1: The now static method

```
package app04a;
import java.util.Date;
public class Util {
    public static Date now() {
        return new Date();
    }
}
```

To call an instance field and method, use this syntax:

```
object.fieldName
```

```
object.methodName(argumentList)
```

Here *object* represents a reference to an Object Stack object. You use the same syntax as when accessing a property. For example, this refers to the first object in the stack:

```
[0]
```

To call the **datePattern** field in **app04.Test2Action** (shown in Listing 4.2), use this expression.

```
[0].datePattern
```

To call the **repeat** method in **app04a.Test2Action**, use this:

```
[0].repeat(3, "Hello")
```

Listing 4.2: The repeat method

```
public String repeat(int count, String s) {
    StringBuilder sb = new StringBuilder();
    for (int i = 0; i < count; i++) {
        sb.append(s);
    }
    return sb.toString();
}
```

Working with Arrays

You can read a property that returns an array the same way you would any property. An array property returns comma-separated elements without brackets. For example, the **colors** property whose get method is shown in Listing 4.3 will return this.

```
blue, green, red
```

Listing 4.3: The getColors method

```java
public String[] getColors() {
    String[] colors = {"blue", "green", "red"};
    return colors;
}
```

You can access individual elements by using the same notation you use to access a Java array element. For instance, this returns the first color in **colors**:

```
colors[0]
```

You can also call an array's length field to find out how many elements it has. For example, this returns 3.

```
colors.length
```

Working with Lists

You can read a property of type **java.util.List** just you would any property. The return value of a **List** is a **String** representation of its comma-separated elements in square brackets. For example, the **countries** property whose get method is shown in Listing 4.4 returns this.

```
[Australia, Fiji, New Zealand, Vanuatu]
```

Listing 4.4: The getCountries method

```java
public List<String> getCountries() {
    List<String> countries = new ArrayList<String>();
    countries.add("Australia");
    countries.add("Fiji");
    countries.add("New Zealand");
    countries.add("Vanuatu");
```

```
    return countries;
}
```

You can access individual elements in a list by using the same notation you would use to access an array element. For instance, this returns the first country in **countries**:

```
countries[0]
```

You can enquiry about a **List**'s size by calling its **size** method or the special keyword **size**. The following returns the number of elements in countries.

```
countries.size
countries.size()
```

The **isEmpty** keyword or a call to its **isEmpty** method tells you whether or not a **List** is empty.

```
countries.isEmpty
countries.isEmpty()
```

You can also use OGNL expressions to create Lists. This feature will come in handy when you're working with form tags that require options such as **select** and **radio**. To create a list, you use the same notation as when declaring an array in Java. For example, the following expression creates a **List** of three **String**s:

```
{"Alaska", "California", "Washington"}
```

This returns the first element in the string array.

```
{"Alaska", "California", "Washington"}[0]
```

The following creates a **List** of two Integers. The primitive elements will be automatically converted to **Integer**s.

```
{6, 8}
```

Working with Maps

Referencing a **Map** property returns all its key/value pairs in this format:

```
{key-1=value-1, key-2=value-2, ... , key-n=value-n}
```

For example, the **cities** property whose getter is shown in Listing 4.5 returns this.

```
{UT=Salt Lake City, CA=Sacramento, WA=Olympia}
```

Listing 4.5: The getCities method

```
public Map<String, String> getCities() {
    Map<String, String> cities = new HashMap<String, String>();
    cities.put("CA", "Sacramento");
    cities.put("WA", "Olympia");
    cities.put("UT", "Salt Lake City");
    return cities;
}
```

To retrieve a **Map**'s value, use this format:

```
map[key]
```

For instance, to get the city whose key is 2, use

```
cities["CA"]
```

or

```
cities['CA']
```

You can use **size** or **size()** to get the number of key/value pairs in a **Map**.

```
cities.size
cities.size()
```

You can use **isEmpty** or **isEmpty** to find out if a **Map** is empty.

```
cities.isEmpty
cities.isEmpty()
```

And yes, you can access the **Map**s in the Context Map too. Just don't forget to use a **#** prefix. For example, the following expression accesses the **application Map** and retrieves the value of "code":

```
#application["code"]
```

You can create a **Map** by using this syntax:

```
#{ key-1:value-1, key-2:value-2, ... key-n:value-n }
```

There can be empty spaces between a key and the colon and between a colon and a value.

For example, the **cities Map** can be rewritten by this OGNL expression:

```
#{ "CA":"Sacramento", "WA":"Olympia", "UT":"Salt Lake City" }
```

This will be useful when you have started working with tags that need options, such as **radio** and **select**.

JSP EL: When OGNL Can't Help

There are times when OGNL and the Struts custom tags are not the best choice. For example, to print a model object on a JSP, you use the **property** tag that is included in the Struts tag library. Like this:

```
<s:property value="serverValue"/>
```

However, you can achieve the same using this shorter JSP Expression Language expression:

```
${serverValue}
```

Also, there's no easy way to use Struts custom tags to print a request header. With EL, it's easy. For instance, the following EL expression prints the value of the host header:

```
${header.host}
```

You will therefore find it practical to use OGNL and EL together. The EL is explained in Appendix B, "The Expression Language."

Summary

The view in the Model-View-Controller (MVC) pattern is responsible for displaying the model and other objects and you use OGNL to access the objects. This chapter discussed the Value Stack that stores the action and context objects and explained how to use OGNL to access them and create arrays, lists, and maps.

Chapter 5
Form Tags

Struts ships with a tag library that incorporates two types of tags: User Interface (UI) tags and non-UI tags. The UI tags are further categorized into two groups, those used for data entry and those for displaying error messages. The UI tags in the first group are called the form tags and are the subject of discussion of this chapter. The UI tags for displaying error messages are explained in Chapter 8, "Input Validation." Non-UI tags help with control flow and data access and are covered in Chapter 6, "Generic Tags." In addition, there are also tags that assist with AJAX programming and are discussed in Chapter 27, "AJAX."

form is the main tag in the form tags category. This tag is rendered as an HTML form element. Other form tags are rendered as input elements. The main benefit of using the form tags is when input validation fails and the form is returned to the user. With manual HTML coding, you have to worry about repopulating the input fields with the values the user previously entered. With the form tags, this is taken care of for you.

Another advantage of using the form tags is that they help with layout and there are several layout templates for each tag. These layout templates are organized into themes and Struts comes with several themes, giving you flexibility to choose a layout that is suitable for your application.

This chapter explains each of the form tags in a separate section. Before you learn the first tag, however, it is beneficial to discuss how to use the Struts tags and peruse the common attributes shared by all the tags. After some basic tags, three attributes—**list**, **listKey**, and **listValue**—are given a separate section because of their importance in tags that use options, including **radio**, **combobox**, **select**, **checkboxlist**, and **doubleselect**. After all form tags are covered, themes are explained at the end of this chapter.

Using Struts Tags

You can use the UI and non-UI tags by declaring this **taglib** directive at the top of your JSP.

```
<%@ taglib prefix="s" uri="/struts-tags" %>
```

A tag attribute can be assigned a static value or an OGNL expression. If you assign an OGNL expression, the expression will be evaluated if you enclose it with %{ and }. For instance, the following **label** attribute is assigned the String literal "userName"

```
label="userName"
```

This one is assigned an OGNL expression userName, and the value will be whatever the value of the userName action property is:

```
label="%{userName}"
```

This one assigns the **label** attribute the value of the session attribute **userName**:

```
label="%{#session.userName}"
```

This **value** attribute is assigned 6:

```
value="%{1 + 5}"
```

Common Attributes

Tag classes of all Struts tags are part of the **org.apache.struts2.components** package and all UI tags are derived from the **UIBean** class. This class defines common attributes that are inherited by the UI tags. Table 5.1 lists the attributes.

An attribute name with an asterisk indicates that the attribute is only available if a non-simple theme is used. Themes are explained toward the end of this chapter.

Name	Data Type	Description
cssClass	String	The CSS class for the rendered element.
cssStyle	String	The CSS style for the rendered element.
title	String	Specifies the HTML **title** attribute.
disabled	String	Specifies the HTML **disabled** attribute.
label*	String	Specifies the label for a form element in the xhtml and ajax theme.
labelPosition*	String	Specifies the label position in the xhtml and ajax theme. Allowed values are **top** and **left** (default).
key	String	The name of the property this input field represents. It is a shortcut for the **name** and **label** attributes
requiredposition*	String	Specifies the required label position of a form element in the xhtml and ajax theme. Possible values are **left** and **right** (default).
name	String	Specifies the HTML **name** attribute that in an input element maps to an action property.
required*	boolean	In the xhtml theme this attribute indicates whether or not an asterisk (*) should be added to the label.
tabIndex	String	Specifies the HTML **tabindex** attribute.
value	String	Specifies the value of a form element.

Table 5.1: The Common attributes

The **name** attribute is probably the most important one. In an input tag it maps to an action property. Other important attributes include **value**, **label**, and **key**. The **value** attribute holds the user value. You seldom use this attribute in an input tag unless the input tag is a hidden field.

By default, each input tag is accompanied by a label element. The **label** attribute specifies the text for the label element. The **key** attribute is a shortcut for the **name** and **label** attributes. If the **key** attribute is used, the value assigned to this attribute will be assigned to the **name** attribute and the **value** returned from the call to **getText(*key*)** will be assigned to the **label** attribute. In other words,

```
key="aKey"
```

is the same as

```
name="aKey" label="%{getText('aKey')}"
```

If both the **key** and **name** attributes are present, the explicit value for **name** takes precedence and the **label** attribute is assigned the result of **getText(*key*)**. If the **key** attribute and the **label** attribute are present, the value assigned to the **label** attribute will be used.

Name	Data Type	Description
templateDir	String	The directory in which the template resides
theme	String	The theme name
template	String	The template name

Table 5.2: Template-related attributes

Name	Data Type	Description
onclick	String	Javascript onclick attribute
ondblclick	String	Javascript ondblclick attribute
onmousedown	String	Javascript onmousedown attribute
onmouseup	String	Javascript onmouseup attribute
onmouseover	String	Javascript onmouseover attribute
onmouseout	String	Javascript onmouseout attribute
onfocus	String	Javascript onfocus attribute
onblur	String	Javascript onblur attribute
onkeypress	String	Javascript onkeypress attribute
onkeyup	String	Javascript onkeyup attribute
onkeydown	String	Javascript onkeydown attribute
onselect	String	Javascript onselect attribute
onchange	String	Javascript onchange attribute

Table 5.3: Javascript-related attributes

Name	Data Type	Description
tooltip	String	The text used as a tooltip.
tooltipIconPath	String	The path to a tooltip icon. The default value is /struts/static/tooltip/tooltip.gif
tooltipDelay	String	The delay (in milliseconds) from the time the mouse hovers over the tooltip icon to the time the tooltip is shown. The default value is 500.

Table 5.4: Tooltip-related attributes

The **key** attribute will be discussed further in Chapter 9, "Message Handling."

In addition to the common attributes in Table 5.1, there are also attributes related to templates, JavaScript, and tooltips. These attributes are given in Table 5.2, Table 5.3, and Table 5.4, respectively.

The form Tag

The **form** tag renders an HTML form. Its attributes are given in Table 5.5. All attributes are optional.

Name	Data Type	Default Value	Description
acceptcharset	String		Comma or space delimited charsets that are accepted for this form.
action	String	current action	The action to submit this form to
enctype	String		The form **enctype** attribute
method	String	post	The form method
namespace		current namespace	The namespace of the action
onsubmit	String		Javascript **onsubmit** attribute
openTemplate	String		Template to use for opening the rendered form
portletMode	String		The portlet mode to display after the form submit
target	String		The form **target** attribute
validate	Boolean	false	Indicates if client-side validation should be performed in xhtml/ajax themes
windowState	String		The window state to display after the form submit

Table 5.5: form tag attributes

The following is an example of the **form** tag:

```
<s:form>
   ...
</s:form>
```

By default a **form** tag is rendered as an HTML form laid out in a table:

```
<form id="..." name="..." method="POST" action="..."
      onsubmit="return true;">
    <table class="wwFormTable">

    </table>
</form>
```

An input field nested within a **form** tag is rendered as a table row. The row has two fields, one for a label and one for the input element. A submit button is translated into a table row with a single cells that occupies two columns. For instance, the following tags

```
<s:form action="...">
    <s:textfield name="userName" label="User Name"/>
    <s:password name="password" label="Password"/>
    <s:submit/>
</s:form>
```

are rendered as

```
<form id="User_login" name="User_login" onsubmit="return true;"
      action="..." method="POST">
<table class="wwFormTable">
<tr>
    <td class="tdLabel">
        <label for="User_login_userName" class="label">
            User Name:
        </label>
    </td>
    <td>
        <input type="text" name="userName" value=""
               id="User_login_userName"/>
    </td>
</tr>
<tr>
    <td class="tdLabel">
        <label for="User_login_password" class="label">
            Password:
        </label>
    </td>
    <td>
        <input type="password" name="password"
               id="User_login_password"/>
    </td>
</tr>
<tr>
```

```
      <td colspan="2">
          <div align="right">
          <input type="submit" id="User_login_0" value="Submit"/>
          </div>
      </td>
</tr>
</table>
</form>
```

You can change the default layout by changing the theme. Themes are discussed in the section "Themes" near the end of this chapter.

The textfield, password, hidden Tags

The **textfield** tag is rendered as an input text field, the **password** tag as a password field, and the **hidden** tag as a hidden field. Attributes common to **textfield** and **password** are given in Table 5.6.

Name	Data Type	Default Value	Description
maxlength	integer		The maximum number of characters the rendered element can accept
readonly	boolean	false	Indicates if the input is read-only
size	integer		The size attribute

Table 5.6: textfield and password tags attributes

The **password** tag extends **textfield** by adding a **showPassword** attribute. This attribute takes a boolean value and its default value is false. It determines whether or not the entered value will be redisplayed when the containing form fails to validate. A value of true redisplays the password when control is redirected back to the form.

For example, the following **password** tag has its **showPassword** attribute set to **true**.

```
<s:form action="Product_save">
    <s:password key="password" showPassword="true"/>
    ...
</s:form>
```

Chapter 5: Form Tags

The **TextField** action in the **app05a** application shows how you can use the **textfield, password,** and **hidden** tags. The action is associated with the **TextFieldTestAction** class in Listing 5.1 and is forwarded to the **TextField.jsp** page in Listing 5.2.

Listing 5.1: The TextFieldTestAction class

```
package app05a;
import com.opensymphony.xwork2.ActionSupport;
public class TextFieldTestAction extends ActionSupport {
    private String userName;
    private String password;
    private String code;

    // getters and setters are not shown to save space
}
```

Listing 5.2: The TextField.jsp page

```
<%@ taglib prefix="s" uri="/struts-tags" %>
<html>
<head>
<title>textfield Tag Example</title>
<style type="text/css">@import url(css/main.css);</style>
</head>
<body>
<div id="global" style="width:150px">
    <h3>Login</h3>
    <s:form>
        <s:hidden name="code" value="1"/>
        <s:textfield name="userName" label="User Name"
                tooltip="Enter User Name"
                labelposition="top"
        />
        <s:password name="password" label="Password"
                tooltip="Enter Password"
                labelposition="top"
        />
        <s:submit value="Login"/>
    </s:form>
</div>
</body>
</html>
```

You can test the action by directing your browser here:

```
http://localhost:8080/app05a/TextField.action
```

The rendered form and input elements are shown in Figure 5.1. The **tooltip** attribute for each input tag results in the default tooltip icon to be displayed.

Figure 5.1: Using textfield, password, and hidden

The submit Tag

The **submit** tag renders a submit button. This tag can have one of three rendering types, depending on the value assigned to its **type** attribute. The following are valid values for the **type** attribute:

- input. Renders **submit** as <input type="submit" .../>
- button. Renders **submit** as <button type="submit" .../>
- image. Renders **submit** as <input type="image" ... />

The attributes for the **submit** tag are listed in Table 5.7.

For example, the following is a submit button whose value is "Login":

```
<s:submit value="Login"/>
```

Name	Data Type	Default Value	Description
action	String		The HTML **action** attribute
align	String		The HTML **align** attribute
method	String		The **method** attribute
type	String	input	The type of the rendered element. The value can be input, button, or image.

Table 5.7: submit tag attributes

The reset Tag

The **reset** tag renders a reset button. It can have one of two rendering types, depending on the value assigned to its **type** attribute. The following are valid values for the **type** attribute:

- input. Renders **reset** as <input type="reset" .../>
- button. Renders **reset** as <button type="reset" .../>

The **reset** tag attributes are given in Table 5.8.

Name	Data Type	Default Value	Description
action	String		The HTML **action** attribute
align	String		The HTML **align** attribute.
method	String		The **method** attribute
type	String	input	The type of the rendered element. The value can be input or button.

Table 5.8: reset tag attributes

The following is a **reset** tag.

```
<s:reset value="Reset to previous values" />
```

The label Tag

The **label** tag is rendered as an HTML label element. Its attribute is given in Table 5.9.

Name	Data Type	Default Value	Description
for	String		The HTML for attribute

Table 5.9: label tag attribute

The head Tag

The **head** tag is rendered as an HTML head element. It is rarely used. However, the identically named tag in the AJAX tag library plays an important role in AJAX programming with Struts.

The textarea Tag

This tag is rendered as a textarea element. Its attributes are shown in Table 5.10.

Name	Data Type	Default Value	Description
cols	integer		The HTML cols attribute.
readonly	boolean	false	Indicates if the textarea is read only.
rows	Integer		The HTML rows attribute.
wrap	boolean		The HTML wrap attribute

Table 5.10: textarea tag attributes

For example, the **TextAreaTestAction** class in Listing 5.3 has a property that is mapped to a **textarea** tag on the **TextArea.jsp** page in Listing 5.4.

Listing 5.3: The TextAreaTestAction class

```
package app05a;
import com.opensymphony.xwork2.ActionSupport;
public class TextAreaTestAction extends ActionSupport {
    private String description;
    //getter and setter not shown
}
```

Listing 5.4: The TextArea.jsp page

```
<%@ taglib prefix="s" uri="/struts-tags" %>
<html>
<head>
```

Chapter 5: Form Tags

```
<title>textfield Tag Example</title>
<style type="text/css">@import url(css/main.css);</style>
</head>
<body>
<div id="global" style="width:450px">
    <s:form>
        <s:textarea name="description" label="Description"
                cols="35" rows="8"
        />
        <s:reset/>
        <s:submit/>
    </s:form>
</div>
</body>
</html>
```

To test this example, direct your browser to this URL:

`http://localhost:8080/app05a/TextArea.action`

Figure 5.2 shows what the **textarea** tag looks like.

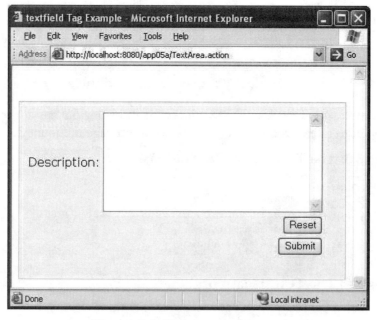

Figure 5.2: Using textarea

The checkbox Tag

The **checkbox** tag renders an HTML checkbox. There is only one attribute specific to this tag, **fieldValue**, which is given in Table 5.11. You will learn at the end of this section that this attribute can be very useful.

Name	Data Type	Default Value	Description
fieldValue	String	true	The actual value of the checkbox.

Table 5.11: checkbox tag attribute

Like other input elements, an HTML checkbox adds a request parameter to the HTTP request when the containing form is submitted. The value of a checked checkbox is "on." If the name of the checkbox element is **subscribe**, for example, the key/value pair of the corresponding request parameter is

```
subscribe=on
```

However, an unchecked checkbox does not add a request parameter. It would be good if it sent this:

```
subscribe=off
```

But it does not.

And here lies the problem: There's no way for the server to know if a checked checkbox has been unchecked. Consider an object in the **HttpSession** that has a boolean property linked with a checkbox. A value of "on" (when the check box is checked) would invoke the property setter and set the value to true. An unchecked checkbox would not invoke the property setter and, as a result, if the previous value was true, it would remain true.

The **checkbox** tag overcomes this limitation by creating an accompanying hidden value. For example, the following **checkbox** tag

```
<s:checkbox label="inStock" key="inStock"/>
```

is rendered as

```
<input type="checkbox" name="inStock" value="true"
       id="ActionName_inStock"/>
<input type="hidden" name="__checkbox_inStock" value="true"/>
```

If the checkbox is checked when the containing form is submitted, both values (the check box and the hidden value) will be sent to the server. If the checkbox is not checked, only the hidden field is sent, and the absence of the checkbox parameter indicates that the checkbox was unchecked. The Checkbox interceptor helps make sure the property setter gets invoke regardless the state of the checkbox. A checked checkbox will pass the String literal "**true**" to the property setter and an unchecked one will pass the String literal "**false.**"

As an example, the **CheckBoxTestAction** class in Listing 5.5 has boolean properties that are mapped to three **checkbox** tags on the **CheckBox.jsp** page in Listing 5.6.

Listing 5.5: The CheckBoxTestAction class

```
package app05a;
import com.opensymphony.xwork2.ActionSupport;
public class CheckBoxTestAction extends ActionSupport {
    private boolean daily;
    private boolean weekly;
    private boolean monthly;

    //getters and setters have been deleted
}
```

Listing 5.6: The CheckBox.jsp page

```
<%@ taglib prefix="s" uri="/struts-tags" %>
<html>
<head>
<title>checkbox Tag Example</title>
<style type="text/css">@import url(css/main.css);</style>
</head>
<body>
<div id="global" style="width:300px">
    <h3>Subscription Type</h3>
    <s:form>
        <s:checkbox name="daily" label="Daily news alert"/>
        <s:checkbox name="weekly" label="Weekly reports"/>
        <s:checkbox name="monthly" label="Monthly reviews"
                value="true" disabled="true"
        />
        <s:submit/>
    </s:form>
</div>
</body>
```

```
</html>
```

You can test the example by using this URL:

```
http://localhost:8080/app05a/CheckBox.action
```

Figure 5.3 shows the checkboxes.

Figure 5.3: Using check boxes

The last checkbox is disabled and its value cannot be changed. Sometimes you may want to display a disabled checkbox to show the user a default selection that cannot be changed.

Now, let's look at another great feature of the **checkbox** tag.

The **checkbox** tag has a **fieldValue** attribute that specifies the actual value that is sent to the server when the containing form of a checked checkbox is submitted. If no **fieldValue** attribute is present, the value of the checkbox is either **"true"** or **"false."** If it is present and the checkbox was checked, the value of the **fieldValue** is sent. If the **fieldValue** attribute is present and the checkbox is unchecked, no request parameter associated with the checkbox will be sent.

This attribute can be used to send selected values of a series of checkboxes. For example, the **CheckBoxTest2Action** class in Listing 5.7 has a getter that returns a list of **Magazine** objects. You can use the **checkbox** tag and the **fieldValue** attribute to construct the same number of checkboxes as the number of magazines on the list, as shown in the CheckBox2.jsp page in Listing 5.8. Each checkbox is assigned a magazine code.

Listing 5.7: The CheckBoxTest2Action class

```
package app05a;
import com.opensymphony.xwork2.ActionSupport;
import java.util.ArrayList;
import java.util.List;

public class CheckBoxTest2Action extends ActionSupport{
    public List<Magazine> getMagazineList() {
        List<Magazine> magazines = new ArrayList<Magazine>();
        magazines.add(new Magazine("034", "The Economist"));
        magazines.add(new Magazine("122", "Business Week"));
        magazines.add(new Magazine("434", "Fortune"));
        magazines.add(new Magazine("906", "Small Business"));
        return magazines;
    }

    public void setMagazines(String[] codes) {
        for (String code : codes) {
            System.out.println(code + " is selected");
        }
    }
}

class Magazine {
    private String code;
    private String name;
    public Magazine(String code, String name) {
        this.code = code;
        this.name = name;
    }
    public String getCode() {
        return code;
    }
    public String getName() {
        return name;
    }
}
```

Listing 5.8: The CheckBox2.jsp page

```
<%@ taglib prefix="s" uri="/struts-tags" %>
<html>
```

```
<head>
<title>CheckBox fieldValue Test</title>
</head>
<body>
<s:form>
<s:iterator value="magazineList">
    <s:checkbox name="magazines"
            label="%{name}"
            fieldValue="%{code}"/>
</s:iterator>
<s:submit/>
</s:form>
</body>
</html>
```

The **iterator** tag will iterate over the magazine list and will be explained in Chapter 6, "Generic Tags." The whole form will be rendered as

```
<form ...>
<input type="checkbox" name="magazines" value="034" .../>
<input type="hidden" name="__checkbox_magazines" value="034" />
      <input type="checkbox" name="magazines" value="122" .../>
<input type="hidden" name="__checkbox_magazines" value="122" />
      <input type="checkbox" name="magazines" value="434" />
<input type="hidden" name="__checkbox_magazines" value="434" />
<input type="checkbox" name="magazines" value="906" />
<input type="hidden" name="__checkbox_magazines" value="906" />
</form>
```

All checkboxes have the same name (magazines) which means their values are linked to an array or a collection. If a checkbox is checked, its value (magazine code) will be sent. If it is not, its value will not be sent. As such, you'll know which magazines have been selected.

You can test this example by using this URL:

```
http://localhost:8080/app05a/CheckBox2.action
```

The checkboxes are shown in Figure 5.4. Note that there are four checkboxes constructed since there are four magazines on the list.

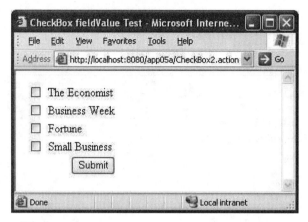

Figure 5.4: Using the fieldValue attribute

Note

The **checkboxlist** tag renders multiple checkboxes too, but its layout is fixed. Using **checkbox** tags, on the other hand, gives you more flexibility in laying out the rendered elements.

The list, listKey, and listValue attributes

The **list**, **listKey**, and **listValue** attributes are important attributes for such tags as **radio**, **combobox**, **select**, **checkboxlist**, **doubleselect** because they help retrieve options for the tags.

A radio set, for example, needs options. Consider these HTML input tags that are rendered as radio buttons shown in Figure 5.5.

```
<input type="radio" name="city" value="1"/>Atlanta
<input type="radio" name="city" value="2"/>Chicago
<input type="radio" name="city" value="3"/>Detroit
```

As you can see, the radio set has a set of values (1, 2, 3) and a set of labels (Atlanta, Chicago, Detroit). The value/label pairs are as follows.

```
1 - Atlanta
2 - Chicago
3 - Detroit
```

○ Atlanta ○ Chicago ○ Detroit

Figure 5.5: Radio buttons

Select elements also need options. This select element (shown in Figure 5.6) features the same options as the radio set.

```
<select name="city">
    <option value="1">Atlanta</option>
    <option value="2">Chicago</option>
    <option value="3">Detroit</option>
</select>
```

Figure 5.6: The city select element

Note

In a select element, the **value** attribute is optional. If it is not present, the label will be sent as the value when the corresponding option is selected. With radio buttons, the value attribute is not required but when the value attribute is absent, **"on"** will be sent, and not the label. Therefore, a radio button must always have the **value** attribute.

This section explains how you can use the **list**, **listKey**, and **listValue** attributes in the **radio**, **select**, and other tags that require options. When you use these tags, you need to have label/value pairs as the source of your options. Of the three attributes, the **list** attribute is required and the other two are optional. You can assign a **String**, an array, a **java.util.Enumeration**, a **java.util.Iterator**, a **java.util.Map**, or a **Collection** to the **list** attribute. The object can be placed in an action object, in the session object, or the **ServletContext** object.

Note

If the object you dynamically assign to the **list** attribute has no options, you must return an empty array/Collection/Map instead of null.

Assigning A String

You can assign a **String** representation of an array. For example, the following **select** tag is assigned a string.

```
<s:select list="{'Atlanta', 'Chicago', 'Detroit'}"/>
```

This **select** tag will be rendered as

```
<select>
    <option value="Atlanta">Atlanta</option>
    <option value="Chicago">Chicago</option>
    <option value="Detroit">Detroit</option>
</select>
```

Note that each string element is used as both the value and the label.

Most of the time, you want to use values that are different from labels for your options. In this case, the syntax is this:

```
#{'value-1':'label-1', 'value-2':'label-2', ... 'value-n':'label-n'}
```

For example, the following select tag:

```
<s:select list="#{'1':'Atlanta', '2':'Chicago', '3':'Detroit'}"/>
```

is rendered as

```
<select>
    <option value="1">Atlanta</option>
    <option value="2">Chicago</option>
    <option value="3">Detroit</option>
</select>
```

Assigning a Map

You use a **Map** as the source for your options if the value of each option needs to be different from the label. Using a **Map** is very straightforward. Put the values as the **Map** keys and the labels as the **Map** values. For example, here is how to populate a **Map** called **cities** with three cities:

```
Map<Integer, String> cities = new HashMap<Integer, String>();
cities.put(1, "Atlanta");
cities.put(2, "Chicago");
cities.put(3, "Detroit");
```

If **cities** is an action property, you can assign it to the list attribute. Like this:

```
<s:select list="cities"/>
```

Or, if **cities** is an application attribute, you use this code.

```
<s:select list="#application.cities"/>
```

Assigning A Collection or An Object Array

You use an array or a **Collection** of objects as the source for options. In this case, you need to use the **list**, **listKey**, and **listValue** attributes. Assign the array or **Collection** to the **list** attribute. Assign to **listKey** the object property that will supply the value of each option and to **listValue** the object property that will supply the label of each option.

For example, assuming that the action object's **getCities** method return a **List** of **City** objects with an **id** and a **name** properties, you would use the following to assign the **List** to a select tag.

```
<s:select list="cities" listKey="id" listValue="name" />
```

You will see more examples in the sections to come.

The radio Tag

The **radio** tag renders a group of radio buttons. The number of radio buttons is the same as the number of options you feed the tag's **list** attribute. Even though the **radio** tag will work with only one option, you should use it to render multiple options from which the user can select one. For a true/false value, use a checkbox instead of **radio**.

Name	Data Type	Default Value	Description
list*	String		An iterable source to populate from
listKey	String		The property of the object in the list that will supply the option values.
listValue	String		The property of the object in the list that will supply the option labels.

Table 5.12: radio tag attributes

The **radio** tag adds three attributes listed in Table 5.12. * indicates a required attribute.

The following example uses two **radio** tags to get the user type and the income level on a club membership form. The first tag gets its options from a hardcoded list and the second tag gets its options from a **Map**.

The **RadioTestAction** class in Listing 5.9 is the action class for this example. Note that the **incomeLevels Map** is a static variable that is populated inside a static block so that it's only populated once for all instances of the action class.

Listing 5.9: The RadioTestAction class

```
package app05a;
import java.util.SortedMap;
import java.util.TreeMap;
import com.opensymphony.xwork2.ActionSupport;

public class RadioTestAction extends ActionSupport {
    private int userType;
    private int incomeLevel;
    private static SortedMap<Integer, String> incomeLevels;
    static {
        incomeLevels = new TreeMap<Integer, String>();
        incomeLevels.put(1, "0 - $10,000");
        incomeLevels.put(2, "$10,001 - $30,000");
        incomeLevels.put(3, "$30,001 - $50,000");
        incomeLevels.put(4, "Over $50,000");
    }
    public int getIncomeLevel() {
        return incomeLevel;
    }
    public void setIncomeLevel(int incomeLevel) {
        this.incomeLevel = incomeLevel;
    }
    public int getUserType() {
        return userType;
    }
    public void setUserType(int userType) {
        this.userType = userType;
    }

    public SortedMap<Integer, String> getIncomeLevels() {
```

```
            return incomeLevels;
        }
    }
}
```

A **SortedMap** is used instead of a **Map** to guarantee that the options are rendered in the same order as the key. Using a **Map** does not provide the same guarantee.

The **Radio.jsp** page in Listing 5.10 shows the **radio** tags.

Listing 5.10: The Radio.jsp page

```
<%@ taglib prefix="s" uri="/struts-tags" %>
<html>
<head>
<title>radio Tag Example</title>
<style type="text/css">@import url(css/main.css);</style>
</head>
<body>
<div id="global" style="width:450px">
    <h3>Membership Form</h3>
    <s:form>
        <s:radio name="userType" label="User Type"
                list="#{'1':'Individual', '2':'Organization'}"
        />
        <s:radio name="incomeLevel" label="Income Level"
                list="incomeLevels"
        />
        <s:submit/>
    </s:form>
</div>
</body>
</html>
```

To run the test, use this URL:

```
http://localhost:8080/app05a/Radio.action
```

Figure 5.7 shows how the radio buttons are rendered.

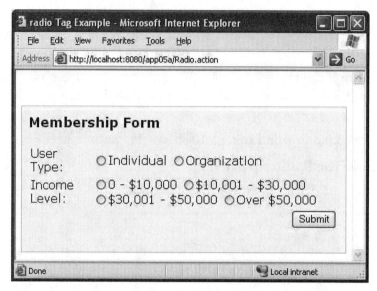

Figure 5.7: Using the radio tag

Note that the first **radio** tag is rendered as two radio buttons, in accordance with the number of hardcoded options. The second **radio** tag translates into four radio buttons because it's linked to a **Map** with four elements.

The select Tag

The **select** tag renders a select element. Its attributes are given in Table 5.13.

The **headerKey** and **headerValue** attributes can be used to insert an option. For instance, the following **select** tag inserts a header.

```
<s:select name="city" label="City"
        headerKey="0" headerValue="[Select a city]"
        list="#{'1':'Atlanta', '2':'Chicago', '3':'Detroit'}"
/>
```

The following example is used to let the user select a country and a city using two select elements. The first select element displays three countries (US, Canada, Mexico) from a **Map** in the **ServletContext** object. You normally put a selection of options in a **ServletContext** if you intend to use the options

from many different points in your application. You use the
ServletContextListener in Listing 5.11 to populate the **Map**.

Name	Data Type	Default Value	Description
emptyOption	boolean	false	Indicates whether or not to insert an empty option after the header.
headerKey	String		The key for the first item in the list.
headerValue	String		The value for the first item in the list.
list*	String		An iterable source to populate from
listKey	String		The property of the object in the list that will supply the option values.
listValue	String		The property of the object in the list that will supply the option labels.
multiple	boolean	false	Indicates whether or not multiple selection is allowed
size	integer		The number of options to show

Table 5.13: select tag attributes

Listing 5.11: The application listener

```
package app05a;
import java.util.HashMap;
import java.util.Map;
import javax.servlet.ServletContext;
import javax.servlet.ServletContextEvent;
import javax.servlet.ServletContextListener;

public class ApplicationListener
        implements ServletContextListener {
    public void contextInitialized(ServletContextEvent cse) {
        Map<Integer, String> countries =
                new HashMap<Integer, String>();
        countries.put(1, "US");
        countries.put(2, "Canada");
        countries.put(3, "Mexico");
        ServletContext servletContext = cse.getServletContext();
        servletContext.setAttribute("countries", countries);
    }
    public void contextDestroyed(ServletContextEvent cse) {
    }
}
```

The second **select** tag dynamically displays cities in the selected country. If the selected country is US, the **select** element displays Atlanta, Chicago, and Detroit. If the selected country is Canada, Vancouver, Toronto, and Montreal are displayed. Because the cities are dynamic, the options are generated in the action class. Note that the selection is presented in an array of **City** object. The **City** class has two properties, **id** and **name**. The action class and the **City** class are shown in Listing 5.12.

Listing 5.12: The SelectTestAction and City classes

```
package app05a;
import com.opensymphony.xwork2.ActionSupport;

public class SelectTestAction extends ActionSupport {
    private int city;
    private int country;

    public City[] getCities() {
        City[] cities = null;
        if (country == 1) {
            cities = new City[3];
            cities[0] = new City(1, "Atlanta");
            cities[1] = new City(2, "Chicago");
            cities[2] = new City(3, "Detroit");
        } else if (country == 2) {
            cities = new City[3];
            cities[0] = new City(4, "Vancouver");
            cities[1] = new City(5, "Toronto");
            cities[2] = new City(6, "Montreal");

        } else if (country == 3) {
            cities = new City[2];
            cities[0] = new City(7, "Mexico City");
            cities[1] = new City(8, "Tijuana");
        } else {
            cities = new City[0];
        }
        return cities;
    }
    public int getCity() {
        return city;
    }
    public void setCity(int city) {
        this.city = city;
    }
```

```
    public int getCountry() {
        return country;
    }
    public void setCountry(int country) {
        this.country = country;
    }
}

class City {
    private int id;
    private String name;
    public City(int id, String name) {
        this.id = id;
        this.name = name;
    }
    public int getId() {
        return id;
    }
    public void setId(int id) {
        this.id = id;
    }
    public String getName() {
        return name;
    }
    public void setName(String name) {
        this.name = name;
    }

}
```

The JSP used for this example is given in Listing 5.13.

Listing 5.13: The Select.jsp page

```
<%@ taglib prefix="s" uri="/struts-tags" %>
<html>
<head>
<title>select Tag Example</title>
<style type="text/css">@import url(css/main.css);</style>
</head>
<body>
<div id="global" style="width:300px">
    <h3>Select Location</h3>
    <s:form>
        <s:select name="country" label="Country" emptyOption="true"
            list="#application.countries"
```

```
            onchange="this.form.submit()"
        />
        <s:select name="city" label="City"
            list="cities" listKey="id" listValue="name"
        />
        <s:submit/>
    </s:form>
</div>
</body>
</html>
```

The **country select** tag has its **emptyOption** attribute set to true to provide an empty option and its **list** attribute set to the **countries** scoped variable in the **application** implicit object. In addition, its **onchange** attribute is assigned a Javascript function that will submit the containing form when the value of the **select** element changes. This way, when the user selects a country, the form will be submitted and invokes the action object that prepares the city options in the **getCities** method.

To run this test, use this URL:

```
http://localhost:8080/app05a/Select.action
```

Figure 5.8 shows the city options when US is selected and Figure 5.9 shows what cities the user can choose when the country is Canada.

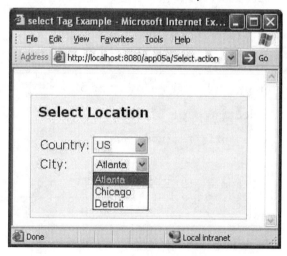

Figure 5.8: The city options for US

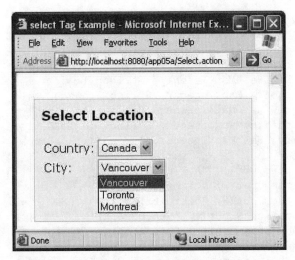

Figure 5.9: The city options for Canada

Select Option Grouping with optgroup

You can group options in a select element by using the **optgroup** tag. Each option group has its own source. The **optgroup** tag's attributes are given in Table 5.14.

Name	Data Type	Default Value	Description
list*	String		An iterable source to populate from
listKey	String		The property of the object in the list that will supply the option values.
listValue	String		The property of the object in the list that will supply the option labels.

Table 5.14: optgroup tag attributes

For example, the **OptGroupTestAction** class in Listing 5.14 is an action class that has three **Map** properties, **usCities**, **canadaCities**, and **mexicoCities**.

Listing 5.14: The OptGroupTestAction class

```
package app05a;
import java.util.HashMap;
import java.util.Map;
import com.opensymphony.xwork2.ActionSupport;
```

```
public class OptGroupTestAction extends ActionSupport {
    private int city;
    private static Map<Integer, String> usCities =
            new HashMap<Integer, String>();
    private static Map<Integer, String> canadaCities =
            new HashMap<Integer, String>();
    private static Map<Integer, String> mexicoCities =
            new HashMap<Integer, String>();
    static {
        usCities.put(1, "Atlanta");
        usCities.put(2, "Chicago");
        usCities.put(3, "Detroit");
        canadaCities.put(4, "Vancouver");
        canadaCities.put(5, "Toronto");
        canadaCities.put(6, "Montreal");
        mexicoCities.put(7, "Mexico City");
        mexicoCities.put(8, "Tijuana");
    }
    public int getCity() {
        return city;
    }
    public void setCity(int city) {
        this.city = city;
    }
    public Map<Integer, String> getUsCities() {
        return usCities;
    }
    public Map<Integer, String> getCanadaCities() {
        return canadaCities;
    }
    public Map<Integer, String> getMexicoCities() {
        return mexicoCities;
    }

}
```

The **OptGroup.jsp** page in Listing 5.15 shows how to use the **optgroup** tag to group options in the **select** element in this example.

Listing 5.15: The OptGroup.jsp page

```
<%@ taglib prefix="s" uri="/struts-tags" %>
<html>
<head>
<title>optgroup Tag Example</title>
```

```
<style type="text/css">@import url(css/main.css);</style>
</head>
<body>
<div id="global" style="width:300px">
    <h3>Select City</h3>
    <s:form>
        <s:select name="city" label="City" emptyOption="true"
                list="usCities">

            <s:optgroup label="Canada" list="canadaCities"/>
            <s:optgroup label="Mexico" list="mexicoCities"/>

        </s:select>
        <s:submit/>
    </s:form>
</div>
</body>
</html>
```

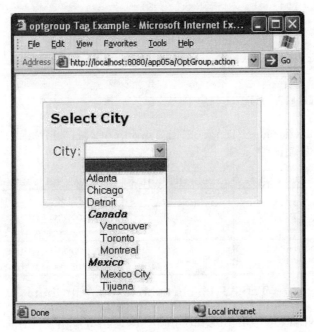

Figure 5.10: Using optgroup

The URL for testing this action is:

`http://localhost:8080/app05a/OptGroup.action`

Figure 5.10 shows the select element with option groups.

If you're curious, you can view the source and see that the select element is rendered as these HTML tags.

```
<select name="city" id="OptGroup_city">
    <option value=""></option>
    <option value="2">Chicago</option>
    <option value="1">Atlanta</option>
    <option value="3">Detroit</option>

    <optgroup label="Canada">
        <option value="4">Vancouver</option>
        <option value="6">Montreal</option>
        <option value="5">Toronto</option>
    </optgroup>
    <optgroup label="Mexico">
        <option value="8">Tijuana</option>
        <option value="7">Mexico City</option>
    </optgroup>
</select>
```

The checkboxlist Tag

The **checkboxlist** tag is rendered as a group of check boxes. Its attributes are listed in Table 5.15.

Name	Data Type	Default Value	Description
list*	String		An iterable source to populate from
listKey	String		The property of the object in the list that will supply the option values.
listValue	String		The property of the object in the list that will supply the option labels.

Table 5.15: checkboxlist tag attribute

A **checkboxlist** tag is mapped to an array of strings or an array of primitives. If no checkbox on the list is selected, the corresponding property will be assigned an empty array, not null.

The following example shows how you can use the **checkboxlist** tag. The property underlying the **checkboxlist** is an array of integers. The options come from a **List** of **Interest** objects.

Listing 5.16 shows the **CheckBoxListTestAction** class, the action class for this example, and the **Interest** class.

Listing 5.16: The CheckBoxListTestAction and Interest classes

```
package app05a;
import java.util.ArrayList;
import java.util.List;
import com.opensymphony.xwork2.ActionSupport;

public class CheckBoxListTestAction extends ActionSupport {
    private int[] interests;
    private static List<Interest> interestOptions =
            new ArrayList<Interest>();
    static {
        interestOptions.add(new Interest(1, "Automotive"));
        interestOptions.add(new Interest(2, "Games"));
        interestOptions.add(new Interest(3, "Sports"));
    }
    public int[] getInterests() {
        return interests;
    }

    public void setInterests(int[] interests) {
        this.interests = interests;
    }
    public List<Interest> getInterestOptions() {
        return interestOptions;
    }

}
class Interest {
    private int id;
    private String description;
    public Interest(int id, String description) {
        this.id = id;
        this.description = description;
    }
    // getters and setters not shown
}
```

Listing 5.17 shows the **CheckBoxList.jsp** page that uses a **checkboxlist** tag.

Listing 5.17: The CheckBoxList.jsp page

```
<%@ taglib prefix="s" uri="/struts-tags" %>
<html>
<head>
<title>checkboxlist Tag Example</title>
<style type="text/css">@import url(css/main.css);</style>
</head>
<body>
<div id="global" style="width:450px">
    <h3>Select Interests</h3>
    <s:form>
        <s:checkboxlist name="interests" label="Interests"
                list="interestOptions"
                listKey="id" listValue="description"
        />
        <s:submit/>
    </s:form>
</div>
</body>
</html>
```

You can run the action by directing your browser to this URL:

```
http://localhost:8080/app05a/CheckBoxList.action
```

The result is shown in Figure 5. 11.

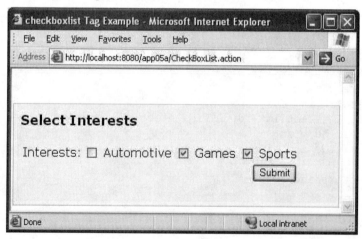

Figure 5.11: Using checkboxlist

The combobox Tag

The **combobox** tag renders as a text input field and a select element. Its attributes are listed in Table 5.16.

Name	Data Type	Default Value	Description
emptyOption	boolean	false	Indicates if an empty option should be inserted.
headerKey	integer		The key for headerValue, should be -1.
headerValue	String		Text that will be added as a select option but is not intended to be selected
list*	String		An iterable source to populate from
listKey	String		The property of the object in the list that will supply the option values.
listValue	String		The property of the object in the list that will supply the option labels.
maxlength	integer		The HTML maxlength attribute.
readonly	boolean	false	Indicates if the rendered element is read only.
size	integer		The size of the rendered element.

Table 5.16: combobox tag attribute

Unlike the **select** tag, the options for a combo box normally do not need keys. Also, the label of the selected option, and not the value, is sent when the containing form is submitted.

As an example, the **ComboBoxTestAction** class in Listing 5.18 is an action class that provides a property (make) linked to the **combobox** tag on the JSP in Listing 5.19.

Listing 5.18: The ComboBoxTestAction class

```
package app05a;
import com.opensymphony.xwork2.ActionSupport;
public class ComboBoxTestAction extends ActionSupport {
```

```
    private String make;
    // getter and setter not shown
}
```

Listing 5.19: The ComboBox.jsp page

```jsp
<%@ taglib prefix="s" uri="/struts-tags" %>
<html>
<head>
<title>combobox Tag Example</title>
<style type="text/css">@import url(css/main.css);</style>
<style type="text/css">
td {
    vertical-align:top;
}
</style>
</head>
<body>
<div id="global" style="width:300px">
    <h3>Select Car Make</h3>
    <s:form>
        <s:combobox name="make" label="Car Make" size="24"
                headerKey="-1" headerValue="Select a make"
                list="{ 'Ford', 'Pontiac', 'Toyota'}"
        />
        <s:submit/>
    </s:form>
</div>
</body>
</html>
```

Use this URL to test the action:

```
http://localhost:8080/app05a/ComboBox.action
```

The result is shown in Figure 5.12.

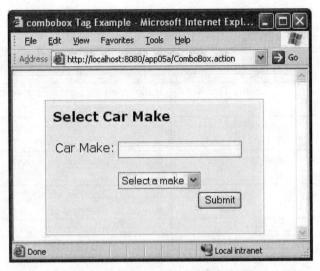

Figure 5.12: Using combobox

The updownselect Tag

The **updownselect** tag functions like a **checkboxlist**, allowing you to select multiple options from a list of options. An **updownselect** tag is rendered as a select element with its **multiple** attribute set to **multiple** and buttons to select all options and reorder options. (See Figure 5.13).

Table 5.17 shows the list of attributes of **updownselect**.

Note

When the form containing the **updownselect** tag fails to validate, the previously selected value(s) of the **updownselect** tag is not retained.

The following example shows how to use **updownselect** to select multiple colors. Listing 5.20 shows an action class (**UpDownSelectTestAction**) for this example and Listing 5.21 the JSP that uses the tag.

Listing 5.20: The UpDownSelectTestAction class

```
package app05a;
import com.opensymphony.xwork2.ActionSupport;
public class UpDownSelectTestAction extends ActionSupport {
    private int[] colors;
```

```
    // getter and setter not shown
}
```

Name	Data Type	Default Value	Description
allowMoveDown	boolean	true	Indicates whether the move down button will be displayed.
allowMoveUp	boolean	true	Indicates whether the move up button will be displayed.
allowSelectAll	boolean	true	Indicates whether the select all button will be displayed.
emptyOption	boolean	false	Indicates whether an empty (--) option should be inserted after the header option.
headerKey	String		The key for the first item on the list.
headerValue	String		The value for the first item on the list.
list*	String		Iterable source to populate from.
listKey	String		The property of the object in the list that will supply the option values.
listValue	String		The property of the object in the list that will supply the option labels.
moveDownLabel	String	v	Text to display on the move down button.
moveUpLabel	String	^	Text to display on the move up button.
multiple	boolean	false	Indicates if a multiple select should be created.
selectAllLabel	String	*	Text to display on the select all button.
size	Integer		The number of options to show.

Table 5.17: updownselect tag attribute

Listing 5.21: The UpDownSelect.jsp page

```jsp
<%@ taglib prefix="s" uri="/struts-tags" %>
<html>
<head>
<title>updownselect Tag Example</title>
<style type="text/css">@import url(css/main.css);</style>
<style type="text/css">
select {
    width:100px;
}
</style>
</head>
<body>
<div id="global" style="width:250px">
```

```
    <h3>Favorite colors</h3>
    <s:form>
        <s:updownselect name="colors" label="Colors" size="5"
                list="#{'1':'Green', '2':'Red', '3':'Yellow'}"
        />
        <s:submit/>
    </s:form>
</div>
</body>
</html>
```

Use this URL to test the example:

```
http://localhost:8080/app05a/UpDownSelect.action
```

The rendered elements are shown in Figure 5.13.

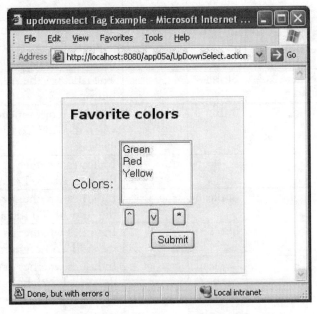

Figure 5.13: Using updownselect

The optiontransferselect Tag

The **optiontransferselect** tag is rendered as two select elements. It includes Javascript functions for transferring options between the two select elements.

Table 5.18 shows the attributes of **optiontransferselect**.

Name	Data Type	Default Value	Description
addAllToLeftLabel	String		The label for the Add All To Left button
addAllToLeftOnclick	String		The Javascript function to invoke when the Add All To Left button is clicked.
addAllToRightLabel	String		The label for the Add All To Right button
addAllToRightOnclick	String		The Javascript function to invoke when the Add All To Right button is clicked.
addToLeftLabel	String		The label for the Add To Left button.
addToLeftOnclick	String		The Javascript function to invoke when the Add To Left button is clicked.
addToRightLabel	String		The label for the Add To Right button.
addToRightOnclick	String		The Javascript function to invoke when the Add To Right button is clicked.
allowAddAllToLeft	boolean	true	Indicates whether or not to enable the Add All To Left button.
allowAddAllToRight	boolean	true	Indicates whether or not to enable the Add All To Right button.
allowAddToLeft	boolean	true	Indicates whether or not to enable the Add To Left button.
allowAddToRight	boolean	true	Indicates whether or not to enable the Add To Right button.
allowSelectAll	boolean	true	Indicates whether or not to enable the Select All button.
allowUpDownOnLeft	boolean	true	Indicates whether or not to enable moving options up and down on the left select element.
allowUpDownOnRight	boolean	true	Indicates whether or not to enable moving options up and down on the right select element.
buttonCssClass	String		The CSS class for the buttons.

buttonCssStyle	String		The CSS style for the buttons.
doubleCssClass	String		The CSS class for the second list.
doubleCssStyle	String		The CSS style for the second list.
doubledDisabled	boolean	false	Indicates if the second list should be disabled.
doubleEmptyOption	boolean	false	Indicates if an empty option should be inserted to the second list.
doubleHeaderKey	String		The header key for the second list.
doubleHeaderValue	String		The header value for the second list.
doubleId	String		The identifier for the second list.
doubleList*	String		The iterable source to populate the second list.
doubleListKey	String		The property of the object in the second list that will supply the option values.
doubleListValue	String		The property of the object in the second list that will supply the option labels.
doubleMultiple	boolean	false	Indicates if the second list should allow multiple selection.
doubleName*	String		The name for the second component.
doubleSize	integer		The size attribute for the second list.
emptyOption	boolean	false	Indicates if an empty option should be inserted to the first list.
formName	String		The name of the form containing this component.
headerKey	String		The header key for the first list.
headerValue	String		The header value for the first list.
leftDownLabel	String		The label for the left Down button.
leftTitle	String		The title for the left selection.
leftUpLabel	String		The label for the left Up button.
list*	String		The iterable source to populate the first list..

listKey	String		The property of the object in the first list that will supply the option values.
listValue	String		The property of the object in the first list that will supply the option labels.
multiple	boolean		Indicates if multiple selection is allowed for the first select element.
rightDownLabel	String		The label for the right Down button.
rightTitle	String		The title for the selection on the right.
rightUpLabel	String		The label for the right Up button.
selectAllLabel	String		The label for the Select All button.
selectAllOnclick	String		The Javascript function to invoke when the Select All button is clicked.
size	integer		The number of elements to show in the first selection.
upDownOnLeftOnclick	String		The Javascript function that will be invoked when the left Up/Down button is clicked.
upDownOnRightOnclick	String		The Javascript function that will be invoked when the right Up/Down button is clicked.

Table 5.18: optiontransferselect tag attributes

Note

Only selected (highlighted) options are sent to the server. Simply transferring an option to the right select element does not make the option selected.

For example, the **OptionTransferSelectTestAction** class in Listing 5.22 is an action class with a **selectedLanguages** property that is mapped to an **optiontransferselect** tag. The tag is used in the **OptionTransferSelect.jsp** page in Listing 5.23.

Listing 5.22: The OptionTransferSelectTestAction

```
package app05a;
import com.opensymphony.xwork2.ActionSupport;

public class OptionTransferSelectTestAction extends ActionSupport {
    private String[] selectedLanguages;
    public String[] getSelectedLanguages() {
        return selectedLanguages;
    }
    public void setSelectedLanguages(String[] selectedLanguages) {
        for (String language : selectedLanguages) {
            System.out.println("Language:" + language);
        }
        this.selectedLanguages = selectedLanguages;
    }
}
```

Listing 5.23: The OptionTransferSelect.jsp page

```
<%@ taglib prefix="s" uri="/struts-tags" %>
<html>
<head>
<title>optiontransferselect Tag Example</title>
<style type="text/css">@import url(css/main.css);</style>
<style>
select {
    width:170px;
}
</style>
</head>
<body>
<div id="global" style="width:550px">
    <s:form>
        <s:optiontransferselect label="Select languages"
                name="allLanguages"
                leftTitle="All languages"
                rightTitle="Selected languages"
                list="{'French', 'Spanish', 'German',
                        'Dutch', 'Mandarin', 'Cantonese'}"
                multiple="true"
                headerKey="headerKey"
                headerValue="--- Please Select ---"
                size="12"

                emptyOption="true"
```

```
                doubleList="{'English'}"
                doubleName="selectedLanguages"
                doubleHeaderKey="doubleHeaderKey"
                doubleMultiple="true"
                doubleSize="5"
        />
        <s:submit/>
      </s:form>
</div>
</body>
</html>
```

To test this example, direct your browser to this URL:

```
http://localhost:8080/app05a/OptionTransferSelect.action
```

The rendered elements are shown in Figure 5.14.

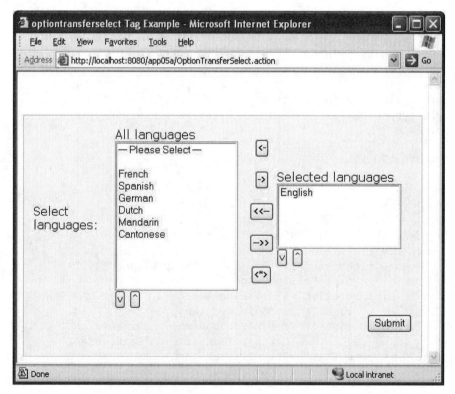

Figure 5.14: Using optiontransferselect

The doubleselect Tag

The **doubleselect** tag renders two select elements that are linked together. Its attributes are listed in Table 5.19.

Name	Data Type	Default Value	Description
doubleCssClass	String		The CSS class for the second select element.
doubleCssStyle	String		The CSS style for the second select element.
doubleDisabled	booelan	false	Indicates if the second select element should be disabled.
doubleEmptyOption		false	Indicates whether an empty option should be inserted to the second select element.
doubleHeaderKey	String		The header key for the second select element.
doubleHeaderValue	String		The header value for the second select element.
doubleId	String		The identifier for the second select element.
doubleList*	String		The iterable object for populating the second select element.
doubleListKey	String		The property of the object in the second list that will supply the option labels.
doubleListValue	String		The property of the object in the second list that will supply the option labels.
doubleMultiple	boolean	false	Indicates whether the second select element should allow multiple selection.
doubleName*	String		The name for the second selection.
doubleSize	interger		The number of options to be shown in the second select element.
doubleValue	String		The value for the second select element.

emptyOption	boolean	false	Indicates whether or not an empty options should be inserted to the first select element.
formName	String		The name of the containing form.
headerKey	String		The header key for the first select element.
headerValue	String		The header value for the first select element.
list			The iterable object that will populate the first select element.
listKey	String		The property of the object in the first list that will supply the option values.
listValue	String		The property of the object in the first list that will supply the option labels.
multiple	boolean	False	Indicates whether or not the first element should allow multiple selection.
size	Integer		The number of options to be displayed in the first element.

Table 5.19: optiontransferselect attributes

As an example, the **DoubleSelectTestAction** class in Listing 5.24 is an action class with two properties linked to the **doubleselect** tag in the **DoubleSelect.jsp** page in Listing 5.25.

Listing 5.24: The DoubleSelectTestAction class

```
package app05a;
import com.opensymphony.xwork2.ActionSupport;
public class DoubleSelectTestAction extends ActionSupport {
    private String country;
    private String city;
    // getters and setters not shown
}
```

Listing 5.25: The DoubleSelect.jsp page

```
<%@ taglib prefix="s" uri="/struts-tags" %>
<html>
<head>
<title>doubleselect Tag Example</title>
<style type="text/css">@import url(css/main.css);</style>
```

```
<style>
select {
    width:170px;
}
</style>
</head>
<body>
<div id="global" style="width:300px">
    <s:form>
        <s:doubleselect label="Select Location"
            name="country"
            list="{'US', 'Canada', 'Mexico'}"
            doubleName="city"
            doubleList="top == 'US' ?
                    {'Atlanta', 'Chicago', 'Detroit'}
                : (top == 'Canada' ?
                    {'Vancouver', 'Toronto', 'Montreal'}
                : {'Mexico City', 'Tijuana'})"
        />

        <s:submit/>
    </s:form>
</div>
</body>
</html>
```

To test the example, use this URL:

`http://localhost:8080/app05a/DoubleSelect.action`

Figure 5.15 shows the rendered **doubleselect** tag.

Figure 5.15: Using doubleselect

Themes

Each UI tag in the Struts Tag Library is rendered to an HTML element or HTML elements. Struts lets you choose how the rendering should happen. For instance, by default the **form** tag is rendered as an HTML **form** element and a **table** element. Therefore,

```
<s:form></s:form>
```

is translated into

```
<form id="..." name="..." onsubmit="return true;" action="..."
        method="post">
<table class="wwFormTable">

</table>
</form>
```

The table element is great for formatting because every input tag, such as **textfield**, **checkbox**, and **submit**, will be rendered as an input element contained within a **tr** element and **td** elements, accompanied by a label.

For example, this **textfield** tag

<s:textfield label="My Label">

will be rendered as

```
<tr>
    <td class="tdLabel">
        <label for="..." class="label">My Label:</label>
    </td>
    <td>
        <input type="text" name="..." id="..."/>
    </td>
</tr>
```

Since most forms are formatted in a table, this kind of rendering helps.

However, sometimes you do not want your **textfield** tag to be rendered as an input element in **tr** and **td**'s and, instead, want it to be translated as a lone **<input>** because you want to apply your own formatting. Can you do this?

You can because each UI tag comes with several rendering templates you can choose. One template renders **<s:form>** as a form and a table elements, but another translates the same **form** tag into a form element, without a <table>. These templates are written in FreeMarker, but you don't have to know FreeMarker to use these templates.

Similar templates are packaged together into a theme. A theme therefore is a collection of templates that produce the same look and feels for all UI tags. There are currently four themes available:

- **simple**. Templates in the simple theme translate UI tags into their simplest HTML equivalents and will ignore the label attribute. For example, using this theme a <s:form> is rendered as a **form** element, without a **table** element. A textfield tag translates into an **input** element without bells and whistles.
- **xhtml**. The xhtml theme is the default theme. Templates in this collection provides automatic formatting using a layout table. That's why a <s:form> is rendered as a <form> and a <table>.
- **css_xhtml**. Templates in this theme are similar to those in the xhtml theme but rewritten to use CSS for layout.
- **ajax**. This theme contains templates based on xhtml templates but provides advanced AJAX features. AJAX programming will be discussed in Chapter 27, "AJAX".

All the templates from the four themes are included in the **struts-core-VERSION.jar** file, under the **template** directory.

Now that you know how UI tags are rendered, it's time to learn how to choose a theme for your UI tags.

As mentioned earlier, if you don't specify a theme, the templates in the xhtml theme will be used. To easiest way to change a theme for a UI tag is by using the theme attribute of that tag. For example, the following **textfield** tag uses the simple theme:

```
<s:textfield theme="simple" name="userId"/>
```

If the **theme** attribute is not present in a form input UI tag, the form's theme will be used. For instance, the following tags all use the css_xhtml theme since the containing form uses that theme, except for the last **checkbox** tag that uses the simple theme.

```
<s:form theme="css_xhtml">
<s:checkbox theme="simple" name="daily" label="Daily news alert"/>
<s:checkbox name="weekly" label="Weekly reports"/>
<s:checkbox theme="simple" name="monthly" label="Monthly reviews"
    value="true" disabled="true"
/>
<s:submit/>
</s:form>
```

In addition to using the **theme** attribute, there are two other ways to select a theme:

1. By adding an attribute named **theme** to the **page, request, session,** or **application** JSP implicit objects.
2. By assigning a theme to the **struts.ui.theme** property in the **struts.properties** file, discussed in Appendix A, "Struts Configuration."

Summary

Struts comes with a tag library that include UI and non-UI tags. Some of the UI tags are used for entering form values and are referred to as the form tags. In this chapter you have learned all the tags in the form tags.

Chapter 6
Generic Tags

As explained in Chapter 5, "Form Tags," Struts comes bundled with a tag library that contains UI and non-UI tags. In this chapter we look at the non-UI tags, which are also known as generic tags.

There two types of generic tags, data tag and control tag. The following are the data tags:

- a
- action
- bean
- date
- debug
- i18n
- include
- param
- push
- set
- text
- url
- property

Note

The **i18n** and **text** tags are related to internationalization and discussed in Chapter 9, "Message Handling." The **debug** tag is used for debugging and explained in Chapter 16, "Debugging and Profiling."

The following are the control tags:

- if
- elseIf
- else
- append
- generator
- iterator
- merge
- sort
- subset

Each of the generic tags is discussed in the following sections. The accompanying samples can be found in the **app06a** application.

The property Tag

You use the **property** tag to print an action property. Its attributes are listed in Table 6.1. All attributes are optional.

Name	Type	Default	Description
default	String		The default value if **value** is null
escape	boolean	true	Whether HTML special characters are escaped
value	String	\<top of stack\>	The value to be displayed

Table 6.1: property tag attributes

For instance, this **property** tag prints the value of the **customerId** action property:

```
<s:property value="customerId"/>
```

The following prints the value of the session attribute **userName**.

```
<s:property value="#session.userName"/>
```

If the **value** attribute is not present, the value of the object at the top of the Value Stack will be printed. By default, the **property** tag escapes HTML special characters in Table 6.2 before printing a value.

Character	Escaped Characters
"	&quot;
&	&amp;
<	&lt;
>	&gt;

Table 6.2: Escaped characters

Note that in many cases, the JSP Expression Language provides shorter syntax. For example, the following EL expression prints the **customerId** action property.

```
${customerId}
```

The **Property** action in **app06a** demonstrates the use of the **property** tag. The action is associated with the **PropertyTestAction** class (in Listing 6.1) that has a property named **temperature**.

Listing 6.1: The PropertyTestAction class

```
package app06a;
import com.opensymphony.xwork2.ActionSupport;
public class PropertyTestAction extends ActionSupport {
    private float temperature = 100.05F;
    // getter and setter not shown
}
```

The **Property.jsp** page in Listing 6.2 prints the value of the **temperature** property and the value of the **degreeSymbol** application attribute. If the **degreeSymbol** attribute is not found, the default **°F** will be used.

Listing 6.2: The Property.jsp page

```
<%@ taglib prefix="s" uri="/struts-tags" %>
<html>
<head>
<title>property Tag Example</title>
<style type="text/css">@import url(css/main.css);</style>
</head>
<body>
<div id="global" style="width:250px">
    Temperature:<s:property value="temperature"/>
    <%-- Default to Fahrenheit--%>
    <s:property value="#application.degreeSymbol"
            escape="false"
            default="&deg;F"
    />
</div>
</body>
</html>
```

Test this example by directing your browser to this URL:

```
http://localhost:8080/app06a/Property.action
```

Figure 6.1 shows the result.

Figure 6.1: Using the property tag

The a Tag

The **a** tag renders an HTML anchor. It can accept all attributes that the a HTML element can. For example, this **a** tag creates an anchor that points to www.example.com.

```
<s:a href="http://www.example.com">Click Here</s:a>
```

This tag is of not much use, however the **a** tag in the AJAX tag library, discussed in Chapter 27, "AJAX," is very powerful.

The action Tag

The **action** tag is used to execute an action and the result for that action. It also adds the action to the Value Stack's context map. Its attributes are shown in Table 6.3.

For example, the following **action** tag causes the **MyAction** action to be executed. The action object will also be accessible through the **obj** variable in the Value Stack's context map.

```
<s:action var="obj" name="MyAction" executeResult="false"/>
```

Name	Type	Default	Description
executeResult	boolean	false	Indicates whether the action result should be executed/rendered.
flush	boolean	true	Indicates whether the writer should be flushed at the end of the action component tag.
ignoreContextParams	boolean	false	Whether request parameters are to be included when the action is invoked.
name*	String		The name of the action to be invoked, without the .action suffix.
namespace	String	the namespace from where the tag is used	The namespace of the action to be invoked.
var	String		The name to be used to reference the action added to the context map.

Table 6.3: action tag attributes

The param Tag

The **param** tag is used to pass a parameter to the containing tag. Its attributes are listed in Table 6.4.

Name	Type	Default	Description
name	String		The name of the parameter to be passed to the containing tag.
value	String		The value of the parameter to be passed to the containing tag.

Table 6.4: param tag attributes

The **value** attribute is always evaluated even if it is written without the %{ and }. For example, the value of the following **param** tag is the **userName** action property:

```
<s:param name="userName" value="userName"/>
```

It is the same as

```
<s:param name="userName" value="%{userName}"/>
```

To send a **String** literal, enclose it with single quotes. For example, the value of this **param** tag is **naomi**.

```
<s:param name="userName" value="'naomi'"/>
```

The **value** attribute can also be written as text between the start and the end tags. Therefore, instead of writing

```
<s:param name="..." value="…"/>
```

you can write

```
<s:param name="...">[value]</s:param>
```

The second form allows you to pass an EL expression. For example, the following passes the current host to the **host** parameter:

```
<s:param name="host">${header.host}</s:param>
```

This will not work:

```
<s:param name="host" value="${header.host}"/>
```

The bean Tag

The **bean** tag creates a JavaBean and stores it in the Value Stack's context map. This tag is similar in functionality to the JSP **useBean** action element. The attributes of the **bean** tag are given in Table 6.5.

Name	Type	Default	Description
name*	String		The fully qualified class name of the JavaBean to be created.
var	String		The name used to reference the value pushed into the Value Stack's context map.

Table 6.5: bean tag attributes

In the following example, the **DegreeConverter** class in Listing 6.3 provides methods to convert Celcius to Fahrenheit and vice versa. The **Bean.jsp** page in Listing 6.4 uses the **bean** tag to instantiate the class.

Listing 6.3: The DegreeConverter class

```
package app06a;
public class DegreeConverter {
    private float celcius;
    private float fahrenheit;
    public float getCelcius() {
        return (fahrenheit - 32)*5/9;
    }
    public void setCelcius(float celcius) {
        this.celcius = celcius;
    }
    public float getFahrenheit() {
        return celcius * 9 / 5 + 32;
    }
    public void setFahrenheit(float fahrenheit) {
        this.fahrenheit = fahrenheit;
    }
}
```

Listing 6.4: The Bean.jsp page

```
<%@ taglib prefix="s" uri="/struts-tags" %>
<html>
<head>
<title>bean Tag Example</title>
<style type="text/css">@import url(css/main.css);</style>
</head>
<body>
<div id="global" style="width:250px">
    <s:bean name="app06a.DegreeConverter" id="converter">
        <s:param name="fahrenheit" value="212"/>
    </s:bean>
    212&deg;F=<s:property value="#converter.celcius"/>&deg;C
</div>
</body>
</html>
```

To test this example, direct your browser to this URL:

```
http://localhost:8080/app06a/Bean.action
```

Figure 6.2 shows the result.

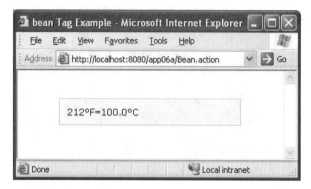

Figure 6.2: Using the bean tag

The date Tag

The **date** tag formats a Java **Date** object. Its attributes are given in Table 6.6.

Name	Type	Default	Description
format	String		The date pattern.
name*	String		The date value to format.
nice	boolean	false	Whether to apply nice formatting.
var	String		The name used to reference the value pushed to the value stack.

Table 6.6: date tag attributes

The **format** attribute conforms to the date and time patterns defined for the **java.text.SimpleDateFormat** class. For example, the **Date.jsp** page in Listing 6.5 uses **date** tags to format dates.

Listing 6.5: The Date.jsp page

```
<%@ taglib prefix="s" uri="/struts-tags" %>
<html>
<head>
<title>date Tag Example</title>
<style type="text/css">@import url(css/main.css);</style>
</head>
<body>
<div id="global" style="width:350px">
    <s:bean name="java.util.Date" var="today"/>
    Today (original format): <s:property value="#today"/>
```

```
    <s:date name="#today" var="format1" format="M/dd/yyyy"/>
    <br/>Today (mm/dd/yyyy): <s:property value="#format1"/>

    <s:date name="#today" var="format2" format="MMM d, yyyy"/>
    <br/>Today (MMM d, yyyy): <s:property value="#format2"/>

    <s:date name="#today" var="format3" format="MMM d, yyyy hh:mm"/>
    <br/>Today (MMM d, yyyy hh:mm): <s:property value="#format3"/>

</div>
</body>
</html>
```

To test the example, direct your browse here:

```
http://localhost:8080/app06a/Date.action
```

The result is shown in Figure 6.3.

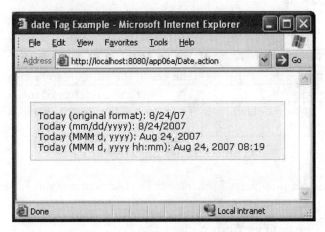

Figure 6.3: Using the date tag

The include Tag

This tag includes the output of a servlet or a JSP. It has one attribute, **value**, that is described in Table 6.7.

Name	Type	Default	Description
value*	String		The servlet/JSP whose output is to be included.

Table 6.7: include tag attrbute

The set Tag

The **set** tag creates a key/value pair in one of the following map:

- the Value Stack's context map
- the session map
- the application map
- the request map
- the page map

The attributes of the **set** tag are given in Table 6.8.

Name	Type	Default	Description
name	String		The key of the attribute to be created
value	String		The object to be referenced by the key.
scope	String	default	The scope of the target variable. The value can be application, session, request, page, or default.

Table 6.8: set tag attributes

The following example, based on the **SetTestAction** class in Listing 6.6, shows the benefit of using **set**.

Listing 6.6: The SetTestAction class

```
package app06a;
import java.util.Map;
import org.apache.struts2.ServletActionContext;
import com.opensymphony.xwork2.ActionSupport;

public class SetTestAction extends ActionSupport {
    public String execute() {
        Map sessionMap = ServletActionContext.
                getContext().getSession();
        Customer customer = new Customer();
        customer.setContact("John Conroy");
        customer.setEmail("info@example.com");
```

```
        sessionMap.put("customer", customer);
        return SUCCESS;
    }

}
class Customer {
    private String contact;
    private String email;
    // getters and setters not shown
}
```

The **SetTestAction** class's **execute** method inserts a **Customer** object to the **Session** object. You could display the **contact** and **email** properties of the **Customer** object using these **property** tags:

```
<s:property value="#session.customer.contact"/>
<s:property value="#session.customer.email"/>
```

However, as you can see from the **Set.jsp** page in Listing 6.7, you could also push the variable **customer** to represents the **Customer** object in the **Session** map.

```
<s:set name="customer" value="#session.customer"/>
```

You can then refer to the **Customer** object simply by using these **property** tags.

```
<s:property value="#customer.contact"/>
<s:property value="#customer.email"/>
```

Listing 6.7: The Set.jsp page

```
<%@ taglib prefix="s" uri="/struts-tags" %>
<html>
<head>
<title>set Tag Example</title>
<style type="text/css">@import url(css/main.css);</style>
</head>
<body>
<div id="global" style="width:250px">
    <h3>Customer Details</h3>
    <s:set name="customer" value="#session.customer"/>
    Contact: <s:property value="#customer.contact"/>
    <br/>Email: <s:property value="#customer.email"/>
</div>
</body>
</html>
```

Test this example by directing your browser to this URL:

`http://localhost:8080/app06a/Set.action`

The result is shown in Figure 6.4.

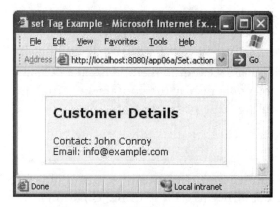

Figure 6.4: Using the set tag

The push Tag

The **push** tag is similar to **set**. The difference is **push** pushes an object to the Value Stack, not the context map. Another unique characteristic of push is that the start tag pushes the object and the end tag pops it. Therefore, if you want to take advantage of **push**, you need to do everything within the start and end tags.

The **push** tag only has one attribute, **value**, described in Table 6.9.

Name	Type	Default	Description
value*	String		The value to be pushed to the value stack.

Table 6.9: push tag attribute

For example, the **PushTestAction** class in Listing 6.8 has an **execute** method that places an **Employee** object in the **HttpSession** object.

Listing 6.8: The PushTestAction class

```
package app06a;
```

```
import java.util.Map;
import org.apache.struts2.interceptor.SessionAware;
import com.opensymphony.xwork2.ActionSupport;
public class PushTestAction extends ActionSupport
        implements SessionAware {
    private Map sessionMap;
    public void setSession(Map sessionMap) {
        this.sessionMap = sessionMap;
    }
    public String execute() {
        Employee employee = new Employee();
        employee.setId(1);
        employee.setFirstName("Karl");
        employee.setLastName("Popper");
        sessionMap.put("employee", employee);
        return SUCCESS;
    }
}

class Employee {
    private int id;
    private String firstName;
    private String lastName;
    // getters and setters not shown
}
```

The **Push.jsp** page in Listing 6.9 uses a **push** tag to push an **Employee** object to the Value Stack.

Listing 6.9: The Push.jsp page

```
<%@ taglib prefix="s" uri="/struts-tags" %>
<html>
<head>
<title>push Tag Example</title>
<style type="text/css">@import url(css/main.css);</style>
</head>
<body>
<div id="global" style="width:250px">
    <h3>Employee Details</h3>
    <s:push value="#session.employee">
        Employee Id: <s:property value="id"/>
        <br/>First Name: <s:property value="firstName"/>
        <br/>Last Name: <s:property value="lastName"/>
    </s:push>
</div>
```

```
</body>
</html>
```

To test this action, direct your browser to this URL:

`http://localhost:8080/app06a/Push.action`

Figure 6.5 shows the result.

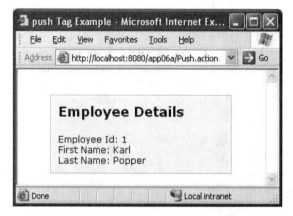

Figure 6.5: Using the push tag

The url Tag

This tag creates a URL dynamically. Its attributes are listed in Table 6.10.

Name	Type	Default	Description
action	String		The action that the created URL will target.
anchor	String		The anchor for the created URL
encode	Boolean	true	Whether to encode parameters.
escapeAmp	Boolean	true	Indicates whether to escape the ampersand character (&)
includeContext	Boolean	true	Indicates whether the actual context should be included
includeParams	String	get	One of these values: **one, get, all**.
method	String		The method of the action.
namespace	String		The target namespace.
portletMode	String		The resulting portlet mode.

portletUrlType	String		Indicates if the created URL should be a portlet render or an action URL.
scheme	String		The scheme ???
value	String		The target value to use, if not using action
var	String		???
windowState	String		When used in a portlet environment, specifies the portlet window state.

Table 6.10: url tag attributes

The **url** tag can be very useful. For example, this **url** tag creates a URL for the HTTPS protocol and includes all the parameters in the current URL.

```
<s:url id="siteUrl" forceAddSchemeHostAndPort="true" value=""
      includeParams="none" scheme="https"/>
```

The if, else, and elseIf Tags

These three tags are used to perform conditional tests and are similar to Java keywords **if**, **else** and **if else**. The **if** and **elseif** tags must have the **test** attribute, which is described in Table 6.11.

Name	Type	Default	Description
test*	Boolean		The test condition.

Table 6.11: if and else tags attribute

For instance, this **if** tag tests if the **ref** request parameter is null:

```
<s:if test="#parameters.ref == null">
```

And this trims the **name** property and tests if the result is empty.

```
<s:if test="name.trim() == ''">
```

In the following cxample, an **if** tag is used to test if the session attribute **loggedIn** exists. If it is not found, a login form is displayed. Otherwise, a greeting is shown. The example relies on the **IfTestAction** class in Listing 6.10 and the **If.jsp** page in Listing 6.11.

Listing 6.10: The IfTestAction class

```
package app06a;
import org.apache.struts2.ServletActionContext;
```

```
import com.opensymphony.xwork2.ActionSupport;
public class IfTestAction extends ActionSupport {
    private String userName;
    private String password;
    // getters and setters not shown
    public String execute() {
        if (userName != null && userName.length() > 0
                && password != null
                && password.length() > 0) {
            ServletActionContext.getContext().
                    getSession().put("loggedIn", true);
        }
        return SUCCESS;
    }
}
```

Listing 6.11: The If.jsp page

```
<%@ taglib prefix="s" uri="/struts-tags" %>
<html>
<head>
<title>if Tag Example</title>
<style type="text/css">@import url(css/main.css);</style>
</head>
<body>
<div id="global" style="width:350px">
    <s:if test="#session.loggedIn == null">
        <h3>Login</h3>
        <s:form>
            <s:textfield name="userName" label="User Name"/>
            <s:password name="password" label="Password"/>
            <s:submit value="Login"/>
        </s:form>
    </s:if>
    <s:else>
      Welcome <s:property value="userName"/>
    </s:else>
</div>
</body>
</html>
```

To test the example, use this URL:

```
http://localhost:8080/app06a/If.action
```

The result is shown in Figure 6.6.

Figure 6.6: Using the if, elseif, and else tags

The iterator Tag

This is the most important tag in the control tag category. It can be used to iterate over an array, a **Collection**, or a **Map** and pushes and pops each element in the iterable object to the Value Stack. Table 6.12 lists the attributes of the **iterator** tag.

Name	Type	Default	Description
value	String		The iterable object to iterate over.
status	org.apache.struts2.views.jsp. IteratorStatus		
var	String		The variable to reference the current element of the iterable object.

Table 6.12: iterator tag attributes

Upon execution, the **iterator** tag pushes an instance of **IteratorStatus** to the context map and updates it at each iteration. The **status** attribute can be assigned a variable that points to this **IteratorStatus** object.

The properties of the **IteratorStatus** object are shown in Table 6.13.

Name	Type	Description
index	integer	The zero-based index of each iteration
count	integer	The current iteration or index + 1.
first	boolean	The value is true if the current element is the first element in the iterable object.
last	boolean	The value is true if the current element is the last element in the iterable object.
even	boolean	The value is true if **count** is an even number
odd	boolean	The value is true if **count** is an odd number
modulus	int	This property takes an integer and returns the modulus of **count**.

Table 6.13: IteratorStatus object attributes

For example, the **IteratorTestAction** class in Listing 6.12 presents an action class with two properties, **interests** and **interestOptions**, that return an array and a **List**, respectively. The **Iterator.jsp** page in Listing 6.13 shows how to use the **iterator** tag to iterate over an array or a **Collection**.

Listing 6.12: The IteratorTestAction class

```
package app06a;
import java.util.ArrayList;
import java.util.List;
import com.opensymphony.xwork2.ActionSupport;

public class IteratorTestAction extends ActionSupport {
    private int[] interests;
    private static List<Interest> interestOptions =
            new ArrayList<Interest>();
    static {
        interestOptions.add(new Interest(1, "Automotive"));
        interestOptions.add(new Interest(2, "Games"));
        interestOptions.add(new Interest(3, "Sports"));
    }
    public int[] getInterests() {
        return interests;
    }

    public void setInterests(int[] interests) {
        this.interests = interests;
    }
    public List<Interest> getInterestOptions() {
```

```
            return interestOptions;
        }

}

class Interest {
    private int id;
    private String description;
    public Interest(int id, String description) {
        this.id = id;
        this.description = description;
    }
    // getters and setters not shown
}
```

Listing 6.13: The Iterator.jsp page

```
<%@ taglib prefix="s" uri="/struts-tags" %>
<html>
<head>
<title>iterator Tag Example</title>
<style type="text/css">@import url(css/main.css);</style>
<style>
table {
    padding:0px;
    margin:0px;
    border-collapse:collapse;
}
td, th {
    border:1px solid black;
    padding:5px;
    margin:0px;
}
.evenRow {
    background:#f8f8ff;
}
.oddRow {
    background:#efefef;
}
</style>
</head>
<body>
<div id="global" style="width:250px">
    First 4 prime number
    <ul>
    <s:iterator value="{2, 3, 5, 7}">
        <li><s:property/></li>
```

```
    </s:iterator>
    </ul>

    <s:set name="car" value="{ 'Chrysler', 'Ford', 'Kia'}"/>
    Cars:
    <s:iterator value="#car" status="status">
        <s:property/><s:if test="!#status.last">,</s:if>
    </s:iterator>
    <p>
    <h3>Interest options</h3>
    <table>
    <tr>
        <th>Id</th>
        <th>Description</th>
    </tr>
    <s:iterator value="interestOptions" status="status">
    <s:if test="#status.odd">
        <tr class="oddRow">
    </s:if>
    <s:if test="#status.even">
        <tr class="evenRow">
    </s:if>
        <td><s:property value="id"/></td>
        <td><s:property value="description"/></td>
    </tr>
    </s:iterator>
    </table>
</div>
</body>
</html>
```

To test this example, direct your browser to this URL:

```
http://localhost:8080/app06a/Iterator.action
```

Figure 6.7 shows the output of the action.

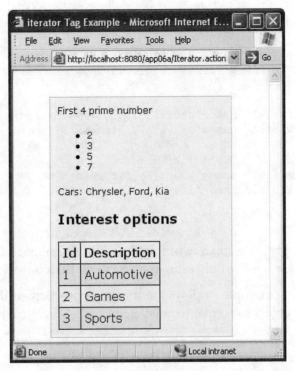

Figure 6.7: Using the iterator tag

Another helpful use of **iterator** is to simulate a loop, similar to the **for** loop in Java. This is easy to do since all an iterator needs is an array or another iterable object. The following code creates a table containing four rows. The cells in each row contain two **textfield** tags whose names are **user[n].firstName** and **user[n].lastName**, respectively. This is useful when you need to generate a variable number of input boxes.

```
<table>
<s:iterator value="new int[3]" status="stat">
<tr>
    <td><s:textfield
            name="%{'users['+#stat.index+'].firstName'}"/></td>
    <td><s:textfield
            name="%{'users['+#stat.index+'].lastName'}"/></td>
</tr>
</s:iterator>
</table>
```

This is the same as writing

```
<table>
<tr>
    <td><s:textfield name="users[0].firstName"/></td>
    <td><s:textfield name="users[0].lastName"/></td>
</tr>
<tr>
    <td><s:textfield name="users[1].firstName"/></td>
    <td><s:textfield name="users[1].lastName"/></td>
</tr>
<tr>
    <td><s:textfield name="users[2].firstName"/></td>
    <td><s:textfield name="users[2].lastName"/></td>
</tr>
</table>
```

In this case, we generate an array of four **int**s. We do not need to initialize the array elements since we're only using the array's **status.count** attribute.

The following example employs the **modulus** property of the **IteratorStatus** object to format iterated elements in a four-column table.

```
<table border="1">
<s:iterator id="item" value="myList" status="status">
    <s:if test="#status.modulus(4)==1">
        <tr>
    </s:if>
    <td>${item}</td>
    <s:if test="#status.modulus(4)==0">
        </tr>
    </s:if>
</s:iterator>

<%-- if the list size is not equally divisible by 4, we need to pad
     with <td></td> and </tr> --%>
<s:if test="myList.size%4!=0">
    <s:iterator value="new int[4 - myList.size%4]">
        <td> </td>
    </s:iterator>
    </tr>
</s:if>
</table>
```

The append Tag

This tag is used to concatenate iterators. Therefore, if you have two lists with 3 elements each, the new list will have these elements:

- List 1, element 1
- List 1, element 2
- List 1, element 3
- List 2, element 1
- List 2, element 2
- List 2, element 3

The **append** tag adds one attribute, **var**, which is described in Table 6.14.

Name	Type	Default	Description
var	String		The variable that will be created to reference the appended iterators.

Table 6.14: append tag attribute

For example, the code in Listing 6.14 uses the **append** tag to concatenate two lists:

Listing 6.14: Using append

```
<s:set var="list1" value="{'one', 'two'}"/>
<s:set var="list2" value="{'1', '2', '3'}"/>

<s:append var="allLists">
    <s:param value="#list1"/>
    <s:param value="#list2"/>
</s:append>

<s:iterator value="#allLists">
    <s:property/><br/>
</s:iterator>
```

The example will print the following on the browser:

```
one
two
1
2
3
```

Also, see the **merge** tag, which is very similar to append. If you replace **append** with **merge** in the example above, you will get

```
one
1
two
2
3
```

The merge Tag

The **merge** tag merges lists and reads an element from each list in succession. Therefore, if you have two lists with 3 elements each, the new list will have these elements:

- List 1, element 1
- List 2, element 1
- List 1, element 2
- List 2, element 2
- List 1, element 3
- List 2, element 3

The **merge** tag adds an attribute, **var**, which is described in Table 6.15.

Name	Type	Default	Description
var	String		The variable that will be created to reference the appended iterators.

Table 6.15: merge tag attribute

In the following example, the action class **MergeTestAction** provides three properties that each returns a **List: americanCars**, **europeanCars**, and **japaneseCars**. The action class is given in Listing 6.15.

Listing 6.15: The MergeTestAction class

```
package app06a;
import java.util.ArrayList;
import java.util.List;
import com.opensymphony.xwork2.ActionSupport;

public class MergeTestAction extends ActionSupport {
```

```
    private static List<String> americanCars;
    private static List<String> europeanCars;
    private static List<String> japaneseCars;
    static {
        americanCars = new ArrayList<String>();
        americanCars.add("Ford");
        americanCars.add("GMC");
        americanCars.add("Lincoln");
        europeanCars = new ArrayList<String>();
        europeanCars.add("Audi");
        europeanCars.add("BMW");
        europeanCars.add("VW");
        japaneseCars = new ArrayList<String>();
        japaneseCars.add("Honda");
        japaneseCars.add("Nissan");
        japaneseCars.add("Toyota");
    }
    public List<String> getAmericanCars() {
        return americanCars;
    }
    public List<String> getEuropeanCars() {
        return europeanCars;
    }
    public List<String> getJapaneseCars() {
        return japaneseCars;
    }
}
```

The **Merge.jsp** page in Listing 6.16 shows the **merge** tag in action.

Listing 6.16: The Merge.jsp page

```
<%@ taglib prefix="s" uri="/struts-tags" %>
<html>
<head>
<title>merge Tag Example</title>
<style type="text/css">@import url(css/main.css);</style>
</head>
<body>
<div id="global" style="width:250px">
    <h3>All cars</h3>
    <s:merge id="cars">
        <s:param value="%{americanCars}"/>
        <s:param value="%{europeanCars}"/>
        <s:param value="%{japaneseCars}"/>
    </s:merge>
```

```
    <ul>
    <s:iterator value="%{#cars}">
        <li><s:property/></li>
    </s:iterator>
    </ul>
</div>
</body>
</html>
```

To test the example, direct your browser to this URL:

`http://localhost:8080/app06a/Merge.action`

Figure 6.8 shows the result

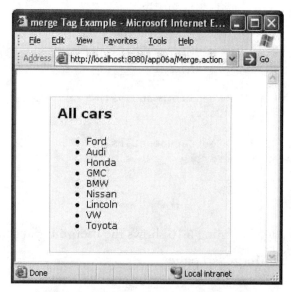

Figure 6.8: Using the merge tag

The generator Tag

This tag is used to generate an iterator and push it to the Value Stack. The closing generator pops the iterator so that any work that needs to be done must be done within the start and end tags. Alternatively, you can create a reference to the iterator as a page attribute. This way, you can access the iterator at a later stage.

The attributes are listed in Table 6.16.

Name	Type	Default	Description
converter	Converter		The converter to convert the String entry parsed from *val* into an object.
count	Integer		The maximum number of elements in the iterator.
separator*	String		The separator for separating the val into entries of the iterator.
val*	String		The source to be parsed into an iterator.
var	String		The variable that references the resulting iterator.

Table 6.16: generator tag attributes

When used, the **converter** attribute must be set to an action property of type **Converter**, an inner interface defined in the **org.apache.struts2.util.IteratorGenerator** class.

The use of the converter is depicted in the second example of this section.

The **Generator.jsp** page in Listing 6.17 illustrates the use of **generator** to create a list of Strings (car makes).

Listing 6.17: The Generator.jsp page

```
<%@ taglib prefix="s" uri="/struts-tags" %>
<html>
<head>
<title>generator Tag Example</title>
<style type="text/css">@import url(css/main.css);</style>
</head>
<body>
<div id="global" style="width:250px">
    <s:generator val="%{'Honda,Toyota,Ford,Dodge'}"
            separator=",">
        <ul>
        <s:iterator>
            <li><s:property/></li>
        </s:iterator>
        </ul>
    </s:generator>

    <s:generator id="cameras"
            count="3"
            val="%{'Canon,Nikon,Pentax,FujiFilm'}"
```

```
            separator=",">
    </s:generator>
    <s:iterator value="#attr.cameras">
        <s:property/>
    </s:iterator>
</div>
</body>
</html>
```

To test the example, direct your browser here:

```
http://localhost:8080/app06a/Generator.action
```

You will see the generated list in Figure 6.8.

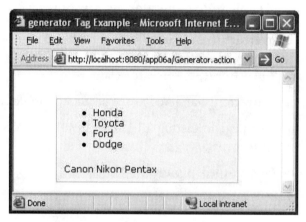

Figure 6.9: Using the generator tag

As a second example, consider the **GeneratorConverterTestAction** class in Listing 6.15. This class has one property, **myConverter**, that returns an implementation of **IteratorGenerator.Converter**. The **Converter** interface defines one method, **convert**, whose signature is given as follows.

```
Object convert(String value) throws Exception
```

In a **generator** tag that has a converter, each element of the generated iterator will be passed to this method.

Listing 6.18: The GeneratorConverterTestAction class

```
package app06a;
import org.apache.struts2.util.IteratorGenerator;
import com.opensymphony.xwork2.ActionSupport;
```

```
public class GeneratorConverterTestAction extends ActionSupport {
    public IteratorGenerator.Converter getMyConverter() {
        return new IteratorGenerator.Converter() {
            public Object convert(String value) throws Exception {
                return value.toUpperCase();
            }
        };
    }
}
```

The **GeneratorConverter.jsp** page in Listing 6.16 uses a **generator** tag whose converter attribute is assigned a converter.

Listing 6.19: The GeneratorConverter.jsp page

```
<%@ taglib prefix="s" uri="/struts-tags" %>
<html>
<head>
<title>Generator Converter Example</title>
<style type="text/css">@import url(css/main.css);</style>
</head>
<body>
<div id="global" style="width:250px">
    <s:generator val="%{'Honda,Toyota,Ford,Dodge'}"
            separator=","
            converter="myConverter">
        <ul>
        <s:iterator>
            <li><s:property/></li>
        </s:iterator>
        </ul>
    </s:generator>
</div>
</body>
</html>
```

You can test the example directing your browser to this URL.

```
http://localhost:8080/app06a/GeneratorConverter.action
```

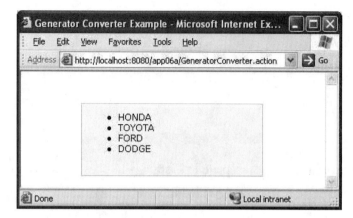

Figure 6.10: The generator converter example

As you can see in Figure 6.10, all elements were converted to upper case.

The sort Tag

This tag sorts the elements of an iterator. Its attributes are given in Table 6.17.

Name	Type	Default	Description
comparator*	java.util.Comparator		The comparator that will be used in the sorting.
source	String		The iterable source to sort.
var	String		The variable that will be created to reference the new iterator.

Table 6.17: sort tag attributes

Note

It is a good design choice to leave data sorting to the presentation layer, even though it may be easier to sort data at the model or data level using the ORDER BY clause in the SQL statement. This is a design decision that should be considered carefully.

For example, the **SortTestAction** class in Listing 6.20 provides a property of type **Comparator** that is used by the **sort** tag in the **Sort.jsp** page (See Listing 6.21.)

Listing 6.20: The SortTestAction class

```
package app06a;
import java.util.Comparator;
import com.opensymphony.xwork2.ActionSupport;

public class SortTestAction extends ActionSupport {
    public Comparator getMyComparator() {
        return new Comparator() {
            public int compare(Object o1, Object o2) {
                return o1.toString().compareTo(o2.toString());
            }
        };
    }
}
```

Listing 6.21: The Sort.jsp page

```
<%@ taglib prefix="s" uri="/struts-tags" %>
<html>
<head>
<title>sort Tag Example</title>
<style type="text/css">@import url(css/main.css);</style>
</head>
<body>
<div id="global" style="width:250px">
    <h4>Computers</h4>
    <s:generator id="computers"
            val="%{'HP,Dell,Asus,Fujitsu,Toshiba'}"
            separator=",">
        <s:sort comparator="myComparator">
            <s:iterator>
                <s:property/>
            </s:iterator>
        </s:sort>
    </s:generator>
    <hr/>

    <h4>Cameras</h4>
    <s:generator id="cameras"
            val="%{'Canon,Nikon,Pentax,FujiFilm'}"
            separator=",">
    </s:generator>
    <s:sort source="#attr.cameras" id="sortedCameras"
            comparator="myComparator">
    </s:sort>
    <s:iterator value="#attr.sortedCameras">
        <s:property/>
    </s:iterator>
```

```
</div>
</body>
</html>
```

To see the elements in the iterators sorted, direct your browser to this URL:

`http://localhost:8080/app06a/Sort.action`

Figure 6.11 shows the result.

Figure 6.11: Using the sort tag

The subset Tag

This tag creates a subset of an iterator. Its attributes are listed in Table 6.18.

You tell the **subset** tag how to create a subset of an iterator by using an instance of the **Decider** class, which is an inner class of **org.apache.struts2.util.SubsetIteratorFilter**. For example, the **SubsetTestAction** class in Listing 6.22 is a **Decider**. It will cause a **subset** tag to include an element if the String representation of the element is more than four characters long. The **Subset.jsp** page in Listing 6.23 employs a **subset** tag that uses the **Decider**.

Name	Type	Default	Description
count	Integer		The number of entries in the resulting iterator.
decider	Decider		An implementation of the **SubsetIteratorFilter.Decider** interface that determines if an entry is to be included in the resulting subset.
source	String		The source iterator to subset.
start	Integer		The starting index of the source iterator to be included in the subset.
var	String		The variable to be created to reference to the subset.

Table 6.18: subset tag attributes

Listing 6.22: The SubsetTestAction class

```
package app06a;
import org.apache.struts2.util.SubsetIteratorFilter;
import com.opensymphony.xwork2.ActionSupport;

public class SubsetTestAction extends ActionSupport {
    public SubsetIteratorFilter.Decider getMyDecider() {
        return new SubsetIteratorFilter.Decider() {
            public boolean decide(Object o1) {
                return o1.toString().length() > 4;
            }
        };
    }
}
```

Listing 6.23: The Subset.jsp page

```
<%@ taglib prefix="s" uri="/struts-tags" %>
<html>
<head>
<title>subset Tag Example</title>
<style type="text/css">@import url(css/main.css);</style>
</head>
<body>
<div id="global" style="width:250px">
    <h4>Computers</h4>
    <s:generator id="computers"
            val="%{'HP,Dell,Asus,Fujitsu,Toshiba'}"
            separator=",">
    </s:generator>
```

```
<s:subset source="#attr.computers" decider="myDecider">
    <s:iterator>
        <s:property/>
    </s:iterator>
</s:subset>
</div>
</body>
</html>
```

Test this example by directing your browser to this URL.

```
http://localhost:8080/app06a/Subset.action
```

Figure 6.12 shows the result.

Figure 6.12: Using the subset tag

Summary

The Struts tag library comes with non-UI tags that are often referred to as generic tags. These tags can be categorized into the data tags and the control tags and you've learned every one of them in this chapter.

Chapter 7
Type Conversion

In Chapter 5, "Form Tags" you learned to use form tags to receive user inputs and submit them to an action object. In Chapter 6, "Generic Tags" you saw how those values could be displayed. In both chapters you witnessed type conversions.

From an HTML form to an action object, conversions are from strings to non-strings. All form inputs are sent to the server as request parameters and each form input is either a **String** or a **String** array because HTTP is type agnostic. At the server side, the web developer or the framework converts the **String** to another data type, such as an **int** or a **java.util.Date**.

As you will learn in this chapter, Struts supports type conversions seamlessly. In addition, this feature is extensible, so you can build your own type converters. Custom converters are covered in this chapter too.

Type Conversion Overview

The Parameters interceptor, one of the interceptors in the default stack, is responsible for mapping request parameters with action properties. Since all request parameters are **String**s, and not all action properties are of type **String**, type conversions must be performed on any non-**String** action properties. The Parameters interceptor uses the OGNL API to achieve this. To be precise, if you happen to be interested in the Struts source code, it is the **ognl.OgnlRuntime** class, which in turn relies on Java reflection. For every property that needs to be set, **OgnlRuntime** creates a **java.lang.reflection.Method** object and calls its **invoke** method.

With the **Method** class, **String**s are automatically converted to other types, enabling user inputs to be assigned to action properties of type **int**, **java.util.Date**, **boolean**, and others. The **String** "123" mapped to an **int** property will be converted to 123, "12/12/2008" mapped to a **Date** property will be converted to December 12, 2008.

> ### Note
>
> As for conversion from **String** to **Date**, the date pattern for parsing the **String** is determined by the locale of the HTTP request. In the United States, the format is MM/dd/yyyy. To accept dates in a different pattern from the locale, you have to use a custom converter.

Type conversions, however, run the risk of failing. Trying to assign "abcd" to a **Date** property will definitely fail. So will assigning a formatted number such as 1,200 to an **int**. In the latter, the comma between 1 and 2 causes it to fail. It is imperative that the user gets notified when a conversion fails so that he or she may correct the input. It's the programmer's job to alert the user, but how do you do that?

A failed conversion will leave a property unchanged. In other words, **int** will retain the value of 0 and a **Date** property will remain null. A zero or null value may be an indication that a type conversion has failed, but it will not be a clear indicator if zero or null is an allowable value for a property. If zero or null is a valid property value, there's no way you can find out that a conversion has produced an error other than by comparing the property value with the corresponding request parameter. Doing so, however, is not recommended. Not only is checking the request parameter an inelegant solution, it also defeats the purpose of using Struts because Struts is capable of mapping request parameters to action properties.

So, what does Struts have to offer?

A failed type conversion will not necessarily stop Struts. There are two possible outcomes for this misbehavior. Which one will happen depends on whether or not your action class implements the **com.opensymphone.xwork2.ValidationAware** interface.

If the action class does not implement this interface, Struts will continue by invoking the action method upon failed type conversions, as if nothing bad had happened.

If the action class does implement **ValidationAware**, Struts will prevent the action method from being invoked. Rather, Struts will enquiry if the corresponding action element declaration contains an **input** result. If so, Struts will forward to the page defined in the **result** element. If no such result was found, Struts will throw an exception.

Customizing Conversion Error Messages

The Conversion Error interceptor, also in the default stack, is responsible for adding conversion errors (provided the action implements **ValidationAware**) and saving the original value of a request parameter so that an incorrect input value can be redisplayed. The input field with the invalid value, provided a non-simple theme is used for the tag rendering the field, will get an error message of this format:

```
Invalid field value for field fieldName.
```

You can override the default error message by providing a key/value pair of this format:

```
invalid.fieldvalue.fieldName=Custom error message
```

Here, *fieldName* is the name of the field for which a custom error message is provided. The key/value pair must be added to a *ClassName*.**properties** file, where *ClassName* is the name of the class that contains the field that is the target of the conversion. Further, the *ClassName*.**properties** file must be located in the same directory as the Java class.

In addition to customizing an error message, you can also customize its CSS style. Each error message is wrapped in an HTML span element, and you can apply formatting to the message by overriding the **errorMessage** CSS style. For example, to make type conversion error messages displayed in red, you can add this to your JSP:

```
<style>
.errorMessage {
    color:red;
}
</style>
```

A type conversion error customization example is given in the **app07a** application. The directory structure of this application is shown in Figure 7.1.

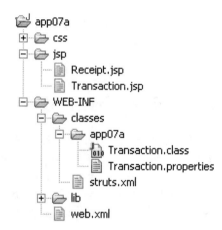

Figure 7.1: app07a directory structure

The **Transaction** action class in Listing 7.1 has four properties: **accountId**
(**String**), **transactionDate** (**Date**), **amount** (**double**), and **transactionType**
(**int**). More important, **Transaction** extends the **ActionSupport** class, thus
indirectly implementing **ValidationAware**.

Listing 7.1: The Transaction action class

```
package app07a;
import java.util.Date;
import com.opensymphony.xwork2.ActionSupport;
public class Transaction extends ActionSupport {

    private String accountId;
    private Date transactionDate;
    private double amount;
    private int transactionType;

    // getters and setters not shown
}
```

Note

We could use **java.util.Currency** for **amount**, but using a **double**
serves as a good example for the type conversions in this example.

There are two actions in this example, **Transaction1** and **Transaction2**. The
following are the declarations for the actions in the **struts.xml** file.

```
<action name="Transaction1">
    <result>/jsp/Transaction.jsp</result>
```

```
</action>
<action name="Transaction2" class="app07a.Transaction">
    <result name="input">/jsp/Transaction.jsp</result>
    <result name="success">/jsp/Receipt.jsp</result>
</action>
```

Transaction1 simply displays the **Transaction.jsp** page, which contains a form and is shown in Listing 7.2. **Transaction2** has two result branches. The first one is executed if the action method returns "input," as is the case when there is a type conversion error. The second one is executed if no type conversion error occurs and forwards to the **Receipt.jsp** page in Listing 7.3.

Listing 7.2: The Transaction.jsp page

```
<%@ taglib prefix="s" uri="/struts-tags" %>
<html>
<head>
<title>Transaction Details</title>
<style type="text/css">@import url(css/main.css);</style>
<style>
.errorMessage {
    color:red;
}
</style>
</head>
<body>
<div id="global" style="width:350px">
    <h4>Transaction Details</h4>
    <s:form action="Transaction2">
        <s:textfield name="accountId" label="Account ID"/>
        <s:textfield name="transactionDate"
                label="Transaction Date"/>
        <s:textfield name="transactionType"
                label="Transaction Type"/>
        <s:textfield name="amount" label="Amount"/>
        <s:submit/>
    </s:form>
</div>
</body>
</html>
```

Listing 7.3: The Receipt.jsp page

```
<%@ taglib prefix="s" uri="/struts-tags" %>
<html>
<head>
<title>Transaction Complete</title>
```

```
<style type="text/css">@import url(css/main.css);</style>
</head>
<body>
<div id="global" style="width:250px">
    <h4>Transaction details:</h4>
    <table>
    <tr>
        <td>Account ID:</td>
        <td><s:property value="accountId"/>
    </tr>
    <tr>
        <td>Transaction Date:</td>
        <td><s:property value="transactionDate"/>
    </tr>
    <tr>
        <td>Transaction Type:</td>
        <td><s:property value="transactionType"/>
    </tr>
    <tr>
        <td>Amount:</td>
        <td><s:property value="amount"/>
    </tr>
    </table>
</div>
<s:debug/>
</body>
</html>
```

The **Transaction.properties** file, shown in Listing 7.4, overrides the type conversion error message for the **transactionDate** field. This file must be located in the same directory as the **Transaction** action class.

Listing 7.4: The Transaction.properties file

```
invalid.fieldvalue.transactionDate=Please enter a date in MM/dd/yyyy
      ➥ format
```

To test this example, invoke the **Transaction1** action by directing your browser here:

```
http://localhost:8080/app07a/Transaction1.action
```

You'll see the form with four input boxes as in Figure 7.2.

Figure 7.2: The Transaction.jsp page

To test the type conversion feature in Struts, I deliberately enter incorrect values in the Transaction Date and Amount boxes. In the Transaction Date box I enter **abcd** and in the Amount box I type **14,999.95**. After the form is submitted, you will see the same form as shown in Figure 7.3.

Figure 7.3: Failed type conversions

What happened was **abcd** could not be converted to a **Date**. **14,999.50** looks like a valid numerical value, but its formatting makes it a bad candidate for a **double**, the type of the **amount** property. Had I entered **14999.50**, Struts would happily have converted it to a **double** and assigned it to the **amount** property.

The Transaction Date field is being adorned with the custom error message specified in the **Transaction.properties** file. The Amount field is being accompanied by a default error message since the **Transaction.properties** file does not specify one for this field.

An important thing to notice is that the wrong values are re-displayed. This is an important feature since the user can easily see what is wrong with his/her form.

Custom Type Converters

Sophisticated as they may be, the built-in type converters are not adequate.
They do not allow formatted numbers (such as 1,200) to be converted to a
java.lang.Number or a primitive. They are not smart enough to permit an
arbitrary date pattern to be used. To overcome this limitation, you need to
build your own converter. Happily, this is not hard to do.

A custom type converter must implement the **ognl.TypeConverter**
interface or extend an implementation class. As you can see in Figure 7.4 there
are two implementation classes available for you to extend,
DefaultTypeConverter and **StrutsTypeConverter**. **DefaultTypeConverter**
is discussed in this section and **StrutsTypeConverter** in the next section.

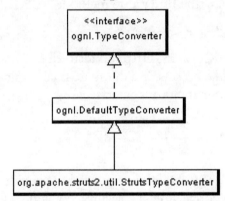

Figure 7.4: TypeConverter and its implementation classes

The **TypeConverter** interface has only one method, **convertValue**, whose
signature is as follows. Struts invokes this method and passes the necessary
parameters whenever it needs the converter's service.

```
java.lang.Object convertValue(java.util.Map context,
        java.lang.Object target, java.lang.reflect.Member member,
        java.lang.String propertyName, java.lang.Object value,
        java.lang.Class toType);
```

The parameters are as follows.

- context. The OGNL context under which the conversion is being
  performed.

- target. The target object in which the property is being set
- member. The class member (constructor, method, or field) being set
- propertyName. The name of the property being set
- value. The value to be converted.
- toType. The type to which the value is to be converted.

The **context** argument is very useful as it contains references to the Value Stack and various resources. For example, to retrieve the Value Stack, use this code:

```
ValueStack valueStack = (ValueStack)
        context.get(ValueStack.VALUE_STACK);
```

And, of course, once you have a reference to the Value Stack, you can obtain a property value by using the **findValue** method:

```
valueStack.findValue(propertyName);
```

To obtain the **ServletContext**, **HttpServletRequest**, and the **HttpServletResponse** objects, use the static finals defined in the **org.apache.struts2.StrutsStatics** interface:

```
context.get(StrutsStatics.SERVLET_CONTEXT);
context.get(StrutsStatics.HTTP_REQUEST);
context.get(StrutsStatics.HTTP_RESPONSE);
```

For a custom converter to function, you need to provide code that works for each supported type conversion. Typically, a converter should support at least two type conversions, from **String** to another type and vice versa. For instance, a currency converter responsible for converting **String** to **double** and **double** to **String** would implement **convertValue** like this:

```
public Object convertValue(Map context, Object target,
        Member member, String propertyName, Object value,
        Class toType) {
    if (toType == String.class) {
        // convert from double to String and return the result
        ...

    } else if (toType == Double.class || toType == Double.TYPE) {
        // convert String to double and return the result
        ...
    }
    return null;
```

```
}
```

Implementing **TypeConverter** is not as easy as extending the
DefaultTypeConverter class, a default implementation of **TypeConverter**.
DefaultTypeConverter, shown in Listing 7.5, provides a default
implementation of **convertValue** that calls another **convertValue** method
with a simpler signature.

Listing 7.5: The DefaultTypeConverter class

```
package ognl;
import java.lang.reflect.Member;
import java.util.Map;
public class DefaultTypeConverter implements TypeConverter {
    public Object convertValue(Map context, Object target,
            Member member, String propertyName, Object value,
            Class toType){
        return convertValue(context, value, toType);
    }
    public Object convertValue(Map context, Object value,
            Class toType) {
        return OgnlOps.convertValue(value, toType);
    }
}
```

Configuring Custom Converters

Before you can use a custom type converter in your application, you must
configure it. Configuration can be either field-based or class-based.

Field-based configuration allows you to specify a custom converter for
each property in an action. You do this by creating a file that must be named
according to the following format.

```
ActionClass-conversion.properties
```

Here, *ActionClass* is the name of the action class. For instance, to configure
custom converters for an action class called **User**, create a filed named **User-
conversion.properties**. The content of this file would look something like
this.

```
field1=customConverter1
field2=customConverter2
...
```

In addition, the configuration file must reside in the same directory as the action class. The **app07b** application shows how you can write a field-based configuration file for your custom converters.

In class-based configuration you specify the converter that will convert a request parameter to an instance of a class. In this case, you create an **xwork-conversion.properties** file under WEB-INF/classes and pair a class with a converter. For example, to use **CustomConverter1** for a class, you'll write

```
fullyQualifiedClassName=CustomConverter1
...
```

app07c teaches you how to use class-based configuration.

Custom Converter Examples

The **app07b** application shows how to implement **TypeConverter** and extend **DefaultTypeConverter**. The directory structure of **app07b** is shown in Figure 7.5. There are two custom converters showcased in this application, one for converting currencies and one for converting dates. The first implements **TypeConverter** and the second extends **DefaultTypeConverter**.

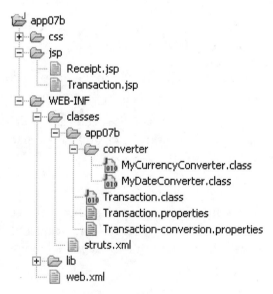

Figure 7.5: app07b directory structure

The currency converter is encapsulated in the **MyCurrencyConverter** class in
Listing 7.6. The first **if** block provides conversion to String by using
NumberFormat and **DecimalFormat**. Conversions from **String** to **double**
are done in the second **if** block by removing all commas in the value.

Listing 7.6: The MyCurrencyConverter class

```
package app07b.converter;
import java.lang.reflect.Member;
import java.text.DecimalFormat;
import java.text.NumberFormat;
import java.util.Map;
import ognl.TypeConverter;
import com.opensymphony.xwork2.util.TypeConversionException;

public class MyCurrencyConverter implements TypeConverter {
    public Object convertValue(Map context, Object target,
            Member member, String propertyName, Object value,
            Class toType) {
        if (toType == String.class) {
            NumberFormat formatter = new DecimalFormat("#,##0.00");
            return formatter.format((Double) value);
        } else if (toType == Double.class
                || toType == Double.TYPE) {
            try {
                String[] s = (String[]) value;
                String doubleValue = s[0];
                // remove commas,
                // we could use a one-line regular expression,
                // String doubleValue = s[0].replaceAll("[,]", "");
                // but regular expressions are comparatively
                // much slower
                return Double.parseDouble(
                        replaceString(doubleValue, ',', ""));
            } catch (NumberFormatException e) {
                System.out.println("Error:" + e);
                throw new TypeConversionException("Wrong");
            }
        }
        return null;
    }

    public static String replaceString(String s, char c,
            String with) {
        if (s == null) {
            return null;
```

```
        }
        int length = s.length();
        StringBuilder sb = new StringBuilder(s.length() * 2);
        for (int i = 0; i < length; i++) {
            char c2 = s.charAt(i);
            if (c2 == c) {
                sb.append(with);
            } else {
                sb.append(c2);
            }
        }
        return sb.toString();
    }
}
```

The date converter is encapsulated in the **MyDateConverter** class in Listing 7.7. Only conversions from **String** to **Date** are catered for. **Date** to **String** is not important since you can use the **date** tag to format and print a **Date** property.

Listing 7.7: The MyDateConverter class

```
package app07b.converter;
import java.text.DateFormat;
import java.text.ParseException;
import java.text.SimpleDateFormat;
import java.util.Date;
import java.util.Map;
import javax.servlet.ServletContext;
import org.apache.struts2.StrutsStatics;
import ognl.DefaultTypeConverter;
import com.opensymphony.xwork2.util.TypeConversionException;

public class MyDateConverter extends DefaultTypeConverter {
    public Object convertValue(Map context, Object value, Class
        toType) {
        if (toType == Date.class) {
            ServletContext servletContext = (ServletContext)
                    context.get(StrutsStatics.SERVLET_CONTEXT);
            String datePattern =
                    servletContext.getInitParameter("datePattern");
            DateFormat format = new SimpleDateFormat(datePattern);
            format.setLenient(false);
            try {
                String[] s = (String[]) value;
                Date date = format.parse(s[0]);
```

```
            return date;
        } catch (ParseException e) {
            System.out.println("Error:" + e);
            throw new
                    TypeConversionException("Invalid
    conversion");
        }
    }
    return null;
    }
}
```

You can use any date pattern for formatting the dates and parsing the **String**s. You pass the date pattern as an initial parameter to the **ServletContext** object. If you open the **web.xml** file of **app07b**, you'll see this **context-param** element, which indicates that the date pattern is yyyy-MM-dd.

```
<context-param>
    <param-name>datePattern</param-name>
    <param-value>yyyy-MM-dd</param-value>
</context-param>
```

As you can see in the **if** block in Listing 7.7, you first need to obtain the date pattern from the **ServletContext** object. After that you employ a **java.text.DateFormat** to convert a **String** to a **Date**.

Finally, the **Transaction-conversion.properties** file (shown in Listing 7.8) registers the two custom converters using field-based configuration.

Listing 7.8: The Transaction-conversion.properties file

```
amount=app07b.converter.MyCurrencyConverter
transactionDate=app07b.converter.MyDateConverter
```

To test this example, direct your browser to this URL:

```
http://localhost:8080/app07b/Transaction1.action
```

Extending StrutsTypeConverter

Since in most type converters you need to provide implementation for **String** to non-**String** conversions and the other way around, it makes sense to provide an implementation class of **TypeConverter** that separates the two

tasks into two different methods. The **StrutsTypeConverter** class, a child of
DefaultTypeConverter, is such a class. There are two abstract methods that
you need to implement when extending **StrutsTypeConverter**,
convertFromString and **convertToString**. See the **StrutsTypeConverter**
class definition in Listing 7.9.

Listing 7.9: The StrutsTypeConverter class

```
package org.apache.struts2.util;
import java.util.Map;
import ognl.DefaultTypeConverter;

public abstract class StrutsTypeConverter
        extends DefaultTypeConverter {
    public Object convertValue(Map context, Object o,
            Class toClass) {
        if (toClass.equals(String.class)) {
            return convertToString(context, o);
        } else if (o instanceof String[]) {
            return convertFromString(context, (String[]) o,
    toClass);
        } else if (o instanceof String) {
            return convertFromString(context,
                    new String[]{(String) o}, toClass);
        } else {
            return performFallbackConversion(context, o, toClass);
        }
    }

    public abstract Object convertFromString(Map context,
            String[] values, Class toClass);

    public abstract String convertToString(Map context, Object o);

    protected Object performFallbackConversion(Map context, Object
        o,
            Class toClass) {
        return super.convertValue(context, o, toClass);
    }
}
```

The implementation of **convertValue** in **StrutsTypeConverter** calls either
convertFromString or **convertToString**, depending on which direction type
conversion must be performed. In addition, the **performFallbackConversion**

method will be called if the object to be converted is not a **String** or the target type (**toClass**) is not a **String** or a **String** array.

The **app07c** application illustrates the use of **StrutsTypeConverter** by featuring a converter for converting **Color** objects to **String**s and vice versa. The user can specify a color by defining its red, green, and blue components in a comma-delimited **String**. For instance, blue is 0,0,255 and green is 0,255,0. Each component value must be an integer in the range of 0 and 255. A **Color** object is an instance of the **Color** class shown in Listing 7.10. A color consists of red, green, and blue components and have a **getHexCode** method that returns the hexadecimal code of the color.

Listing 7.10: The Color class

```
package app07c;
import com.opensymphony.xwork2.ActionSupport;

public class Color extends ActionSupport {
    private int red;
    private int green;
    private int blue;

    // getters and setters not shown

    public String getHexCode() {
        return (red < 16? "0" : "")
                + Integer.toHexString(red)
                + (green < 16? "0" : "")
                + Integer.toHexString(green)
                + (blue < 16? "0" : "")
                + Integer.toHexString(blue);
    }
}
```

The directory structure of **app07c** is shown in Figure 7.6. There are two actions defined in it, **Design1** and **Design2**, as described in the **struts.xml** file accompanying **app07c**. The action declarations are printed in Listing 7.11.

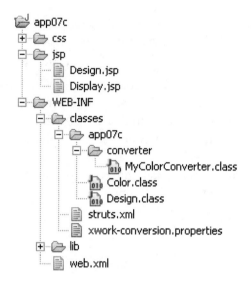

Figure 7.6: app07c directory structure

Listing 7.11: The action declaration

```
<package name="app07c" extends="struts-default">
    <action name="Design1">
        <result>/jsp/Design.jsp</result>
    </action>
    <action name="Design2" class="app07c.Design">
        <result name="input">/jsp/Design.jsp</result>
        <result name="success">/jsp/Display.jsp</result>
    </action>
</package>
```

The **Design1** action is used to take a design from the user. A design is modeled as an instance of the **Design** class in Listing 7.12. It is a simple class that has two properties, **designName** and **color**.

Listing 7.12: The Design class

```
package app07c;
import com.opensymphony.xwork2.ActionSupport;
public class Design extends ActionSupport {
    private String designName;
    private Color color;
    // getters and setters not shown
}
```

The **MyColorConverter** class in Listing 7.13 is derived from
StrutsTypeConverter that provides services for converting a **String** to a
Color and a **Color** to a **String**. Its **convertFromString** method splits a **String**
representation of a color into its red, green, and blue components and
constructs a Color object. Its **convertToString** method takes a **Color** object
and constructs a **String**.

Listing 7.13: The MyColorConverter class

```
package app07c.converter;
import java.util.Map;
import org.apache.struts2.util.StrutsTypeConverter;
import app07c.Color;
import com.opensymphony.xwork2.util.TypeConversionException;

public class MyColorConverter extends StrutsTypeConverter {
    public Object convertFromString(Map context, String[] values,
            Class toClass) {
        boolean ok = false;
        String rgb = values[0];
        String[] colorComponents = rgb.split(",");
        if (colorComponents != null
                && colorComponents.length == 3) {
            String red = colorComponents[0];
            String green = colorComponents[1];
            String blue = colorComponents[2];
            int redCode = 0;
            int greenCode = 0;
            int blueCode = 0;
            try {
                redCode = Integer.parseInt(red.trim());
                greenCode = Integer.parseInt(green.trim());
                blueCode = Integer.parseInt(blue.trim());
                if (redCode >= 0 && redCode < 256
                        && greenCode >= 0 && greenCode < 256
                        && blueCode >= 0 && blueCode < 256) {
                    Color color = new Color();
                    color.setRed(redCode);
                    color.setGreen(greenCode);
                    color.setBlue(blueCode);
                    ok = true;
                    return color;
                }
            } catch (NumberFormatException e) {
            }
        }
```

```
        if (!ok) {
            throw new
                    TypeConversionException("Invalid color codes");
        }
        return null;
    }

    public String convertToString(Map context, Object o) {
        Color color = (Color) o;
        return color.getRed() + ","
                + color.getGreen() + ","
                + color.getBlue();
    }
}
```

To use **MyColorConverter**, you must configure it. The **xwork-conversion.properties** file in Listing 7.14 is the class-based configuration file. There is only one entry in this file, mapping the **Color** class with **MyColorConverter**. If you're mapping more than one class, feel free to add more entries in this file.

Listing 7.14: The xwork-conversion.properties file

```
app07c.Color=app07c.converter.MyColorConverter
```

Alternatively, you could also do field-based configuration by creating a **Design-conversion.properties** file in the **WEB-INF/classes/app07c** directory with one entry:

```
color=app07c.converter.MyColorConverter
```

To test the color converter, direct your browser to this URL:

```
http://localhost:8080/app07c/Design1.action
```

You will see a form with two text fields like the one in Figure 7.7. Enter a design name and a color.

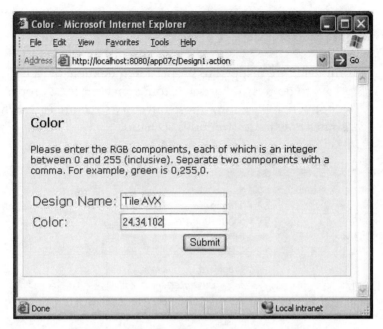

Figure 7.7: Using a color converter

If you enter a valid color and submit the form, you will invoke the **Design2** action and have the color displayed as in Figure 7.8.

Figure 7.8: Displaying a color

Working with Complex Objects

Oftentimes, form fields are mapped to properties in multiple objects. Thanks to OGNL, it is easy to do this and use a custom converter for a property in any object. The **app07d** application, whose directory structure is shown in Figure 7.9, illustrates how to deal with this scenario.

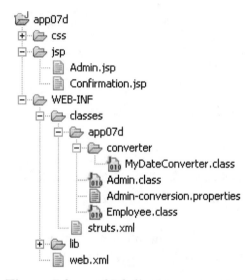

Figure 7.9: app07d directory structure

This sample application has two actions, **Admin1** and **Admin2**, that can be used to add an Employee to the database. Every time a new employee is added, the admin id must also be noted because there are multiple users in the admin role. The action declarations in the **struts.xml** are shown in Listing 7.15.

Listing 7.15: The action declaration

```
<package name="app07d" extends="struts-default">
    <action name="Admin1">
        <result>/jsp/Admin.jsp</result>
    </action>
    <action name="Admin2" class="app07d.Admin">
        <result name="input">/jsp/Admin.jsp</result>
        <result name="success">/jsp/Confirmation.jsp</result>
    </action>
```

```
</package>
```

The **Admin** class (See Listing 7.16) has two properties, **adminId** and **employee**. **adminId** is a **String**, but employee is of type **Employee**, another class (shown in Listing 7.17) with its own properties (**firstName**, **lastName**, and **birthDate**). With one HTML form, how do you populate an **Admin** and an **Employee** and at the same time use a custom converter for the **birthDate** property?

Listing 7.16: The Admin class

```
package app07d;
import com.opensymphony.xwork2.ActionSupport;
public class Admin extends ActionSupport {
    private Employee employee;
    private String adminId;
    // getters and setters not shown

    public String execute() {
        // code to insert the employee to the database here

        return SUCCESS;
    }
}
```

Listing 7.17: The Employee class

```
package app07d;
import java.util.Date;

public class Employee {
    private String firstName;
    private String lastName;
    private Date birthDate;

    // getters and setters not shown
}
```

The answer is simple: OGNL. A **form** tag can be mapped to a property's property. For example, to map a field to the **firstName** property of the **employee** property of the action, use the OGNL expression **employee.firstName**. The **Admin.jsp** page in Listing 7.18 shows the form whose fields map to two objects.

Chapter 7: Type Conversion

Listing 7.18: The Admin.jsp page

```
<%@ taglib prefix="s" uri="/struts-tags" %>
<html>
<head>
<title>Add Employee</title>
<style type="text/css">@import url(css/main.css);</style>
<style>
.errorMessage {
    color:red;
}
</style>
</head>
<body>
<div id="global" style="width:450px">
      <h4>Add Employees</h4>
      <s:form action="Admin2">
          <s:textfield name="adminId" label="Admin ID"/>
          <s:textfield name="employee.firstName"
                  label="Employee First Name"/>
          <s:textfield name="employee.lastName"
                  label="Employee Last Name"/>
          <s:textfield name="employee.birthDate"
                  label="Employee Birth Date (yyyy-MM-dd)"/>
        <s:submit/>
      </s:form>
</div>
</body>
</html>
```

The **Confirmation.jsp** page in Listing 7.19 shows how to display the **adminId** property as well as the properties of the **employee** property.

Listing 7.19: The Confirmation.jsp page

```
<%@ taglib prefix="s" uri="/struts-tags" %>
<html>
<head>
<title>Employee Details</title>
<style type="text/css">@import url(css/main.css);</style>
</head>
<body>
<div id="global" style="width:350px">
    Admin Id: <s:property value="adminId"/>
    <h4>Employee Created:</h4>
    <s:property value="employee.firstName"/>
    <s:property value="employee.lastName"/>
```

```
    (<s:date name="employee.birthDate"
            format="MMM dd, yyyy"/>)
</div>
</body>
</html>
```

Last but not least, the **birthDate** property of the **Employee** class must be configured to use the **MyDateConverter** converter. Listing 7.20 shows the **Admin-conversion.properties** file that registers **MyDateConverter** for **birthDate**.

Listing 7.20: The Admin-conversion.properties file

```
employee.birthDate=app07d.converter.MyDateConverter
```

To test this application, direct your browser here:

```
http://localhost:8080/app07d/Admin1.action
```

Working with Collections

Struts also allows you to populate objects in a **Collection**. Normally, you would want to do this for faster data entry. Instead of adding one employee at a time as we did in **app07d**, **app07e** enables multiple employees to be added at the same time.

The directory structure of **app07e** is shown in Figure 7.10 and the action declarations in Listing 7.21.

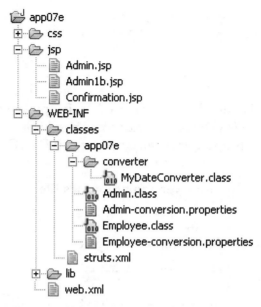

Figure 7.10: app07e directory structure

Listing 7.21: The action declaration

```
<package name="app07e" extends="struts-default">
    <action name="Admin1">
        <result>/jsp/Admin.jsp</result>
    </action>
    <action name="Admin2" class="app07e.Admin">
        <result name="input">/jsp/Admin.jsp</result>
        <result name="success">/jsp/Confirmation.jsp</result>
    </action>
    <action name="Admin1b">
        <result>/jsp/Admin1b.jsp</result>
    </action>
</package>
```

The **Admin1** action displays the form for entering two employees and
Admin2 inserts the employees to the database and displays the added data.
The **Admin1b** action is additional and allows any number of employees.
Admin1b will be discussed at the end of this section.

The **Admin** class and the **Employee** class are given in Listing 7.22 and
Listing 7.23, respectively. Note that the **Admin** class contains an **employee**
property that is of **Collection** type.

Listing 7.22: The Admin class

```java
package app07e;
import java.util.Collection;
import com.opensymphony.xwork2.ActionSupport;

public class Admin extends ActionSupport {
    private Collection employees;
    public Collection getEmployees() {
        return employees;
    }
    public void setEmployees(Collection employees) {
        this.employees = employees;
    }
}
```

Listing 7.23: The Employee class

```java
package app07e;
import java.util.Date;

public class Employee {
    private String firstName;
    private String lastName;
    private Date birthDate;

    // getters and setters not shown

    public String toString() {
        return firstName + " " + lastName;
    }
}
```

The **Admin.jsp** page in Listing 7.24 contains a form that allows you to enter two employees. The first employee will become the first element of the **Collection employees** property in the **Admin** action. It is denoted by **employees[0]**, and the second employee is **employees[1]**. Consequently, the **textfield** tag mapped to the **lastName** property of the first employee has its **name** property assigned **employees[0].lastName**.

Listing 7.24: The Admin.jsp page

```jsp
<%@ taglib prefix="s" uri="/struts-tags" %>
<html>
<head>
<title>Add Employees</title>
<style type="text/css">@import url(css/main.css);</style>
```

```
<style>
.errorMessage {
    color:red;
}
</style>
</head>
<body>
<div id="global" style="width:450px">
    <h4>Add Employees</h4>
    <s:fielderror/>
    <s:form theme="simple" action="Admin2">
    <table>
    <tr>
        <th>First Name</th>
        <th>Last Name</th>
        <th>Birth Date</th>
    </tr>
    <tr>
        <td><s:textfield name="employees[0].firstName"/></td>
        <td><s:textfield name="employees[0].lastName"/></td>
        <td><s:textfield name="employees[0].birthDate"/></td>
    </tr>
    <tr>
        <td><s:textfield name="employees[1].firstName"/></td>
        <td><s:textfield name="employees[1].lastName"/></td>
        <td><s:textfield name="employees[1].birthDate"/></td>
    </tr>
    <tr>
        <td colspan="3"><s:submit/></td>
    </tr>
    </table>
    </s:form>
</div>
</body>
</html>
```

The **Confirmation.jsp** page, shown in Listing 7.25, uses the **iterator** tag to iterate over the employees property in the **Admin** action. It also employs the **date** tag to format the birthdates.

Listing 7.25: The Confirmation.jsp page

```
<%@ taglib prefix="s" uri="/struts-tags" %>
<html>
<head>
<title>Confirmation</title>
```

```
<style type="text/css">@import url(css/main.css);</style>
</head>
<body>
<div id="global" style="width:350px">
    <h4>Employee Created:</h4>
    <table>
    <s:iterator value="employees">
        <tr>
            <td><s:property value="firstName"/>
            <s:property value="lastName"/>
            (<s:date name="birthDate" format="MMM dd, yyyy"/>)
            </td>
        </tr>
    </s:iterator>
    </table>
</div>
<s:debug/>
</body>
</html>
```

You can test this example by directing your browser to this URL.

```
http://localhost:8080/app07e/Admin1.action
```

Figure 7.11 shows the form.

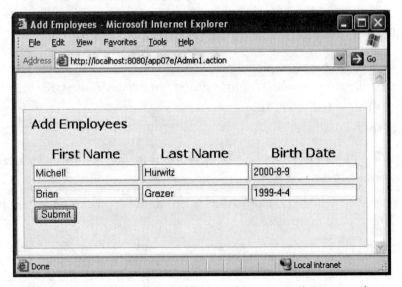

Figure 7.11: Adding multiple employees at the same time

Go ahead and add data to the form and submit it. Figure 7.12 shows the data displayed.

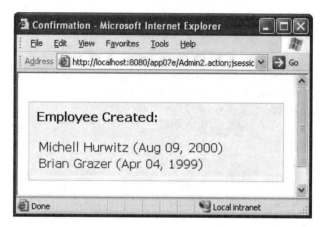

Figure 7.12: Displaying added employees

Being able to add two employees is great, but you probably want more. The rest of the section discusses how get more flexibility.

Instead of hardcoding the text fields for employees as we did in the **Admin.jsp** page, we use an **iterator** tag to dynamically build text fields. For example, to create four sets of fields, you need an **iterator** tag with four elements like this.

```
<s:iterator value="new int[4]" status="stat">
```

Or, better still, you can pass a **count** request parameter to the URL and use the value to build the iterator:

```
new int[#parameters.count[0]]
```

Note that the **[0]** is necessary because **parameters** always returns an array of **String**s, not a **String**.

Here are the tags that build text fields on the fly. You can find them in the **Admin1b.jsp** page in **app07e**.

```
<s:iterator value="new int[#parameters.count[0]]" status="stat">
<tr>
    <td><s:textfield
            name="%{'employees['+#stat.index+'].firstName'}"/></td>
    <td><s:textfield
```

```
            name="%{'employees['+#stat.index+'].lastName'}"/></td>
      <td><s:textfield
            name="%{'employees['+#stat.index+'].birthDate'}"/></td>
</tr>
</s:iterator>
```

Invoke the action by using this URL, embedding a **count** request parameter.

```
http://localhost:8080/app07e/Admin1b.action?count=n
```

where *n* is the number of rows you want created. You can now enter as many employees as you want in one go.

Working with Maps

Most of the times you'll probably be happy with populating objects in a **Collection**. In some rare cases, however, you might need to populate objects in a **Map**. Even though it's harder, it's something Struts will happily do for you too, as you can see in the **app07f** application. As usual, I begin by presenting the directory structure of the application. It is shown in Figure 7.13.

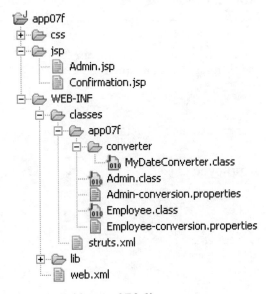

Figure 7.13: app07f directory structure

The action declarations, shown in Listing 7.26, are similar to those in **app07e**. **Admin1** displays a multiple record entry form, **Admin2** displays the entered data, and **Admin1b** can be used to add any number of employees.

Listing 7.26: The action declaration

```
<package name="app07f" extends="struts-default">
    <action name="Admin1">
        <result>/jsp/Admin.jsp</result>
    </action>
    <action name="Admin2" class="app07f.Admin">
        <result name="input">/jsp/Admin.jsp</result>
        <result name="success">/jsp/Confirmation.jsp</result>
    </action>
    <action name="Admin1b">
        <result>/jsp/Admin1b.jsp</result>
    </action>
</package>
```

The **Admin** class is given in Listing 7.27. Note that the **employees** property is a **Map**. The **Employee** class is presented in Listing 7.28 and is a template for employees.

Listing 7.27: The Admin class

```
package app07f;
import java.util.Map;
import com.opensymphony.xwork2.ActionSupport;
public class Admin extends ActionSupport {
    private Map employees;
    private String[] userName;

    // getters and setters not shown
}
```

Listing 7.28: The Employee class

```
package app07f;
import java.util.Date;
public class Employee {
    private String firstName;
    private String lastName;
    private Date birthDate;
    public String toString() {
        return firstName + " " + lastName;
    }
}
```

```
    // getters and setters not shown
}
```

To populate a **Map** property, which **employees** is, you need to tell Struts what class to instantiate for each entry. The **Admin-conversion.properties** file in Listing 7.29 is a field-based configuration file that indicates that every element of the **employees** property is an instance of **app07f.Employee** and that it should create a new **Map** if **employees** is null.

Listing 7.29: The Admin-conversion.properties file

```
Element_employees=app07f.Employee
CreateIfNull_employees=true
```

On top of that, we want to use a date converter for the **birthDate** property in **Employee**. Listing 7.30 shows the field-based configuration file for the **Employee** class.

Listing 7.30: The Employee-conversion.properties file

```
birthDate=app07f.converter.MyDateConverter
```

The **Admin.jsp** page in Listing 7.31 contains a form for entering two employees. **employees['user0'].lastName** indicates the **lastName** property of the entry in the **employees Map** whose key is **user0**.

Listing 7.31: The Admin.jsp page

```
<%@ taglib prefix="s" uri="/struts-tags" %>
<html>
<head>
<title>Add Employees</title>
<style type="text/css">@import url(css/main.css);</style>
<style>
.errorMessage {
    color:red;
}
</style>
</head>
<body>
<div id="global" style="width:450px">
    <h4>Add Employees</h4>
    <s:fielderror/>
    <s:form theme="simple" action="Admin2">
    <table>
    <tr>
```

```
        <th>First Name</th>
        <th>Last Name</th>
        <th>Birth Date</th>
    </tr>
    <tr>
        <td><s:textfield name="employees['user0'].firstName"/></td>
        <td><s:textfield name="employees['user0'].lastName"/></td>
        <td><s:textfield name="employees['user0'].birthDate"/></td>
    </tr>
    <tr>
        <td><s:textfield name="employees['user1'].firstName"/></td>
        <td><s:textfield name="employees['user1'].lastName"/></td>
        <td><s:textfield name="employees['user1'].birthDate"/></td>
    </tr>
    <tr>
        <td colspan="3"><s:submit/></td>
    </tr>
    </table>
    </s:form>
</div>
</body>
</html>
```

Listing 7.32 shows the **Confirmation.jsp** page that displays entered data by iterating over the **employees Map**.

Listing 7.32: The Confirmation.jsp page

```
<%@ taglib prefix="s" uri="/struts-tags" %>
<html>
<head>
<title>Confirmation</title>
<style type="text/css">@import url(css/main.css);</style>
</head>
<body>
<div id="global" style="width:350px">
    <h4>Employees Created:</h4>
    <ul>
    <s:iterator value="employees.keySet()" var="key" status="stat">
        <li><s:property value="#key"/>:
            <s:property value="employees[#key].firstName"/>
            <s:property value="employees[#key].lastName"/>
        </li>
    </s:iterator>
    </ul>
</div>
```

```
</body>
</html>
```

To test the application, direct your browser here:

```
http://localhost:8080/app07f/Admin1.action
```

You will see a form like the one in Figure 7.14. Enter values in the text fields and submit the form, and you will see the entered data displayed, as shown in Figure 7.15.

To have a form for entering n employees, use the technique described in **app07e**.

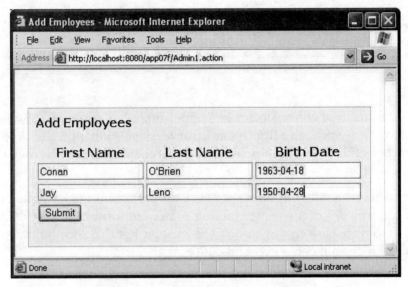

Figure 7.14: Populating a Map

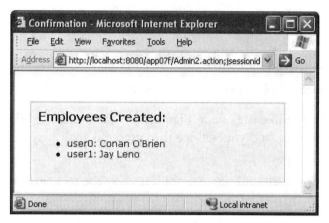

Figure 7.15: Displaying a Map's elements

Summary

Struts performs type conversions when populating action properties. When a conversion fails, Struts also displays an error message so that the user knows how to correct the input. You've learned in this chapter how to override the error message.

Sometimes default type conversions are not sufficient. For example, if you have a complex object or you want to use a different format than the default, you need to write custom converters. This chapter has also shown how to write various custom converters and configure them.

Chapter 8
Input Validation

A robust web application must ensure that user input is valid. For instance, you may want to make sure that user information entered in a form will only be stored in the database if the selected password is at least n characters long and the birth date is a date that is no later than today's date. Struts makes input validation easy by providing built-in validators that are based on the XWork Validation Framework. Using these validators does not require programming. Instead, you declare in an XML file how a validator should work. Among the things to declare are what field needs to be validated and what message to send to the browser if a validation fails.

In more complex scenarios, built-in validators can help little and you have to write code to validate input. This is called programmatic validation and, along with built-in validators, is discussed in this chapter.

Validator Overview

There are two types of validators, field validators and plain validators (non-field validators). A field validator is associated with a form field and works by verifying a value before the value is assigned to an action property. Most bundled validators are field validators. A plain validator is not associated with a field and is used to test if a certain condition has been met. The validation interceptor, which is part of the default stack, is responsible for loading and executing registered validators.

Using a validator requires these three steps:

1. Determine the action whose input is to be validated.
2. Write a validator configuration file. The file name must follow one of these two patterns:

```
ActionClass-validation.xml
```

`ActionClass-alias-validation.xml`

The first pattern is more common. However, since an action class can be used by multiple actions, there are cases whereby you only want to apply validation on certain actions. For example, the **UserAction** class may be used with **User_create** and **User_edit** actions. If both actions are to be validated using the same rules, you can simply declare the rules in a **UserAction-validation.xml** file. However, if **User_create** and **User_edit** use different validation rules, you must create two validator configuration files, **UserAction-User_create-validation.xml** and **UserAction-User_edit-validation.xml**.

3. Determine where the user should be forwarded to when validation fails by defining a **<result name="input">** element in the **struts.xml** file. Normally, the value of the **result** element is the same JSP that contains the validated form.

Note on Validator Registration

All bundled validators are registered by default and can be used without you having to worry about registration. Registration becomes an issue if you're using a custom validator. If this is the case, read the section "Writing Custom Validators" later in this chapter.

Validator Configuration

The task of configuring validators centers around writing validator configuration files, which are XML documents that must comply with the XWork validator DTD.

A validator configuration file always starts with this **DOCTYPE** statement.

```
<!DOCTYPE validators PUBLIC
    "-//OpenSymphony Group//XWork Validator 1.0.2//EN"
    "http://www.opensymphony.com/xwork/xwork-validator-1.0.2.dtd">
```

The root element of a validator configuration file is **validators**. **<validators>** may have any number of **field** and **validator** elements. A **field** element represents a form field to which one or more field validators will be applied. A **validator** element represents a plain validator. Here is the skeleton of a typical validator configuration file.

```
<!DOCTYPE validators PUBLIC
    "-//OpenSymphony Group//XWork Validator 1.0.2//EN"
    "http://www.opensymphony.com/xwork/xwork-validator-1.0.2.dtd">
<validators>
    <field name="...">
        ...
    </field>
    <field name="...">
        ...
    </field>

    ...

    <validator type="...">
        ...
    </validator>
    <validator type="...">
        ...
    </validator>

    ...

</validators>
```

The **name** attribute in a **field** element specifies the form field to be validated.

You can apply any number of validators to a form field by nesting **field-validator** elements within the **field** element. For instance, the following **field** element indicates that the **userEmail** field must be validated by required and email validators.

```
<field name="userEmail">
    <field-validator type="required">
    </field-validator>
    <field-validator type="email">
    </field-validator>
</field>
```

A **field-validator** element must have a **type** attribute, which points to a validator. In addition, it can have a **short-circuit** attribute. The value of **short-circuit** is either true or false (default). A value of true indicates that if the current validator fails, the next validators for the same field will not be executed. For example, in the configuration below, if the required validator fails, the email validator will not be executed.

```
<field name="userEmail">
    <field-validator type="required" short-circuit="true">
    </field-validator>
    <field-validator type="email">
    </field-validator>
</field>
```

You can pass parameters to a validator by nesting **param** elements within the **field-validator** element. You can also define a validation error message by using the **message** element within the **field-validator** element. As an example, this **stringlength** field validator receives two parameters, **minLength** and **maxLength**, and the error message that must be displayed when validation fails.

```
<field-validator type="stringlength">
    <param name="minLength">6</param>
    <param name="maxLength">14</param>
    <message>
        User name must be between 6 and 14 characters long
    </message>
</field-validator>
```

A **field-validator** element can have zero or more **param** element and at most one **message** element.

The **validator** element is used to represent a plain validator. It can also contain multiple **param** element and a **message** element. For example, the following **validator** element dictates that the **max** field must be greater than the **min** field or validation will fail.

```
<validator type="expression">
    <param name="expression">
        max > min
    </param>
    <message>
        Maximum temperature must be greater than Minimum temperature
    </message>
</validator>
```

Like **field-validator**, the **validator** element must have a **type** attribute and may have a **short-circuit** attribute.

Bundled Validators

Struts comes with these built-in validators.

- required validator.
- requiredstring validator
- int validator
- date validator
- expression validator
- fieldexpression validator
- email validator
- url validator
- visitor validator
- conversion validator
- stringlength validator
- regex validator

Each of the validators is discussed in a separate section below.

required Validator

This validator makes sure that a field value is not null. An empty string is not null and therefore will not raise an exception.

For instance, the **RequiredTestAction** class in Listing 8.1 has two properties, **userName** and **password**, and employs a validator configuration file presented in Listing 8.2.

Listing 8.1: The RequiredTestAction class

```
package app08a;
import com.opensymphony.xwork2.ActionSupport;
public class RequiredTestAction extends ActionSupport {
    private String userName;
    private String password;
    // getters and setters not shown
}
```

Listing 8.2: The RequiredTestAction-validation.xml file

```
<!DOCTYPE validators PUBLIC
```

```
    "-//OpenSymphony Group//XWork Validator 1.0.2//EN"
    "http://www.opensymphony.com/xwork/xwork-validator-1.0.2.dtd">

<validators>
    <field name="userName">
        <field-validator type="required">
            <message>Please enter a user name</message>
        </field-validator>
    </field>
    <field name="password">
        <field-validator type="required">
            <message>Please enter a password</message>
        </field-validator>
    </field>
</validators>
```

When you submit a form to **RequiredTestAction,** two fields are required.
Listing 8.3 shows the JSP used to demonstrate the required validator. The
userName textfield tag has been commented out to trigger the validator.

Listing 8.3: The Required.jsp page

```
<%@ taglib prefix="s" uri="/struts-tags" %>
<html>
<head>
<title>required Validator Example</title>
<style type="text/css">@import url(css/main.css);</style>
<style>
.errorMessage {
    color:red;
}
</style>
</head>
<body>
<div id="global" style="width:350px">
    <h3>Enter user name and password</h3>
    <s:fielderror/>
    <s:form action="Required2">
<%--    <s:textfield name="userName" label="User Name"/>
--%>
        <s:password name="password" label="Password"/>
        <s:submit/>
    </s:form>
</div>
</body>
</html>
```

You can use this URL to display the page:

`http://localhost:8080/app08a/Required2.action`

Figure 8.1 shows the form after a failed validation. It is rejected since the **userName** field is missing.

Figure 8.1: The required validator

requiredstring validator

The requiredstring validator ensures a field value is not null and not empty. It has a **trim** parameter that by default has a value of true. If **trim** is true, the validated field will be trimmed prior to validation. If **trim** is false, the value of the validated field will not be trimmed. The **trim** parameter is described in Table 8.1.

Name	Data Type	Description
trim	boolean	Indicates whether or not trailing spaces will be trimmed prior to validation.

Table 8.1: requiredstring validator parameter

With **trim** true, a field that contains only spaces will fail to be validated.

Chapter 8: Input Validation

The following example validates the fields associated with the properties of the **RequiredStringTestAction** class in Listing 8.4. The validation configuration file in Listing 8.5 assigns the requiredstring validator to the userName and password fields.

Listing 8.4: The RequiredStringTestAction class

```
package app08a;
import com.opensymphony.xwork2.ActionSupport;
public class RequiredStringTestAction extends ActionSupport {
    private String userName;
    private String password;
    // getters and setters deleted
}
```

Listing 8.5: The RequiredStringTestAction-validation.xml file

```
<!DOCTYPE validators PUBLIC
    "-//OpenSymphony Group//XWork Validator 1.0.2//EN"
    "http://www.opensymphony.com/xwork/xwork-validator-1.0.2.dtd">

<validators>
    <field name="userName">
        <field-validator type="requiredstring">
            <param name="trim">true</param>
            <message>Please enter a user name</message>
        </field-validator>
    </field>
    <field name="password">
        <field-validator type="requiredstring">
            <param name="trim">false</param>
            <message>Please enter a password</message>
        </field-validator>
    </field>
</validators>
```

Note that the requiredstring validator for the userName has its **trim** parameter set to **true**, which means a space or spaces do not qualify. The **RequiredString.jsp** page in Listing 8.6 shows the form for this example.

Listing 8.6: The RequiredString.jsp page

```
<%@ taglib prefix="s" uri="/struts-tags" %>
<html>
<head>
<title>requiredstring Validator Example</title>
<style type="text/css">@import url(css/main.css);</style>
```

```
<style>
.errorMessage {
    color:red;
}
</style>
</head>
<body>
<div id="global" style="width:350px">
    <h3>Enter user name and password</h3>
    <s:form action="RequiredString2">
        <s:textfield name="userName" label="User Name"/>
        <s:password name="password" label="Password"/>
        <s:submit/>
    </s:form>
</div>
</body>
</html>
```

To test this example, direct your browser to this URL:

```
http://localhost:8080/app08a/RequiredString1.action
```

Submitting the form without first entering values to the fields will result in the form being returned.

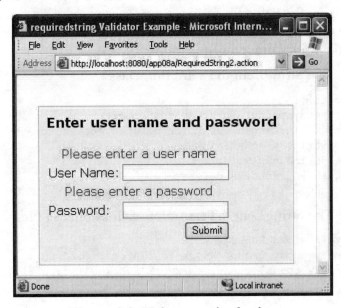

Figure 8.2: Using requiredstring

stringlength Validator

You use stringlength to validate that a non-empty field value is of a certain length. You specify the minimum and maximum lengths through the **minLength** and **maxLength** parameters. The complete list of parameters is given in Table 8.2.

Name	Data Type	Description
minLength	int	The maximum length allowed. If this parameter is not present, there will be no maximum length restriction for the associated field.
maxLength	int	The minimum length allowed for the associated field. If this parameter is not present, there will be no minimum length restriction for the field.
trim	boolean	Indicates whether or not trailing spaces will be trimmed prior to validation.

Table 8.2: stringlength validator parameters

For example, the **StringLengthTestAction** class in Listing 8.7 defines two properties, **userName** and **password**. A user name must be between six to fourteen characters long and the stringlength validator is used to ensure this. The validator configuration file for this example is presented in Listing 8.8. The **StringLength.jsp** page in Listing 8.9 shows the form whose field is mapped to the **userName** property.

Listing 8.7: The StringLengthTestAction class

```
package app08a;
import com.opensymphony.xwork2.ActionSupport;
public class StringLengthTestAction extends ActionSupport {
    private String userName;
    private String password;
    // getters and setters deleted
}
```

Listing 8.8: The StringLengthTestAction-validation.xml file

```
<!DOCTYPE validators PUBLIC
    "-//OpenSymphony Group//XWork Validator 1.0.2//EN"
    "http://www.opensymphony.com/xwork/xwork-validator-1.0.2.dtd">

<validators>
    <field name="userName">
        <field-validator type="stringlength">
```

```
            <param name="minLength">6</param>
            <param name="maxLength">14</param>
            <message>
                User name must be between 6 and 14 characters long
            </message>
        </field-validator>
    </field>
</validators>
```

Listing 8.9: The StringLength.jsp page

```
<%@ taglib prefix="s" uri="/struts-tags" %>
<html>
<head>
<title>stringlength Validator Example</title>
<style type="text/css">@import url(css/main.css);</style>
<style>
.errorMessage {
    color:red;
}
</style>
</head>
<body>
<div id="global" style="width:480px">
    <h3>Select a user name</h3>
    <s:form action="StringLength2">
        <s:textfield name="userName"
                label="User Name (6-14 characters)"/>
        <s:submit/>
    </s:form>
</div>
</body>
</html>
```

To test this example, direct your browser to this URL:

```
http://localhost:8080/app08a/StringLength1.action
```

Figure 8.3 shows the form.

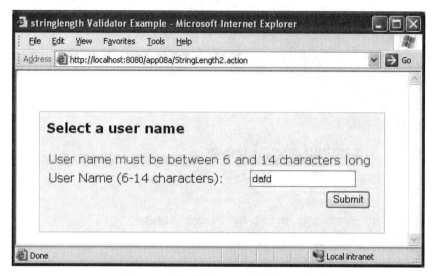

Figure 8.3: Using stringlength

int Validator

The int validator checks if a field value can be converted into an int and, if the min and max parameters are used, if its value falls within the specified range. The int validator's parameters are listed in Table 8.3.

Name	Data Type	Description
min	int	The maximum value allowed. If this parameter is not present, there's no maximum value.
max	int	The minimum value allowed. If this parameter is not present, there's no minimum value.

Table 8.3: int validator parameters

As an example, consider the **IntTestAction** class in Listing 8.10. It exposes one property, **year**, which is an int representing the year part of a date.

Listing 8.10: The IntTestAction class

```
package app08a;
import com.opensymphony.xwork2.ActionSupport;
public class IntTestAction extends ActionSupport {
    private int year;
```

```
        // getter and setter not shown
}
```

The validator configuration file in Listing 8.11 guarantees that any year value submitted to an **IntTestAction** object must be between 1990 and 2009 (inclusive).

Listing 8.11: The IntTestAction-validation.xml file

```
<!DOCTYPE validators PUBLIC
    "-//OpenSymphony Group//XWork Validator 1.0.2//EN"
    "http://www.opensymphony.com/xwork/xwork-validator-1.0.2.dtd">

<validators>
    <field name="year">
        <field-validator type="int">
            <param name="min">1990</param>
            <param name="max">2009</param>
            <message>Year must be between 1990 and 2009</message>
        </field-validator>
    </field>
</validators>
```

The **Int.jsp** page in Listing 8.12 shows a form with a **textfield** tag named **year**. Upon the form submit, the validator will kick in to make sure the value of **year** is within the prescribed range.

Listing 8.12: The Int.jsp page

```
<%@ taglib prefix="s" uri="/struts-tags" %>
<html>
<head>
<title>int Validator Example</title>
<style type="text/css">@import url(css/main.css);</style>
<style>
.errorMessage {
    color:red;
}
</style>
</head>
<body>
<div id="global" style="width:350px">
    <h3>Enter a year</h3>
    <s:form action="Int2">
    <s:textfield name="year" label="Year (1990-2009)"/>
    <s:submit/>
```

```
        </s:form>
</div>
</body>
</html>
```

Direct your browser to this URL to test the int validator.

`http://localhost:8080/app08a/Int1.action`

You will see the form as shown in Figure 8.14.

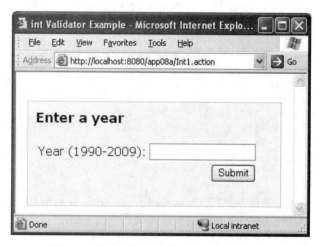

Figure 8.4: Using the int validator

date Validator

This validator checks if a specified date field falls within a certain range. Table 8.4 lists all possible parameters of the date validator.

Name	Data Type	Description
max	date	The maximum value allowed. If this parameter is not present, there will be no maximum value.
min	date	The minimum value allowed. If this parameter is not present, there will be no minimum value.

Table 8.4: date validator parameters

Note
The date pattern used to validate a date is dependant on the current locale.

For example, the **DateTestAction** class in Listing 8.13 is used to test the date validator. The **DateTestAction-validation.xml** configuration file in Listing 8.14 assigns the date validator to the **birthDate** field.

Listing 8.13: The DateTestAction class

```
package app08a;
import java.util.Date;
import com.opensymphony.xwork2.ActionSupport;
public class DateTestAction extends ActionSupport {
    private Date birthDate;
    // getter and setter deleted
}
```

Listing 8.14: The DateTestAction-validation.xml file

```
<!DOCTYPE validators PUBLIC
    "-//OpenSymphony Group//XWork Validator 1.0.2//EN"
    "http://www.opensymphony.com/xwork/xwork-validator-1.0.2.dtd">

<validators>
    <field name="birthDate">
        <field-validator type="date">
            <param name="max">1/1/2000</param>
            <message>
            You must have been born before the year 2000 to register
            </message>
        </field-validator>
    </field>
</validators>
```

The configuration file specifies that the year value must be before January 1, 2000. The date pattern used here is **US_en**.

The **Date.jsp** page in Listing 8.15 contains a form that submits the **birthDate** field to the **DateTestAction** action.

Listing 8.15: The Date.jsp page

```
<%@ taglib prefix="s" uri="/struts-tags" %>
<html>
<head>
<title>date Validator Example</title>
```

```
<style type="text/css">@import url(css/main.css);</style>
<style>
.errorMessage {
        color:red;
}
</style>
</head>
<body>
<div id="global" style="width:350px">
    <h3>Enter your birthdate</h3>
    <s:form action="Date2">
        <s:textfield name="birthDate" label="Birth Date"/>
        <s:submit/>
    </s:form>
</div>
</body>
</html>
```

To test the date validator, direct your browser to this URL:

```
http://localhost:8080/app08a/Date1.action
```

The form will be shown in your browser and will look like that in Figure 8.5.

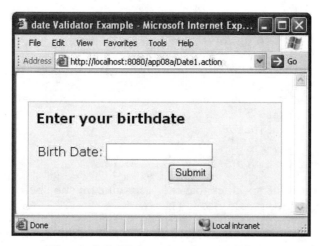

Figure 8.5: Using the date validator

email Validator

The email validator can be used to check if a **String** evaluates to an email address. This validator uses the Java Regular Expression API and use the following pattern:

```
"\\b(^[_A-Za-z0-9-]+(\\.[_A-Za-z0-9-]+)*@([A-Za-z0-9-])+(\\.[A-Za-
z0-9-]+)*((\\.[A-Za-z0-9]{2,})|(\\.[A-Za-z0-9]{2,}\\.[A-Za-z0-
9]{2,}))$)\\b"
```

This means an email can start with any combination of letters and numbers that is followed by any number of periods and letters and numbers. It must have a @ character followed by a valid host name.

As an example, the **EmailTestAction** class in Listing 8.16 defines an **email** property that will be validated using the email validator. The validator configuration file is given in Listing 8.17 and the JSP that contains a form with the corresponding field in printed in Listing 8.18.

Listing 8.16: The EmailTestAction class

```
package app08a;
import com.opensymphony.xwork2.ActionSupport;
public class EmailTestAction extends ActionSupport {
    private String email;
    //getter and setter not shown
}
```

Listing 8.17: The EmailTestAction-validation.xml file

```
<!DOCTYPE validators PUBLIC
    "-//OpenSymphony Group//XWork Validator 1.0.2//EN"
    "http://www.opensymphony.com/xwork/xwork-validator-1.0.2.dtd">

<validators>
    <field name="email">
        <field-validator type="email">
            <message>Invalid email</message>
        </field-validator>
    </field>
</validators>
```

Listing 8.18: The Email.jsp page

```
<%@ taglib prefix="s" uri="/struts-tags" %>
<html>
<head>
```

```
<title>email Validator Example</title>
<style type="text/css">@import url(css/main.css);</style>
<style>
.errorMessage {
    color:red;
}
</style>
</head>
<body>
<div id="global" style="width:350px">
    <h3>Enter your email</h3>
    <s:form action="Email2">
        <s:textfield name="email" label="Email"/>
        <s:submit/>
    </s:form>
</div>
</body>
</html>
```

To test the email validator, direct your browser to this URL:

```
http://localhost:8080/app08a/Email1.action
```

Figure 8.6 shows the form that contains a **textfield** tag named **email**.

Figure 8.6: Using the email validator

url Validator

The url validator can be used to check if a **String** qualifies as a valid URL. The validator does it work by trying to create a **java.net.URL** object using the String. If no exception is thrown during the process, validation is successful.

The following are examples of valid URLs:

```
http://www.google.com
https://hotmail.com
ftp://yahoo.com
file:///C:/data/V3.doc
```

This one is invalid because there is no protocol.

```
java.com
```

As an example, consider the **UrlTestAction** class in Listing 8.19 has a **url** property that will be validated using the url validator. The validation configuration file is given in Listing 8.20.

Listing 8.19: The UrlTestAction class

```
package app08a;
import com.opensymphony.xwork2.ActionSupport;
public class UrlTestAction extends ActionSupport {
    private String url;
    // getter and setter not shown
}
```

Listing 8.20: The UrlTestAction-validation.xml file

```
<!DOCTYPE validators PUBLIC
    "-//OpenSymphony Group//XWork Validator 1.0.2//EN"
    "http://www.opensymphony.com/xwork/xwork-validator-1.0.2.dtd">
<validators>
    <field name="url">
        <field-validator type="url">
            <message>Invalid URL</message>
        </field-validator>
    </field>
</validators>
```

The **Url.jsp** page in Listing 8.21 contains a form with a **textfield** tag named **url**.

Listing 8.21: The Url.jsp page

```
<%@ taglib prefix="s" uri="/struts-tags" %>
<html>
<head>
<title>url Validator Example</title>
<style type="text/css">@import url(css/main.css);</style>
<style>
.errorMessage {
    color:red;
}
</style>
</head>
<body>
<div id="global" style="width:350px">
    <h3>What is your website?</h3>
    <s:form action="Url2">
        <s:textfield name="url" label="URL" size="40"/>
        <s:submit/>
    </s:form>
</div>
</body>
</html>
```

To test this example, direct your browser here.

```
http://localhost:8080/app08a/Url1.action
```

Figure 8.7 shows the form.

Figure 8.7: Using the url validator

regex Validator

This validator checks if a field value matches the specified regular expression pattern. Its parameters are listed in Table 8.5. See the documentation for the **java.lang.regex.Pattern** class for more details on Java regular expression patterns.

Name	Data Type	Description
expression*	String	The regular expression pattern to match.
caseSensitive	boolean	Indicates whether or not the matching should be done in a case sensitive way. The default value is true.
trim	boolean	Indicates whether or not the field should be trimmed prior to validation. The default value is true.

Table 8.5: regex validator parameters

expression and fieldexpression Validators

The expression and fieldexpression validators are used to validate a field against an OGNL expression. expression and fieldexpression are similar, except that the former is not a field validator whereas the latter is. The other difference is a failed validation of the expression validator will generate an action error. fieldexpression will raise a field error on a failed validation. The parameter for these validators is given in Table 8.6.

Name	Data Type	Description
expression*	String	The OGNL expression that governs the validation process.

Table 8.6: expression and fieldexpression validators' parameter

There are two examples in this section. The first one deals with the expression validator, the second with the fieldexpression validator.

The expression Validator Example

The **ExpressionTestAction** class in Listing 8.22 has two properties, **min** and **max**, that will be used in the OGNL expression of an expression validator instance. Listing 8.23 shows a validator configuration file that uses the expression validator and specifies that the value of the **max** property must be

Chapter 8: Input Validation

greater than the value of **min**. Listing 8.24 shows a JSP with a form with two fields.

Listing 8.22: The ExpressionTestAction class

```
package app08a;
import com.opensymphony.xwork2.ActionSupport;
public class ExpressionTestAction extends ActionSupport {
    private int min;
    private int max;
    // getters and setters not shown
}
```

Listing 8.23: The ExpressionTestAction-validation.xml file

```
<!DOCTYPE validators PUBLIC
    "-//OpenSymphony Group//XWork Validator 1.0.2//EN"
    "http://www.opensymphony.com/xwork/xwork-validator-1.0.2.dtd">

<validators>
    <validator type="expression">
        <param name="expression">
            max > min
        </param>
        <message>
            Maximum temperature must be greater than Minimum
    temperature
        </message>
    </validator>
</validators>
```

Listing 8.24: The Expression.jsp page

```
<%@ taglib prefix="s" uri="/struts-tags" %>
<html>
<head>
<title>expression Validator Example</title>
<style type="text/css">@import url(css/main.css);</style>
<style>
.errorMessage {
    color:red;
}
</style>
</head>
<body>
<div id="global" style="width:400px">
    <s:actionerror/>
```

```
    <h3>Enter the minimum and maximum temperatures</h3>
    <s:form action="Expression2">
        <s:textfield name="min" label="Minimum temperature"/>
        <s:textfield name="max" label="Maximum temperature"/>
        <s:submit/>
    </s:form>
</div>
</body>
</html>
```

To test this example, direct your browser to this URL.

```
http://localhost:8080/app08a/Expression1.action
```

You'll see a form like the one in Figure 8.8. You can only submit the form successfully if you entered integers in the input fields and the value of **min** was less than the value of **max**.

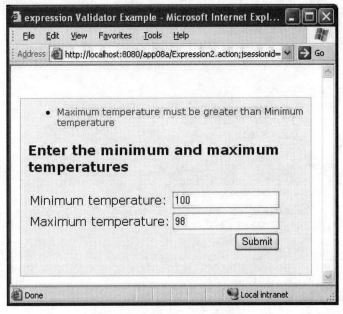

Figure 8.8: Using expression

The fieldexpression Validator Example

The **FieldExpressionTestAction** class in Listing 8.25 defines two properties, **min** and **max**, that will have to meet a certain criteria, namely **min** must be less than **max**. The validator configuration file in Listing 8.26 specifies an OGNL expression for the fieldexpression validator. Listing 8.27 shows the JSP used in this example.

Listing 8.25: The FieldExpressionTestAction class

```
package app08a;
import com.opensymphony.xwork2.ActionSupport;
public class FieldExpressionTestAction extends ActionSupport {
    private int min;
    private int max;
    // getters and setters not shown
}
```

Listing 8.26: The FieldExpressionTestAction-validation.xml file

```
<!DOCTYPE validators PUBLIC
    "-//OpenSymphony Group//XWork Validator 1.0.2//EN"
    "http://www.opensymphony.com/xwork/xwork-validator-1.0.2.dtd">
<validators>
    <field name="max">
        <field-validator type="fieldexpression">
            <param name="expression">
                max > min
            </param>
            <message>
                Maximum temperature must be greater than Minimum
    temperature
            </message>
        </field-validator>
    </field>
</validators>
```

Listing 8.27: The FieldExpression.jsp page

```
<%@ taglib prefix="s" uri="/struts-tags" %>
<html>
<head>
<title>fieldexpression Validator Example</title>
<style type="text/css">@import url(css/main.css);</style>
<style>
.errorMessage {
```

```
      color:red;
}
</style>
</head>
<body>
<div id="global" style="width:400px">
    <h3>Enter the minimum and maximum temperatures</h3>
    <s:form action="FieldExpression2">
        <s:textfield name="min" label="Minimum temperature"/>
        <s:textfield name="max" label="Maximum temperature"/>
        <s:submit/>
    </s:form>
</div>
</body>
</html>
```

Test this example by directing your browser here:

```
http://localhost:8080/app08a/FieldExpression1.action
```

Figure 8.9 shows the fieldexpression validator in action.

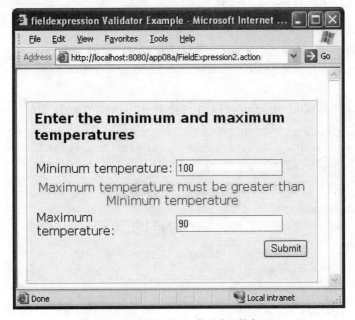

Figure 8.9: Using fieldvalidator

conversion Validator

The conversion validator tells you if the type conversion for an action property generated a conversion error. The validator also lets you add a custom message on top of the default conversion error message. Here is the default message for a conversion error:

```
Invalid field value for field "fieldName".
```

With the conversion validator, you can add another message:

```
Invalid field value for field "fieldName".
[Your custom message]
```

For example, the **ConversionTestAction** class in Listing 8.28 has one property, **age**, which is an int. The validator configuration file in Listing 8.29 configures the conversion validator for the **age** field and adds an error message for a failed conversion.

Listing 8.28: The ConversionTestAction class

```
package app08a;
import com.opensymphony.xwork2.ActionSupport;
public class ConversionTestAction extends ActionSupport {
    private int age;
    // getter and setter deleted
}
```

Listing 8.29: The ConversionTestAction-validation.xml file

```
<!DOCTYPE validators PUBLIC
    "-//OpenSymphony Group//XWork Validator 1.0.2//EN"
    "http://www.opensymphony.com/xwork/xwork-validator-1.0.2.dtd">

<validators>
    <field name="age">
        <field-validator type="conversion">
            <message>
                An age must be an integer.
            </message>
        </field-validator>
    </field>
</validators>
```

The **Conversion.jsp** page in Listing 8.30 contains a form with a field mapped to the **age** property.

Listing 8.30: The Conversion.jsp page

```
<%@ taglib prefix="s" uri="/struts-tags" %>
<html>
<head>
<title>conversion Validator Example</title>
<style type="text/css">@import url(css/main.css);</style>
<style>
.errorMessage {
    color:red;
}
</style>
</head>
<body>
<div id="global" style="width:350px">
    <h3>Enter your age</h3>
    <s:form action="Conversion2">
        <s:textfield name="age" label="Age"/>
        <s:submit/>
    </s:form>
</div>
</body>
</html>
```

You can test this example by directing your browser to this URL.

```
http://localhost:8080/app08a/Conversion1.action
```

Figure 8.10 shows the conversion validator in action. There are two error messages displayed, the default one and the one that you added using the conversion validator.

Figure 8.10: The conversion validator in action

visitor Validator

The visitor validator introduces some level of reusability, enabling you to use the same validator configuration file with more than one action. Consider this scenario.

Suppose you have an action class (say, **Customer**) that has an **address** property of type **Address**, which in turn has five properties (**streetName**, **streetNumber**, **city**, **state**, and **zipCode**). To validate the **zipCode** property in an **Address** object that is a property of the **Customer** action class, you would write this **field** element in a **Customer-validation.xml** file .

```
<field name="address.zipCode">
    <field-validator type="requiredstring">
        <message>Zip Code must not be empty</message>
    </field-validator>
</field>
```

Note how OGNL makes it possible to reference a complex object?

Suppose also that you have an **Employee** action class that uses **Address** as a property type. If the **address** property of **Employee** requires the same validation rules as the **address** property in **Customer**, you would have an

Employee-validation.xml file that is an exact copy of the **Customer-validation.xml** file.

This is redundant and the visitor validator can help you isolate identical validation rules into a file. Every time you need to use the validation rules, you simply need to reference the file. In this example, you would isolate the validation rules for the **Address** class into an **Address-validation.xml** file. Then, in your **Customer-validation.xml** file you would write

```
<field name="address">
    <field-validator type="visitor">
        <message>Address: </message>
    </field-validator>
</field>
```

This **field** element says, for the **address** property, use the validation file that comes with the property type (**Address**). In other words, Struts would use the **Address-validation.xml** file for validating the **address** property. If you use **Address** in multiple action classes, you don't need to write the same validation rules in every validator configuration file for each action.

Another feature of the visitor validator is the use of context. If one of the actions that use **Address** needs other validation rules than the ones specified the **Address-validation.xml** file, you can create a new validator configuration file just for that action. The new validator configuration file would be named:

```
Address-context-validation.xml
```

Here, *context* is the alias of the action that needs specific validation rules for the Address class. If the **AddEmployee** action needed special validation rules for its **address** property, you would have this file:

```
Address-AddEmployee-validation.xml
```

That's not all. If the context name is different from the action alias, for example, if the **AddManager** action also requires the validation rules in the **Address-AddEmployee-validaton.xml** instead of the ones in **Address-validation.xml**, you can tell the visitor validator to look at a different context by writing this field element.

```
<field name="address">
    <field-validator type="visitor">
        <param name="context">specific</param>
        <message>Address: </message>
```

```
    </field-validator>
</field>
```

This indicates to the visitor validator that to validate the **address** property, it should use **Address-specific-validation.xml** and not **Address-AddManager-validation.xml**.

Now let's look at the three sample applications (**app08b**, **app08c**, and **app08d**) that illustrate the use of the visitor validator. The **app08b** application shows a **Customer** action that has an **address** property of type **Address** and uses a conventional way to validate address. The **app08c** application features the same **Customer** and **Address** classes, but use the visitor validator to validate the **address** property. The **app08d** application employs the visitor validator and uses a different context.

Validating a Complext Object (app08b)

In this example, a **Customer** class has an **address** property of type **Address**. It is shown how you can validate a complex object with the help of OGNL expressions. The example is given in **app08b** and its directory structure is shown in Figure 8.11. The **Customer** class and the **Address** class are shown in Listings 8.31 and 8.32, respectively.

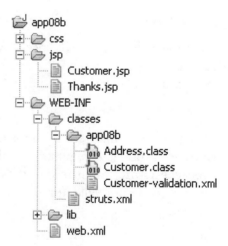

Figure 8.11: app08b directory structure

Listing 8.31: The Customer class

```
package app08b;
import com.opensymphony.xwork2.ActionSupport;
public class Customer extends ActionSupport {
    private String firstName;
    private String lastName;
    private Address address;
    // getters and setter not shown
}
```

Listing 8.32: The Address class

```
package app08b;
public class Address {
    private String streetName;
    private String streetNumber;
    private String city;
    private String state;
    private String zipCode;
    // getters and setters not shown
}
```

To validate the Customer action class, use the **Customer-validation.xml** file in Listing 8.33. Note that you can specify the validators for the properties in the **Address** object here.

Listing 8.33: The Customer-validation.xml

```
<!DOCTYPE validators PUBLIC
    "-//OpenSymphony Group//XWork Validator 1.0.2//EN"
    "http://www.opensymphony.com/xwork/xwork-validator-1.0.2.dtd">

<validators>
    <field name="firstName">
        <field-validator type="requiredstring">
            <message>First Name must not be empty</message>
        </field-validator>
    </field>
    <field name="lastName">
        <field-validator type="requiredstring">
            <message>Last Name must not be empty</message>
        </field-validator>
    </field>
    <field name="address.streetName">
        <field-validator type="requiredstring">
            <message>Street Name must not be empty</message>
```

```
            </field-validator>
        </field>
        <field name="address.streetNumber">
            <field-validator type="requiredstring">
                <message>Street Number must not be empty</message>
            </field-validator>
        </field>
        <field name="address.city">
            <field-validator type="requiredstring">
                <message>City must not be empty</message>
            </field-validator>
        </field>
        <field name="address.state">
            <field-validator type="requiredstring">
                <message>State must not be empty</message>
            </field-validator>
        </field>
        <field name="address.zipCode">
            <field-validator type="requiredstring">
                <message>Zip Code must not be empty</message>
            </field-validator>
        </field>
</validators>
```

The **Customer.jsp** page in Listing 8.34 contains a form with fields that map to the properties in the **Customer** action.

Listing 8.34: The Customer.jsp page

```
<%@ taglib prefix="s" uri="/struts-tags" %>
<html>
<head>
<title>Add Customer</title>
<style type="text/css">@import url(css/main.css);</style>
<style>
.errorMessage {
    color:red;
}
</style>
</head>
<body>
<div id="global" style="width:350px">
    <h3>Enter customer details</h3>
    <s:form action="Customer2">
        <s:textfield name="firstName" label="First Name"/>
        <s:textfield name="lastName" label="Last Name"/>
```

```
        <s:textfield name="address.streetName" label="Street Name"/>
        <s:textfield name="address.streetNumber"
            label="Street Number"/>
        <s:textfield name="address.city" label="City"/>
        <s:textfield name="address.state" label="State"/>
        <s:textfield name="address.zipCode" label="Zip Code"/>
        <s:submit/>
    </s:form>
</div>
</body>
</html>
```

Test this example by directing your browser to this URL.

```
http://localhost:8080/app08b/Customer1.action
```

The form is shown in Figure 8.12.

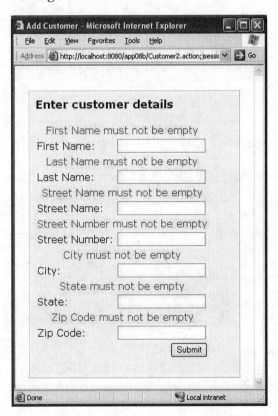

Figure 8.12: Validations for a complex object

Using the visitor Validator (app08c)

app08c, whose directory structure is shown in Figure 8.13, is similar to **app08b**. It has **Address** and **Customer** classes and a **Customer.jsp** page that are identical to the ones in **app08b**. However, the validation rules for the **Address** class have been moved to an **Admin-validation.xml** file (See Listing 8.35).

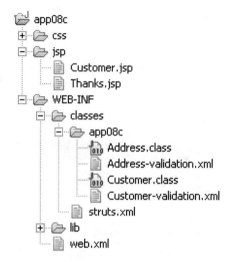

Figure 8.13: app08c directory structure

Listing 8.35: The Address-validation.xml file

```
<!DOCTYPE validators PUBLIC
    "-//OpenSymphony Group//XWork Validator 1.0.2//EN"
    "http://www.opensymphony.com/xwork/xwork-validator-1.0.2.dtd">

<validators>
    <field name="streetName">
        <field-validator type="requiredstring">
            <message>Street Name must not be empty</message>
        </field-validator>
    </field>
    <field name="streetNumber">
        <field-validator type="requiredstring">
            <message>Street Number must not be empty</message>
        </field-validator>
    </field>
    <field name="city">
```

```
            <field-validator type="requiredstring">
                <message>City must not be empty</message>
            </field-validator>
        </field>
        <field name="state">
            <field-validator type="requiredstring">
                <message>State must not be empty</message>
            </field-validator>
        </field>
        <field name="zipCode">
            <field-validator type="requiredstring">
                <message>Zip Code must not be empty</message>
            </field-validator>
        </field>
</validators>
```

The **Customer-validation.xml** file (shown in Listing 8.36) is now shorter, since the validation rules for the **address** property are no longer here. Instead, it uses the visitor validator to point to the **Address-validation.xml** file.

Listing 8.36: The Customer-validation.xml file

```
<!DOCTYPE validators PUBLIC
    "-//OpenSymphony Group//XWork Validator 1.0.2//EN"
    "http://www.opensymphony.com/xwork/xwork-validator-1.0.2.dtd">

<validators>
    <field name="firstName">
        <field-validator type="requiredstring">
            <message>First Name must not be empty</message>
        </field-validator>
    </field>
    <field name="lastName">
        <field-validator type="requiredstring">
            <message>Last Name must not be empty</message>
        </field-validator>
    </field>
    <field name="address">
        <field-validator type="visitor">
            <message>Address: </message>
        </field-validator>
    </field>
</validators>
```

Test this example by directing your browser here.

```
http://localhost:8080/app08c/Customer1.action
```

Using the visitor Validator in different contexts (app08d)

app08d is similar to **app08c** and its directory structure is shown in Figure 8.14. Its **Address-validation.xml** and **Customer-validation.xml** files are the same as the ones in **app08c**.

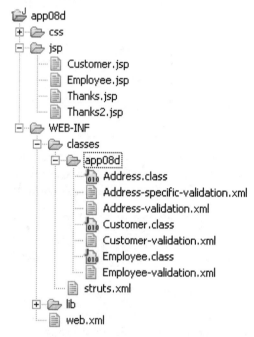

Figure 8.14: app08d directory structure

In addition to the **Customer** class, there is an **Employee** class that has an **address** property. There is a new validator configuration file for the **Address** class, **Address-specific-validation.xml**, which is shown in Listing 8.37.

Listing 8.37: The Address-specific-validation.xml file

```
<!DOCTYPE validators PUBLIC
    "-//OpenSymphony Group//XWork Validator 1.0.2//EN"
    "http://www.opensymphony.com/xwork/xwork-validator-1.0.2.dtd">

<validators>
    <field name="zipCode">
        <field-validator type="regex">
            <param name="expression">
                <![CDATA[\d\d\d\d\d]]>
```

```
            </param>
            <message>
                Invalid zip code or invalid format
            </message>
        </field-validator>
    </field>
</validators>
```

The **address** property in **Employee** uses the validation rules in **Address-specific-validation.xml**, and not the ones in **Address-validation.xml**. This is indicated in the **Employee-validation.xml** file in Listing 8.38. The **context** parameter instructs Struts to use the **specific** context.

Listing 8.38: The Employee-validation.xml file

```
<!DOCTYPE validators PUBLIC
    "-//OpenSymphony Group//XWork Validator 1.0.2//EN"
    "http://www.opensymphony.com/xwork/xwork-validator-1.0.2.dtd">

<validators>
    <field name="firstName">
        <field-validator type="requiredstring">
            <message>First Name must not be empty</message>
        </field-validator>
    </field>
    <field name="lastName">
        <field-validator type="requiredstring">
            <message>Last Name must not be empty</message>
        </field-validator>
    </field>
    <field name="address">
        <field-validator type="visitor">
            <param name="context">specific</param>
            <message>Address: </message>
        </field-validator>
    </field>
</validators>
```

To test this application, direct your browser to this URL:

```
http://localhost:8080/app08d/Employee1.action
```

Writing Custom Validators

Using the bundled validators does not require you to know anything about the validators' underlying classes. If you wish to write your own validator, however, you need to know both the classes and the registration mechanism for Struts validators.

A validator must implement the **Validator** interface that is part of the **com.opensymphony.xwork2.validator** package. Figure 8.15 shows this interface, its subinterface, and implementing classes.

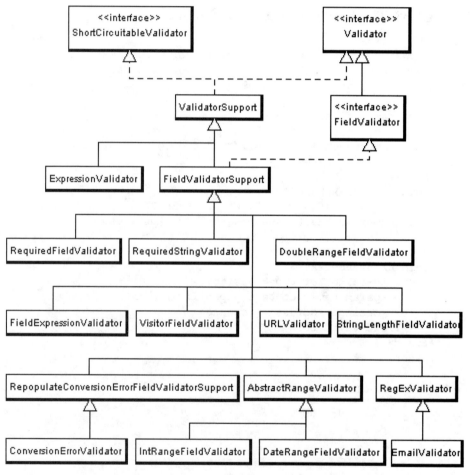

Figure 8.15: The Validator interface and supporting types

The package names in Figure 8.15 have been omitted. The **Validator**, **FieldValidator**, and **ShortCircuitableValidator** interfaces belong to the **com.opensymphony.xwork2.validator** package. The rest are part of the **com.opensymphony.xwork2.validator.validators** package. The **Validator** interface is printed in Listing 8.39.

Listing 8.39: The Validator interface

```
package com.opensymphony.xwork2.validator;
public interface Validator {
    void setDefaultMessage(String message);
    String getDefaultMessage();
    String getMessage(Object object);
    void setMessageKey(String key);
    String getMessageKey();
    void setValidatorType(String type);
    String getValidatorType();

    void setValidatorContext(ValidatorContext validatorContext);
    ValidatorContext getValidatorContext();
    void validate(Object object) throws ValidationException;
}
```

The Validation interceptor is responsible for loading and executing validators. After it loads a validator, the interceptor will call the validator's **setValidatorContext** method and pass the current **ValidatorContext**, which will allow access to the current action. The interceptor will then invoke the **validate** method, passing the object to be validated. The **validate** method is the method you need to override when writing a custom validator.

It is much easier to extend one of the convenience classes **ValidatorSupport** and **FieldValidatorSupport** than to implement **Validator**. Extend **ValidatorSupport** if you're creating a plain validator. Subclass **FieldValidatorSupport** if you're writing a field validator. If you design your validator to be able to accept a parameter, add a property for the parameter too. For example, if your validator allows a **minValue** parameter, you need the getter and setter for the **minValue** property.

The **ValidatorSupport** class adds several methods, of which three are convenience methods you can call from your validation class.

```
protected java.lang.Object getFieldValue(java.lang.String name,
        java.lang.Object object) throws ValidationException
```
Returns the field value named name from object.

```
protected void addActionError(java.lang.Object actionError)
```
Adds an action error.

```
protected void addFieldError(java.lang.String propertyName,
        java.lang.Object object)
```
Adds a field error.

From your **validate** method you call the **addActionError** when a plain validator fails or the **addFieldError** when a field validator fails.

FieldValidatorSupport extends **ValidatorSupport** and adds two properties, **propertyType** and **fieldName**.

Listing 8.40 shows the **RequiredStringValidator** class, the underlying class for the requiredstring validator.

Listing 8.40: The RequiredStringValidator class

```java
package com.opensymphony.xwork2.validator.validators;
import com.opensymphony.xwork2.validator.ValidationException;
public class RequiredStringValidator extends FieldValidatorSupport {
    private boolean doTrim = true;
    public void setTrim(boolean trim) {
        doTrim = trim;
    }
    public boolean getTrim() {
        return doTrim;
    }
    public void validate(Object object) throws ValidationException {
        String fieldName = getFieldName();
        Object value = this.getFieldValue(fieldName, object);

        if (!(value instanceof String)) {
            addFieldError(fieldName, object);
        } else {
            String s = (String) value;

            if (doTrim) {
                s = s.trim();
            }

            if (s.length() == 0) {
                addFieldError(fieldName, object);
            }
        }
    }
}
```

}

The requiredstring validator can accept a **trim** parameter, therefore its underlying class needs to have a **trim** property. The setter will be called by the validation interceptor if a trim parameter is passed to the validator.

The **validate** method does the validation. If validation fails, this method must call the **addFieldError** method.

Registration

As mentioned at the beginning of this chapter, bundled validators are already registered so you don't need to register them before use. They are registered in the **com/opensymphony/xwork2/validator/validators/default.xml** file (shown in Listing 8.41), which is included in the xwork jar file. If you are using a custom or third party validator, you need to register it in a **validators.xml** file deployed under WEB-INF/classes or in the classpath.

Note
The Struts website maintains, at the time of writing, that if you have a **validators.xml** file in your classpath, you must register all bundled validators in this file because Struts will not load the **default.xml** file. My testing revealed otherwise. You can still use the bundled validators without registering them in a **validators.xml** file.

Listing 8.41: The default.xml file

```
<?xml version="1.0" encoding="UTF-8"?>
<!DOCTYPE validators PUBLIC
    "-//OpenSymphony Group//XWork Validator Config 1.0//EN"
    "http://www.opensymphony.com/xwork/xwork-validator-config-
        ➥1.0.dtd">

<validators>
    <validator name="required"
        class="com.opensymphony.xwork2.validator.validators.
RequiredFieldValidator"/>
        <validator name="requiredstring" class="com.opensymphony.xwork2.
            ➥validator.validators.RequiredStringValidator"/>
        <validator name="int" class="com.opensymphony.xwork2.validator.
            ➥validators.IntRangeFieldValidator"/>
        <validator name="double" class="com.opensymphony.xwork2.
            ➥validator.validators.DoubleRangeFieldValidator"/>
```

```
<validator name="date" class="com.opensymphony.xwork2.validator.
    ➥validators.DateRangeFieldValidator"/>
<validator name="expression" class="com.opensymphony.xwork2.
    ➥validator.validators.ExpressionValidator"/>
<validator name="fieldexpression" class="com.opensymphony.
    ➥xwork2.validator.validators.FieldExpressionValidator"/>
<validator name="email" class="com.opensymphony.xwork2.
    ➥validator.validators.EmailValidator"/>
<validator name="url" class="com.opensymphony.xwork2.validator.
    ➥validators.URLValidator"/>
<validator name="visitor" class="com.opensymphony.xwork2.
    ➥validator.validators.VisitorFieldValidator"/>
<validator name="conversion" class="com.opensymphony.xwork2.
    ➥validator.validators.ConversionErrorFieldValidator"/>
<validator name="stringlength" class="com.opensymphony.xwork2.
    ➥validator.validators.StringLengthFieldValidator"/>
<validator name="regex" class="com.opensymphony.xwork2.
    ➥validator.validators.RegexFieldValidator"/>
</validators>
```

Example

The following example teaches you how to write a custom validator and register it. This example showcases a strongpassword validator that checks the strength of a password. A password is considered strong if it contains at least one digit, one lowercase character, and one uppercase character. In addition, the validator can accept a **minLength** parameter that the user can pass to set the minimum length of an acceptable password.

Figure 8.16 shows the directory structure of the application (**app08e**).

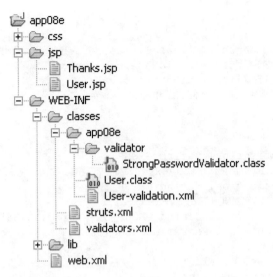

Figure 8.16: app08e directory structure

The supporting class for **strongpassword** is the
app08e.validator.StrongPasswordValidator class. This class extends the
FieldValidatorSupport class and is shown in Listing 8.42. The **validate**
method uses the **isPasswordStrong** method to test the strength of a
password.

Listing 8.42: The StrongPasswordValidator class

```
package app08e.validator;
import com.opensymphony.xwork2.validator.ValidationException;
import com.opensymphony.xwork2.validator.validators.
FieldValidatorSupport;

public class StrongPasswordValidator extends FieldValidatorSupport {
    private int minLength = -1;
    public void setMinLength(int minLength) {
        this.minLength = minLength;
    }
    public int getMinLength() {
        return minLength;
    }
    public void validate(Object object) throws ValidationException {
        String fieldName = getFieldName();
        String value = (String) getFieldValue(fieldName, object);
        if (value == null || value.length() == 0) {
            // use a required validator for these
```

```
            return;
        }
        if ((minLength > -1) && (value.length() < minLength)) {
            addFieldError(fieldName, object);
        } else if (!isPasswordStrong(value)) {
            addFieldError(fieldName, object);
        }
    }

    private static final String GROUP_1 =
        "abcdefghijklmnopqrstuvwxyz";
    private static final String GROUP_2 =
        "ABCDEFGHIJKLMNOPQRSTUVWXYZ";
    private static final String GROUP_3 = "0123456789";
    protected boolean isPasswordStrong(String password) {
        boolean ok1 = false;
        boolean ok2 = false;
        boolean ok3 = false;
        int length = password.length();
        for (int i = 0; i < length; i++) {
            if (ok1 && ok2 && ok3) {
                break;
            }
            String character = password.substring(i, i + 1);
            if (GROUP_1.contains(character)) {
                ok1 = true;
                continue;
            }
            if (GROUP_2.contains(character)) {
                ok2 = true;
                continue;
            }
            if (GROUP_3.contains(character)) {
                ok3 = true;
            }
        }
        return (ok1 && ok2 && ok3);
    }
}
```

The **validators.xml** file in Listing 8.43 registers the **strongpassword** validator.

Listing 8.43: The validators.xml file

```
<?xml version="1.0" encoding="UTF-8"?>
```

```
<!DOCTYPE validators PUBLIC
    "-//OpenSymphony Group//XWork Validator Config 1.0//EN"
    "http://www.opensymphony.com/xwork/xwork-validator-config-
        ➦1.0.dtd">

<validators>
    <validator name="strongpassword"
        class="app08e.validator.StrongPasswordValidator"/>
</validators>
```

Now that you've registered your custom validator, you can use it the same way
you would a bundled validator. For example, the **User** class in Listing 8.44 has
a **password** property that can only be assigned a strong password. The **User-
validation.xml** file in Listing 8.45 configures the validators for the **User** class.

Listing 8.44: The User class

```
package app08e;
import com.opensymphony.xwork2.ActionSupport;
public class User extends ActionSupport {
    private String userName;
    private String password;
    // getters and setters not shown
}
```

Listing 8.45: The User-validation.xml file

```
<!DOCTYPE validators PUBLIC
    "-//OpenSymphony Group//XWork Validator 1.0.2//EN"
    "http://www.opensymphony.com/xwork/xwork-validator-1.0.2.dtd">

<validators>
    <field name="userName">
        <field-validator type="requiredstring">
            <message>User Name must not be empty</message>
        </field-validator>
    </field>
    <field name="password">
        <field-validator type="requiredstring">
            <message>Password must not be empty</message>
        </field-validator>
    </field>
    <field name="password">
        <field-validator type="strongpassword">
            <param name="minLength">8</param>
            <message>
                Password must be at least 8 characters long
```

```
                    and contains at least one lower case character,
                    one upper case character, and a digit.
                </message>
            </field-validator>
        </field>
    </validators>
```

Listing 8.46: The User.jsp page

```
<%@ taglib prefix="s" uri="/struts-tags" %>
<html>
<head>
<title>Select user name and password</title>
<style type="text/css">@import url(css/main.css);</style>
<style>
.errorMessage {
    color:red;
}
</style>
</head>
<body>
<div id="global" style="width:350px">
    <h3>Please select your user name and password</h3>
    <s:form action="User2">
        <s:textfield name="userName" label="User Name"/>
        <s:password name="password" label="Password"/>
        <s:submit/>
    </s:form>
</div>
</body>
</html>
```

The **User.jsp** page in Listing 8.47 features a form that accepts a user name and a password. Direct your browser here to test this example.

```
http://localhost:8080/app08e/User1.action
```

Figure 8.17 shows the strongpassword validator in action.

Figure 8.17: The strongpassword validator in action

Programmatic Validation Using Validateable

So far we've looked at using and writing validators that can be used declaratively. In some cases, validation rules are too complex to be specified in a declarative validation and you need to write code for that. In other words, you need to perform programmatic validation.

Struts comes with the **com.opensymphony.xwork2.Validateable** interface that an action class can implement to provide programmatic validation. There is only one method in this interface, **validate**.

```
void validate()
```

If an action class implements **Validateable**, Struts will call its **validate** method. You write code that validates user input within this method. Since the **ActionSupport** class implements this interface, you don't have to implement **Validateable** directly if your class extends **ActionSupport**.

The **app08f** application demonstrates how to write programmatic validation rules. The **User** action (See Listing 8.47) overrides the **validate** method and adds a field error if the **userName** value entered by the user is already in the **userNames** list.

Listing 8.47: The User class

```
package app08f;
import java.util.ArrayList;
import java.util.List;
import com.opensymphony.xwork2.ActionSupport;
public class User extends ActionSupport {
    private String userName;
    private String password;
    private static List<String> userNames = new ArrayList<String>();
    static {
        userNames.add("harry");
        userNames.add("sally");
    }
    // getters and setters not shown
    public void validate() {
        if (userNames.contains(userName)) {
            addFieldError("userName",
                    "'" + userName + "' has been taken.");
        }
    }
}
```

Even when employing programmatic validation, you can still use the bundled validators. In this example, the **userName** field is also "guarded" by a stringrequired validator, as shown in the **User-validation.xml** file in Listing 8.48.

Listing 8.48: The User-validation.xml file

```
<!DOCTYPE validators PUBLIC
    "-//OpenSymphony Group//XWork Validator 1.0.2//EN"
    "http://www.opensymphony.com/xwork/xwork-validator-1.0.2.dtd">

<validators>
    <field name="userName">
        <field-validator type="requiredstring">
            <message>User Name must not be empty</message>
        </field-validator>
    </field>
    <field name="password">
```

```
        <field-validator type="requiredstring">
            <message>Password must not be empty</message>
        </field-validator>
    </field>
</validators>
```

To test this example, direct your browser to this URL.

```
http://localhost:8080/app08f/User1.action
```

Figure 8.18 shows the programmatic validator at work.

Figure 8.18: Programmatic validation

Summary

Input validation is one of the features Struts offer to expedite web application development. In fact, Struts comes with built-in validators that are available for use in most cases. As you've learned in this chapter, you can also write custom validators to cater for validations not already covered by any of the bundled validators. In addition, you can perform programmatic validation in more complex situations.

Chapter 9
Message Handling and
Internationalization

Message handling is an important task in application development. For example, it is almost always mandatory that text and messages be editable without source recompile. In addition, nowadays it is often a requirement that an application be able to "speak" many languages. A technique for developing applications that support multiple languages and data formats without having to rewrite programming logic is called *internationalization*. Internationalization is abbreviated **i18n** because the word starts with an *i* and ends with an *n*, and there are 18 characters between the first *i* and the last *n*. In addition, localization is a technique for adapting an internationalized application to support a specific locale. A locale is a specific geographical, political, or cultural region. An operation that takes a locale into consideration is said to be *locale-sensitive*. For example, displaying a date is locale-sensitive because the date must be in the format used by the country or region of the user. The 15th day of November 2005 is written as 11/15/2005 in the US, but printed as 15/11/2005 in Australia. Localization is abbreviated **l10n** because the word starts with an *l* and ends with an *n* and there are 10 letters between the *l* and the *n*.

With internationalization, you can change visual text in an application quickly and easily. Java has built-in supports for internationalization and Struts makes use of this feature and has been designed from the outset to support easy message handling and internationalization. For instance, the **com.opensymphony.xwork2.ActionSupport** class, which was introduced in Chapter 3, "Actions and Results," has **getText** methods for reading messages from a text file and selecting messages in the correct language. A custom tag can display a localized message simply by calling one of these methods.

This chapter explains how to use Struts' support for internationalization and localization. Two tags, **text** and **i18n**, are also discussed.

Note
Even if you're developing a monolingual site, you should take advantage of the Struts internationalization support for better message handling.

Locales and Java Resource Bundles

A locale is a specific geographical, political, or cultural region. There are three main components of a locale: language, country, and variant. The language is obviously the most important part; however, sometimes the language itself is not sufficient to differentiate a locale. For example, the German language is spoken in countries such as Germany and Switzerland. However, the German language spoken in Switzerland is not exactly the same as the one used in Germany. Therefore, it is necessary to specify the country of the language. As another example, the English language used in the United States is slightly different from that spoken in England. It's *favor* in the United States, but *favour* in England.

The variant argument is a vendor- or browser-specific code. For example, you use WIN for Windows, MAC for Macintosh, and POSIX for POSIX. If there are two variants, separate them with an underscore, and put the most important one first. For example, a Traditional Spanish collation might construct a locale with parameters for the language, the country, and the variant as **es**, **ES**, **Traditional_WIN**, respectively.

The language code is a valid ISO 639 language code. Table 9.1 displays some of the country codes. The complete list can be found at http://www.w3.org/WAI/ER/IG/ert/iso639.htm.

The country argument is also a valid ISO code, which is a two-letter, uppercase code specified in ISO 3166. Table 9.2 lists some of the country codes in ISO 3166. The complete list can be found at http://userpage.chemie.fu-berlin.de/diverse/doc/ISO_3166.html or http://www.iso.org/iso/en/prods-services/iso3166ma/02iso-3166-code-lists/list-en1.html.

Code	Language
de	German
el	Greek
en	English
es	Spanish
fr	French
hi	Hindi
it	Italian
ja	Japanese
nl	Dutch
pt	Portuguese
ru	Russian
zh	Chinese

Table 9.1: Examples of ISO 639 language codes

Country	Code
Australia	AU
Brazil	BR
Canada	CA
China	CN
Egypt	EG
France	FR
Germany	DE
India	IN
Mexico	MX
Switzerland	CH
Taiwan	TW
United Kingdom	GB
United States	US

Table 9.2: Examples of ISO 3166 Country Codes

An internationalized application stores its textual elements in a separate properties file for each locale. Each file contains key/value pairs, and each key uniquely identifies a locale-specific object. Keys are always strings, and values can be strings or any other type of object. For example, to support American English, German, and Chinese, you will have three properties files, all with the same keys.

Here is the English version of the properties file. Note that it has two keys: greetings and farewell:

```
greetings = Hello
farewell = Goodbye
```

The German version would be as follows:

```
greetings = Hallo
farewell = Tschüß
```

And the properties file for the Chinese language would be this:

```
greetings=\u4f60\u597d
farewell=\u518d\u89c1
```

Converting Chinese Characters (or Other Language Special Characters) to Unicode

The following applies to all languages that have special characters. Chinese is taken as an example.

In Chinese, the most common greeting is □ □ (represented by the Unicode codes 4f60 and 597d, respectively), and farewell is □ □ (represented by Unicode codes 518d and 89c1, respectively). Of course, no one remembers the Unicode code of each Chinese character. Therefore, you create the .properties file in two steps:

1. Using your favorite Chinese text editor, create a text file like this:
   ```
   greetings=□□
   farewell=□□
   ```
2. Convert the content of the text file into the Unicode representation. Normally, a Chinese text editor has a feature for converting Chinese characters into Unicode codes. You will get this end result.
   ```
   greetings=\u4f60\u597d
   farewell=\u518d\u89c1
   ```

This is the content of the properties file you use in your Java application.

Note
With Struts you don't need to know any more than writing properties files in multiple languages. However, if interested, you may want to learn about the **java.util.ResourceBundle** class and study how it selects and reads a properties file specific to the user's locale.

Each of the properties files in an internationalized application must be named according to this format.

```
basename_languageCode_countryCode
```

For example, if the base name is **MyAction** and you define three locales **US-en**, **DE-de**, **CN-zh**, you would have these properties files:

- MyAction_en_US.properties
- MyAction_de_DE.properties
- MyAction_zh_CN.properties

Now, let's take a look at message resources in Struts.

Internationalization Support in Struts

Struts has a built-in support for internationalization and localization. You'll get most of this support simply by extending the **ActionSupport** class. Inside the class is an implementation of **com.opensymphony.xwork2.TextProvider**, an interface that provides access to resource bundles and their underlying text messages. Calls to the **getText** methods in **ActionSupport** are delegated to this **TextProvider**. Most of the time you don't need to know anything about **TextProvider**.

Here are the more important overloads of **getText**.

```
public java.lang.String getText(java.lang.String key)
```
Gets the message associated with the key and returns null if the message cannot be found.

```
public java.lang.String getText(java.lang.String key,
        java.lang.String defaultValue)
```
Gets the message associated with the key and returns the specified default value if the message cannot be found.

```
public java.lang.String getText(java.lang.String key,
        java.lang.String[] args)
```
Gets the message associated with the key and formats it using the specified arguments in accordance with the rules defined in **java.text.MessageFormat**.

```
public java.lang.String getText(java.lang.String key,
```

```
        java.util.List args)
```
Gets the message associated with the key and formats it using the specified arguments in accordance with the rules defined in **java.text.MessageFormat**.

```
public java.lang.String getText(java.lang.String key,
        java.lang.String defaultValue, java.lang.String[] args)
```
Gets the message associated with the key and formats it using the specified arguments in accordance with the rules defined in **java.text.MessageFormat**. If the message cannot be found, this method returns the specified default value.

```
public java.lang.String getText(java.lang.String key,
        java.lang.String defaultValue, java.util.List args)
```
Gets the message associated with the key and formats it using the specified arguments in accordance with the rules defined in **java.text.MessageFormat**. If the message cannot be found, this method returns the specified default value.

When you call a **getText** method, it searches for the appropriate properties file in this order.

1. The action class properties file, i.e. one whose basename is the same as the name of the corresponding action class and located in the same directory as the action class. For example, if the action class is **app09a.Customer**, the relevant file for the default locale is **Customer.properties** in **WEB-INF/classes/app09a**.
2. The properties file for each interface that the action class implements. For example, if the action class implements a **Dummy** interface, the default properties file that corresponds to this interface is **Dummy.properties**.
3. The properties file for each of its parent class followed by each interface the parent class implements. For instance, if the action class extends **ActionSupport**, the **ActionSupport.properties** file will be used. If the message is not found, the search moves up to the next parent in the hierarchy, up to **java.lang.Object**.
4. If the action class implements **com.opensymphony.xwork2.ModelDriven**, Struts calls the **getModel** method and does a class hierarchy search for the class of the model object. **ModelDriven** is explained in Chapter 10, "Model Driven and Prepare Interceptors."

5. The default package properties file. If the action class is **app09a.Customer**, the default package **ResourceBundle** is **package** in **app09a**.
6. The package resource bundle in the next parent package.
7. Global resources

You can display a localized message using the **property** tag or the **label** attribute of a form tag by calling **getText**. The syntax for calling it is

```
%{getText('key')}
```

For example, to use a **textfield** tag to retrieve the message associated with key **customer.name**, use this:

```
<s:textfield name="name" label="%{getText('customer.name')}"/>
```

The following **property** tag prints a message associated with the key **customer.contact**.

```
<s:property value="%{getText('customer.contact')}"/>
```

The following sample application shows how to use the message handling feature in a monolingual application. It is shown here how easy it is to change messages across the application by simply editing properties files.

The application centers around the **Customer** action class, which implements an interface named **Dummy**. This interface does not define any method and is used to demonstrate the order of properties file search.

The directory structure of the example (**app09a**) is shown in Figure 9.1.

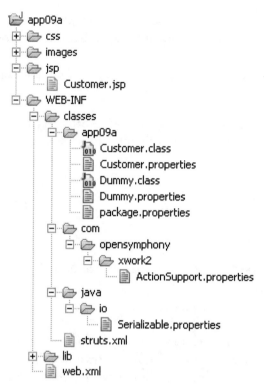

Figure 9.1: app09a directory structure

The **Customer** class is given in Listing 9.1 and the **Customer.jsp** page in Listing 9.2.

Listing 9.1: The Customer action class

```
package app09a;
import com.opensymphony.xwork2.ActionSupport;
public class Customer extends ActionSupport implements Dummy {
    private String name;
    private String contact;
    private String address;
    private String city;
    private String state;
    private String zipCode;

    // getters and setters not shown

}
```

Listing 9.2: The Customer.jsp page

```jsp
<%@ taglib prefix="s" uri="/struts-tags" %>
<html>
<head>
<title>Customers</title>
<style type="text/css">@import url(css/main.css);</style>
</head>
<body>
<div id="global" style="width:350px">
<h4>Customer</h4>
<s:form>
    <s:textfield name="name" label="%{getText('customer.name')}"/>
    <s:textfield name="contact"
            label="%{getText('customer.contact')}"/>
    <s:textfield name="address"
            label="%{getText('customer.address')}"/>
    <s:textfield name="city" label="%{getText('customer.city')}"/>
    <s:textfield name="zipCode"
            label="%{getText('customer.zipCode', 'Zip Code')}"/>
    <s:submit/>
</s:form>
</div>
</body>
</html>
```

You can test the application using this URL.

```
http://localhost:8080/app09a/Customer.action
```

You can experiment with the localized messages by editing the properties files.

The text Tag

The **text** tag is a data tag for rendering an internationalized message. It is equivalent to calling **getText** from the **property** tag. The attributes of the **text** tag are given in Table 9.3.

Name	Data Type	Description
name*	String	The key of the message to be retrieved.
var	String	The name of the variable that references the value to pushed to the stack context.

Table 9.3: text tag attributes

For example, the following **text** tag prints the message associated with the key **greetings**:

```
<s:text name="greetings"/>
```

If the **var** attribute is present, however, the message is not printed but pushed to the Value Stack's context map. For instance, the following pushes the message associated with **greetings** to the context map and creates a variable named **msg** that references the message.

```
<s:text name="greetings" id="msg"/>
```

You can then use the **property** tag to access the message.

```
<s:text name="greetings" id="msg"/>
<s:property value="#msg"/>
```

You can pass parameters to a **text** tag. For example, if you have the following key in a properties file

```
greetings=Hello {0}
```

You can use this **text** tag to pass a parameter.

```
<s:text name="greetings">
    <s:param>Visitor</s:param>
</s:text>
```

The tag will print this message:

```
Hello Visitor
```

A parameter can be a dynamic value too. For example, the following code passes the value of the **firstName** property to the **text** tag.

```
<s:text name="greetings">
    <s:param><s:property value="firstName"/></s:param>
</s:text>
```

The **app09b** application shows how to use the **text** tag in a multilingual site. Three languages are supported: English (default), German, and Chinese.

Figure 9.2 shows the directory structure of **app09b**.

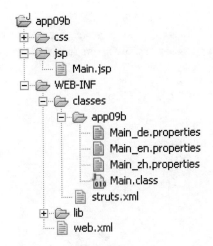

Figure 9.2: app09b directory structure

Note that three properties files correspond to the **Main** class. The properties files are given in Listings 9.3 to 9.5.

Listing 9.3: The Main_en.properties file

```
greetings=\u4f60\u597d {0}
farewell=\u518d\u89c1
```

Listing 9.4: The Main_de.properties file

```
greetings=Hallo {0}
farewell=Tschüß
```

Listing 9.5: The Main_zh.properties file

```
greetings=\u4f60\u597d {0}
farewell=\u518d\u89c1
```

The **Main** class is shown in Listing 9.6 and the **Main.jsp** page in Listing 9.7.

Listing 9.6: The Main class

```
package app09b;
import com.opensymphony.xwork2.ActionSupport;
public class Main extends ActionSupport {
}
```

Listing 9.7: The Main.jsp page

```
<%@ taglib prefix="s" uri="/struts-tags" %>
<html>
```

```
<head>
<title>I18N</title>
<style type="text/css">@import url(css/main.css);</style>
</head>
<body>
<div id="global" style="width:350px">

<s:text name="greetings">
    <s:param>Jon</s:param>
</s:text>.
<s:text name="farewell"/>

</div>
</body>
</html>
```

To test this example, direct your browser to this URL:

`http://localhost:8080/app09b/Main.action`

Figure 9.3 shows the messages in German locale.

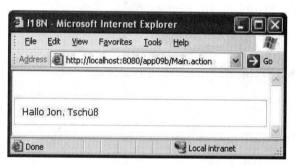

Figure 9.3: The German locale

The i18n Tag

The **i18n** tag loads a custom **ResourceBundle**. You may want to provide a custom **ResourceBundle** for one of these reasons.

- You want to use a **ListResourceBundle** so that you can associate a key with a non-String object.
- You wish to pre-process a key.
- The message comes from an unconventional source.

The tag falls back to the default resource bundle if the specified custom **ResourceBundle** cannot be found.

The **i18n** tag has one attribute, name, which is described in Table 9.4.

Name	Data Type	Description
name	String	The fully qualified Java class to load.

Table 9.4: i18n tag attribute

For example, the **app09c** application features two custom **ResourceBundles** that extend **ListResourceBundle**, **MyCustomResourceBundle** and **MyCustomResourceBundle_de**. The custom **ResourceBundles** are shown in Listings 9.8 and 9.9, respectively. These **ResourceBundles** return one of two message arrays. If the current time is before 12 am, it will return the first array. Otherwise, the second array will be returned. Therefore, the user will get a different message depending on the current time.

Listing 9.8: The MyCustomResourceBundle class

```
package app09c.resourcebundle;
import java.util.Calendar;
import java.util.ListResourceBundle;

public class MyCustomResourceBundle extends ListResourceBundle {
    public Object[][] getContents() {
        if (Calendar.getInstance().get(Calendar.HOUR_OF_DAY) < 12) {
            return contents1;
        } else {
            return contents2;
        }
    }
    static final Object[][] contents1 = {
            { "greetings", "Good morning {0}" },
            { "farewell", "Good bye" } };

    static final Object[][] contents2 = {
            { "greetings", "Hello {0}" },
            { "farewell", "Good bye" } };
}
```

Listing 9.9: The MyCustomResourceBundle_de class

```
package app09c.resourcebundle;
import java.util.Calendar;
import java.util.ListResourceBundle;
```

```java
public class MyCustomResourceBundle_de extends ListResourceBundle {
    public Object[][] getContents() {
        if (Calendar.getInstance().get(Calendar.HOUR_OF_DAY) < 12) {
            return contents1;
        } else {
            return contents2;
        }
    }
    static final Object[][] contents1 = {
            { "greetings", "Guten Morgen {0}" },
            { "farewell", "Tschüß" } };

    static final Object[][] contents2 = {
            { "greetings", "Hallo {0}" },
            { "farewell", "Tschüß" } };
}
```

The **Main.jsp** page in Listing 9.10 uses an **i18n** tag to select a custom **ResourceBundle** and employs two **text** tags to display the localized messages.

Listing 9.10: The Main.jsp page

```jsp
<%@ taglib prefix="s" uri="/struts-tags" %>
<html>
<head>
<title>I18N</title>
<style type="text/css">@import url(css/main.css);</style>
</head>
<body>
<div id="global" style="width:350px">

<s:i18n name="app09c.resourcebundle.MyCustomResourceBundle">
    <s:text name="greetings">
        <s:param>Jon</s:param>
    </s:text>.
    <s:text name="farewell"/>
</s:i18n>
</div>
</body>
</html>
```

You can test the application by directing your browser to this URL.

```
http://localhost:8080/app09c/Main.action
```

Manually Selecting A Resource Bundle

The **ResourceBundle** that gets picked up depends on the browser's locale. If you want to let the user select one that is not browser-dependant, you can. You just need to pass a request parameter **request_locale**. For example, the following request parameter indicates to the server that the user wanted to be served in German language.

```
request_locale=de
```

The locale will be retained throughout the session.

As an example, the app09d application illustrates how you can create an application that lets the user select a language. The actions in this application are declared in Listing 9.11.

Listing 9.11: The action declarations

```
<package name="app09d" extends="struts-default">
    <action name="Language">
        <result>/jsp/Language.jsp</result>
    </action>
    <action name="Main1" class="app09d.Main">
        <result>/jsp/Main1.jsp</result>
    </action>
    <action name="Main2" class="app09d.Main">
        <result>/jsp/Main2.jsp</result>
    </action>
</package>
```

The first action, **Language**, displays the **Language.jsp** page (shown in Listing 9.12) that shows two links that let the user select a language.

Listing 9.12: The Language.jsp page

```
<%@ taglib prefix="s" uri="/struts-tags" %>
<html>
<head>
<title>Select Language</title>
<style type="text/css">@import url(css/main.css);</style>
</head>
<body>
<div id="global" style="width:350px">

<s:url action="Main1" id="enUrl">
```

```
        <s:param name="request_locale">en</s:param>
</s:url>
<s:url action="Main1" id="deUrl">
        <s:param name="request_locale">de</s:param>
</s:url>

<h3>Select Language</h3>
        <ul>
            <li><s:a href="%{enUrl}">English</s:a></li>
            <li><s:a href="%{deUrl}">Deutsch</s:a></li>
        </li>
</div>
</body>
</html>
```

Selecting the first link invokes the **Main1** action and passes the **request_locale=en** request parameter to the server. Selecting the second link invokes **Main2** and passes **request_locale=de**. The **Main1.jsp** and **Main2.jsp** pages, associated with actions **Main1** and **Main2**, are shown in Listing 9.13 and 9.14, respectively.

Listing 9.13: The Main1.jsp page

```
<%@ taglib prefix="s" uri="/struts-tags" %>
<html>
<head>
<title>I18N</title>
<style type="text/css">@import url(css/main.css);</style>
<style type="text/css">
img {
        border:none;
}
</style>
</head>
<body>
<div id="global" style="width:350px">
<s:text name="greetings">
    <s:param>Jon</s:param>
</s:text>
</div>

<s:url action="Main2" id="url"/>
<s:a href="%{url}"><img src="images/next.png"/></s:a>
</body>
</html>
```

Listing 9.14: The Main2.jsp page

```
<%@ taglib prefix="s" uri="/struts-tags" %>
<html>
<head>
<title>I18N</title>
<style type="text/css">@import url(css/main.css);</style>
</head>
<body>
<div id="global" style="width:350px">
<s:text name="farewell"/>
</div>
</body>
</html>
```

To test the example, direct your browser to this URL:

```
http://localhost:8080/app09d/Language.action
```

You will see something similar to Figure 9.4.

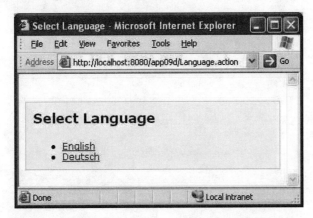

Figure 9.4: Letting the user select a language

Summary

Message handling is one of the most important tasks in application development. Today applications also often require that applications be able to display internationalized and localized messages. Struts has been designed with i18n and l10n in mind, and the tags in the Struts tag library support internationalized message handling.

Chapter 10
Model Driven and Prepare Interceptors

This chapter explains the Model Driven and Prepare interceptors, two very important interceptors that help with separating the action and the model. It starts with a discussion of why separating the action and the model is a good idea and continues with two sample applications that illustrate the roles of the interceptors.

Separating the Action and the Model

Web applications are normally multi-tiered. There are the presentation tier, the logic tier, and the data tier. Communication between two tiers is conducted by invoking methods and passing data in the form of transfer objects. Also known as a value object, a transfer object is simple and has no methods. In fact, there is a pattern that governs the design and use of transfer objects: the Data Transfer Object (DTO) pattern.

Struts resides mainly in the presentation tier and since you can write business logic in Struts actions, you can argue that Struts encapsulates the logic tier too. In an enterprise application, however, it is less often that you write business logic in action classes. Rather, you will call methods in another tier from your action classes.

A Struts action has methods and properties and can definitely act as a transfer object. However, is it really appropriate to send an action object to another tier?

The answer is no. An action class has methods that are useful only in the presentation tier. What would an **execute** method that returns "success" do in an EJB container, for example? Transferring an action object to another tier is not only awkward but could be dangerous too.

Now, if you accept this, you'll acknowledge that there needs to be a clear separation between the action and the model in an enterprise application that uses Struts as the front-end. There will be action classes that don't represent model objects and whose functions are limited to serve the presentation tier. The names of such action classes should end with **Action**. Model classes, on the other hand, should have no suffix. An action class that manages products should be called **ProductAction** whereas an instance of a **Product** class should be used as a transfer object that encapsulates information about a product.

By now you've probably grown used to receiving the Struts service that maps form fields with action properties. You'll probably ask, if you are to create a model that is not an instance of the action class, how do you map form fields with the transfer object's properties? The answer is by employing the Model Driven interceptor.

The Model Driven Interceptor

As mentioned in the preceding section, you often need to worry about a model that is separate from an action class. If you have a **ProductAction** class that handles products, you will have to think about creating and populating the model. The Model Driven interceptor works on any action that implements the **com.opensymphony.xwork2.ModelDriven** interface. This interface is shown in Listing 10.1.

Listing 10.1: The ModelDriven interface

```
package com.opensymphony.xwork2;
/**
 * ModelDriven Actions provide a model object to be pushed onto the
 * ValueStack in addition to the Action itself, allowing a FormBean
 * type approach like Struts 1.
 */
public interface ModelDriven<T> {
    /**
     * @return the model to be pushed onto the ValueStack instead of
     * the Action itself
     */
```

```
        T getModel();
}
```

An action class that implements **ModelDriven** must override the **getModel** method. As an example, the **ProductAction** class in Listing 10.2 implements **ModelDriven** and its **getModel** method returns an instance of the **Product** class (given in Listing 10.3).

Listing 10.2: A ModelDriven action

```
public class ProductAction extends ActionSupport
        implements ModelDriven {
    public String execute() throws Exception {
        return SUCCESS;
    }
    public Object getModel() {
        return new Product();
    }
}
```

Listing 10.3: The Product class

```
public class Product {
    private String productName;
    private String description;
    private float price;

    // getters and setters not shown
}
```

When the user invokes the **ProductAction** action, the Model Driven interceptor will call its **getModel** method on **ProductAction** and push the returned model (in this case, an instance of **Product**) to the Value Stack. If the basic stack or the default stack has been configured to kick in after the Model Driven interceptor, the Parameters interceptor will then map form fields to the properties of the objects in the Value Stack. Since now the model (the **Product** object) is at the top of the Value Stack, it will get populated. If a field does not have a matching property in the model, the Param interceptor will try the next object in the Value Stack. In this case, the **ProductAction** object will be used.

As an example, the **app10a** application shows how you can separate an action and a model. This simple application manages employees and comes with two actions:

- **Employee_list** that shows all employees in the system
- **Employee_create** that is used to add a new employee

The action declarations for this application are given in Listing 10.4.

Listing 10.4: The struts.xml file

```
<package name="app10a" extends="struts-default">
    <action name="Employee_list" method="list"
            class="app10a.EmployeeAction">
        <result>/jsp/Employee.jsp</result>
    </action>
    <action name="Employee_create" method="create"
            class="app10a.EmployeeAction">
        <result type="redirect-action">Employee_list</result>
        <result name="input">/jsp/Employee.jsp</result>
    </action>
</package>
```

As you can see in Listing 10.4, both actions are handled by the
EmployeeAction class. The **list** method is used to handle the **Employee_list**
action and the **create** method is for creating a new employee.

The **EmployeeAction** class is shown in Listing 10.5.

Listing 10.5: The EmployeeAction class

```
package app10a;
import com.opensymphony.xwork2.ActionSupport;
import com.opensymphony.xwork2.ModelDriven;
import java.util.List;

public class EmployeeAction extends ActionSupport
        implements ModelDriven {

    private Employee employee;
    private List<Employee> employees;

    public Object getModel() {
        employee = new Employee();
        return employee;
    }

    public List<Employee> getEmployees() {
        employees = EmployeeManager.getEmployees();
        return employees;
    }
```

```
public Employee getEmployee() {
    return employee;
}

public void setEmployee(Employee employee) {
    this.employee = employee;
}

public void setEmployees(List<Employee> employees) {
    this.employees = employees;
}

public String list() {
    employees = EmployeeManager.getEmployees();
    return SUCCESS;
}
public String create() {
    EmployeeManager.create(employee);
    return SUCCESS;
}
}
```

The model used in this application is the **Employee** class in Listing 10.6.

Listing 10.6: The Employee model class

```
package app10a;
public class Employee {
    private int id;
    private String firstName;
    private String lastName;

    public Employee() {
    }
    public Employee(int id, String firstName, String lastName) {
        this.id = id;
        this.firstName = firstName;
        this.lastName = lastName;
    }

    // getters and setters not shown
}
```

Note that a model class must have a no-argument constructor. Since the **Employee** class has a constructor that accepts three arguments, a no-argument constructor must be explicitly defined. The **Employee** class itself is very simple with three properties, **id**, **firstName**, and **lastName**.

Both the **list** and **create** methods in **EmployeeAction** rely on an **EmployeeManager** class that hides the complexity of the business logic that manages employees. In a real-world solution, **EmployeeManager** could be a business service that reads from and writes to a database. In this application, **EmployeeManager** provides a simple repository of **Employee** objects in a **List**.

Note
Chapter 11, "Persistence Layer" explains the Data Access Object design pattern for data access.

The **EmployeeManager** class is shown in Listing 10.7.

Listing 10.7: The EmployeeManager classs

```java
package app10a;
import java.util.ArrayList;
import java.util.List;

public class EmployeeManager {
    private static List<Employee> employees;
    public static int id;
    static {
        employees = new ArrayList<Employee>();
        employees.add(new Employee(++id, "Ken", "Cornell"));
        employees.add(new Employee(++id, "Cindy", "Huang"));
        employees.add(new Employee(++id, "Ross", "Geller"));
        employees.add(new Employee(++id, "George", "Michael"));
        employees.add(new Employee(++id, "Bruce", "Santiago"));
    }

    public static List<Employee> getEmployees() {
        return employees;
    }

    public static void create(Employee employee) {
        employee.setId(++id);
        employees.add(employee);
    }
}
```

You can run the application by directing your browser to this URL:

```
http://localhost:8080/app10a/Employee_list.action
```

Figure 10.1 shows how the employee list looks like.

Figure 10.1: Using the Model Driven interceptor

If you click the Submit button, the create method in the action object will be invoked. A validation file (named **EmployeeAction-Employee_create-validation.xml**) is used to make sure that the first name and the last name are not empty. Listing 10.8 shows the **EmployeeAction-Employee_create-validation.xml** file.

Listing 10.8: The EmployeeAction-Employee_create-validation.xml file

```
<!DOCTYPE validators PUBLIC
    "-//OpenSymphony Group//XWork Validator 1.0.2//EN"
    "http://www.opensymphony.com/xwork/xwork-validator-1.0.2.dtd">

<validators>
    <field name="firstName">
```

```
            <field-validator type="requiredstring">
                <message>Please enter a first name</message>
            </field-validator>
        </field>
        <field name="lastName">
            <field-validator type="requiredstring">
                <message>Please enter a last name</message>
            </field-validator>
        </field>
</validators>
```

Now, pay attention to the **result** elements for the **Employee_create** action in the configuration file:

```
<action name="Employee_create" method="create"
        class="app10a.EmployeeAction">
    <result type="redirect-action">Employee_list</result>
    <result name="input">/jsp/Employee.jsp</result>
</action>
```

After a successful create, the user will be redirected to the **Employee_list** action. Why didn't we do a forward that would have been faster?

The Create Employee form is submitted to this URI:

```
/Employee_create.action
```

If we had used a forward, then the URI would have remained the same after the action and result were executed. As a result, if the user clicked the browser's Refresh/Reload button, the form (and its contents) would be submitted again and a new employee would be created.

By redirecting, the URI after **Employee_create** will be the following, which will not cause another create if the user (accidentally) reloads the page.

```
/Employee_list.action
```

The Preparable Interceptor

As you can see in the preceding section, the **getModel** method of a **ModelDriven** action always returns a new object. However, as models are sometimes retrieved from a database, you cannot simply return a new instance every time you override **getModel**. In the latter case, the Preparable interceptor can help. This interceptor calls the **prepare** method of any action object whose class implements the **com.opensymphony.xwork2.Preparable** interface. This interface is shown in Listing 10.9.

Listing 10.9: The Preparable interface

```
package com.opensymphony.xwork2;
public interface Preparable {
    void prepare() throws Exception;
}
```

Let's continue with an example.

The **app10b** application extends **app10a** by adding three actions:

- Employee_edit
- Employee_update
- Employee_delete

The declarations for the actions in **app10b** are given in Listing 10.10.

Listing 10.10: The action declarations in app10b

```
<package name="app10b" extends="struts-default">
    <action name="Employee_list" method="list"
            class="app10b.EmployeeAction">
        <result>/jsp/Employee.jsp</result>
        <result name="input">/jsp/Employee.jsp</result>
    </action>
    <action name="Employee_create" method="create"
            class="app10b.EmployeeAction">
        <result type="redirect-action">Employee_list</result>
        <result name="input">/jsp/Employee.jsp</result>
    </action>

    <action name="Employee_edit" method="edit"
            class="app10b.EmployeeAction">
        <interceptor-ref name="paramsPrepareParamsStack"/>
        <result>/jsp/EditEmployee.jsp</result>
    </action>
    <action name="Employee_update" method="update"
            class="app10b.EmployeeAction">
        <result type="redirect-action">Employee_list</result>
    </action>
    <action name="Employee_delete" method="delete"
            class="app10b.EmployeeAction">
```

```
            <result>/jsp/Employee.jsp</result>
        </action>
</package>
```

The **EmployeeAction** class, shown in Listing 10.11, handles all the actions in **app10b**.

Listing 10.11: The EmployeeAction class

```java
package app10b;
import com.opensymphony.xwork2.ActionSupport;
import com.opensymphony.xwork2.ModelDriven;
import com.opensymphony.xwork2.Preparable;
import java.util.List;

public class EmployeeAction extends ActionSupport
        implements Preparable, ModelDriven {
    private Employee employee;
    private int employeeId;
    private List<Employee> employees;

    public void prepare() throws Exception {
        if (employeeId == 0) {
            employee = new Employee();
        } else {
            employee = EmployeeManager.find(employeeId);
        }
    }

    public Object getModel() {
        return employee;
    }

    public List<Employee> getEmployees() {
        employees = EmployeeManager.getEmployees();
        return employees;
    }

    public Employee getEmployee() {
        return employee;
    }

    public void setEmployee(Employee employee) {
        this.employee = employee;
    }
```

```java
    public void setEmployees(List<Employee> employees) {
        this.employees = employees;
    }

    public String list() {
        employees = EmployeeManager.getEmployees();
        return SUCCESS;
    }
    public String create() {
        EmployeeManager.create(employee);
        return SUCCESS;
    }
    public String edit() {
        return SUCCESS;
    }
    public String update() {
        EmployeeManager.update(employee);
        return SUCCESS;
    }
    public String delete() {
        EmployeeManager.delete(employeeId);
        return SUCCESS;
    }

    public int getEmployeeId() {
        return employeeId;
    }

    public void setEmployeeId(int employeeId) {
        this.employeeId = employeeId;
    }
}
```

Note that the **prepare** method in the **EmployeeAction** class will create a new **Employee** object only if **employeeId** is 0. If an action invocation populates the **employeeId** property of the action object, the **prepare** method will attempt to find an **Employee** object through the **EmployeeManager** class.

This is why the **Employee_edit** action uses the **paramsPrepareParamsStack** stack that calls the Params interceptor twice, as shown below:

```xml
<interceptor-stack name="paramsPrepareParamsStack">
    ...
    <interceptor-ref name="params"/>
    ...
```

```
    <interceptor-ref name="prepare"/>
    <interceptor-ref name="model-driven"/>
    ...
    <interceptor-ref name="params"/>
    ...
</interceptor-stack>
```

The first time the Parameters interceptor is invoked, it populates the
employeeId property on the **EmployeeAction** object, so that the **prepare**
method knows how to retrieve the **Employee** object to be edited. After the
Prepare and Model Driven interceptors are invoked, the Parameters
interceptor is called again, this time giving it the opportunity to populate the
model.

The model class (**Employee**) for this application is exactly the same as the
one in **app10a** and will not be reprinted here. However, the
EmployeeManager class has been modified and is given in Listing 10.12.

Listing 10.12: The EmployeeManager class

```
package app10b;
import java.util.ArrayList;
import java.util.List;

public class EmployeeManager {
    private static List<Employee> employees;
    public static int id;
    static {
        employees = new ArrayList<Employee>();
        employees.add(new Employee(++id, "Ken", "Cornell"));
        employees.add(new Employee(++id, "Cindy", "Huang"));
        employees.add(new Employee(++id, "Ross", "Geller"));
        employees.add(new Employee(++id, "George", "Michael"));
        employees.add(new Employee(++id, "Bruce", "Santiago"));
    }

    public static List<Employee> getEmployees() {
        return employees;
    }

    public static void create(Employee employee) {
        employee.setId(++id);
        employees.add(employee);
    }
    public static void delete(int employeeId) {
        for (Employee employee : employees) {
```

```
                if (employee.getId() == employeeId) {
                    employees.remove(employee);
                    break;
                }
            }
        }
    public static Employee find(int employeeId) {
        for (Employee employee : employees) {
            if (employee.getId() == employeeId) {
                System.out.println("found");
                return employee;
            }
        }
        return null;
    }
    public static void update(Employee employee) {
        int employeeId = employee.getId();
        for (Employee emp : employees) {
            if (emp.getId() == employeeId) {
                emp.setFirstName(employee.getFirstName());
                emp.setLastName(employee.getLastName());
                break;
            }
        }

    }
}
```

You can invoke the application by using this URL:

`http://localhost:8080/app08b/Employee_list.action`

Figure 10.2 shows the list of employees. It's similar except that there are now Edit and Delete links for each employee.

Figure 10.2: Using the Prepare interceptor

Summary

It is often necessary to separate the action and the model, especially in an enterprise application and in a more complex Struts application. This chapter showed how the Model Driven and Prepare interceptors could help.

Chapter 11
The Persistence Layer

At some stage, application data needs to be persisted or saved to secondary storage. Several methods are available, including storing them into files, relational databases, XML documents, and so on. Of these, persisting data to a relational database is the most reliable and the most popular. In addition, object-to-relational database mapping tools can be purchased off the shelf to help Java programmers persist Java objects.

Without a mapping tool, you have other options in hand. These include the Data Access Object (DAO) pattern, Java Data Objects (JDO), open source libraries such as Hibernate, and so on. Of these, the DAO pattern in the easiest to learn and is sufficient in most applications. This chapter shows you how to implement the DAO pattern for data persistence.

Also note that because many parts of an application may need to persist objects, a good design dictates that you create a dedicated layer for data persistence. This persistence layer provides methods that can be called by any component that needs to persist objects. In addition to simplifying your application architecture (because now object persistence is handled by only one component), the persistence layer also hides the complexity of accessing the relational database. The persistence layer is depicted in Figure 11.1.

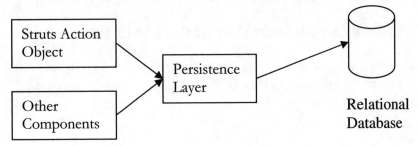

Figure 11.1: The persistence layer

The persistence layer provides public methods for storing, retrieving, and manipulating value objects, and the client of the persistence layer does not have to know how the persistence layer accomplishes this. All they care is their data is safe and retrievable.

The Data Access Object Pattern

With this pattern, you write a class for each type of object you need to persist. For example, if your application needs to persist three types of transfer objects—**Product**, **Customer**, and **Order**—you need three DAO classes, each of which takes care of an object type. Therefore, you would have the following classes: **ProductDAO**, **CustomerDAO**, and **OrderDAO**. The DAO suffix at the end of the class name indicates that the class is a DAO class. It is a convention that you should follow unless you have compelling reasons not to do so.

A typical DAO class takes care of the addition, deletion, modification, and retrieval of an object, and the searching for those objects. For example, a **ProductDAO** class may support the following methods:

```
void addProduct(Product product)
void updateProduct(Product product)
void deleteProduct(int productId)
Product getProduct(int productId)
List<Product> findProducts(SearchCriteria searchCriteria)
```

There are many variants of the DAO pattern. You will learn the three most common variants: from the most basic to the most flexible.

The Simplest Implementation of the DAO Pattern

In this implementation, a client instantiates the DAO class directly and call its methods. Figure 11.2 shows the **ProductDAO** class in this variant of the DAO pattern.

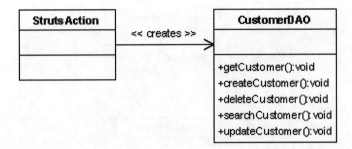

Figure 11.2: The simplest implementation of the DAO pattern

When a Struts action object needs to access product information, it instantiates the **ProductDAO** class and calls its methods.

The DAO Pattern with A DAO Interface

A typical Struts application has more than one DAO class. The instances of the DAO classes need a uniform way of getting a connection object to access the data source. It is therefore convenient to have a **DAO** interface that provides the **getConnection** method and a **DAOBase** class that provides the implementation of the method. All the DAO classes then extend the **DAOBase** class, as depicted in Figure 11.3.

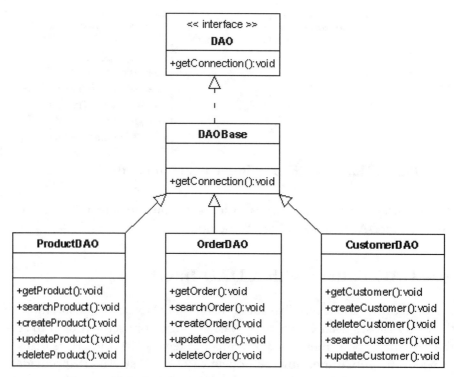

Figure 11.3: DAO pattern with a DAO interface

The DAO Pattern with the Abstract Factory Pattern

Each method in the DAO class accesses the database by using an SQL statement. Unfortunately, the SQL statement may vary depending on the database type. For example, to insert a record into a table, Oracle databases support the notion of sequences to generate sequential numbers for new records. Therefore, in Oracle, you would perform two operations: generate a sequential number and insert a new record. MySQL, by contrast, supports auto numbers that get generated when new records are inserted. In this case, an **insert** method will depend on the database it is persisting data to. To allow your application to support multiple databases, you can modify your DAO pattern implementation to employ the Abstract Factory pattern. Figure 11.4 shows the **CustomerDAO** interface that defines the methods that need to exist in a **CustomerDAO** object. A **CustomerDAO** implementation will be tied to a database type. In Figure 11.4 two implementation classes are available,

CustomerDAOMySQLImpl and **CustomerDAOOracleImpl**, which supports persisting objects to the MySQL database and the Oracle database, respectively.

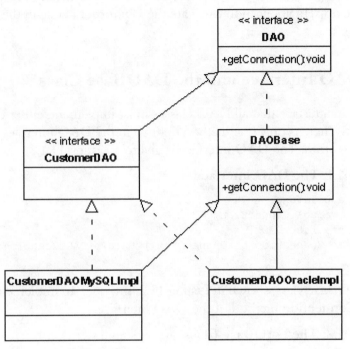

Figure 11.4: DAO pattern with Abstract Factory pattern

Implementing the DAO Pattern

The **app11a** application exemplifies the DAO pattern. In this application you can search customers, add, update, and delete customers. The **CustomerDAO** interface provides methods for manipulating **CustomerTO** objects. The class diagram is the same as the one in Figure 11.4. The **CustomerDAO** interface has one implementation, **CustomerDAOMySQLImpl**.

In order to discuss the application thoroughly, I split the applications into subsections.

Note

To run the **app11a** application, you need to have a MySQL database installed on your machine and run the **MySQLScript.sql** file included in the **app11a** application to create the **Customers** table in the **test** database.

The DAO Interface and the DAOBase Class

DAO is an interface that all DAO classes must implement, either directly or indirectly. There is only one method defined in the **DAO** interface, **getConnection**. The **DAO** interface is given in Listing 11.1.

Listing 11.1: The DAO interface

```
package app11a.dao;
import java.sql.Connection;
public interface DAO {
    public Connection getConnection() throws DAOException;
}
```

The **DAOBase** class, shown in Listing 11.2, provides an implementation of the **getConnection** method of the **DAO** interface.

Listing 11.2: The DAOBase Class

```
package app11a.dao;
import java.sql.Connection;
import java.sql.SQLException;
import javax.servlet.ServletContext;
import javax.sql.DataSource;
import org.apache.struts2.ServletActionContext;

public class DAOBase implements DAO {
    public Connection getConnection() throws DAOException {
        ServletContext servletContext = ServletActionContext.
                getServletContext();
        DataSource dataSource = (DataSource)
                servletContext.getAttribute("dataSource");
        Connection connection = null;
        if (dataSource != null) {
            try {
                connection = dataSource.getConnection();
            } catch (SQLException e) {
                System.out.println("DAOBase");
```

```
                    throw new DAOException();
                }
            }
        return connection;
        }
}
```

The **getConnection** method returns a **java.sql.Connection** that can be used by DAO objects to access the database. In Java SE, you can obtain a **Connection** object via **java.sql.DriverManager**. In Java EE, however, scalability is very important and you definitely want to use connection pooling to obtain **Connection** objects quickly. The **javax.sql.DataSource** supports connection pooling and all Java EE containers must provide a **DataSource** object from which **Connection** objects can be obtained. Connection pooling is so important that you can even find this feature in Tomcat, even though Tomcat is not a Java EE container.

In Java EE, you obtain a **DataSource** object by employing a JNDI lookup using this boilerplate code:

```
try {
    Context context = new InitialContext();
    DataSource dataSource = (DataSource)
            context.lookup(dataSourceJndiName);
    ...
```

JNDI lookups are expensive operations, and, as such, obtaining a **DataSource** is resource intensive. Therefore, you may want to cache this object and the **ServletContext** object will be an ideal location to cache it. In **app11a** we use the application listener in Listing 11.3 to obtain a **DataSource** object and store it in the **ServletContext** object. Afterwards, in the **DAOBase** class in Listing 11.2 you can obtain a **DataSource** by using this code:

```
ServletContext servletContext = ServletActionContext.
        getServletContext();
DataSource dataSource = (DataSource)
        servletContext.getAttribute("dataSource");
```

Listing 11.3: The AppListener class

```
package app11a.listener;
import javax.naming.Context;
import javax.naming.InitialContext;
import javax.naming.NamingException;
import javax.servlet.ServletContext;
```

```java
import javax.servlet.ServletContextEvent;
import javax.servlet.ServletContextListener;
import javax.sql.DataSource;
public class AppListener implements ServletContextListener {
    public void contextInitialized(ServletContextEvent sce) {
        ServletContext servletContext = sce.getServletContext();
        String dataSourceJndiName = servletContext
                .getInitParameter("dataSourceJndiName");
        try {
            Context context = new InitialContext();
            DataSource dataSource = (DataSource)
        context.lookup(dataSourceJndiName);
            servletContext.setAttribute("dataSource", dataSource);
        } catch (NamingException e) {
            throw new RuntimeException();
        }
    }
    public void contextDestroyed(ServletContextEvent cse) {
    }
}
```

Connection Pooling in Tomcat

To configure connection pooling in Tomcat, add this **Context** element under **<Host>** in Tomcat's **server.xml** file.

```xml
<Context path="/app11a" docBase="app11a" reloadable="true"
        debug="8">
    <Resource name="jdbc/myDataSource" auth="Container"
    type="javax.sql.DataSource"/>
    <ResourceParams name="jdbc/myDataSource">
        <parameter>
            <name>factory</name>
            <value>
                org.apache.commons.dbcp.BasicDataSourceFactory
            </value>
        </parameter>
        <parameter>
            <name>maxActive</name>
            <value>100</value>
        </parameter>
        <parameter>
            <name>maxIdle</name>
```

```
                <value>30</value>
            </parameter>
            <parameter>
                <name>maxWait</name>
                <value>10000</value>
            </parameter>
            <parameter>
                <name>username</name>
                <value>root</value>
            </parameter>
            <parameter>
                <name>password</name>
                <value></value>
            </parameter>
            <parameter>
                <name>driverClassName</name>
                <value>com.mysql.jdbc.Driver</value>
            </parameter>
            <parameter>
                <name>url</name>
                <value>jdbc:mysql://localhost/test</value>
            </parameter>
        </ResourceParams>
</Context>
```

The **Context** element above facilitates the creation of a **DataSource** object
from which you can get **java.sql.Connection** objects from the pool. The
specifics of the **DataSource** object are given in the **parameter** elements of
the **ResourceParams** element. The **username** and **password** parameters
specify the user name and password used to access the database, the
driverClassName parameter specifies the JDBC driver, and the **url**
parameter specifies the database URL for accessing the MySQL database.
The **url** parameter indicates that the database server resides in the same
machine as Tomcat (the use of **localhost** in the URL) and the database the
DataSource object references is the test database.

Also, for your DAO implementation, you may want to extend the **java.lang.Exception** class to have your own DAO-specific exception. Methods in DAO objects can throw this specific exception so that you can provide code that deals with data access and data manipulation failures.

A simple DAO-specific exception class, named **DAOException**, is given in Listing 11.4.

Listing 11.4: The DAOException Class

```
package app11a.dao;
public class DAOException extends Exception {

}
```

The EmployeeDAO Interface

The **app11a** application uses one DAO class, **EmployeeDAO**. To support multiple databases, **EmployeeDAO** is written as an interface that defines the methods for **EmployeeDAO** objects. Listing 11.5 presents the **EmployeeDAO** interface.

Listing 11.5: The EmployeeDAO interface

```
package app11a.dao;
import app11a.Employee;
import app11a.EmployeeSearchCriteria;
import java.util.List;

public interface EmployeeDAO {
    public void createEmployee(Employee employee)
            throws DAOException;
    public void updateEmployee(Employee customer)
            throws DAOException;
    public Employee getEmployee(int employeeId) throws DAOException;
    public void deleteEmployee(int employeeId) throws DAOException;
    public List<Employee> searchEmployees(EmployeeSearchCriteria
            searchCriteria) throws DAOException;
}
```

The **createEmployee** and **updateEmployee** methods accept an **Employee** object to be inserted or updated. The getEmployee and **deleteEmployee** methods accept an employee identifier, and the **searchEmployees** method accepts an **EmployeeSearchCriteria**.

In **app11a** the **EmployeeSearchCriteria** class is similar to the **Employee** class, however in other applications it may include search-related properties, such as **sortOrder** and **maximumSearchResults**, that do not exist in **Employee**. Hence, the need for another class that encapsulates user search criteria.

The EmployeeDAOMySQLImpl Class

The **EmployeeDAOMySQLImpl** class, presented in Listing 11.6, is an implementation of the **EmployeeDAO** interface. To support another database, you can create another **EmployeeDAO** implementation, such as **EmployeeDAOOracleImpl**, **EmployeeDAOSQLServerImpl**, etc.

Listing 11.6: The EmployeeDAOMySQLImpl Interface

```
package app11a.dao;
import java.sql.SQLException;
import java.sql.Connection;
import java.sql.PreparedStatement;
import java.sql.ResultSet;
import java.sql.Statement;
import java.util.ArrayList;
import java.util.List;
import app11a.Employee;
import app11a.EmployeeSearchCriteria;
import app11a.dao.DAOException;
import app11a.dao.DBUtil;

public class EmployeeDAOMySQLImpl extends DAOBase
        implements EmployeeDAO {
    private static final String CREATE_EMPLOYEE_SQL =
        "INSERT INTO employees (firstName,lastName) VALUES (?, ?)";
    public void createEmployee(Employee customer)
            throws DAOException {
        Connection connection = null;
        PreparedStatement pStatement = null;
        try {
            connection = getConnection();
            // Prepare a statement to insert a record
            pStatement = connection.prepareStatement(
                    CREATE_EMPLOYEE_SQL);
            pStatement.setString(1, customer.getFirstName());
            pStatement.setString(2, customer.getLastName());
            pStatement.executeUpdate();
```

```
            pStatement.close();
    } catch (SQLException ex) {
        throw new DAOException();
    } finally {
        try {
            connection.close();
        } catch (SQLException ex) {
            throw new DAOException();
        }
    }
}

private static final String UPDATE_EMPLOYEE_SQL =
    "UPDATE employees SET firstName=?, lastName=? WHERE id = ?";
public void updateEmployee(Employee employee)
        throws DAOException {
    Connection connection = null;
    PreparedStatement pStatement = null;
    try {
        connection = getConnection();
        pStatement = connection.prepareStatement(
                UPDATE_EMPLOYEE_SQL);
        pStatement.setString(1, employee.getFirstName());
        pStatement.setString(2, employee.getLastName());
        pStatement.setInt(3, employee.getId());
        pStatement.executeUpdate();
        pStatement.close();
    } catch (SQLException e) {
        throw new DAOException();
    } finally {
        try {
            connection.close();
        } catch (SQLException ex) {
        }
    }
}

private static final String GET_EMPLOYEE_SQL =
    "SELECT firstName, lastName FROM employees WHERE id = ?";
public Employee getEmployee(int employeeId)
        throws DAOException {
    Connection connection = null;
    PreparedStatement pStatement = null;
    ResultSet rs = null;
    Employee employee = new Employee();
    try {
```

```
            connection = getConnection();
            pStatement = connection.prepareStatement(
                    GET_EMPLOYEE_SQL);
            pStatement.setInt(1, employeeId);
            rs = pStatement.executeQuery();
            if (rs.next()) {
                employee.setFirstName(rs.getString("firstName"));
                employee.setLastName(rs.getString("lastName"));
                employee.setId(employeeId);
            }
            rs.close();
            pStatement.close();
        } catch (SQLException ex) {
            throw new DAOException();
        } finally {
            try {
                connection.close();
            } catch (SQLException ex) {
            }
        }
        return employee;
    }

private static final String DELETE_EMPLOYEE_SQL =
    "DELETE FROM employees WHERE id = ?";
public void deleteEmployee(int employeeId) throws DAOException {
    Connection connection = null;
    PreparedStatement pStatement = null;
    try {
        connection = getConnection();
        pStatement =
  connection.prepareStatement(DELETE_EMPLOYEE_SQL);
        pStatement.setInt(1, employeeId);
        pStatement.executeUpdate();
        pStatement.close();
    } catch (SQLException e) {
        throw new DAOException();
    } finally {
        try {
            connection.close();
        } catch (SQLException ex) {
        }
    }
}

private static final String SEARCH_EMPLOYEES_SQL =
```

```java
        "SELECT id, firstName, lastName FROM employees WHERE ";
public List<Employee> searchEmployees(
        EmployeeSearchCriteria searchCriteria)
        throws DAOException {
    List<Employee> employees = new ArrayList<Employee>();
    Connection connection = null;
    Statement statement = null;
    ResultSet resultSet = null;

    // Build the search criterias
    StringBuilder criteriaSql = new StringBuilder(512);
    criteriaSql.append(SEARCH_EMPLOYEES_SQL);
    if (searchCriteria.getFirstName() != null) {
        criteriaSql.append("firstName LIKE '%" +
        DBUtil.fixSqlFieldValue(searchCriteria.getFirstName())
        + "%' AND ");
    }
    if (searchCriteria.getLastName() != null) {
        criteriaSql.append("lastName LIKE '%" +
        DBUtil.fixSqlFieldValue(searchCriteria.getLastName())
        + "%' AND ");
    }
    // Remove unused 'And' & 'WHERE'
    if (criteriaSql.substring(criteriaSql.length() - 5).
            equals(" AND "))
        criteriaSql.delete(criteriaSql.length() - 5,
                criteriaSql.length() - 1);
    if (criteriaSql.substring(criteriaSql.length() - 7).
            equals(" WHERE "))
        criteriaSql.delete(criteriaSql.length() - 7,
                criteriaSql.length() - 1);

    try {
        connection = getConnection();
        statement = connection.createStatement();
        resultSet = statement.executeQuery(
                criteriaSql.toString());
        while (resultSet.next()) {
            Employee employee = new Employee();
            employee.setId(resultSet.getInt("id"));
            employee.setFirstName(
                    resultSet.getString("firstName"));
            employee.setLastName(
                    resultSet.getString("lastName"));
            employees.add(employee);
        }
```

```
            resultSet.close();
            statement.close();
        } catch (SQLException e) {
            throw new DAOException();
        } finally {
            try {
                connection.close();
            } catch (SQLException ex) {
            }
        }
        return employees;
    }
}
```

The SQL statements for all the methods, except **searchEmployees**, are
defined as static final **String**s because they will never change. Making them
static final avoids creating the same **String**s again and again. Also, all those
methods use a **PreparedStatement** instead of a **java.sql.Statement** even
though the **PreparedStatement** object is only executed once. The use of
PreparedStatement saves you from having to check if one of the arguments
contains a single quote. With a **Statement**, you must escape any single quote
in the argument.

The **searchEmployees** method, on the other hand, is based on a dynamic
SQL statement. This necessitates us to use a **Statement** object. Consequently,
you must check for single quotes in the arguments using the **DbUtil** class's
fixSqlFieldValue method. Listing 11.7 presents the **fixSqlFieldValue**
method.

Listing 11.7: The fixSqlFieldValue method

```
package app11a.dao;

public class DBUtil {
    public static String fixSqlFieldValue(String value) {
        if (value == null) {
            return null;
        }
        int length = value.length();
        StringBuilder fixedValue = new StringBuilder((int) (length *
    1.1));
        for (int i = 0; i < length; i++) {
            char c = value.charAt(i);
            if (c == '\'') {
                fixedValue.append("''");
```

```
        } else {
            fixedValue.append(c);
        }
    }
    return fixedValue.toString();
  }
}
```

Note

You could replace the **fixSqlFieldValue** method with the **replaceAll** method of the **String** class like this.

```
String t= s.replaceAll("[\']", "'");
```

However, this method is compute intensive because it uses regular expressions and should be avoided in applications designed to be scalable.

The DAOFactory Class

The **DAOFactory** class helps the client instantiate a DAO class. Also, the necessity for a **DAOFactory** class in the application stems from the fact that the implementation class name is not known at design time, e.g. whether it is **EmployeeDAOMySQLImpl** or **EmployeeDAOOracleImpl**. As such, the **DAOFactory** class hides the complexity of creating a DAO object.

The **DAOFactory** class is presented in Listing 11.8.

Listing 11.8: The DAOFactory Class

```
package app11a.dao;
import javax.servlet.ServletContext;
import org.apache.struts2.ServletActionContext;

public class DAOFactory {
    private String databaseType;
    private static DAOFactory instance;
    static {
        instance = new DAOFactory();
    }
    private DAOFactory() {
        ServletContext servletContext = ServletActionContext
                .getServletContext();
        databaseType = servletContext.getInitParameter("dbType");
    }
```

```
    public static DAOFactory getInstance() {
        return instance;
    }
    public EmployeeDAO getEmployeeDAO() {
        if ("mysql".equalsIgnoreCase(databaseType)) {
            return new EmployeeDAOMySQLImpl();
        } else if ("oracle".equalsIgnoreCase(databaseType)) {
            // return new EmployeeDAOOracleImpl();
        } else if ("mssql".equalsIgnoreCase(databaseType)) {
            // return new EmployeeDAOMsSQLImpl();
        }
        return null;
    }
}
```

You can use the **DAOFactory** if you know the implementation classes for all your DAOs when the application is written. This means, if you are thinking of only supporting two databases, MySQL and Oracle, you know beforehand the type for the **EmployeeDAO** class is either **EmployeeDAOMySQLImpl** or **EmployeeDAOOracleImpl**. If in the future your application needs to support Microsoft SQL Server, you must rewrite the **DAOFactory** class, i.e. add another **if** statement in the **getCustomerDAO** class.

You can add support of more databases without recompiling the **DAOFactory** class if you use reflection to create the DAO object. Instead of the **dbType** parameter in your **web.xml** file, you'd have **employeeDAOType**. Then, you would have the following code in your **DAOFactory** class's **getCustomerDAO** method.

```
String customerDAOType = Config.getCustomerDAOType();
Class customerDAOClass = Class.forName(customerDAOType);
CustomerDAO customerDAO = customerDAOClass.newInstance();
```

The EmployeeManager Class

The **EmployeeManager** class (shown in Listing 11.9) is the client of the DAO classes. This class provides another layer between the Struts actions and the DAO classes.

Listing 11.9: The EmployeeManager class

```
package app11a;
import java.util.List;
import app11a.Employee;
```

```
import app11a.dao.DAOException;
import app11a.dao.DAOFactory;
import app11a.dao.EmployeeDAO;

public class EmployeeManager {
    public static List<Employee> getEmployees() {
        return search(new EmployeeSearchCriteria());
    }

    public static void create(Employee employee) {
        EmployeeDAO employeeDAO =
                DAOFactory.getInstance().getEmployeeDAO();
        try {
            employeeDAO.createEmployee(employee);
        } catch (DAOException e) {
        }
    }

    public static void delete(int employeeId) {
        EmployeeDAO employeeDAO =
                DAOFactory.getInstance().getEmployeeDAO();
        try {
            employeeDAO.deleteEmployee(employeeId);
        } catch (DAOException e) {
        }
    }

    public static Employee find(int employeeId) {
        EmployeeDAO employeeDAO =
                DAOFactory.getInstance().getEmployeeDAO();
        try {
            return employeeDAO.getEmployee(employeeId);
        } catch (DAOException e) {
        }
        return null;
    }

    public static void update(Employee employee) {
        EmployeeDAO employeeDAO =
                DAOFactory.getInstance().getEmployeeDAO();
        try {
            employeeDAO.updateEmployee(employee);
        } catch (DAOException e) {
        }
    }
```

```
public static List<Employee> search(
        EmployeeSearchCriteria criteria) {
    EmployeeDAO employeeDAO =
            DAOFactory.getInstance().getEmployeeDAO();
    try {
        return employeeDAO.searchEmployees(criteria);
    } catch (DAOException e) {
    }
    return null;
}
}
```

Running the Application

The **app11a** application provides the action classes for creating a new employee, updating and deleting an existing employee, and searching for employees. The main entry point is the **Employee_list** action. To invoke this action, use the following URL.

```
http://localhost:8080/app11a/Employee_list.action
```

You will see something similar to Figure 11.5.

Figure 11.5: The Employee form

When you run this application for the first time, you will not see the list of existing employees.

Hibernate

Hibernate has gained popularity in the past few years as an add-on for Java EE and other applications. Its web site (www.hibernate.org) advertises this free product as "a powerful, ultra-high performance object/relational persistence and query service for Java." Using Hibernate, you do not need to implement your own persistence layer. Instead, you use a tool to create databases and related tables and determine how your objects should be persisted. Hibernate virtually supports all kinds of database servers in the market today, and its

Hibernate Query Language provides "an elegant bridge between the object and relational worlds".

More people will be using Hibernate in the near future. If you have time, invest in it.

Summary

Most applications need a persistence layer for persisting value objects. The persistence layer hides the complexity of accessing the database from its clients, notably the action objects. The persistence layer can be implemented as entity beans, the DAO pattern, by using Hibernate, etc.

This chapter shows you in detail how to implement the DAO pattern. There are many variants of this pattern and which one you choose depends on the project specification. The most flexible DAO pattern is preferable because you can extend your application easily should it need to change in the future.

Chapter 12
File Upload

HTTP file upload is specified in Request For Comments (RFC) 1867. Struts' File Upload interceptor supports HTTP file upload by seamlessly incorporating the Jakarta Commons FileUpload library that contains a multipart parser. This chapter discusses file upload in general and how you can do single and multiple file uploads in Struts.

File Upload Overview

When using an HTML form to upload a file or multiple files, the **enctype** attribute of the form must be assigned **multipart/form-data** and the form method must be **post**. The form should look like this.

```
<form action="anAction" enctype="multipart/form-data" method="post">
...
</form>
```

To enable the user to select a file you must have an **<input type="file">** field. Here is an example of a form used for selecting a file. In addition to a **file** field, the form also contains a text box named **description** and a submit button.

```
<form action="Upload.action" enctype="multipart/form-data"
        method="post">
    Select file to upload <input type="file" name="filename"/><br/>
    Description: <input type="text" name="description"/><br/>
    <input type="submit" value="Upload"/>
</form>
```

Figure 12.1 shows how the **file** input field is rendered as a text box and a Browse button.

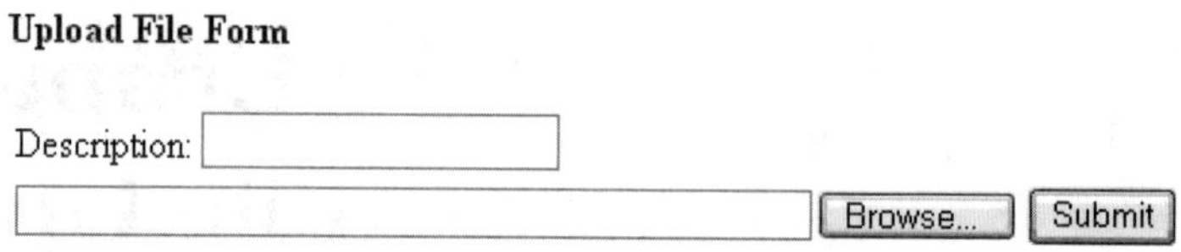

Upload File Form

Description:

Browse... Submit

Figure 12.1: Rendered visual elements of <input type=file>

Without Struts or the Java Commons FileUpload library, you would have to call the **getInputStream** method on **HttpServletRequest** and parse the resulting **InputStream** object to retrieve the uploaded file. This is a tedious and error-prone task. Luckily, Struts makes it very easy to retrieve uploaded files.

File Upload in Struts

In Struts, the File Upload interceptor and the Jakarta Commons FileUpload library help parse uploaded files. Basically, there are only two things you need to do.

First, use the **file** tag in a form on your JSP. Give it a descriptive name such as **attachment** or **upload**. For multiple file upload, use multiple **file** tags and give them the same name. For instance, the following form contains three **file** tags named **attachment**.

```
<s:form action="File_multipleUpload"
        enctype="multipart/form-data">
    <s:file name="attachment" label="Attachment 1"/>
    <s:file name="attachment" label="Attachment 2"/>
    <s:file name="attachment" label="Attachment 3"/>
    <s:submit />
</s:form>
```

A **file** tag will be rendered as the following **input** element in the browser:

```
<input type="file" name="inputName"/>
```

Second, create an action class with three properties. The properties must be named according to these patterns:

- [inputName]File
- [*inputName*]FileName

- [*inputName*]ContentType

Here [*inputName*] is the name of the file tag(s) on the JSP. For example, if the **file** tag's name is **attachment**, you will have these properties in your action class:

- attachmentFile
- attachmentFileName
- attachmentContentType

For single file upload, the type of [***inputName***]**File** is **java.io.File** and references the uploaded file. The second and third properties are **String** and refer to the uploaded file name and the content type, respectively.

For multiple file upload, you can either use arrays or **java.util.List**s. For instance, the following properties are arrays of **File**s and **String**s.

```
private File[] attachmentFile;
private String[] attachmentFileName;
private String[] attachmentContentType;
```

If you decide to use **List**s, you must assign an empty list to each of the properties:

```
private List<File> attachmentFile = new ArrayList<File>();
private List<String> attachmentFileName = new ArrayList<String>();
private List<String> attachmentContentType =
        new ArrayList<String>();
```

You can access these properties from your action method. Normally, you would want to save the uploaded file into a folder or a database and you would iterate over the **File** array, if an array is being used:

```
ServletContext servletContext =
        ServletActionContext.getServletContext();
String dataDir = servletContext.getRealPath("/WEB-INF");
for (int i=0; i < attachment.length; i++) {
    File savedFile = new File(dataDir, attachmentFileName[i]);
    attachment[i].renameTo(savedFile);
}
```

Since you often need to access both the uploaded file and the file name at each iteration, using arrays is easier because an array lets you iterate over its elements by index. On the other hand, iterating over a list would be more difficult.

The File Upload Interceptor

This interceptor is responsible for file upload and is included in the default stack. Even if you know nothing about this interceptor, you can still manage uploaded files easily. However, understanding how this interceptor works allows you to make full use of the file upload feature in Struts.

There are two important properties that you may want to set on the interceptor. You can limit the size of the uploaded file as well as determine the allowable content type by setting the following properties of the File Upload interceptor.

- **maximumSize**. The maximum size (in bytes) of the uploaded file. The default is about 2MB.
- **allowedTypes**. A comma-separated list of allowable content types.

For example, the following action imposes a size limit and the type of the uploaded file. Only files up to 1,000,000 bytes in size and JPEG, GIF, and PNG files can be uploaded.

```
<action name="File_upload" class="app14a.FileUploadAction">
    <interceptor-ref name="fileUpload"/>
        <param name="maximumSize">1000000</param>
        <param name="allowedTypes">
            image/gif,image/jpeg,image/png
        </param>
        </interceptor-ref>
    </interceptor-ref>
    <interceptor-ref name="basicStack"/>
    ...
</action>
```

If the user uploaded a file that is larger than the specified maximum size or a type not in the allowedTypes parameter, an error message will be displayed. File upload-related error messages are predefined in the **struts-messages.properties** file which is included in the core Struts JAR file. Here are the contents of the file:

```
struts.messages.error.uploading=Error uploading: {0}
struts.messages.error.file.too.large=File too large: {0} "{1}" {2}
struts.messages.error.content.type.not.allowed=Content-Type not
allowed: {0} "{1}" {2}
```

To override the messages here, create a **struts-messages.properties** file that contains values that you want to override the default values and place the file under **WEB-INF/classes/org/apache/struts2**. If you create a new **struts-messages.properties** file, the default one will not be examined. This means, if you override one message key and decide to use the other default ones, you must copy the latter to your properties file.

Single File Upload Example

The **app12a** application is a Struts application for uploading a file. The directory structure is shown in Figure 12.2.

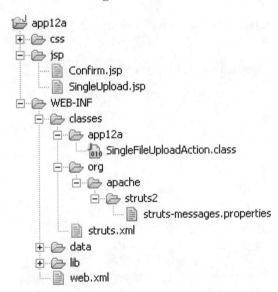

Figure 12.2: app12a directory structure

There are two actions in this application, one for displaying a file upload form and one for receiving the uploaded file. The action declarations are printed in Listing 12.1.

Listing 12.1: The struts.xml file

```
<package name="app12a" extends="struts-default">
    <action name="File">
        <result>/jsp/SingleUpload.jsp</result>
```

```
    </action>

    <action name="File_singleUpload"
            class="app12a.SingleFileUploadAction" method="upload">
        <interceptor-ref name="fileUpload">
            <param name="maximumSize">100000</param>
            <param name="allowedTypes">
                image/gif,image/jpeg,image/png
            </param>
        </interceptor-ref>
        <interceptor-ref name="basicStack"/>
        <result name="input">/jsp/SingleUpload.jsp</result>
        <result>/jsp/SingleUpload.jsp</result>
    </action>
</package>
```

The **SingleUpload.jsp** page (shown in Listing 12.2) contains a form with a **file** tag.

Listing 12.2: The SingleUpload.jsp page

```
<%@ taglib prefix="s" uri="/struts-tags" %>
<html>
<head>
<title>File Upload</title>
<style type="text/css">@import url(css/main.css);</style>
</head>
<body>
<div id="global">
    <h1>Single File Upload</h1>
    <s:fielderror />
    <s:form action="File_singleUpload"
            enctype="multipart/form-data">
        <s:textfield name="description" label="Description"/>
        <s:file name="attachment" label="Attachment"/>
        <s:submit />
    </s:form>
</div>
</body>
</html>
```

When the user submits the form, the **File_singleUpload** action will be invoked. The **SingleFileUploadAction** class in Listing 12.3 handles this action.

Listing 12.3: The SingleFileUploadAction class

```
package app12a;
import java.io.File;
import javax.servlet.ServletContext;
import org.apache.struts2.ServletActionContext;
import com.opensymphony.xwork2.ActionSupport;

public class SingleFileUploadAction extends ActionSupport {
    private File attachment;
    private String attachmentFileName;
    private String attachmentContentType;
    private String description;

    // getters and setters not shown

    public String upload() throws Exception {
        System.out.println(description);
        ServletContext servletContext =
                ServletActionContext.getServletContext();
        if (attachment != null) {
            // attachment will be null if there's an error,
            // such as if the uploaded file is too large
            String dataDir = servletContext.getRealPath("/WEB-INF");
            File savedFile = new File(dataDir, attachmentFileName);
            attachment.renameTo(savedFile);
        }
        return SUCCESS;
    }
}
```

The action class has three properties, **attachmentFileName**, **attachmentContentType**, and **description**, the first two of which are related to the uploaded file. It saves the uploaded file under **WEB-INF**, but you can choose a different location.

The **app12a** application also overrides the custom error messages by providing a new **struts-messages.properties** file in Listing 12.4.

Listing 12.4: The struts-messages.properties file

```
struts.messages.error.content.type.not.allowed=Error. File type not
allowed.
struts.messages.error.file.too.large=Error. File too large.
```

Run the **app12a** application by invoking this URL.

```
http://localhost:8080/app12a/File.action
```

You'll see the upload form like the one in Figure 12.3.

Figure 12.3: Single file upload

Multiple File Upload Example

The **app12b** application demonstrates multiple file upload. There are two actions in **app12b**, **File** (for displaying a file upload form) and **File_multipleUpload** (for handling the uploaded files). The action declarations are shown in Listing 12.5.

Listing 12.5: The action declarations

```
<package name="app12b" extends="struts-default">
    <action name="File">
        <result>/jsp/MultipleUpload.jsp</result>
    </action>
    <action name="File_multipleUpload"
            class="app12b.MultipleFileUploadAction" method="upload">
        <result name="input">/jsp/MultipleUpload.jsp</result>
        <result>/jsp/MultipleUpload.jsp</result>
    </action>
</package>
```

The **File** action displays the **MultipleUpload.jsp** page in Listing 12.6.

Listing 12.6: The MultipleUpload.jsp page

```
<%@ taglib prefix="s" uri="/struts-tags" %>
<html>
<head>
<title>File Upload</title>
<style type="text/css">@import url(css/main.css);</style>
</head>
<body>
<div id="global">
    <h1>Multiple File Upload</h1>
        <s:actionerror />
        <s:fielderror />
    <s:form action="File_multipleUpload"
            enctype="multipart/form-data">
        <s:file name="attachment" label="Attachment 1"/>
        <s:file name="attachment" label="Attachment 2"/>
        <s:file name="attachment" label="Attachment 3"/>
        <s:submit />
    </s:form>
</div>
</body>
</html>
```

When the file upload form is submitted, the **File_multipleUpload** action is invoked. This action is handled by the **MultipleFileUploadAction** class in Listing 12.7. Note that arrays are used for the uploaded files, file names, and content types.

Listing 12.7: The MultipleFileUploadAction class

```
package app12b;
import java.io.File;
import java.util.Map;
import javax.servlet.ServletContext;
import javax.servlet.http.HttpServletRequest;
import org.apache.struts2.ServletActionContext;
import com.opensymphony.xwork2.ActionContext;
import com.opensymphony.xwork2.ActionSupport;

public class MultipleFileUploadAction extends ActionSupport {
    private File[] attachment;
    private String[] attachmentFileName;
    private String[] attachmentContentType;

    // getters and setters not shown
```

```
public String upload() throws Exception {
    ServletContext servletContext =
            ServletActionContext.getServletContext();
    String dataDir = servletContext.getRealPath("/WEB-INF");
    for (int i=0; i < attachment.length; i++) {
        File savedFile = new File(dataDir,
                attachmentFileName[i]);
        attachment[i].renameTo(savedFile);
    }
    return SUCCESS;
}
}
```

You can start uploading multiple files by directing your browser here.

`http://localhost:8080/app12b/File.action`

You'll see a form similar to the one in Figure 12.4.

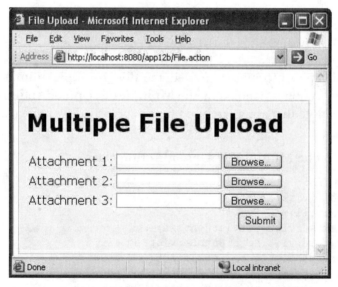

Figure 12.4: Multiple file upload

You can also use **List**s instead of arrays. The MultipleFileUploadAction2 class in Listing 12.8 shows how to use **List**s. Note that you must instantiate a **List** implementation for the **List** variables.

Listing 12.8: Using Lists

```
package app12a;
import com.opensymphony.xwork2.ActionSupport;
import java.io.File;
import java.util.ArrayList;
import java.util.List;
public class MultipleFileUploadAction2 extends ActionSupport {
    private List<File> attachment =
            new ArrayList<File>();
    private List<String> attachmentFileName =
            new ArrayList<String>();
    private List<String> attachmentContentType =
            new ArrayList<String>();

    // getters and setters not shown

    public String upload() throws Exception {
        for (String fileName : attachmentFileName) {
            System.out.println(fileName);
        }
        return SUCCESS;
    }
}
```

Using arrays are better than **List**s because with arrays you can iterate over the uploaded files over by index.

Summary

This chapter discussed file upload. Struts supports file upload through the File Upload interceptor that incorporates the Jakarta Commons FileUpload library. Two examples that illustrated single file upload and multiple file upload were presented in this chapter

.

Chapter 13
File Download

This chapter discusses file download, an important topic that does not often get enough attention in web programming books, and how Struts supports programmatic file download by providing the Stream result type. Two examples illustrate the use of the stream result type.

File Download Overview

Downloading files is a day-to-day activity for an Internet surfer. Writing a web application that allows only authorized users to download certain files is a different story. A solution would be to use the operating system's or the web container's authentication system. This authentication mechanism lets you password-protect files so that file downloading is allowed only after the user has entered the correct user name and password. However, if you have more than one user, the password must be shared, greatly reducing the effectiveness of the password. The more people know the password, the less secure it is. Furthermore, when many users use the same password, it is almost impossible to record who downloads what.

In other applications, you may want to dynamically send a file when the name or location of the file is not known at design time. For instance, in a product search form, you display the products found as the result of the search. Each product has a thumbnail image. Since you do not know at design time which product will be searched for, you do not know which image files to send to the browser.

In another scenario, you have a large and expensive image that should only be displayed on your web pages. How do you prevent other web sites from cross referencing it? You can by checking the **referer** header of each request for this image before allowing the image to be downloaded and only allowing access if the **referer** header contains your domain name.

Programmable file download can help solve all the problems detailed above. In short, programmable file download lets you select a file to send to the browser.

Note
To protect a file so that someone who knows its URL cannot download it, you must store the file outside the application directory or under **WEB-INF** or in external storage such as a database.

To send a file to the browser, do the following.

1. Set the response's content type to the file's content type. The **Content-Type** header specifies the type of the data in the body of an entity and consists of the media type and subtype identifiers. Visit http://www.iana.org/assignments/media-types to find all standard content types. If you do not know what the content type is or want the browser to always display the File Download dialog, set it to **Application/Octet-stream**. This value is case insensitive.
2. Add an HTTP response header named **Content-Disposition** and give it the value **attachment; filename=***theFileName*, where *theFileName* is the default name for the file that appears in the File Download dialog box. This is normally the same name as the file, but does not have to be so.

For instance, this code sends a file to the browser.

```
FileInputStream fis = new FileInputStream(file);
BufferedInputStream bis = new BufferedInputStream(fis);
byte[] bytes = new byte[bis.available()];
response.setContentType(contentType);
OutputStream os = response.getOutputStream();
bis.read(bytes);
os.write(bytes);
```

First, you read the file as a **FileInputStream** and load the content to a byte array. Then, you obtain the **HttpServletResponse** object's **OutputStream** and call its **write** method, passing the byte array.

The Stream Result Type

Struts provides the Stream result type specifically for file download. When using a Stream result, you don't need a JSP because the output will be flushed from an **InputStream**. The parameters a Stream result can take are listed in Table 13.1. All parameters are optional.

Name	Data Type	Default Value	Description
inputName	String	inputStream	The name of the action class property that returns the InputStream object to be flushed to the browser.
bufferSize	int	1024	The buffer size used when reading the InputStream and the OutputStream used for flushing data to the browser.
contentType	String	text/plain	Sets the Content-Type response header
contentLength	int		Sets the Content-Length response header
contentDisposition	String	inline	Sets the Content-Disposition response header

Table 13.1: Stream result parameters

Take the **app13a** application as an example. There are two actions that are related to file download, **ViewCss** and **DownloadCss**. **ViewCss** sends a CSS file to the browser and instructs the browser to display its content. **DownloadCss** file sends the CSS file as a file download. You can modify this example to work with other file types, not only CSS.

Whether the browser will show a file content or display a File Download dialog depends on the value you set the **Content-Type** header. Setting it to "text/css" tells the browser that the file is a CSS file and should be displayed. Assigning "application/octet-stream" tells the browser that the user should be given the chance to save the file. Listing 13.1 shows the action declarations in **app13a**. The **Menu** action displays the **Menu.jsp** page from which the user can select whether to view or download a CSS file.

Listing 13.1: The action declarations

```
<package name="app13a" extends="struts-default">
    <action name="Menu">
        <result>/jsp/Menu.jsp</result>
    </action>
    <action name="ViewCss" class="app13a.FileDownloadAction">
        <result name="success" type="stream">
            <param name="inputName">inputStream</param>
            <param name="contentType">text/css</param>
            <param name="contentDisposition">
                filename="main.css"</param>
            <param name="bufferSize">2048</param>
        </result>
    </action>
    <action name="DownloadCss" class="app13a.FileDownloadAction">
        <result name="success" type="stream">
            <param name="inputName">inputStream</param>
            <param name="contentType">
                application/octet-stream
            </param>
            <param name="contentDisposition">
                filename="main.css"
            </param>
            <param name="bufferSize">2048</param>
        </result>
    </action>
</package>
```

Note that the main difference between **ViewCss** and **DownloadCss** lies in the value of the **contentType** parameter. Both use the **FileDownloadAction** class in Listing 13.2. This class implements **ServletContextAware** because it needs access to the **ServletContext** object and use its **getResourceAsStream** method. Using this method is an easy way to return a resource as a **java.io.InputStream**.

Listing 13.2: The FileDownloadAction class

```
package app13a;
import java.io.InputStream;
import javax.servlet.ServletContext;
import org.apache.struts2.util.ServletContextAware;
import com.opensymphony.xwork2.ActionSupport;

public class FileDownloadAction extends ActionSupport
        implements ServletContextAware {
```

```
    private String filePath;
    private ServletContext servletContext;

    public void setServletContext(
            ServletContext servletContext) {
        this.servletContext = servletContext;
    }
    public void setFilePath(String filePath) {
        this.filePath = filePath;
    }
    public InputStream getInputStream() throws Exception {
        return servletContext.getResourceAsStream(filePath);
    }
}
```

The **FileDownloadAction** class has a **filePath** property that indicates the file path of the requested resource. You must set this property from your JSP, the **Menu.jsp** page shown in Listing 13.3.

Listing 13.3: The Menu.jsp file

```
<%@ taglib prefix="s" uri="/struts-tags" %>
<html>
<head>
<title>File Download</title>
<style type="text/css">@import url(css/main.css);</style>
</head>
<body>
<div id="global" style="width:200px">

    <s:url id="url1" action="ViewCss">
        <s:param name="filePath">css/main.css</s:param>
    </s:url>
    <s:a href="%{url1}">View CSS</s:a>

    <br/>
    <s:url id="url2" action="DownloadCss">
        <s:param name="filePath">css/main.css</s:param>
    </s:url>
    <s:a href="%{url2}">Download CSS</s:a>

</div>
</body>
</html>
```

The **Main.jsp** page employs two **url** tags with different parameters. The URLs are then used by the **a** tags on the page.

To test this example, point your browser to this URL:

```
http://localhost:8080/app13a/Menu.action
```

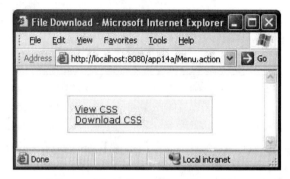

Figure 13.1: Downloading files

You'll see two links as shown in Figure 13.1. If you click the first link, the content of the **main.css** file will be displayed. If you click the second link, the File Download dialog of your browser will open and you can save the file.

Programmatic File Download

The preceding example showed how to use the **stream** result. On both actions, the user had to know the name of the resource and the path to the resource. The **app13b** application in this section shows how you can perform programmatic file download, in the case where the resource name is not known by the user. Here you can also restrict access to certain resources if you so wish.

Consider the **DisplayProducts** and **GetImage** actions declared in Listing 13.4.

Listing 13.4: Action declarations

```
<package name="app13b" extends="struts-default">
    <action name="DisplayProducts"
            class="app13b.DisplayProductsAction">
        <result>/jsp/Product.jsp</result>
```

```
    </action>
    <action name="GetImage" class="app13b.GetImageAction">
        <result name="success" type="stream">
            <param name="inputName">inputStream</param>
        </result>
    </action>
</package>
```

A product is represented by the **Product** class in Listing 13.5 and **DisplayProducts** obtains a list of products and displays the details of each product. The **DisplayProductsAction** class, the action class for **DisplayProducts**, is given in Listing 13.6.

Listing 13.5: The Product class

```
package app13b;
import java.io.Serializable;
public class Product implements Serializable {
    private int id;
    private String name;
    public Product() {
    }
    public Product (int id, String name) {
        this.id = id;
        this.name = name;
    }
    // getters and setters not shown
}
```

Listing 13.6: The DisplayProductsAction class

```
package app13b;
import java.util.ArrayList;
import java.util.List;
import com.opensymphony.xwork2.ActionSupport;

public class DisplayProductsAction extends ActionSupport {
    public List<Product> getProducts() {
        List<Product> products = new ArrayList<Product>();
        products.add(new Product(1, "Television"));
        products.add(new Product(2, "Computer"));
        products.add(new Product(3, "VCR"));
        products.add(new Product(4, "Game Console"));
        return products;
    }
}
```

The **Product.jsp** page in Listing 13.7 is used to display the product list.

Listing 13.7: The Product.jsp page

```
<%@ taglib prefix="s" uri="/struts-tags" %>
<html>
<head>
<title>File Download</title>
<style type="text/css">@import url(css/main.css);</style>
</head>
<body>
<div id="global" style="width:200px">

    <h3>Products</h3>
    <table>
    <tr>
        <th>Name</th>
        <th>Picture</th>
    </tr>
    <s:iterator value="products" id="product">
        <tr>
            <td><s:property value="#product.name"/></td>
            <td>
                <s:url id="url" action="GetImage">
                    <s:param name="productId">
                        <s:property value="#product.id"/>
                    </s:param>
                </s:url>
                <img src="<s:property value='#url'/>"
                        width="100" height="50"/>
        </td>
        </tr>
    </s:iterator>
    </table>
</div>
</body>
</html>
```

A product may have an image stored in the **images** directory of the application. A product image is named according to the product identifier in a web-friendly format (one of jpeg, gif, or png). For product identifier 3, the image name would be **3.gif** or **3.jpg** or **3.png**. Because the image file name is not stored, you have to find a way to display the image.

The **GetImage** action flushes an image to the browser. Note that in the **Product.jsp** page the **iterator** tag contains an **img** element whose source is a

URL that references to the **GetImage** action and passes a **productId** parameter.

Now, let's focus on the **GetImageAction** class in Listing 13.8.

Listing 13.8: The GetImageAction class

```
package app13b;
import java.io.IOException;
import java.io.InputStream;
import java.io.File;
import java.io.FileInputStream;
import javax.servlet.ServletContext;
import javax.servlet.http.HttpServletResponse;
import org.apache.struts2.ServletActionContext;
import org.apache.struts2.dispatcher.StreamResult;
import org.apache.struts2.interceptor.ServletResponseAware;
import org.apache.struts2.util.ServletContextAware;

import com.opensymphony.xwork2.ActionContext;
import com.opensymphony.xwork2.ActionSupport;
import com.opensymphony.xwork2.Result;

public class GetImageAction extends ActionSupport implements
        ServletResponseAware, ServletContextAware {

    private String productId;
    private HttpServletResponse servletResponse;
    private ServletContext servletContext;
    public void setServletResponse(HttpServletResponse
            servletResponse) {
        this.servletResponse = servletResponse;
    }
    public void setServletContext(ServletContext servletContext) {
        this.servletContext = servletContext;
    }
    public InputStream getInputStream() throws Exception {
        String contentType = "image/gif";
        String imageDirectory =
                servletContext.getRealPath("images");
        // The images can be a jpg or gif,
        // retrieve default image if no file was found
        File file = new File(imageDirectory, productId + ".gif");
        if (!file.exists()) {
            file = new File(imageDirectory, productId + ".jpg");
            contentType = "image/jpeg";
        }
```

```
        if (!file.exists()) {
            file = new File(imageDirectory, "noimage.jpg");
        }
        if (file.exists()) {
            Result result = ActionContext.getContext().
            getActionInvocation().getResult();
            if (result != null && result instanceof StreamResult) {
                StreamResult streamResult = (StreamResult) result;
                streamResult.setContentType(contentType);
            }
            try {
                return new FileInputStream(file);
            } catch (IOException ex) {
            }
        }
        return null;
    }

    public String getProductId() {
        return productId;
    }

    public void setProductId(String productId) {
        this.productId = productId;
    }
}
```

This class is similar to the **FileDownloadAction** class in **app13a**. However, **GetImage** class has a **productId** property that is set by the **productId** request parameter. The **getInputStream** method retrieves the image as a file and wraps it in a **FileInputStream**.

You can test this application by directing your browser to this URL.

```
http://localhost:8080/app13b/DisplayProducts.action
```

You'll see something similar to Figure 13.2.

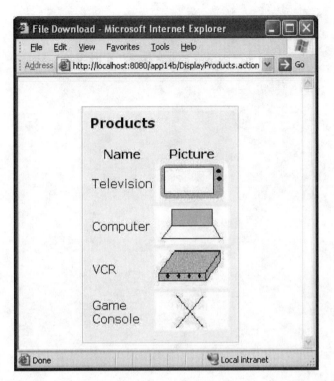

Figure 13.2: The images sent from the GetImageAction object.

Summary

In this chapter you have learned how file download work in web applications. You have also learned how to select a file and sent it to the browser.

Chapter 14
Securing Struts Applications

Security is one of the most critical issues in web application development. As for servlet applications, there are two ways to secure application resources, by configuring the application and by writing Java code. The former is more popular because of its flexibility. By editing your deployment descriptor (**web.xml** file), you can change your security policy without rewriting code. For instance, you can restrict access to certain roles and HTTP methods, determine how users can authenticate themselves, and so forth. Since Struts is based on the Servlet technology, securing a Struts application will center on this configuration plus the security feature in Struts itself.

To be good at security configuration, you need to be familiar with the concepts of principal and roles, therefore this chapter starts with a discussion of both. Afterwards, the chapter explains how to write a security policy and deals with authentication methods. After a section on how to hide resources and another on Struts-specific security features, this chapter concludes with the second way of security servlet applications: by writing code.

Principals and Roles

A principal is an entity which can be either an individual or an organization. A role is an abstract grouping of users. Regard a role as a position. Vera, Chuck and Dave are users. Administrator, Director, Manager, Programmer are roles. Any user can be in no role or in many roles. For example, Vera can be in the Manager and Programmer roles, Chuck can be in the Administrator role, and so on.

Every servlet container provides you with a different mechanism of managing users and roles. You should consult the documentation that accompanies the servlet container on this.

In Tomcat you manage principal and roles in the **tomcat-users.xml** file under the **conf** directory of the deployment directory. Here is an example of the **tomcat-users-xml** file.

```
<tomcat-users>
    <role rolename="manager"/>
    <role rolename="admin"/>
    <user username="vera" password="arev" roles="manager"/>
    <user username="chuck" password="chuck" roles="admin"/>
    <user username="dave" password="secret" roles="manager,admin"/>
</tomcat-users>
```

The file says that there are two roles (admin and manager) and three users (vera, chuck, and dave). You can add as many roles and users as you want to the **tomcat-users.xml** file.

Writing Security Policies

Writing a security policy involves the following tasks:

- Protecting resources
- Determining the login method for user authentication.

These tasks are discussed in the following subsections.

Protecting Resources

You enforce the security policy by using the **security-constraint** element in the deployment descriptor. Here is the description of this element.

```
<!ELEMENT security-constraint (display-name?,
    web-resource-collection+, auth-constraint?,
    user-data-constraint?)>
```

This means that the **security-constraint** element can have an optional **display-name** subelement, one or many **web-resource-collection** subelements, an optional **auth-constraint** subelement, and an optional **user-data-constraint** subelement.

You specify the set of web resources that you want to protect in the **web-resource-collection** element, and you use the **auth-constraint** element to define the user roles allowed to access them. The subelements are described further below.

You use the **web-resource-collection** element to specify which resources must be protected by specifying a URL pattern for those resources. In addition, you can also specify what HTTP methods (GET, POST, etc) should be allowed access to the protected resources. The **web-resource-collection** element can have the following subelements.

- **web-resource-name**. A resource identifier. This element is required.
- **decription**. A description of the resource. This element is optional.
- **url-pattern**. Specifies a URL pattern which the restriction must be applied to. There can be zero or more **url-pattern** elements in a **web-resource-collection** element. For example, if you want to protect the resources in the **members** and **trading** directories, you need two **url-pattern** elements.
- **http-method**. Specifies the restricted method. For example, if the value of the **http-method** element is **GET**, then all **GET** requests will be restricted.

The **auth-constraint** element can have the following subelements.

- **description**. A description. This is an optional element.
- **role-name**. The user role allowed access to the restricted resource. There can be zero to many **role-name** elements in an **auth-constraint** element.

The **user-data-constraint** element can contain the following elements:

- **description**. A description. This is an optional subelement.
- **transport-guarantee**. The possible values are **NONE, INTEGRAL, CONFIDENTIAL. NONE** means the application does not require any transport guarantees. **INTEGRAL** means the data must be transported in such a way that it cannot be changed in transit. **CONFIDENTIAL** means that the transmitted data must be encrypted.

The following is a **security-constraint** element.

```
<security-constraint>
    <web-resource-collection>
        <web-resource-name>Manager Area</web-resource-name>
        <url-pattern>/manager/*.do</url-pattern>
```

```
    </web-resource-collection>
    <auth-constraint>
        <role-name>manager</role-name>
    </auth-constraint>
</security-constraint>
```

The **security-constraint** element will cause the web container to block any request that match the pattern **/manager/*.do** that does not come from a user belonging to the manager role. Because no **http-method** element is used, the web container will attempt to block all requests regardless the HTTP method being used to access the resource.

In addition, you should also register all roles used to access the restricted resources by using the **security-role** element. Inside a **security-role** element, you write a **role-name** element for each role. For example, the following **security-role** element defines two roles, admin and manager.

```
<security-role>
    <role-name>admin</role-name>
    <role-name>manager</role-name>
</security-role>
```

Specifying the Login Method

After you specify which resources are restricted and which roles may access them, you must specify how a user can login to prove that he or she is in the allowed role(s). You specify the login method by using the **login-config** element. Here is the description of the **login-config** element.

```
<!ELEMENT login-config (auth-method?, realm-name?,
        form-login-config?)>
<!ELEMENT auth-method (#PCDATA)>
<!ELEMENT realm-name (#PCDATA)>
<!ELEMENT form-login-config (form-login-page, form-error-page)>
```

The **auth-method** element specifies the method for authenticating users. Its possible values are **BASIC**, **DIGEST**, **FORM**, or **CLIENT-CERT**. The next section, "Authentication Methods," explains more about these methods.

The **realm-name** element specifies a descriptive name that will be displayed in the standard Login dialog when using the BASIC authentication method.

The **form-login-config** element is used when the value of **<auth-method>** is FORM. It specifies the login page to be used and the error page to be displayed if authentication failed.

Here is a **login-config** element.

```
<login-config>
  <auth-method>BASIC</auth-method>
  <realm-name>User Basic Authentication</realm-name>
</login-config>
```

Authentication methods are the subject of discussion on the next section.

Authentication Methods

There are several authentication methods: basic, form-based, digest, Secure Socket Layer (SSL), and client certificate authentication. With the basic authentication, the web container asks the browser to display the standard Login dialog box which contains two fields: the user name and the password. The standard Login dialog box will look different in different browsers. In Internet Explorer, it looks like the one in Figure 14.1

Figure 14.1: The standard Login dialog box in Internet Explorer

If the user enters the correct user name and password, the server will display the requested resource. Otherwise, the Login dialog box will be redisplayed, asking the user to try again. The server will let the user try to log in three times, after which an error message is sent. The drawback of this method is that the user name and password are transmitted to the server using base64 encoding, which is a very weak encryption scheme. However, you can use SSL to encrypt the user's credential.

Form-based authentication is similar to Basic authentication. However, you specify a login page yourself. This gives you a chance to customize the look and feel of your login dialog. This authentication method will also display a custom Error page written by the developer on a failed attempt to login. Again, you can use SSL to encrypt users' credentials.

Digest authentication works like Basic authentication; however, the login information is not transmitted. Instead, the hash of the passwords is sent. This protects the information from malicious sniffers.

Basic and digest authentication methods are specified in RFC 2617, which you can find at ftp://ftp.isi.edu/in-notes/rfc2617.txt. More information about SSL can be found at http://home.netscape.com/eng/ssl3/3-SPEC.HTM.

The following subsections provide examples of the basic and form-based authentication methods.

Note
There are two possible error messages with regard to authentication, 401 and 403. The user will get a 401 if he or she cannot supply the correct user name and password of any user. A user is normally given three chances, but this is browser specific. The user will get a 403 if he or she can enter the correct user name and password of a user but the user is not in the allowed role list.

Using Basic Authentication

The **app14a** application presents an example of how to use basic authentication. There are two actions defined, **User_input** and **User**, as shown in Listing 14.1.

Listing 14.1: Action declarations

```
<package name="app14a" extends="struts-default">
    <action name="User_input">
        <result>/jsp/User.jsp</result>
    </action>
```

```
    <action name="User" class="app15a.User">
        <result>/jsp/Thanks.jsp</result>
    </action>
</package>
```

What is special is the way these resources are protected using configuration in the **web.xml** file, which is shown in Listing 14.2.

Listing 14.2: The deployment descriptor (web.xml file)

```
<?xml version="1.0" encoding="ISO-8859-1"?>
<web-app xmlns="http://java.sun.com/xml/ns/javaee"
    xmlns:xsi="http://www.w3.org/2001/XMLSchema-instance"
    xsi:schemaLocation="http://java.sun.com/xml/ns/javaee
       http://java.sun.com/xml/ns/javaee/web-app_2_5.xsd"
    version="2.5">

<filter>
    <filter-name>struts2</filter-name>
    <filter-
    class>org.apache.struts2.dispatcher.FilterDispatcher</filter-
    class>
</filter>
<filter-mapping>
    <filter-name>struts2</filter-name>
    <url-pattern>/*</url-pattern>
</filter-mapping>

<!-- Restrict direct access to JSPs.
     For the security constraint to work, the auth-constraint
     and login-config elements must be present -->
<security-constraint>
    <web-resource-collection>
        <web-resource-name>JSPs</web-resource-name>
        <url-pattern>/jsp/*</url-pattern>
    </web-resource-collection>
    <auth-constraint/>
</security-constraint>

<security-constraint>
    <web-resource-collection>
        <web-resource-name>Admin Area</web-resource-name>
        <url-pattern>/User_input.action</url-pattern>
        <url-pattern>/User.action</url-pattern>
    </web-resource-collection>
    <auth-constraint>
```

```
        <role-name>admin</role-name>
    </auth-constraint>
</security-constraint>
<login-config>
    <auth-method>BASIC</auth-method>
    <realm-name>User Basic Authentication</realm-name>
</login-config>
<security-role>
    <role-name>admin</role-name>
</security-role>

<error-page>
    <error-code>403</error-code>
    <location>/403.html</location>
</error-page>
</web-app>
```

Pay attention to the sections in bold. Practically, the URLs for invoking the two actions are protected. Using Tomcat with the following **tomcat-users.xml** file, you know that the actions can be accessed by Chuck and Dave, but not by Vera.

```
<?xml version='1.0' encoding='utf-8'?>
<tomcat-users>
    <role rolename="manager"/>
    <role rolename="admin"/>
    <user username="vera" password="arev" roles="manager"/>
    <user username="dave" password="secret" roles="manager,admin"/>
    <user username="chuck" password="chuck" roles="admin"/>
</tomcat-users>
```

Only users in the admin role can access it. Use this URL to test it:

```
http://localhost:8080/app14a/User_input.action
```

The first time you try to access this resource, you'll see a Basic authentication page that prompts you to enter the user name and password. If you do not enter the user name and password of a user in the admin role, you'll get a 403 error. The **error-page** section in the **web.xml** file tells the servlet container to display the **403.html** file upon a 403 error occurring. Without the **error-page** declaration, you'll get a standard servlet container error page, as shown in Figure 14.2.

You can use the following URL to test the application.

```
http://localhost:8080/app14a/displayAddOrderForm.do
```

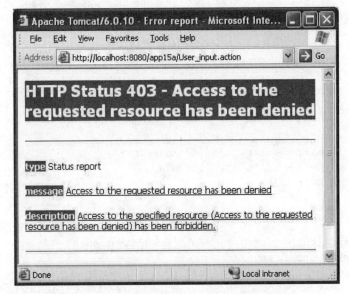

Figure 14.2: Tomcat default error page

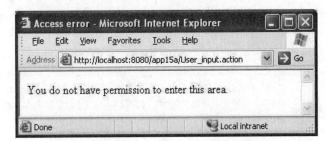

Figure 14.3: Custom error page

Using Form-Based Authentication

The **app14b** application is similar to **app14a**, except that **app14b** uses form-based authentication. Listing 14.3 shows the **web.xml** file.

Listing 14.3: The web.xml file for app14b

```
<?xml version="1.0" encoding="ISO-8859-1"?>
<web-app xmlns="http://java.sun.com/xml/ns/javaee"
    xmlns:xsi="http://www.w3.org/2001/XMLSchema-instance"
```

```
xsi:schemaLocation="http://java.sun.com/xml/ns/javaee
   http://java.sun.com/xml/ns/javaee/web-app_2_5.xsd"
version="2.5">

<filter>
    <filter-name>struts2</filter-name>
    <filter-
   class>org.apache.struts2.dispatcher.FilterDispatcher</filter-
   class>
</filter>
<filter-mapping>
    <filter-name>struts2</filter-name>
    <url-pattern>/*</url-pattern>
</filter-mapping>

<!-- Restrict direct access to JSPs.
    For the security constraint to work, the auth-constraint
    and login-config elements must be present -->
<security-constraint>
    <web-resource-collection>
        <web-resource-name>JSPs</web-resource-name>
        <url-pattern>/jsp/*</url-pattern>
    </web-resource-collection>
    <auth-constraint/>
</security-constraint>

<security-constraint>
    <web-resource-collection>
        <web-resource-name>Admin Area</web-resource-name>
        <url-pattern>/User_input.action</url-pattern>
        <url-pattern>/User.action</url-pattern>
    </web-resource-collection>
    <auth-constraint>
        <role-name>admin</role-name>
    </auth-constraint>
</security-constraint>
<login-config>
    <auth-method>FORM</auth-method>
    <form-login-config>
        <form-login-page>/login.html</form-login-page>
        <form-error-page>/loginError.html</form-error-page>
    </form-login-config>
</login-config>
<security-role>
    <role-name>admin</role-name>
</security-role>
```

```
<error-page>
    <error-code>403</error-code>
    <location>/403.html</location>
</error-page>

</web-app>
```

For the login form, the user name field must be **j_username**, the password
field must be **j_password**, and the form's action must be **j_security_check**.
Listing 14.4 presents the login form used in **app14b**.

Listing 14.4: The login page in app14b

```
<html>
<title>Authentication Form</title>
</head>
<body>
<form method="post" action="j_security_check">
    <table>
    <tr>
        <td colspan="2">Login:</td>
    </tr>
    <tr>
        <td>User Name:</td>
        <td><input type="text" name="j_username"/></td>
    </tr>
    <tr>
        <td>Password:</td>
        <td><input type="password" name="j_password"/></td>
    </tr>
    <tr>
        <td><input type="submit"/></td>
        <td><input type="reset"/></td>
    </tr>
    </table>
</form>
</body>
</html>
```

You can test the **app14b** application using the following URL:

```
http://localhost:8080/app14b/User_input.action
```

Like the **app14a** application, Chuck and Dave can access the restricted
resources but Vera cannot.

The first time you request the action, you'll see the login page in Figure 14.4.

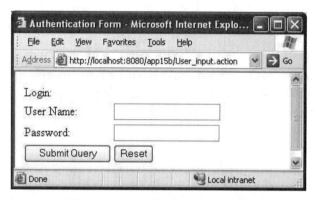

Figure 14.4: The Login page

There are two error pages provided in **app14b**. The **loginError.html**, declared in the **web.xml** file, is shown if the user cannot enter the correct user name and password. The **403.html** file is shown if the user can produce a correct user name and password but the user is not on the allowed role list.

Hiding Resources

An observant reader would notice that all access should go through the Struts action servlet and JSPs should not be accessible directly. Protecting JSPs from direct access can be easily achieved in several ways.

1. By placing the resources, i.e. JSPs, under **WEB-INF**, which makes the JSPs not accessible by typing their URLs. This way, the JSPs can only be displayed if they are a forward destination from the action servlet. However, you have also noticed that throughout this book all JSPs are not in the **WEB-INF** directory. This is because some containers (such as WebLogic) will not be able to forward control to a JSP under **WEB-INF**. Storing JSPs in WEB-INF may also change how other resources, such as image and JavaScript files, can be referenced from the JSPs.
2. By using a filter to protect the JSPs outside the **WEB-INF** directory. It is easy to implement such a filter. All you need to do is apply the filter so

that it will redirect access to a user page if the URL ends with .jsp. However, this is not as easy as the trick explained in Step 3.

3. By using the **security-constraint** element in the **web.xml** file to protect all JSPs but without providing a legitimate user role to access them. For example, in both **app14a** and **app14b**, you have two **security-constraint** elements in the **web.xml** files. One to prevent all JSPs from being accessed directly, another to protect actions.

```
<security-constraint>
    <web-resource-collection>
        <web-resource-name>
            Direct Access to JSPs
        </web-resource-name>
        <url-pattern>*.jsp</url-pattern>
    </web-resource-collection>
    <auth-constraint>
        <role-name>none</role-name>
    </auth-constraint>
</security-constraint>
<security-constraint>
    <web-resource-collection>
        <web-resource-name>Admin Area</web-resource-name>
        <url-pattern>/User_input.action</url-pattern>
        <url-pattern>/User.action</url-pattern>
    </web-resource-collection>
    <auth-constraint>
        <role-name>admin</role-name>
    </auth-constraint>
</security-constraint>
```

All URLs ending with .jsp can only be accessed by users in the **none** role. If you do not have a user in this role, no one can access the JSPs directly.

Struts Security Configuration

Struts adds a feature that allows you to specify which role(s) may access an action through the Roles interceptor. This interceptor can accept these parameters:

- **allowedRoles**. A list of roles that are allowed to access the corresponding action. Roles can be comma-delimited.

- **disallowedRoles**. A list of roles that are not allowed to access the corresponding action. Roles can be comma-delimited.

The **app14c** application provides an example of using the **roles** attribute. To be specific, you use the deployment descriptor in Listing 14.5, in which you restrict access to all URLs ending with **.action**, in effect restricting access to all Struts actions.

Listing 14.5: The deployment descriptor

```
<?xml version="1.0" encoding="ISO-8859-1"?>
<web-app xmlns="http://java.sun.com/xml/ns/javaee"
    xmlns:xsi="http://www.w3.org/2001/XMLSchema-instance"
    xsi:schemaLocation="http://java.sun.com/xml/ns/javaee
        http://java.sun.com/xml/ns/javaee/web-app_2_5.xsd"
    version="2.5">

<filter>
    <filter-name>struts2</filter-name>
    <filter-
    class>org.apache.struts2.dispatcher.FilterDispatcher</filter-
    class>
</filter>
<filter-mapping>
    <filter-name>struts2</filter-name>
    <url-pattern>/*</url-pattern>
</filter-mapping>

<!-- Restrict direct access to JSPs.
    For the security constraint to work, the auth-constraint
    and login-config elements must be present -->
<security-constraint>
    <web-resource-collection>
        <web-resource-name>JSPs</web-resource-name>
        <url-pattern>/jsp/*</url-pattern>
    </web-resource-collection>
    <auth-constraint/>
</security-constraint>

<security-constraint>
    <web-resource-collection>
        <web-resource-name>Admin Area</web-resource-name>
        <url-pattern>*.action</url-pattern>
    </web-resource-collection>
    <auth-constraint>
        <role-name>admin</role-name>
```

```
            <role-name>manager</role-name>
        </auth-constraint>
    </security-constraint>
    <login-config>
        <auth-method>BASIC</auth-method>
        <realm-name>User Basic Authentication</realm-name>
    </login-config>
    <security-role>
        <role-name>admin</role-name>
        <role-name>manager</role-name>
    </security-role>
</web-app>
```

You also specify that two roles may access the application, admin and manager.

Now, you have the following actions in the **app14c** application: **User_input** and **User**. You want both to be accessible by all managers and admins. The elements shown in Listing 14.6 shows you how to declare the actions and interceptors in both actions.

Listing 14.6: Action declarations

```
<package name="app14c" extends="struts-default">
    <action name="User_input">
        <interceptor-ref name="completeStack"/>
        <interceptor-ref name="roles">
            <param name="allowedRoles">admin,manager</param>
        </interceptor-ref>
        <result>/jsp/User.jsp</result>
    </action>
    <action name="User" class="app14c.User">
        <interceptor-ref name="completeStack"/>
        <interceptor-ref name="roles">
            <param name="allowedRoles">admin,manager</param>
        </interceptor-ref>
        <result>/jsp/Thanks.jsp</result>
    </action>
</package>
```

To test the **app14c** application, direct your browser to this URL.

```
http://localhost:8080/app14c/User_input.action
```

Programmatic Security

Even though configuring the deployment descriptor and specifying roles in the **tomcat-users.xml** file means that you do not need to write Java code, sometimes coding is inevitable. For example, you might want to record all the users that logged in. The **javax.servlet.http.HttpServletRequest** interface provides several methods that enable you to have access to portions of the user's login information. These methods are **getAuthType**, **isUserInRole**, **getPrincipal**, and **getRemoteUser**. The methods are explained in the following subsections.

The getAuthType Method

The **getAuthType** method has the following signature.

```
public String getAuthType()
```

This method returns the name of the authentication scheme used to protect the servlet. The return value is one of the following values: **BASIC_AUTH**, **FORM_AUTH**, **CLIENT_CERT_AUTH**, and **DIGEST_AUTH**. It returns **null** if the request was not authenticated.

The isUserInRole Method

Here is the signature of the **isUserInRole** method.

```
public boolean isUserInRole(String role)
```

This method indicates whether the authenticated user is included in the specified role. If the user has not been authenticated, the method returns false.

The getUserPrincipal Method

The signature of **getUserPrincipal** is as follows.

```
public java.security.Principal getUserPrincipal()
```

This method returns a **java.security.Principal** object containing the name of the current authenticated user. If the user has not been authenticated, the method returns **null**.

The getRemoteUser Method

The **getRemoteUser** method has the following signature.

```
public String getRemoteUser()
```

This method returns the name of the user making this request, if the user has been authenticated. Otherwise, it returns null. Whether the user name is sent with each subsequent request depends on the browser and type of authentication.

Summary

In this chapter, you have learned how to configure the deployment descriptor to restrict access to some or all of the resources in your servlet applications. The configuration means that you need only to modify your deployment descriptor file—no programming is necessary. In addition, you have also learned how to use the **roles** attribute in the **action** elements in your Struts configuration file.

Writing Java code to secure Web applications is also possible through the following methods of the **javax.servlet.http.HttpServletRequest** interface: **getRemoteUser**, **getPrincipal**, **getAuthType**, and **isUserInRole**.

Chapter 15
Preventing Double Submits

Double form submits normally happen by accident or by the user's not knowing what to do when it is taking a long time to process a form. Some double submits have fatal consequences, some simply unpleasant. For instance, when submitting an online payment in which a credit card will be charged, the user may click the submit button for the second time if the server's response time is too slow. This may result in his/her credit card being charged twice. Other less critical examples include forms that add a new product and doubly submitting these forms will cause a product to be added twice.

Browsers' behaviors are different with regard to preventing double submits. Mozilla Firefox will not respond to subsequent clicks on the same button, providing you with some kind of protection. Other browsers, including Internet Explorer, do not yet implement the feature to prevent double submits. In addition, in Mozilla and non-Mozilla browsers, if the user presses the browser Refresh/Reload button after the request is processed, the same request will be submitted again, effectively causing double submits. As such, you should always take action if double submits may cause inadvertent consequences in your business logic.

Struts has built-in support for preventing double submits. It employs a technique that you can also find in other web application development technologies. This technique involves storing a unique token in the server and inserting a copy of the token into a form. When the form is submitted, this token is also sent to the server. The server application will compare the token with its own copy for the current user. If they match, form submission is considered valid and the token is reset. Subsequent (accidental) submits of the same form will fail because the token on the server have been reset.

This chapter explains how to use Struts' built-in feature for preventing double submits.

Managing Tokens

Struts provides the **token** tag that generates a unique token. This tag, which must be enclosed in a **form** tag, inserts a hidden field into the form and stores the token in the **HttpSession** object. If you use the **debug** tag on the same page as the form, you'll see a session attribute **session.token** with a 32 character value.

The use of **token** must be accompanied by one of two interceptors, Token and Token Session, that are capable of handling tokens. The Token interceptor, upon a double submit, returns the result "invalid.token" and adds an action error. The default message for this error is

```
The form has already been processed or no token was supplied, please
try again.
```

This is confusing for most users. Should they try again by resubmitting the form? Hasn't the form been processed?

To override the message, you can create a validation file and add a value for the key **struts.messages.invalid.token**. The supporting class for the Token interceptor is **org.apache.struts2.interceptor.TokenInterceptor**. Therefore, to override the message, you must place your key/value pair in a **TokenInterceptor.properties** file and place it under this directory:

```
/WEB-INF/classes/org/apache/struts2/interceptor
```

The Token Session interceptor extends the Token interceptor and provides a more sophisticated service. Instead of returning a special result and adding an action error, it simply blocks subsequent submits. As a result, the user will see the same response as if there were only one submit.

The following sections provide examples on both interceptors.

Using the Token Interceptor

The **app15a** application shows how you can use the Token interceptor. The directory structure of **app15a** is shown in Figure 15.1.

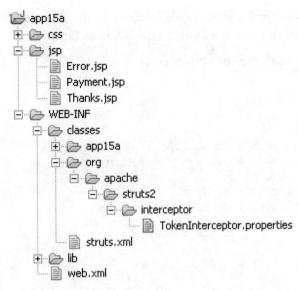

Figure 15.1: app15a directory structure

There are two actions in the application, **Pay_input** and **Pay**. The declarations for these actions are shown in Listing 15.1. **Pay_input** displays the **Payment.jsp** page, which contains a form to take payment details. Submitting the form invokes the **Pay** action. The **Pay** action is protected by the Token interceptor.

Listing 15.1: The action declarations

```
<package name="app15a" extends="struts-default">
    <action name="Pay_input">
        <result>/jsp/Payment.jsp</result>
    </action>
    <action name="Pay" class="app15a.Payment">
        <interceptor-ref name="token"/>
        <interceptor-ref name="basicStack"/>
        <result name="invalid.token">/jsp/Error.jsp</result>
        <result name="input">/jsp/Payment.jsp</result>
        <result>/jsp/Thanks.jsp</result>
    </action>
</package>
```

The **Pay** action provides three results. The **invalid.token** result, executed if a token is invalid, forwards to the **Error.jsp** page. The **input** result, which will be executed if input validation failed, forwards to the **Payment.jsp** page. Finally, the **success** result forwards to the **Thanks.jsp** page.

Listing 15.2: The Payment action class

```
package app15a;
import java.util.ArrayList;
import java.util.List;

import com.opensymphony.xwork2.ActionSupport;
public class Payment extends ActionSupport {
    private double amount;
    private int creditCardType;
    private String nameOnCard;
    private String number;
    private String expiryDate;

    // getters and setters not shown

    public String execute() {
        // simulate a long processing task
        try {
            Thread.sleep(4000);
        } catch (InterruptedException e) {
        }
        return SUCCESS;
    }
}
```

The **Pay** action uses the **Payment** class in Listing 15.2 as its action class. The class simulates a long processing task that will take four seconds, giving you a chance to double submit the form.

The **TokenInterceptor.properties** file in Listing 15.3 overrides the message upon an invalid token. The **Payment.jsp** page, the **Error.jsp** page, and the **Thanks.jsp** page are shown in Listings 15.4, 15.5, and 15.6, respectively.

Listing 15.3: The TokenInterceptor.properties file

```
struts.messages.invalid.token=You have submitted the form the second
time. Please contact the administrator.
```

Listing 15.4: The Payment.jsp page

```
<%@ taglib prefix="s" uri="/struts-tags" %>
<html>
```

```
<head>
<title>Check out</title>
<style type="text/css">@import url(css/main.css);</style>
<style>
.errorMessage {
    color:red;
}
</style>
</head>
<body>
<div id="global" style="width:350px">
    <h3>Please enter the amount and your credit card details</h3>
    <s:form action="Pay">
        <s:token/>
        <s:textfield name="amount" label="Amount"/>
        <s:select name="creditCardType" label="Credit Card"
list="#{'1':'Visa', '2':'Mastercard', '3':'American Express'}"/>
        <s:textfield name="nameOnCard" label="Name on Credit Card"/>
        <s:textfield name="number" label="Credit Card Number"/>
        <s:textfield name="expiryDate" label="Expiry Date (mm/yy)"/>
        <s:submit/>
    </s:form>
</div>
</body>
</html>
```

Listing 15.5: The Error.jsp page

```
<%@ taglib prefix="s" uri="/struts-tags" %>
<html>
<head>
<title>Thank you</title>
<style type="text/css">@import url(css/main.css);</style>
</head>
<body>
<div id="global">
    <s:actionerror/>
</div>
</body>
</html>
```

Listing 15.6: The Thanks.jsp page

```
<%@ taglib prefix="s" uri="/struts-tags" %>
<html>
<head>
<title>Thank you</title>
```

```
<style type="text/css">@import url(css/main.css);</style>
</head>
<body>
<div id="global">
Thank you. We will ship your order within 24 hours.
</div>
</body>
</html>
```

To test this application, direct your browser to this URL.

```
http://localhost:8080/app15a/Pay_input.action
```

Figure 15.2 shows the form.

Figure 15.2: The Payment form

Click the Submit button and quickly click it again. You will see an error message displayed on your browser.

Using the Token Session Interceptor

The **app15b** application illustrates the use of the Token Session interceptor. This example is very similar to **app15a,** however there is no longer a properties file for handling error messages or a JSP for displaying an error message. Figure 15.3 shows the directory structure of **app15b.**

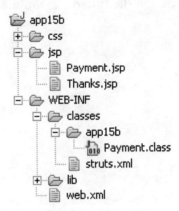

Figure 15.3: app15b directory structure

Listing 15.7 shows the action declarations. Instead of the Token interceptor for the **Pay** action, we use the Token Session interceptor. The JSPs are the same as those in **app15a** and will not be reprinted here.

Listing 15.7: The action declarations of app15b

```
<package name="app15b" extends="struts-default">
    <action name="Pay_input">
        <result>/jsp/Payment.jsp</result>
    </action>
    <action name="Pay" class="app15b.Payment">
        <interceptor-ref name="tokenSession"/>
        <interceptor-ref name="basicStack"/>
        <result name="invalid.token">/jsp/Error.jsp</result>
        <result name="input">/jsp/Payment.jsp</result>
        <result>/jsp/Thanks.jsp</result>
    </action>
</package>
```

To test this application, direct your browser to this URL.

```
http://localhost:8080/app15b/Pay_input.action
```

Summary

Double form submits normally happen by accident or by the user's not knowing what to do when it is taking a long time to process a form. The technique to prevent a form from being submitted twice is by employing a token which is reset at the first submit of a form. Struts has built-in support for handling this token, through the **token** tag and the Token and Token Session interceptors.

Chapter 16
Debugging and Profiling

This chapter discusses two related topics that can help you debug your application, debugging and profiling. Debugging is made easy by the introduction of the **debug** tag in the Struts tag library and the Debugging interceptor. Profiling lets you profile your application courtesy of the Profiling interceptor.

This chapter starts with the **debug** tag and proceeds with the Debugging interceptor. It then concludes with profiling.

The debug Tag

The **debug** tag displays the content of the Value Stack and other objects. Using **debug** is a no-brainer as you need only write:

```
<s:debug/>
```

This tag has one attribute, **id**, but you hardly need to use it.

The code in Listing 16.1 is a JSP that uses a **debug** tag.

Listing 16.1: The Debug.jsp page

```
<%@ taglib prefix="s" uri="/struts-tags" %>
<html>
<head>
<title>debug Tag Example</title>
<style type="text/css">@import url(css/main.css);</style>
</head>
<body>
    <s:debug/>
</body>
</html>
```

You can direct your browser to this URL to test the **debug** tag.

`http://localhost:8080/app16a/Debug.action`

The page in Figure 16.1 shows how the tag is initially rendered.

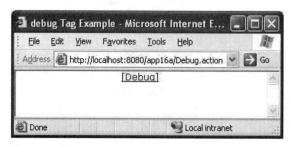

Figure 16.1: The Debug tag

If you click the **[Debug]** link, you'll see the stack objects and the objects in the context map, as shown in Figure 16.2.

You can use the **debug** tag to see the values of action properties and the contents of objects such as the session and application maps. This will help you pinpoint any error in your application quickly.

The Debugging Interceptor

The Debugging interceptor, which is part of the default stack, allows you to look into the Value Stack and other objects. You can invoke this interceptor by adding **debug=xml** or **debug=console** to the URL that invokes an action.

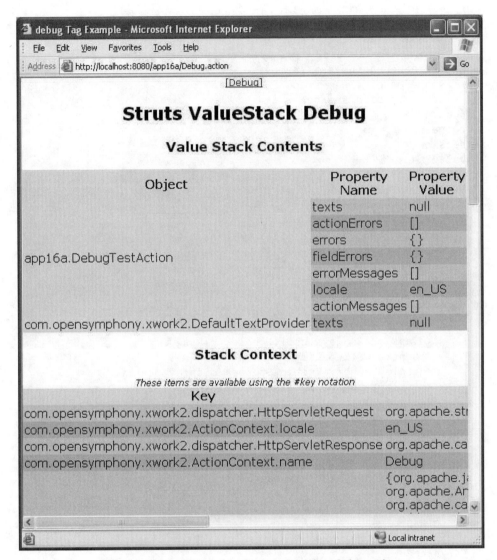

Figure 16.2: Useful information for debugging

Appending **debug=xml** will result in an XML that contains the values of the Value Stack and other objects, such as the following:

```
<debug>
  <parameters/>
  <context>
    <attr/>
    <report.conversion.errors>false</report.conversion.errors>
```

```
        <struts.actionMapping>
          <class>class
           org.apache.struts2.dispatcher.mapper.ActionMapping</class>
          <name>DebuggingTest</name>
          <namespace>/</namespace>
        </struts.actionMapping>
      </context>
      <request/>
      <session/>
      <valueStack>
        <value>
          <actionErrors/>
          <actionMessages/>
          <amount>0.0</amount>
          <class>class app16a.Profiling</class>
          <errorMessages/>
          <errors/>
          <fieldErrors/>
          <locale>
            <ISO3Country>USA</ISO3Country>
            <ISO3Language>eng</ISO3Language>
            <class>class java.util.Locale</class>
            <country>US</country>
            <displayCountry>United States</displayCountry>
            <displayLanguage>English</displayLanguage>
            <displayName>English (United States)</displayName>
            <displayVariant></displayVariant>
            <language>en</language>
            <variant></variant>
          </locale>
          <transactionType>0</transactionType>
        </value>
        <value>
          <class>class
           com.opensymphony.xwork2.DefaultTextProvider</class>
        </value>
      </valueStack>
    </debug>
```

Using **debug=console** displays a console like the one shown in Figure 16.3. You can enter an OGNL expression to the bottom of the page and the value will be displayed.

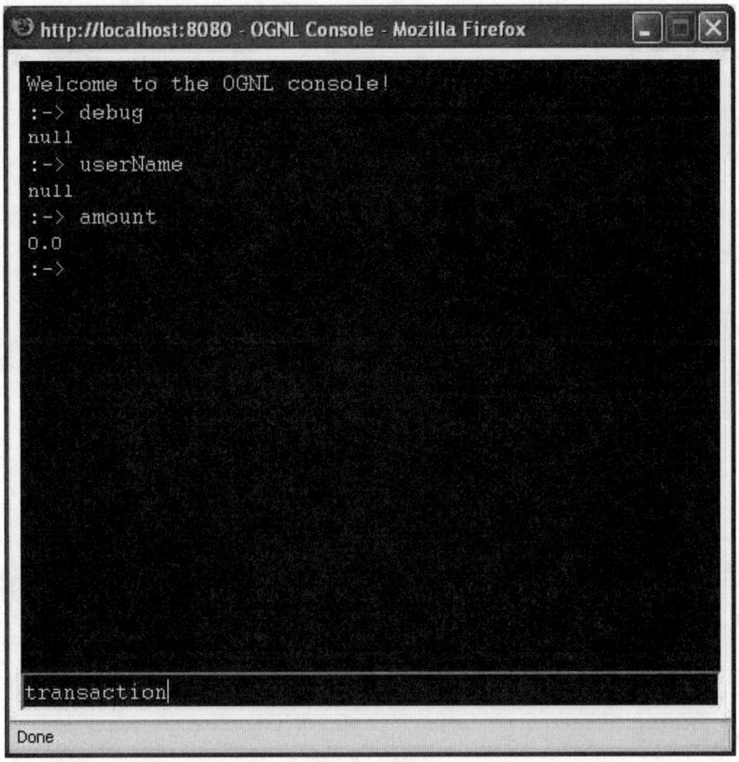

Figure 16.3: The OGNL console

Note

When I tested this feature, it did not work with Internet Explorer but worked perfectly with Mozilla Firefox.

Profiling

Struts supports profiling that can potentially identify any bottleneck in your program. Struts keeps track the time taken by its filter dispatcher, each interceptor, action execution, and result execution with the help of a class called **UtilTimerStack** (a member of the **com.opensymphony.xwork2.util.profiling** package). By default, however, the profiling result is not shown. The Profiling interceptor, which is part of the default stack, can help activate profiling. When profiling is activated for a particular action, the profiling result is printed by an internal logger in

UtilTimerStack on the container console or to a log file, depending on the setting of your container. If you're using Tomcat, this will be the console (on Windows) or the **catalina.out** file (on Unix and Linux).

Here is an example of a profiling result for an action that uploads a file.

```
INFO: [80ms] - FilterDispatcher_doFilter:
  [40ms] - Handling request from Dispatcher
    [0ms] - create DefaultActionProxy:
      [0ms] - create DefaultActionInvocation:
        [0ms] - actionCreate: SingleUpload2
    [40ms] - invoke:
    [40ms] - interceptor: fileUpload
      [20ms] - invoke:
        [20ms] - interceptor: exception
          [20ms] - invoke:
            [20ms] - interceptor: servletConfig
              [20ms] - invoke:
                [20ms] - interceptor: prepare
                  [20ms] - invoke:
                    [20ms] - interceptor: checkbox
                      [20ms] - invoke:
                        [20ms] - interceptor: params
                          [10ms] - invoke:
                            [10ms] - interceptor: conversionError
                              [10ms] - invoke:
                                [0ms] - invokeAction: Upload2
                                [10ms] - executeResult: success
```

Each line represents an activity. On the left of each line is the accumulated time taken to invoke the activity. For example, the bottommost line says that executing the result took 10ms, whereas invoking the **Upload2** action took 0ms. Of course it does not mean that there was no time at all to execute the action, it's just that it took less than what the timer can measure.

The Conversion Error interceptor's accumulated time is also 10ms, which means the invocation of this interceptor took 0ms because the activities invoked after it consumed 10ms. The File Upload interceptor took 20ms to execute (40ms – 20ms), and so on.

There are a few ways to activate profiling. Once it is active, it will stay active until it's turned off or until the application is restarted.

1. Through the request parameter, by adding **profiling=true** or **profiling=yes** to the URL that invokes the action to be profiled. For

this to take effect, the **struts.devMode** property must be **true**. For example, this URL turns on profiling.

```
http://localhost:8080/app16a/Test.action?profiling=true
```

To turn profiling off, use this URL.

```
http://localhost:8080/app16a/Test.action?profiling=false
```

Note that "profiling" is the default profiling key defined in the Profiling interceptor. You can override this if you have to, for example because you have a form input with the same name, by using the **param** element. For instance, this changes the profiling key to **pf** so that you can turn on and off profiling by adding the request parameter **pf=true** or **pf=false**.

```
<action name="ProfilingTest" class="app16a.Profiling">
    <interceptor-ref name="profiling">
        <param name="profilingKey">pf</param>
    </interceptor-ref>
    <interceptor-ref name="basicStack"/>
    <result>/jsp/OK.jsp</result>
</action>
```

2. By setting the active property of the **UtilTimerStack** object through code in a servlet listener or your action method.

```
public String execute() {
    UtilTimerStack.setActive(true);

    // do something
    return SUCCESS;
}
```

3. By setting the **UtilTimerStack.ACTIVATE_PROPERTY** to true:

```
System.setProperty(UtilTimerStack.ACTIVATE_PROPERTY, "true");
```

You can also monitor a certain activity in your action code. To do this, you need to call the **push** and **pop** methods on **UtilTimerStack**:

```
String activityName = "database access";
UtilTimerStack.push(activityName);
try {
    // do some code
} finally {
    UtilTimerStack.pop(activityName);
}
```

Summary

This chapter discusses two important topics that can help you make more robust applications, debugging and profiling. For debugging you use the **debug** tag and the Debugging interceptor. Profiling is a bundled feature in Struts that just needs activation. The Profiling interceptor can be used to activate profiling. Alternatively, you can use code to activate it.

Chapter 17
Progress Meters

What do you do if one of your actions takes five minutes to complete and you don't want your user worried or sleepy? Show a progress meter! In a web application writing a progress meter is not an easy task, you would spend at least days on it. Happily, Struts has an easy to use interceptor, Execute and Wait, that is good at emulating a progress meter for heavy tasks.

This chapter shows you how to use this interceptor.

The Execute and Wait Interceptor

Time consuming tasks, ones that take minutes, should be handled differently in web applications than they are in desktop programs. They pose more risks in the former because HTTP connections may time out, something not possibly occurring in the latter.

The Execute and Wait interceptor was designed to handle such situations. Since it's not part of the default stack, actions that need this interceptor must declare it and it must come last after in the interceptor stack.

This interceptor runs on a per-session basis, which means the same user may not cause two instances of this interceptor (recall that each action has its own instance of any declared interceptor) to run in parallel. An action backed by this interceptor will execute normally. However, Execute and Wait will assign a background thread to handle the action and forward the user to a wait result before the execution finishes and schedule the result to hit the same action again. On subsequent requests, if the first action has not finished executing, the wait result is sent again. If it has finished, the user will get a final result for that action.

A wait result acts like a dispatcher result. However, the view it forwards to has this meta tag that reloads the same URL after n seconds:

```
<meta http-equiv="refresh" content="n;url"/>
```

By default *n* is 5 and *url* is the same URL used to invoke the current action.

You can create your own wait view if you don't like the default. If no wait result is found under the action declaration, the default will be used.

The Execute and Wait interceptor can take these parameters, all optional.

- **threadPriority**. The priority to assign the thread. The default value is **Thread.NORM_PRIORITY**.
- **delay**. The number of milliseconds to wait before the user is forwarded the wait result. The default is 0.
- **delaySleepInterval**. Specifies the number of milliseconds the main thread (the one that creates a background thread to handle the action) has to wake up to check if the background process has been completed. The default is 100 and this parameter only takes effect if the delay is not zero.

The delay can be used if you don't want to send the wait result right away. For example, you can set it to 2,000 so that the wait result will only be sent if the action takes longer than two seconds.

Let's have a look at two examples in the section to follow.

Using the Execute and Wait Interceptor

Two examples are given to illustrate how to use Execute and Wait to emulate a progress meter. The first example uses the default wait result and the second uses a custom one. Both examples use the action class shown in Listing 17.1.

Listing 17.1: The HeavyDuty action class

```
package app17a;
import com.opensymphony.xwork2.ActionSupport;

public class HeavyDuty extends ActionSupport {
    public String execute() {
        try {
```

```
            Thread.sleep(12000);
        } catch (Exception e) {
        }
        return SUCCESS;
    }
    private int complete = 0;
    public int getComplete() {
        complete += 10;
        return complete;
    }

}
```

The **execute** method of the action class takes twelve seconds to complete, enough to show off the progress meter. The complete field and its getter are only used by the second example.

The action declaration for the first example is given in Listing 17.2.

Listing 17.2: The action declaration for the first example

```
<package name="app17a" extends="struts-default">
    <action name="HeavyDuty1" class="app17a.HeavyDuty">
        <interceptor-ref name="defaultStack"/>
        <interceptor-ref name="execAndWait">
            <param name="delay">1500</param>
        </interceptor-ref>
        <result>/jsp/OK.jsp</result>
    </action>
</package>
```

Since Execute and Wait is not part of the default stack, you must declare it explicitly and it must be the last interceptor to run. No wait result is declared and the final result is a dispatcher that forwards to the **OK.jsp** page. The delay is set to 1,500 milliseconds, which means the wait result will be sent after 1,5 seconds.

To test the example, direct your browser to this URL.

```
http://localhost:8080/app17a/HeavyDuty1.action
```

The wait page is shown in Figure 17.1. Pretty standard and uninspiring.

Figure 17.1: The standard wait page

If you're interested enough to check, you'll see the source of the wait page as follows.

```html
<html>
    <head>
        <meta http-equiv="refresh"
                content="5;url=/app17a/HeavyDuty1.action"/>
    </head>
    <body>
        Please wait while we process your request...
        <p/>
        This page will reload automatically and display your request
        when it is completed.
    </body>
</html>
```

Notice the meta tag? That's the one that forces the page to refresh every five seconds.

Using A Custom Wait Page

The second example is similar to the first one and uses the action class in Listing 17.1. It also uses the **complete** property of the action class to show the progress to the user. The second example also differs from the first in that it employs a custom wait page, as shown in the action declaration in Listing 17.3.

Listing 17.3: The action declaration for the second example

```
<package name="app17a" extends="struts-default">
```

```
<action name="HeavyDuty2" class="app17a.HeavyDuty">
    <interceptor-ref name="defaultStack"/>
    <interceptor-ref name="execAndWait">
        <param name="delay">1500</param>
    </interceptor-ref>
    <result name="wait">/jsp/Wait.jsp</result>
    <result>/jsp/OK.jsp</result>
</action>
</package>
```

Note that a wait result is present that forwards to a **Wait.jsp** page (See Listing 17.4). It is an ordinary JSP that has a meta tag that refreshes the page every two seconds. Since the URL part is not present in the meta tag, the same page will be reloaded.

Listing 17.4: The Wait.jsp page

```
<%@ taglib prefix="s" uri="/struts-tags" %>
<html>
<head>
<head>
<meta http-equiv="refresh" content="2;"/>
<title>Wait</title>
<style type="text/css">@import url(css/main.css);</style>
<style>
.errorMessage {
    color:red;
}
</style>
</head>
<body>
<div id="global" style="width:350px">
    Please wait... (<s:property value="complete"/>% complete)
</div>
</body>
</html>
```

Another thing to note is that it displays the value of **complete**. Its getter increments its value by 10 every time it is called.

```
private int complete = 0;
public int getComplete() {
    complete += 10;
    return complete;
}
```

To test the example, direct your browser here.

```
http://localhost:8080/app17a/HeavyDuty2.action
```

The wait page is shown in Figure 17.2. Notice that it looks more like a progress meter that indicates how much progress is being made?

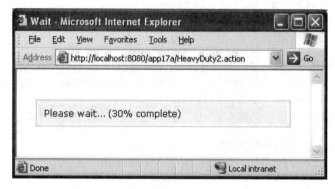

Figure 17.2: A custom wait page

Summary

This chapter discusses how you can use the Execute and Wait interceptor to handle time-consuming tasks. The trick is to create a background thread that executes the action and forward the user to a temporary wait page that keeps hitting the same action until the background thread finishes its task.

Chapter 18
Custom Interceptors

There are more than a dozen default interceptors that come with Struts. Input validation, for instance, is handled by the Validation interceptor. Unplug this interceptor and validation will stop working. File upload is so smooth thanks to another interceptor, the File Upload interceptor. Some of the interceptors may prevent the action from being executed if certain conditions are not met. For example, the Validation interceptor keeps an action from firing if an error occurs during the validation of that action.

For most applications, the default interceptors are sufficient. However, there are times when you need to create your own interceptor. This chapter explains how.

The Interceptor Interface

Technically, an interceptor is a Java class that implements the **com.opensymphony.xwork2.interceptor.Interceptor** interface. The interface is shown in Listing 18.1.

Listing 18.1: The Interceptor interface

```
package com.opensymphony.xwork2.interceptor;
import com.opensymphony.xwork2.ActionInvocation;
import java.io.Serializable;

public interface Interceptor extends Serializable {
    void destroy();
    void init();
    String intercept(ActionInvocation invocation) throws Exception;
}
```

This interface has three lifecycle methods:

- **init**. This method is called once right after the interceptor is created. An interceptor author overrides this method to perform resource initialization.
- **intercept**. This method is called every time the request for an action is invoked, giving the interceptor a chance to do something before and after the action is executed.
- **destroy**. The method is called before the interceptor is destroyed. Code to release resources should be written here.

Struts calls the **intercept** method of each interceptor registered for an action. Each time this method is called, Struts passes an instance of the **com.opensymphony.xwork2.ActionInvocation** interface. An **ActionInvocation** represents the execution state of an action, from which an interceptor can obtain the **Action** object as well as the **Result** object associated with the action. To let the execution chain proceed to the next level, the interceptor calls the **invoke** method on **ActionInvocation**.

You can also attach **PreResultListener** listeners to an **ActionInvocation**, by calling the **addPreResultListener** method on the **ActionInvocation**. The **com.opensymphony.xwork2.interceptor.PreResultListener** interface allows you to do something after the action is executed but before the execution of the result. This interface has one callback method, **beforeResult**:

```
void beforeResult(com.opensymphony.xwork2.ActionInvocation
        invocation, java.lang.String resultCode)
```

The **AbstractInterceptor** class implements **Interceptor** and provides empty implementations of the **init** and **destroy** methods. Since not all interceptors need to initialize resources or do anything when they are destroyed, extending **AbstractInterceptor** saves your from implementing **init** and **destroy**.

The **AbstractInterceptor** class is shown in Listing 18.2.

Listing 18.2: The AbstractInterceptor class

```
package com.opensymphony.xwork2.interceptor;
import com.opensymphony.xwork2.ActionInvocation;
public abstract class AbstractInterceptor implements Interceptor {
    public void init() {
    }
    public void destroy() {
    }
```

```
    public abstract String intercept(ActionInvocation invocation)
        throws Exception;
}
```

Writing A Custom Interceptor

As an example, application **app18a** contains a custom interceptor named
DataSourceInjectorInterceptor. This interceptor injects a **DataSource** to an
action object. The action can in turn inject the **DataSource** to a Data Access
Object class (See the discussion of the DAO pattern in Chapter 11, "The
Persistence Layer"). The **DataSourceInjectorInterceptor** class is presented in
Listing 18.3. In this example, the **DataSource** is obtained once from a JNDI
lookup and is stored in a static variable.

Listing 18.3: The DataSourceInjectorInterceptor class

```
package interceptor;
import javax.naming.Context;
import javax.naming.InitialContext;
import javax.naming.NamingException;
import javax.sql.DataSource;

import com.opensymphony.xwork2.ActionInvocation;
import com.opensymphony.xwork2.interceptor.AbstractInterceptor;

public class DataSourceInjectorInterceptor extends
        AbstractInterceptor {
    private static DataSource dataSource;
    private String dataSourceName;
    public void setDataSourceName(String dataSourceName) {
        this.dataSourceName = dataSourceName;
    }

    public void init() {
        // init() is called AFTER properties are set
        if (dataSource == null) {
            System.out.println("Interceptor. init DS" );
            try {
                Context context = new InitialContext();
                dataSource = (DataSource)
                        context.lookup(dataSourceName);
            } catch (NamingException e) {
            }
```

```
        }
    }

    public String intercept(ActionInvocation invocation)
            throws Exception {
        Object action = invocation.getAction();
        if (action instanceof DataSourceAware) {
            ((DataSourceAware) action).setDataSource(dataSource);
        }
        return invocation.invoke();
    }

}
```

Every time an action backed by this interceptor is invoked, the interceptor injects the **DataSource** object. Not all actions will get this object, only those whose classes implement the **DataSourceAware** interface will. This interface is given in Listing 18.4.

Listing 18.4: The DataSourceAware interface

```
package interceptor;
import javax.sql.DataSource;

public interface DataSourceAware {
    void setDataSource(DataSource dataSource);
}
```

Using DataSourceInjectorInterceptor

Now that you have a custom interceptor, it is a good idea to put it to use. The **app18a** application employs a **Product_list** action that uses this interceptor. Note that since this is a custom interceptor, you must register it with the struts.xml file before you can use it. The action and interceptor declarations for **app18a** are shown in Listing 18.5.

Listing 18.5: The action declarations

```
<package name="app18a" extends="struts-default">
    <interceptors>
        <interceptor name="dataSourceInjector"
                class="interceptor.DataSourceInjectorInterceptor">
```

```
            <param name="dataSourceName">
                java:/comp/env/jdbc/myDataSource
            </param>
        </interceptor>
    </interceptors>

    <action name="Product_list" class="app18a.ListProductAction">
        <interceptor-ref name="dataSourceInjector"/>
        <interceptor-ref name="defaultStack"/>
        <result>/jsp/Products.jsp</result>
    </action>
</package>
```

The **Product_list** action lists products from a database. The database can be accessed by using the **DataSource** injected by the custom interceptor. The **ListProductAction** class in Listing 18.6 handles the action.

Listing 18.6: The ListProductAction class

```
package app18a;
import interceptor.DataSourceAware;
import java.util.List;
import javax.sql.DataSource;
import com.opensymphony.xwork2.ActionSupport;
public class ListProductAction extends ActionSupport implements
        DataSourceAware {
    private DataSource dataSource;
    private List<Product> products;

    public void setDataSource(DataSource dataSource) {
        this.dataSource = dataSource;
    }
    public List<Product> getProducts() {
        return products;
    }
    public void setProducts(List<Product> products) {
        this.products = products;
    }

    public String execute() {
        ProductDAO productDAO = new ProductDAO();
        productDAO.setDataSource(dataSource);
        products = productDAO.getAllProducts();
        return SUCCESS;
    }
}
```

There are two things to note. A product is represented by the **Product** class in Listing 18.7. A **Product** is a transfer object that encapsulates four properties, **productId, name, description,** and **price**. The **ListProductAction** class implements **DataSourceAware** so an instance of **ListProductAction** can be injected a **DataSource**.

Listing 18.7: The Product class

```
package app18a;
public class Product {
    private int productId;
    private String name;
    private String description;
    private double  price;
    // getters and setters not shown
}
```

The **ListProductAction** class uses the **ProductDAO** class (shown in Listing 18.8) to retrieve data from the **Products** table in the database. You must of course first create this table and populates it with data. The action injects the **ProductDAO** the **DataSource** by calling the **ProductDAO**'s **setDataSource** method.

Listing 18.8: The ProductDAO class

```
package app18a;
import java.sql.Connection;
import java.sql.PreparedStatement;
import java.sql.ResultSet;
import java.sql.SQLException;
import java.util.ArrayList;
import java.util.List;
import javax.sql.DataSource;

public class ProductDAO {
    private DataSource dataSource;
    public void setDataSource(DataSource dataSource) {
        this.dataSource = dataSource;
    }
    private static final String sql =
        "SELECT productId, name, description, price FROM Products";

    public List<Product> getAllProducts() {
        List<Product> products = new ArrayList<Product>();
        Connection connection = null;
        PreparedStatement pStatement = null;
```

```
            ResultSet resultSet = null;
            try {
                connection = dataSource.getConnection();
                pStatement = connection.prepareStatement(sql);
                resultSet = pStatement.executeQuery();
                while (resultSet.next()) {
                    Product product = new Product();
                    product.setProductId(resultSet.getInt("productId"));
                    product.setName(resultSet.getString("name"));
                    product.setDescription(
                            resultSet.getString("description"));
                    product.setPrice(resultSet.getDouble("price"));
                    products.add(product);
                }
            } catch (SQLException e) {
                e.printStackTrace();
            } finally {
                if (resultSet != null) {
                    try {
                        resultSet.close();
                    } catch (SQLException e) {
                    }
                }
                if (pStatement != null) {
                    try {
                        pStatement.close();
                    } catch (SQLException e) {
                    }
                }
                if (connection != null) {
                    try {
                        connection.close();
                    } catch (SQLException e) {
                    }
                }
            }
            return products;
    }
}
```

Direct your browser to this URL to invoke the custom interceptor.

```
http://localhost:8080/app18a/Product_list.action
```

You will see the results shown in your browser, like those in Figure 18.1. What you see depends on the content of the Products table in your database.

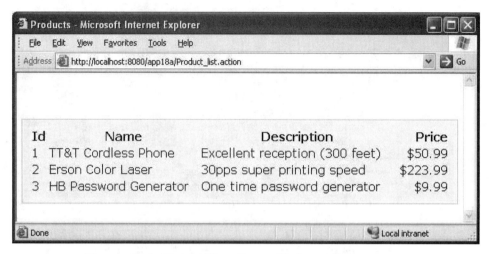

Figure 18.1: Using DataSourceInjectorInterceptor

Summary

You can write custom interceptors by implementing the **Interceptor** interface or extending the **AbstractInterceptor** class. In this chapter you learned how to write a custom interceptor and how to register it in an application.

Chapter 19
Custom Result Types

Struts ships with standard result types such as Dispatcher and Stream. This chapter explains how you can write a custom result type. An example, a CAPTCHA image producing result type, is also discussed.

Overview

A result type must implement the **com.opensymphony.xwork2.Result** interface. This interface has one method, **execute**, whose signature is as follows.

```
void execute(ActionInvocation invocation)
```

This method gets called when the result is executed. A result type author can write the code that will be run when an instance of the result type executes.

> ### Note
> **ActionInvocation** was explained in Chapter 18, "Custom Interceptors."

The **org.apache.struts2.dispatcher.StrutsResultSupport** class is a base class that implements the **Result** interface. Many result types extend this class instead of implementing **Result** directly.

Writing A Custom Plugin

This section shows you how to write your own result type. An instance of the custom result type developed in this chapter sends a CAPTCHA image. If you are not familiar with CAPTCHA, read the explanation below.

CAPTCHA is a slightly contrived acronym for "Completely Automated Public Turing test to tell Computers and Humans Apart." CAPTCHA images are often used in web forms. For example, a login form, such as the one in Figure 19.1, can use a CAPTCHA image in addition to the usual user name and password fields to make it more secure. A user who wishes to log in is asked to type in his/her user name and password plus the word displayed by the CAPTCHA image. Login is successful if the user entered the correct username and password as well as typed in the correct image word. A login form equipped with a CAPTCHA image is more secure because brute force, attempts to log in by using automatically generated pairs of user names and passwords until one successfully logs the offending computer in, will be less likely to be successful.

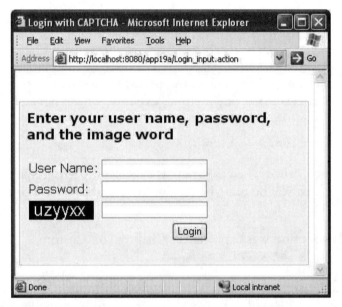

Figure 19.1: The CAPTCHA-facilitated login page

Another common use of CAPTCHA is to prevent spammers from sending messages to form owners. CAPTCHA forms may be used to frustrate automatic programs that submit forms because submission will only be successful if the correct word is also supplied.

The idea behind using CAPTCHA in forms is that computers are good with characters and numbers but not so with images. Therefore, if you ask the computer what the word in the image in Figure 19.1 reads, chances are the computer will not have a clue. Unless of course you use a program designed to recognize images, which are already in existence but are not so commonplace. In other words, CAPTCHA makes your login form more secure but there's no 100% guarantee that it will protect you from the most determined people.

In a web form, CAPTCHA works by producing a pair of words. The first word is converted into an image and the second word is produced using an algorithm in such a way that different instances of the same word always produce the same second word. However, knowing the second word is not good enough to find out what the first word is. Many implementations of CAPTCHA use a hash algorithm to produce the second word.

There are several ways of producing CAPTCHA-facilitated forms. One way would be to generate hundreds or thousands of word pairs and store them in a database. When you send the form to the browser, you also send the image version of the first word and the second word in a hidden field. When the form is submitted, the server matches the hidden field value and the word typed in by the user. If the two match, the user passed the CAPTCHA test.

Another way, one that does not require a database, is by using cookies. A Struts action specializes in generating a word and its hash and converts the word to an image. At the same time, the second word or the hash is sent to the browser as a cookie. When the form is submitted, the server will match the value entered by the user and the cookie. The server will do this by using the same algorithm that produces the word pair in the first place.

It sounds complicated, but I have written a Java library, free for download from brainysoftware.com and free to use commercially or non-commercially, that can generate random words and produce CAPTCHA images. The library is included in the ZIP that accompanies this book.

There's only one class in the library, the **com.brainysoftware.captcha.CaptchaUtil** class, with the following methods, all static:

```
public static String getRandomWord(int length)
```
Returns a random word of a specified length.

```
public static String getHash(java.lang.String word)
```
Returns an irreversible hash of the specified word.

```
public static java.awt.image.BufferedImage getCaptchaImage(
        java.lang.String word, int width, int height, int type)
```

Returns an image representation of the specified word. The width and height arguments specify the image size in pixel. The last argument is currently reserved for future use.

```
public static boolean validate(java.lang.String word,
        java.lang.String hash)
```
Returns true if the specified hash is the hash of the specified word. Otherwise, returns false.

Now, let's see how we can create a result type that returns a CAPTCHA image with the help of this library.

The **CaptchaResult** class in Listing 19.1 is the brain of the new result type. It extends the **StrutsResultSupport** class and overrides its **doExecute** method.

Listing 19.1: The CaptchaResult class

```
package com.brainysoftware.captcha;
import java.awt.image.BufferedImage;
import javax.imageio.ImageIO;
import javax.servlet.http.Cookie;
import javax.servlet.http.HttpServletResponse;
import org.apache.struts2.dispatcher.StrutsResultSupport;
import com.opensymphony.xwork2.ActionInvocation;

public class CaptchaResult extends StrutsResultSupport {
    private String hashCookieName = "hash";
    private int wordLength = 6;
    private int imageWidth = 200;
    private int imageHeight = 70;

    // getters and setters not shown

    protected void doExecute(String finalLocation,
            ActionInvocation invocation) throws Exception {
        HttpServletResponse response = (HttpServletResponse)
            invocation.getInvocationContext().get(HTTP_RESPONSE);
        response.setContentType("image/jpg");
        String word = CaptchaUtil.getRandomWord(wordLength);
        String hash = CaptchaUtil.getHash(word);
        Cookie hashCookie = new Cookie(hashCookieName, hash);
        response.addCookie(hashCookie);
        BufferedImage image = CaptchaUtil.getCaptchaImage(word,
                imageWidth, imageHeight, 0);
        ImageIO.write(image, "jpg", response.getOutputStream());
```

```
        }
    }
```

The **doExecute** method generates a random word and a corresponding hash and creates a **Cookie** that contains the hash. It then appends the cookie to the **HttpServletResponse** object, generates a **BufferedImage** of the random word, and sends the image to the browser.

Using the New Result Type

The **app19a** application presents a CAPTCHA login form that uses the result type in Listing 191. The action declarations are given in Listing 19.2.

Listing 19.2: Action declarations

```xml
<?xml version="1.0" encoding="UTF-8" ?>
<!DOCTYPE struts PUBLIC
    "-//Apache Software Foundation//DTD Struts Configuration 2.0//EN"
    "http://struts.apache.org/dtds/struts-2.0.dtd">

<struts>
    <package name="app19a" extends="struts-default">
        <result-types>
            <result-type name="captcha"
                class="com.brainysoftware.captcha.CaptchaResult"
            />
        </result-types>
        <action name="Login_input">
            <result>/jsp/Login.jsp</result>
        </action>
        <action name="Login" class="app19a.Login">
            <param name="hashCookieName">hashCookie</param>
            <result name="success">/jsp/Thanks.jsp</result>
            <result name="input">/jsp/Login.jsp</result>
        </action>
        <action name="GetCaptchaImage">
            <result type="captcha">
                <param name="hashCookieName">hashCookie</param>
                <param name="wordLength">6</param>
                <param name="imageWidth">90</param>
                <param name="imageHeight">25</param>
            </result>
        </action>
```

```
    </package>
</struts>
```

The captcha result type is declared under **<result-types>** and there are three **action** elements. The **Login_input** action shows the login form and the **Login** action verifies the user name and password and the CAPTCHA word. The **GetCaptchaImage** action returns a CAPTCHA image.

The **Login** action class is given in Listing 19.3.

Listing 19.3: The Login class

```
package app19a;
import javax.servlet.http.Cookie;
import javax.servlet.http.HttpServletRequest;
import org.apache.struts2.interceptor.ServletRequestAware;
import com.brainysoftware.captcha.CaptchaUtil;
import com.opensymphony.xwork2.ActionSupport;

public class Login extends ActionSupport
        implements ServletRequestAware {
    private String userName;
    private String password;
    private String word;
    private String hashCookieName = "hash";
    private HttpServletRequest httpServletRequest;

    // getters and setters not shown

    public void setServletRequest(HttpServletRequest
       httpServletRequest) {
       this.httpServletRequest = httpServletRequest;
    }
    public String execute() {
       Cookie[] cookies = httpServletRequest.getCookies();
       String hash = null;
       for (Cookie cookie : cookies) {
           if (cookie.getName().equals(hashCookieName)) {
               hash = cookie.getValue();
               break;
           }
       }
       if (hash != null
               && userName.equals("don")
               && password.equals("secret")
               && CaptchaUtil.validate(word, hash)) {
```

```
            return SUCCESS;
        } else {
            addActionError("Login failed.");
            return INPUT;
        }
    }
}
```

The **execute** method verifies the user name and password and validates the word and the hash. The hash is obtained from a cookie and the word is what the user types in the third text field in the Login form.

The **Login.jsp** page is given in Listing 19.4 and the **Thanks.jsp** page in Listing 19.5.

Listing 19.4: The Login.jsp page

```
<%@ taglib prefix="s" uri="/struts-tags" %>
<html>
<head>
<title>Login with CAPTCHA</title>
<style type="text/css">@import url(css/main.css);</style>
</head>
<body>
<div id="global">
    <h3>Enter your user name, password, and the image word</h3>
    <s:actionerror/>
    <s:form action="Login">
        <s:textfield name="userName" label="User Name"/>
        <s:password name="password" label="Password"/>
        <tr>
            <td><img src="GetCaptchaImage.action"/></td>
            <td>
                <s:textfield theme="simple" name="word"
                        value=""/>
            </td>
        </tr>
        <s:submit value="Login"/>
    </s:form>
</div>
</body>
</html>
```

Note that the **img** element's **src** attribute in the **Login.jsp** page points to the **GetCaptchaImage** action.

Listing 19.5: The Thanks.jsp page

```
<%@ taglib prefix="s" uri="/struts-tags" %>
<html>
<head>
<title>Thank you</title>
<style type="text/css">@import url(css/main.css);</style>
</head>
<body>
<div id="global">
You're logged in.
</div>
</body>
</html>
```

Note

You must copy both the **brainycaptcha.jar** and **brainycaptchaplugin.jar** files in your **WEB-INF/lib** directory. Both JAR files are included in the zip file that bundles the sample applications that accompany this book.

To test the application, direct your browser to this URL:

```
http://localhost:8080/app19a/Login_input.action
```

You'll see a CAPTCHA image similar to the one in Figure 19.1.

Summary

This chapter explained how you could write a custom result type. It also presented an example of result type that streamed a CAPTCHA image to the browser.

Chapter 20
Velocity

The Apache Velocity Engine is an open source templating engine that supports a simple and powerful template language to reference Java objects. The Apache Velocity Project is an Apache project responsible for creating and maintaining the Apache Velocity Engine. The software is available for free download from http://velocity.apache.org. Struts includes the latest version of Velocity so there's no need to download Velocity separately.

This chapter provides a brief tutorial on how to use Velocity in Struts.

Overview

Most Struts applications use JSP as the view technology. However, JSP is not the only view technology Struts supports. Velocity and FreeMarker (discussed in Chapter 21, "FreeMarker") can also be used to display data.

Velocity is a template language. A template is text that provides a basis for documents and allows for words to be dynamically inserted into certain parts of it. For example, JSP can serve as a template because it lets you insert values through the use of the Expression Language. Since you already know JSP then it should not be hard to learn Velocity as both are similar.

Unlike JSP, however, Velocity does not permit Java code to be used and only allows rudimentary access to data. As such, developers are forced to separate presentation from the business logic. In the past this "feature," the inability to use Java code, was often cited by Velocity proponents as a reason to leave JSP and embrace Velocity. However, starting from Servlet 2.0 you can now configure your servlet applications to disallow Java code in JSPs and hence promote separation of presentation and logic.

Another point to note is that Velocity templates can be placed within the application or in the class path. Contrast this with JSPs that can only be found if placed within the application. Velocity will first search the application, if the template could not be found, it will search the class path. In addition, Velocity templates can be loaded from a JAR while JSPs cannot. Therefore, if you are deploying a component as a Struts plug-in, Velocity is a great choice because you can include the templates in the same JAR as the other part of the component.

Velocity supports simple control structures such as loops and if-else statements, though. The dollar sign ($) has a special meaning in Velocity. It is used to indicate what follows is a variable name that needs to be replaced at run-time.

The **struts-default.xml** file already defines the velocity result type, you can use Velocity in Struts without writing additional configurations.

```
<result-type name="velocity"
        class="org.apache.struts2.dispatcher.VelocityResult"/>
```

You just need to make sure that the following JAR files are copied to your **WEB-INF/lib** directory: **velocity-*VERSION*.jar**, **velocity-dep-*VERSION*.jar**, and **velocity-tools-*VERSION*.jar**. In addition, Velocity relies on the Digester project, so the **commons-digester-*VERSION*.jar** file, included with Struts deployment, is also needed.

The **default.properties** file specifies the following entry that indicates that Velocity configuration file must be named **velocity.properties**.

```
struts.velocity.configfile = velocity.properties
```

Velocity Implicit Objects

In Struts, Velocity searches for data in this order:

1. The Value Stack
2. The action context
3. Built-in variables

Just like JSP, Velocity allows access to important objects such as the
ServletContext and **HttpServletRequest**. Table 20.1 lists the implicit objects
in Velocity.

Name	Description
stack	The value stack
action	The action object
response	The **HttpServletResponse** object
res	The alias for **response**
request	The **HttpServletRequest** object
req	The alias for **request**
session	The **HttpSession** object
application	The **ServletContext** object
base	The request's context path

Table 20.1: Velocity implicit objects

Tags

Velocity in Struts extends the tags in the Struts tag library. Velocity tags are
similar to the Struts tags but the syntax for using them is slightly different. To
start, you don't need this **taglib** directive that you need when using JSP:

```
<%@ taglib prefix="s" uri="/struts-tags" %>
```

In JSP, a start tag is enclosed with < and > and an end tag with </ and >. In
Velocity a start tag starts with **#s** followed by the tag name. Most tags are
inline and do not need an end tag. For example:

```
#stextfield
```

Some tags, including **form**, require an #end.

```
#sform ...
    #stextfield ...
    #ssubmit ...
#end
```

Velocity tag attributes are enclosed in brackets. Each attribute name/value are
enclosed in double quotes and separated by an equal sign.

```
#stagName ("attribute-1=value-1" "attribute-2=value-2" ... )
```

For example:

```
#stextfield ("name=userName" "label=User Name")
```

Velocity Example

The **app20a** application illustrates the use of Velocity in Struts. It features two actions, **Product_input** and **Product_save**, as declared using the **action** elements in Listing 20.1.

Listing 20.1: Action declarations

```
<package name="app20a" extends="struts-default">
    <action name="Product_input">
        <result type="velocity">/template/Product.vm</result>
    </action>
    <action name="Product_save" class="app20a.Product">
        <result name="input" type="velocity">
            /template/Product.vm
        </result>
        <result type="velocity">/template/Details.vm</result>
    </action>
</package>
```

The **Product_input** action forwards to the **Product.vm** template in Listing 20.2. This template contains a form for inputting product information.

Listing 20.2: The Product.vm template

```
<html>
<head>
<title>Add Product</title>
<style type="text/css">@import url(css/main.css);</style>
</head>
<body>
<div id="global" style="width:330px">

<h3>Add Product</h3>
#sform ("action=Product_save")
    #stextfield ("name=name" "label=Product Name")
    #stextfield ("name=description" "label=Description")
    #stextfield ("name=price" "label=Price")
    #ssubmit ("value=Add Product")
#end
```

```
</div>
</body>
```

The **Product_save** action invokes the **Product** action class in Listing 20.3 and forwards to the **Details.vml** template in Listing 20.4.

Listing 20.3: The Product class

```java
package app20a;
import com.opensymphony.xwork2.ActionSupport;
public class Product extends ActionSupport {
    private String productId;
    private String name;
    private String description;
    private double price;

    // getters and setters not shown

    public String save() {
        return SUCCESS;
    }
}
```

Listing 20.4: The Details.vm template

```html
<html>
<head>
<title>Details</title>
<style type="text/css">@import url(css/main.css);</style>
</head>
<body>
<div id="global" style="width:300px">
<h3>Product Details</h3>
<table>
<tr>
    <td>Name:</td>
    <td>#sproperty ("value=name")</td>
</tr>
<tr>
    <td>Description:</td>
    <td>${description}</td>
</tr>
<tr>
    <td>Price:</td>
    <td>${price}</td>
</tr>
</table>
```

```
</div>
</body>
```

To test this application, direct your browser to this URL.

```
http://localhost:8080/app20a/Product_input.action
```

You will see a form like that in Figure 20.1.

Figure 20.1: The form in the Product.vm template

If you click the Add Product button, you will see the content of the **Details.vm** template.

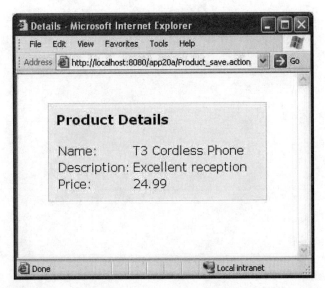

Figure 20.1: The content of the Details.vm template

Summary

JSP is not the only view technology that can be used in Struts. Velocity and FreeMarker can too, and so can XSLT. This chapter explained how you can use Velocity as a view technology.

Chapter 21
FreeMarker

FreeMarker is a template engine written in Java that can be used with Struts. In fact, the Struts tag library uses FreeMarker as the default template language. FreeMarker supports more features than Velocity. For detailed comparison between FreeMarker and Velocity, read this:

```
http://freemarker.org/fmVsVel.html
```

This chapter provides a brief tutorial on how to use FreeMarker in Struts.

Overview

To use FreeMarker in Struts, you don't need to install additional software. The JAR file that contains the FreeMarker engine, the **freemarker-*VERSION*.jar** file, is already included in Struts deployment. In fact, without this file your Struts application won't work because FreeMarker is the default template for the Struts tag library.

FreeMarker templates can be placed within the application directory or the class path. The application directory will be searched first. The fact that the FreeMarker engine also searches the class path makes this technology perfect for Struts because it enables FreeMarker templates to be packaged in JAR files. As you'll learn in Chapter 23, "Plug-ins", plug-ins are distributed as JAR files. You cannot package JSPs in a JAR and hope the web container will translate and compile them.

In Struts the FreeMarker engine searches for data in this order:

1. Built-in variables
2. The Value Stack
3. The action context
4. Request scope

5. Session scope
6. Application scope

Just like JSP, FreeMarker allows access to important objects such as the **ServletContext** and **HttpServletRequest**. Table 21.1 lists the implicit objects in FreeMarker.

Name	Description
Stack	The Value Stack
action	The action object
response	The **HttpServletResponse** object
res	The alias for **response**
request	The **HttpServletRequest** object
req	The alias for **request**
session	The **HttpSession** object
application	The **ServletContext** object
base	The request's context path

Table 21.1: FreeMarker implicit objects

FreeMarker Tags

Struts provides FreeMarker tags that are extensions to the tags in the Struts tag library. The syntax is very similar to that in JSP. You use **<@s.*tag*** as the start tag and **</@s.*tag*>** as the end tag, where ***tag*** is the tag name. For example, here is the **form** tag:

```
<@s.form action="...">

</@s.form>
```

Now, compare these JSP tags

```
<s:form action="Product_save">
    <s:textfield name="name" label="Product Name"/>
    <s:textfield name="description" label="Description"/>
    <s:textfield name="price" label="Price"/>
    <s:submit value="Add Product"/>
</s:form>
```

with their equivalents in FreeMarker:

Example 411

```
<@s.form action="Product_save">
    <@s.textfield name="name" label="Product Name"/>
    <@s.textfield name="description" label="Description"/>
    <@s.textfield name="price" label="Price"/>
    <@s.submit value="Add Product"/>
</@s.form>
```

FreeMarker supports dynamic attributes, a feature missing in JSP. In JSP, you can use the **param** tag to pass values to the containing tag. For instance:

```
<s:url value="myResource">
    <s:param name="userId" value="%{userId}"/>
</s:url>
```

In FreeMarker you don't need to pass the parameter using the param tag. Instead, you can treat the parameter as a dynamic attribute. The FreeMarker equivalent of the **url** tag above will be:

```
<@s.url value="myResource" userId="${userId}"/>
```

Example

As an example, consider the **app21a** application that has two actions, **Product_input** and **Product_save**. The application uses FreeMarker templates instead of JSPs.

The actions are declared in the **struts.xml** as shown in Listing 21.1.

Listing 21.1: Action declarations

```
<package name="app21a" extends="struts-default">
    <action name="Product_input">
        <result type="freemarker">/template/Product.ftl</result>
    </action>
    <action name="Product_save" class="app21a.Product">
        <result name="input" type="freemarker">
            /template/Product.ftl
        </result>
        <result type="freemarker">/template/Details.ftl</result>
    </action>
</package>
```

The **Product_save** action uses the **Product** action class given in Listing 21.2. This is exactly the same action class you would have for a dispatcher result.

Listing 21.2: The Product class

```
package app21a;
import com.opensymphony.xwork2.ActionSupport;
public class Product extends ActionSupport {
    private String productId;
    private String name;
    private String description;
    private double price;

    // getters and setters not shown

    public String save() {
        return SUCCESS;
    }
}
```

Listings 21.3 and 21.4 shows two templates that sport FreeMarker tags.

Listing 21.3: The Product.ftl template

```
<html>
<head>
<title>Add Product</title>
<style type="text/css">@import url(css/main.css);</style>
</head>
<body>
<div id="global" style="width:330px">

<h3>Add Product</h3>

<@s.form action="Product_save">
    <@s.textfield name="name" label="Product Name"/>
    <@s.textfield name="description" label="Description"/>
    <@s.textfield name="price" label="Price"/>
    <@s.submit value="Add Product"/>
</@s.form>
</div>
</body>
```

Listing 21.4: The Details.ftl template

```
<html>
<head>
<title>Details</title>
```

Example   413

```
<style type="text/css">@import url(css/main.css);</style>
</head>
<body>
<div id="global" style="width:300px">

<h3>Product Details</h3>
<table>
<tr>
    <td>Name:</td>
    <td><@s.property value="name"/></td>
</tr>
<tr>
    <td>Description:</td>
    <td>${description}</td>
</tr>
<tr>
    <td>Price:</td>
    <td>${price}</td>
</tr>
</table>

</div>
</body>
```

Note that to access an action property, you can use the **property** tag or the notation **${ … }**.

To test the application, direct your browser to this URL.

```
http://localhost:8080/app21a/Product_input.action
```

You'll see the Product form like the one in Figure 21.1.

Figure 21.1: The Product form

Submitting the form invokes the **Product_save** action that forwards to the **Details.ftl** template. The result is shown in Figure 21.2.

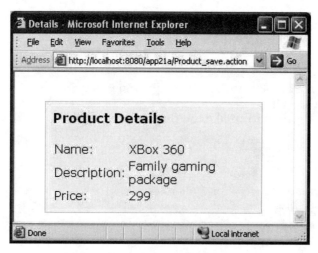

Figure 21.2: The Details page

Summary

FreeMarker is the template language used to render tags in the Struts tag library. It is also a good alternative to JSP and allows templates to reside in the class path, in addition to a directory under the application directory. Because of this feature, FreeMarker templates can be deployed in a JAR file, which makes FreeMarker suitable for plug-ins.

Chapter 22
XSLT Results

Extensible Stylesheet Language (XSL) is a World Wide Web Consortium specification that deals with XML formatting. XSL defines how an XML document should be displayed. XSL to XML is what CSS to HTML. There are two technologies defined in the XSL specification: XSL Formatting Objects and XSL Transformations (XSLT). The latter is the main focus of this chapter as the Struts XSLT result type is intended to support this technology.

The XSLT specification can be downloaded from

```
http://www.w3.org/TR/xslt
```

Overview

XML documents are used for easy data exchange. Unlike proprietary databases where data is stored in proprietary formats that make exchanging data difficult, XML documents are plain text and can be understood by just reading the documents. For example, this XML document is self-explanatory, it contains information about an employee.

```
<employee>
    <employeeId>34</employeeId>
    <firstName>Jen</firstName>
    <lastName>Goodhope</lastName>
    <birthDate>2/25/1980</birthDate>
    <hiredDate>3/22/2006</hiredDate>
</employee>
```

If you send this XML document, the receiving party can easily understand it and probably manipulate it with their own tools. However, it's probably not as straightforward as you may think. The other party may have XML documents containing details on employees, but the format is slightly different. Instead of

employeeId they might use **id** and instead of **employee** they might call it
worker.

```
<worker>
    <id>50</employeeId>
    <firstName>Max</firstName>
    <lastName>Ocean</lastName>
    <birthDate>12/13/1977</birthDate>
    <hiredDate>10/5/2005</hiredDate>
</worker>
```

If the data from the first XML document is to be merged into the second
XML document, for example, there must be some kind of transformation that
converts **<employee>** to **<worker>** and **<employeeId>** to **<id>**. This is
where XSLT plays a role.

Figure 22.1 shows how XSLT works. At the core is an XSLT processor
that reads the source XML and uses a stylesheet to transform an XML
document into something else.

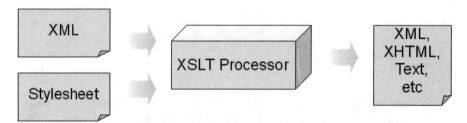

Figure 22.1: How XSLT works

An XSL stylesheet is an XML file with an xsl or xslt extension. The root
element of an XSL stylesheet is either **<xsl:stylesheet>** or **<xsl:transform>**.
Here is the skeleton of an XSL stylesheet:

```
<?xml version="1.0" encoding="UTF-8"?>
<xsl:stylesheet version="1.0"
    xmlns:xsl="http://www.w3.org/1999/XSL/Transform">

    . . .

</xsl:stylesheet>
```

The **xsl:stylesheet** element has two attributes in this case. The first attribute declares the version, which currently is 1.0. The second attribute declares the XML namespace. It points to the official W3C XSLT namespace. The prefix **xsl** is preferred for an XSL stylesheet but could be anything you like.

The list of elements can be found in the specification. Here are some of the more important ones:

- **xsl:template**. Defines a template. Its **match** attribute associates the template with an element in the source XML. For example, this **xsl:template** element matches the root of the source XML:

```
<xsl:template match="/">
```

- **xsl:value-of**. Reads the value of an XML element and appends it to the output stream of the transformation. You select an XML element by using the **select** attribute. For instance, the following prints the value of the name element under **<result>**.

```
<xsl:value-of select="/result/name"/>
```

- **xsl:for-each**. Iterates over a node set. Again, use the **select** attribute to specify an XML element. For example, this **xsl:for-each** element iterates over the **result/supplier** elements and prints the details of each supplier and formats them in an HTML table.

```
<table>
<xsl:for-each select="/result/supplier">
<tr>
    <td><xsl:value-of select="supplierName"/></td>
    <td><xsl:value-of select="address"/></td>
</tr>
</xsl:for-each>
</table>
```

The XSLT Result Type

XML to XML conversion is not the only transformation XSLT can do. XML to XHTML conversion is often done with XSLT too. Actually, XSLT can transform XML to any plain text.

The Struts XSLT result type inspects the Value Stack and produces a raw XML with a **result** root element. Nested within this element are all the action properties and other information, such as the locale. The XSLT result will then use the supplied XSLT stylesheet to convert the raw XML to another XML or XHTML.

The XSLT result can take these parameters:

- **stylesheetLocation**. The location of the stylesheet file.
- **excudingPattern**. Specifies excluded elements. Note that there's a typo (there is no l in excluding) that has not been fixed until Struts version 2.0.9.
- **matchingPattern**. Specifies the matching pattern. By default it matches everything.
- **parse**. Indicates whether or not the **stylesheetLocation** parameter should be parsed for OGNL expressions. The default value is false.

Note there is also a deprecated **location** parameter that does the same thing as **stylesheetLocation**.

Note
By default XSLT stylesheets are cached. In development mode it's easier if they are not. You can change this behavior by setting **struts.xslt.nocache** to true in the **struts.properties** file.

Consider the **Product** action class in Listing 22.1. The **supplier** property of **Product** is of type **Supplier**, shown in Listing 22.2.

Listing 22.1: The Product action class

```
package app22a;
import com.opensymphony.xwork2.ActionSupport;
public class Product extends ActionSupport {
    private String productId;
    private String name;
    private String description;
    private double price;
    private Supplier supplier;

    // getters and setters not shown

    public String execute() {
        productId = "345";
        name = "Epson";
        description = "Super printer";
        price = 12.34;
        supplier = new Supplier();
        supplier.setSupplierId("20a");
```

```
        supplier.setName("Online Business Ltd.");
        supplier.setAddress("Oakville, Ontario");
        return SUCCESS;
    }

}
```

Note that the **execute** method populates the properties. However, in a real world application, the data could come from anywhere.

Listing 22.2: The Supplier class

```
package app22a;
public class Supplier {
    private String supplierId;
    private String name;
    private String address;

    // getters and setters not shown

}
```

The XSLT result would produce the following raw XML out of a **Product** action.

```
<result>
    <actionErrors></actionErrors>
    <actionMessages></actionMessages>
    <description>
        <#text>Super printer</#text>
    </description>
    <errorMessages></errorMessages>
    <errors></errors>
    <fieldErrors></fieldErrors>
    <locale>
        <ISO3Country>
            <#text>USA</#text>
        </ISO3Country>
        <ISO3Language>
            <#text>eng</#text>
        </ISO3Language>
        <country>
            <#text>US</#text>
        </country>
        <displayCountry>
            <#text>United States</#text>
        </displayCountry>
```

```
        <displayLanguage>
            <#text>English</#text>
        </displayLanguage>
        <displayName>
            <#text>English (United States)</#text>
        </displayName>
        <displayVariant>
            <#text></#text>
        </displayVariant>
        <language>
            <#text>en</#text>
        </language>
        <variant>
            <#text></#text>
        </variant>
    </locale>
    <name>
        <#text>Epson</#text>
    </name>
    <price>
        <#text>12.34</#text>
    </price>
    <productId>
        <#text>345</#text>
    </productId>
    <supplier>
        <address>
            <#text>Oakville, Ontario</#text>
        </address>
        <name>
            <#text>Online Business Ltd. </#text>
        </name>
        <supplierId>
            <#text>20a</#text>
        </supplierId>
    </supplier>
    <texts>
        <#text>null</#text>
    </texts>
</result>
```

The action properties are printed in bold.

Example   423

Example

As an example, the **app22a** application features an action that uses an XSLT result. The action, XSLT, converts the **Product** action to XHTML. The Product class is the same class shown in Listing 22.1. The action declaration is shown in Listing 22.3.

Listing 22.3: The action declaration

```
<package name="app22a" extends="struts-default">
    <action name="XSL" class="app22a.Product">
        <result name="success" type="xslt">
            <param name="stylesheetLocation">
                /xsl/Product.xsl
            </param>
        </result>
    </action>
</package>
```

The XSL action uses an XSLT result that employs the **Product.xsl** template in Listing 22.4.

Listing 22.4: The Product.xsl template

```
<?xml version="1.0" encoding="UTF-8"?>
<xsl:stylesheet version="1.0"
    xmlns:xsl="http://www.w3.org/1999/XSL/Transform">
    <xsl:template match="/">
    <product>
        <productName>
            <xsl:value-of select="/result/name"/>
        </productName>
        <productDescription>
            <xsl:value-of select="/result/description"/>
        </productDescription>
        <price>
            <xsl:value-of select="/result/price"/>
        </price>
        <supplierName>
            <xsl:value-of select="/result/supplier/name"/>
        </supplierName>
    </product>
    </xsl:template>
</xsl:stylesheet>
```

You can test the application by directing your browser to this URL:

```
http://localhost:8080/app22a/XSL.action
```

The result is this:

```
<?xml version="1.0" encoding="UTF-8"?>
<product>
    <productName>Epson</productName>
    <productDescription>Super printer</productDescription>
    <price>12.34</price>
    <supplierName>Online Business Ltd.</supplierName>
</product>
```

Note

A modified **org.apache.struts2.views.xslt.XSLTResult** class is included in the **app22a** example. For debugging purpose, I added a method that prints the raw XML to the console or the **Catalina.out** file. The **XSLTResult** class is the underlying class of the XSLT result type.

Summary

The XSLT result type transforms action objects to XML. This result type is not as common as Dispatcher but may be used in applications that require XML outputs, such as web services.

In this chapter you learned how it works and how to use it in your Struts applications.

Chapter 23
Plug-ins

The Struts plug-in provides an elegant mechanism to promote code reuse. A plug-in is essentially a JAR. It may contain Java classes, FreeMarker or Velocity templates, and a **struts-plugin.xml** file. The latter, if present, can be used to configure applications that use the plug-in.

In this chapter you will learn how to write plug-ins.

Overview

Struts has been designed to be extensible through plug-ins. Using a plug-in is as easy as copying the plug-in JAR file to the **WEB-INF/lib** directory. Unlike an ordinary JAR file, a plug-in may contain a **struts-plugin.xml** file that complies with the same rules as a **struts.xml** file. It is possible to include configuration settings in a plug-in because Struts loads configuration files in this order:

1. The **struts-default.xml** in the **struts2-core-*VERSION*.jar** file.
2. All **struts-plugin.xml** files in plug-ins deployed in the application.
3. The **struts.xml** file.

This means, you can override values defined in the **struts-default.xml** file in your **struts-plugin.xml**, even though the application will have the final say since anything defined in the **struts.xml** file overrides similar settings in other configuration files.

You can distribute any type of Struts component in your plug-in, including new packages, new result types, custom interceptors, actions, new tag libraries, and others.

The Plug-in Registry

Struts comes bundled with several plug-ins, including the Tiles plug-in, the JFreeChart plug-in, and the SiteMesh plug-in. However, the Struts community is buzzing with third-party plug-ins, most of which are free. This site maintains a registry of Struts 2 plug-ins:

```
http://cwiki.apache.org/S2PLUGINS/home.html
```

At my last visit there were close to forty plug-ins available. I suspect there are others that are not listed here.

Writing A Custom Plugin

Plug-ins are easy to write. If you know how to create a JAR file, you can create a plug-in. The **app23a** application contains the new result type **CaptchaResult** class discussed in Chapter 19, "Custom Result Types." Please read Chapter 19 now if you haven't done so.

The CAPTCHA result type is based on the **CaptchaResult** class that extends **StrutsResultSupport**. In order for the result type to be easily used in applications, you need to package it as a plug-in. Since it is a result type, you need to register it in a **struts-plugin.xml**. Listing 23.1 shows the XML file.

Listing 23.1: The struts-plugin.xml file

```
<?xml version="1.0" encoding="UTF-8" ?>
<!DOCTYPE struts PUBLIC
    "-//Apache Software Foundation//DTD Struts Configuration 2.0//EN"
    "http://struts.apache.org/dtds/struts-2.0.dtd">

<struts>
    <package name="captcha-default" extends="struts-default">
        <result-types>
            <result-type name="captcha"
                    class="com.brainysoftware.captcha.CaptchaResult"
            />
        </result-types>
    </package>
</struts>
```

The directory structure of our plug-in application is shown in Figure 23.1. There are one class and one XML file.

Figure 23.1: The directory structure of the captcha plugin

Now, create a JAR. The standard way, albeit not the easiest, is to use the **jar** program that comes with your JDK by following these steps. This assumes that your JDK has been added to the path directory so that you can invoke the **jar** program from anywhere in your computer.

1. Change directory to the directory where the **struts-plugin.xml** resides. This directory will also contain the **com** directory.
2. Type this command and press Enter.

```
jar -cvf captchaplugin.jar *
```

A JAR named **captchaplugin.jar** will be created. This JAR is your plug-in.

Using the Captcha Plug-in

The **app23b** application illustrates how to use the Captcha plug-in discussed earlier. All you need to do is make sure the JAR file is copied to the **WEB-INF/lib** directory of the application. In addition, since the plug-in uses classes in Brainy Software's CAPTCHA component, you must copy the **brainycaptcha.jar** file too. This file is distributed with the ZIP file that bundles the sample applications for this book.

There are three actions defined in **app23b**, **Login_input**, **Login**, and **GetCaptchaImage**. These action declarations are shown in Listing 23.2.

Listing 23.2: Action declarations

```
<package name="app23b" extends="captcha-default">
    <action name="Login_input">
        <result>/jsp/Login.jsp</result>
    </action>
```

```
<action name="Login" class="app23b.Login">
    <result name="success">/jsp/Thanks.jsp</result>
    <result name="input">/jsp/Login.jsp</result>
    <param name="hashCookieName">hashCookie</param>
</action>
<action name="GetCaptchaImage">
    <result type="captcha">
        <param name="hashCookieName">hashCookie</param>
        <param name="wordLength">6</param>
        <param name="imageWidth">90</param>
        <param name="imageHeight">25</param>
    </result>
</action>
</package>
```

The first thing that should catch your attention is the **extends** attribute of the **package** element. Its value is **captcha-default**, which represents a package in Captcha plug-in. Since **captcha-default** extends **struts-default**, you inherit all the settings from the latter in the package. In addition, you can use the new result type captcha. Note that the action **GetCaptchaImage** has a captcha result type.

There is only one action class, the **Login** class, which is shown in Listing 23.3.

Listing 23.3 The Login class

```
package app23b;
import javax.servlet.http.Cookie;
import javax.servlet.http.HttpServletRequest;
import org.apache.struts2.interceptor.ServletRequestAware;
import com.brainysoftware.captcha.CaptchaUtil;
import com.opensymphony.xwork2.ActionSupport;

public class Login extends ActionSupport
        implements ServletRequestAware {
    private String userName;
    private String password;
    private String word;
    private String hashCookieName = "hash";
    private HttpServletRequest httpServletRequest;
    public void setServletRequest(HttpServletRequest
            httpServletRequest) {
        this.httpServletRequest = httpServletRequest;
    }
```

```
    // getters and setters not shown

    public String execute() {
        Cookie[] cookies = httpServletRequest.getCookies();
        String hash = null;
        for (Cookie cookie : cookies) {
            if (cookie.getName().equals(hashCookieName)) {
                hash = cookie.getValue();
                break;
            }
        }
        if (hash != null
                && userName.equals("don")
                && password.equals("secret")
                && CaptchaUtil.validate(word, hash)) {
            return SUCCESS;
        } else {
            addActionError("Login failed.");
            return INPUT;
        }
    }
}
```

Pay special attention to the **execute** method. How it works was explained in **Chapter 19**. All I'll say here is the user can log in by using **don** and **secret** as the user name and password and entering the word in the CAPTCHA image.

The **Login.jsp** page displays the Login form. This page is given in Listing 23.4 and the **Thanks.jsp**, the page you'll see after a successful login, in Listing 23.5

Listing 23.4: The Login.jsp page

```
<%@ taglib prefix="s" uri="/struts-tags" %>
<html>
<head>
<title>Login with CAPTCHA</title>
<style type="text/css">@import url(css/main.css);</style>
</head>
<body>
<div id="global">
    <h3>Enter your user name, password, and the image word</h3>
    <s:actionerror/>
    <s:form action="Login">
        <s:textfield name="userName" label="User Name"/>
        <s:password name="password" label="Password"/>
```

```
        <tr>
            <td><img src="GetCaptchaImage.action"/></td>
            <td><s:textfield theme="simple" name="word"
    value=""/></td>
        </tr>
        <s:submit value="Login"/>
    </s:form>
</div>
</body>
</html>
```

Listing 23.5: The Thanks.jsp page

```
<%@ taglib prefix="s" uri="/struts-tags" %>
<html>
<head>
<title>Thank you</title>
<style type="text/css">@import url(css/main.css);</style>
</head>
<body>
<div id="global">
You're logged in.
</div>
</body>
</html>
```

Note
You must copy both the **brainycaptcha.jar** and **captchaplugin.jar** files in your **WEB-INF/lib** directory

To test the application, direct your browser to this URL:

```
http://localhost:8080/app23b/Login_input.action
```

You'll see the captcha image on the Login page as shown in Figure 23.2.

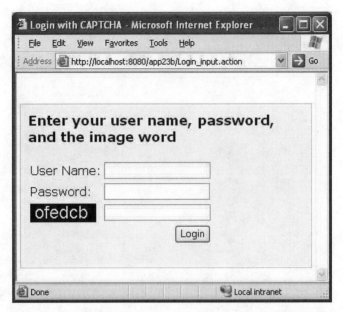

Figure 23.2: The CAPTCHA-facilitated login page

Summary

Struts provides an elegant way to distribute code: through plug-ins. This chapter showed how easy it is to write and use one.

Chapter 24
The Tiles Plug-in

Web applications need a consistent look, which you can achieve by using the same layout for all the pages. A typical layout has a header, a footer, a menu, an ad section, and a body content. Normally, many parts—such as the header, the footer, and the menu—look the same in all pages. To support component reuse, a common part can be implemented as an external resource. You then have the choice of using a frameset, a layout table, or div elements to include these external resources. With a frameset, you reference each common external resource using a frame. If layout tables or div elements are used, each JSP in your application will employ several include files: one for the header, one for the footer, one for the menu, one for the body content, and so on. The JSP technology provides the **include** directive (**<%@ include %>** to include static files and the **include** tag (**<jsp:include>**) to include dynamic resources. However, as will be discussed in the first section of this chapter, both JSP includes are not without shortcomings. If the layout needs changing, you will have to change all your JSPs.

Tiles overcomes these failings and adds more features to enable you to lay out your pages more easily and flexibly. First and foremost, Tiles provides a tag library that allows you to create a layout JSP that defines the layout for all JSPs in an application. Changes to a layout JSP will be reflected in all the JSPs referencing it. This means, only one page needs to be edited should the layout change.

In addition to layout JSPs, Tiles allows you to write definition pages, which are more powerful than the former. A definition page can have one of the two formats, JSP and XML.

This chapter teaches you how to make full use of Tiles by presenting a sample application that uses Tiles.

Note
The Tiles framework provides its services through a series of tags in the Tiles Tag Library. Tiles used to be a component of Struts 1. After it gained popularity, Tiles was extracted from Struts as Tiles 2 and is now an independent Apache project. Its website is http://tiles.apache.org/. The classes that make up Tiles are deployed in three JAR files, **tiles-core-*VERSION*.jar**, **tiles-api-*VERSION*.jar**, and **tiles-jsp-*VERSION*.jar**. In addition, to use Tiles with Struts, you need the **struts2-tiles-plugin-*VERSION*..jar**. All these JARs are deployed with Struts 2. You must copy these JARs to your **WEB-INF/lib** directory

The Problem with JSP Includes

Figure 24.1 shows a page layout with a header, a footer, a menu, an ad section, and a body content. All parts, with the exception of the body content, are common to all the JSPs. The header comes from the **header.jsp** page, the footer from the **footer.jsp** page, the menu from the **menu.jsp** page, and the ad section from the **ad.jsp** page.

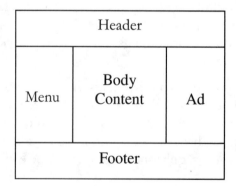

Figure 24.1: A typical layout of a web page

To achieve a consistent look, each of your JSPs must contain a layout table such as this.

```
<html>
<head><title>Page title</title></head>
<body>
<table>
```

```
<tr>
    <td colspan="3"><%@include file="header.jsp"%></td>
</tr>
<tr>
    <td width="120"> <%@include file="menu.jsp"%></td>
    <td>

    body content

    </td>
    <td width="120"> <%@include file="ad.jsp"%></td>
</tr>
<tr>
    <td colspan="3"><%@include file="footer.jsp"%></td>
</tr>
</table>
</body>
</html>
```

Note

A layout table is used just for illustration. You should always use CSS instead.

With this approach, what differentiates one JSP from another is the body content.

Now, what if you want to change the layout? For example, what if you want to make the menu wider by 30 pixels? Or, what if you want the ad to appear on top of the menu? This would require changing all your JSPs, which of course is a tedious and error-prone chore. Tiles can help solve this problem.

Tiles Layout and Definition

This section explains how Tiles resolves the problems with JSP includes in defining a page layout. There are two concepts explained in this section, layout and definition.

The Layout Page

A layout page is a template JSP that defines a layout. You can have as many layout JSPs as you deem necessary. Each JSP that needs to use a layout will only need to reference the layout JSP indirectly. If you need to change the layout of the whole application, you need only change one file, the layout JSP.

Note

JSPs that need to use a layout do not directly reference the layout page. Instead, they refer to a definition that references the layout page. You'll learn more about Tiles definitions in the next subsection.

An example of a layout JSP is given in Listing 24.1. The JSP is named **MyLayout.jsp**.

Listing 24.1: The MyLayout.jsp Tiles layout JSP

```
<%@ taglib uri="http://tiles.apache.org/tags-tiles" prefix="tiles"%>
<html>
<head>
<title><tiles:getAsString name="pageTitle"/></title>
<style type="text/css">@import url(css/main.css);</style>
</head>
<body>
    <tiles:insertAttribute name="header"/>
    <tiles:insertAttribute name="body"/>
    <tiles:insertAttribute name="footer"/>
</body>
</html>
```

There are two tags from the Tiles Tag Library used here, **insertAttribute** and **getAsString**. The **insertAttribute** tag defines an insert point into which an attribute will be inserted. The **name** attribute specifies the logical name of the resource that will be inserted.

The list of attributes for **insertAttribute** is given in Table 24.1.

The **getAsString** tag specifies a variable whose **String** value will be passed by objects referencing the layout JSP. You would imagine that the **getAsString** tag in Listing 24.1 would be passed a different page title by each JSP using this layout.

Attribute	Type	Description
name	String	The name of the attribute to insert. It will be ignored if the **value** attribute is present.
value	String	The attribute object to render.
flush	boolean	A value of true causes the current page output stream to be flushed before insertion.
ignore	boolean	A value of **true** indicates that no exception will be thrown if the attribute specified by the **name** attribute cannot be found. The default value for this attribute is false.
role	String	Specifies the role that the current user must belong to in order for this tag to be executed.
preparer	String	The fully qualified name of the preparer.

Table 24.1: insertAttribute tag's attributes

The complete list of **getAsString** attributes is given in Table 24.2.

Attribute	Type	Description
name	String	A required attribute that specifies the name of the attribute.
ignore	boolean	A value of **true** indicates that no exception will be thrown if the attribute specified by the name attribute cannot be found. The default value for this attribute is false.
role	String	Specifies the role that the current user must belong to in order for this tag to be executed.

Table 24.2: getAsString tag's attributes

Tiles Definitions

The second thing you need to grasp before you can use Tiles is definitions. A definition is a layer between a layout page and a JSP using the layout. In Struts a Tiles definition corresponds to a view. The view is normally a JSP, but Velocity or FreeMarker can also be used.

By analogy, a layout page is like a Java interface and a definition page is a base class that provides default method implementations of the interface. Any Java class that needs to implement the interface can extend the base class, so that the class does not need to implement a method unless it needs to override the default. By the same token, a JSP references a definition page instead of a layout JSP. The diagram in Figure 12.2 provides comparison between Java inheritance and Tiles' layout and definition pages.

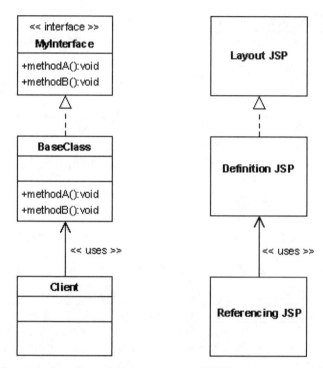

Figure 24.2: Comparing Java inheritance and Tiles' layout and definition

Tiles definitions are defined in a **tiles.xml** file located in the **WEB-INF** directory of your Struts application. A **tiles.xml** file must comply with the DTD file defined in the following DOCTYPE declaration that must precede the root element.

```
<!DOCTYPE tiles-definitions PUBLIC
    "-//Apache Software Foundation//DTD Tiles Configuration 2.0//EN"
    "http://struts.apache.org/dtds/tiles-config_2_0.dtd">
```

The root element for a tiles definition file is **tiles-definition**. Under it you write one or more **definition** element, each of which defines a definition.

Here is a definition that references the **MyLayout.jsp** page.

```
<definition name="MyDefinition" template="/jsp/MyLayout.jsp"/>
```

The **name** attribute specifies a name that will be used by a view to refer to this definition. The **template** attribute specifies the template or layout page. In the example above, the definition name is **MyDefinition** and the layout page is **MyLayout.jsp**.

A **definition** element is only useful if it contains one or several **put-attribute** elements. A **put-attribute** element is used to pass a value to the layout page referenced by the definition. For example, the **definition** elements below use the **MyLayout.jsp** page and pass four values:

```
<definition name="Product" template="/jsp/MyLayout.jsp">
    <put-attribute name="pageTitle" value="Product Info"/>
    <put-attribute name="header" value="/jsp/Header.jsp"/>
    <put-attribute name="footer" value="/jsp/Footer.jsp"/>
    <put-attribute name="body" value="/jsp/Product.jsp"/>
</definition>

<definition name="Thanks" template="/jsp/MyLayout.jsp">
    <put-attribute name="pageTitle" value="Thank You"/>
    <put-attribute name="header" value="/jsp/Header.jsp"/>
    <put-attribute name="footer" value="/jsp/Footer.jsp"/>
    <put-attribute name="body" value="/jsp/Thanks.jsp"/>
</definition>
```

The **Product** definition passes "Product Info" to the **getAsString** tag in the **MyLayout.jsp** page and inserts the **Header.jsp**, **Footer.jsp**, and **Product.jsp** to the header, footer, body **insertAttribute** tags, respectively. The **Thanks** definition passes "Thanks You" to the **getAsString** tag and inserts the **Header.jsp**, **Footer.jsp**, and **Thanks.jsp** to the header, footer, body **insertAttribute** tags, respectively.

A Struts result that needs to forward to a definition can refer to it by its name like this.

```
<action name="Product_input">
    <result name="success" type="tiles">Product</result>
</action>
<action name="Product_add">
    <result name="success" type="tiles">Thanks</result>
</action>
```

Contrast these tiles results with dispatcher results that forward to a JSP.

Struts Tiles Plugin

The Struts Tiles plug-in is meant to enable the use of Tiles in Struts applications. You need to do the following to use Tiles.

1. Copy the Tiles JARs (tiles-core-*VERSION*.jar, tiles-api-*VERSION*.jar, tiles-jsp-*VERSION*.jar) and the struts2-tiles-plugin-*VERSION*.jar files to WEB-INF/lib.
2. Register the **StrutsTilesListener** in your **web.xml** file.

```
<listener>
    <listener-class>
        org.apache.struts2.tiles.StrutsTilesListener
    </listener-class>
</listener>
```

3. Extend the **tiles-default** package in your package or define the following in your package:

```
<result-types>
    <result-type name="tiles"
        class="org.apache.struts2.views.tiles.TilesResult"/>
</result-types>
```

4. Use tiles results in your actions.

Now let's look at an example.

Struts Tiles Example

The **app24a** application has two actions, **Product_input** and **Product_add**. Figure 24.3 shows the directory structure of this application.

The action declarations for this application are shown in Listing 24.2.

Listing 24.2: Action declarations

```
<package name="app24a" extends="tiles-default">
    <action name="Product_input">
        <result name="success" type="tiles">Product</result>
    </action>
    <action name="Product_add">
        <result name="success" type="tiles">Thanks</result>
    </action>
</package>
```

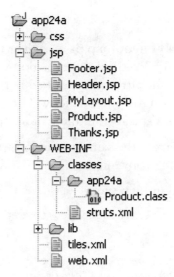

Figure 24.3: app24a directory structure

The actions look like any ordinary actions, except that their results are of type **tiles**. Also, instead of forwarding to JSPs, these results forward to definitions. The **Product** and **Thanks** definitions are defined in the **tiles.xml** file shown in Listing 24.3.

Listing 24.3: The tiles.xml file

```
<?xml version="1.0" encoding="ISO-8859-1" ?>
<!DOCTYPE tiles-definitions PUBLIC
    "-//Apache Software Foundation//DTD Tiles Configuration 2.0//EN"
    "http://struts.apache.org/dtds/tiles-config_2_0.dtd">

<tiles-definitions>
    <definition name="Product" template="/jsp/MyLayout.jsp">
        <put-attribute name="pageTitle" value="Product Input"/>
        <put-attribute name="header" value="/jsp/Header.jsp"/>
        <put-attribute name="footer" value="/jsp/Footer.jsp"/>
        <put-attribute name="body" value="/jsp/Product.jsp"/>
    </definition>

    <definition name="Thanks" template="/jsp/MyLayout.jsp">
        <put-attribute name="pageTitle" value="Thank You"/>
        <put-attribute name="header" value="/jsp/Header.jsp"/>
        <put-attribute name="footer" value="/jsp/Footer.jsp"/>
        <put-attribute name="body" value="/jsp/Thanks.jsp"/>
    </definition>
```

```
</tiles-definitions>
```

Both definitions use the **MyLayout.jsp** page as their template. It's clear that the result associated with the **Product_input** action will be forwarded to the **MyLayout.jsp** page using the attributes specified in the **Product** definition. The **Product_add** action, on the other hand, will be forwarded to the same template using the attributes specified in the **Thanks** definition.

The **MyLayout.jsp** page is the same as that in Listing 24.1 but reprinted in Listing 24.4 for your reading convenience.

Listing 24.4: The MyLayout.jsp page

```
<%@ taglib uri="http://tiles.apache.org/tags-tiles" prefix="tiles"%>
<html>
<head>
<title><tiles:getAsString name="pageTitle"/></title>
<style type="text/css">@import url(css/main.css);</style>
</head>
<body>
    <tiles:insertAttribute name="header"/>
    <tiles:insertAttribute name="body"/>
    <tiles:insertAttribute name="footer"/>
</body>
</html>
```

The other JSPs are given in Listings 24.5 to 24.8.

Listing 24.5: The Product.jsp page

```
<%@ taglib prefix="s" uri="/struts-tags" %>
<div id="global">
    <h3>Add Product</h3>
    <s:form action="Product_add">
        <s:textfield name="name" label="Product Name"/>
        <s:textfield name="description" label="Description"/>
        <s:textfield name="price" label="Price"/>
        <s:submit/>
    </s:form>
</div>
```

Listing 24.6: The Thanks.jsp page

```
<%@ taglib prefix="s" uri="/struts-tags" %>
<div id="global">
The product has been added.
</div>
```

Listing 24.7: The Header.jsp page

```
<div style="border:1px solid black;height:60px;background:#dedede">
<h1>Administration Page</h1>
</div>
```

Listing 24.8: The Footer.jsp page

```
<div style="text-align:right;border:1px solid black">
&copy;2008 Company Co.
</div>
```

You can run the application by invoking this URL.

```
http://localhost:8080/app24a/Product_input.action
```

Figure 24.4 shows how the layout is rendered.

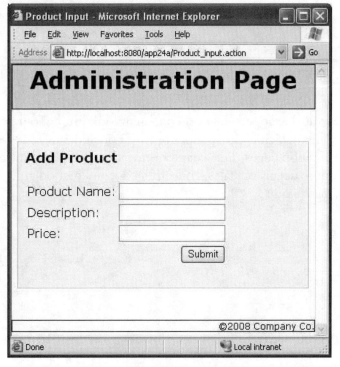

Figure 24.4: Tiles in action

The same consistent layout is used for the **Product_add** action, as shown in Figure 24.5.

Figure 24.5: The Thank You page

Summary

Tiles helps Struts developers create a consistent look throughout an application. Tiles, which is vastly superior to JSP includes, allows you to write layout and definition pages. This chapter is meant to be a brief introduction to Tiles 2. For more details on Tiles, consult the documentation at its website http://tiles.apache.org/.

Chapter 25
JFreeChart Plug-ins

JFreeChart is a Java open source library for creating charts. Thanks to the two plug-ins discussed in this chapter, you can too tap the power of this popular library. This chapter is focused on how to use the plug-ins and not a tutorial on JFreeChart itself, even though a brief introduction is given.

JFreeChart must be downloaded separately as its LGPL license does not permit it to be distributed with Struts. Information on how to download it is available from its website:

```
http://www.jfree.org/jfreechart,
```

The JFreeChart component is packaged into a JAR file named **jfreechart-VERSION.jar**. In addition to this JAR file, you need the **jcommon-VERSION.jar** file that contains dependencies needed by JFreeChart. The latter is included in the JFreeChart package, so you don't need to download JCommon separately.

This chapter explains the standard JFreeChart plug-in that comes with Struts and a more flexible plug-in from BrainySoftware that I wrote.

The JFreeChart API

This section discusses the most important types in the API. The complete list can be found here:

```
http://www.jfree.org/jfreechart/api/javadoc/index.html
```

The JFreeChart Class

JFreeChart is a class in the **org.jfree.chart** package. A **JFreeChart** object represents a chart. When using the JFreeChart plug-in in your Struts application, you produce a chart by creating an instance of this class.

For example, you can create an instance of **JFreeChart**, hence a web chart, just by having an instance of **Plot**, which will be discussed in the next subsection. Here are the constructors of **JFreeChart**.

```
public JFreeChart(Plot plot)

public JFreeChart(java.lang.String title, Plot plot)

public JFreeChart(java.lang.String title, java.awt.Font titleFont,
        Plot plot, boolean createLegend)
```

Plot

This abstract class is the main member of the **org.jfree.chart.plot** package. An instance of **Plot** represents a plot that draws a chart. There are many subclasses of **Plot** that you can use, one of which you'll see in the **app25a** application.

Using the Standard Plugin

Struts comes with a plug-in that utilizes JFreeChart. To use it, follow these steps.

1. Download the JFreeChart component and copy the **jfreechart-VERSION.jar** and **jcommon-VERSION.jar** files to your application's **WEB-INF/lib** directory.
2. Copy the struts-jfreechart-plugin-*VERSION*.jar file to the WEB-INF/lib directory.
3. Make sure that your Struts package extends **jfreechart-default**.
4. Use chart as the result type and pass the **width** and **height** parameters to the result.
5. Your action class must have a **chart** property that returns the **JFreeChart** object to be displayed.

The plug-in sends the chart as a PNG image. You may want to use an **img** element to request the chart so that you can include the chart in an HTML page.

The plug-in accepts two parameters, **width** and **height**, to give you a chance to change the chart size, which by default is 200px X 150px.

As an example, the **app25a** application shows an action that uses JFreeChart. The action declarations for the application are given in Listing 25.1.

Listing 25.1: The action declarations

```
<package name="chart" extends="jfreechart-default">
    <action name="chart" class="app20a.GetChartAction">
        <result name="success" type="chart">
            <param name="width">400</param>
            <param name="height">300</param>
        </result>
    </action>
</package>
<package name="app25a" extends="struts-default">
    <action name="main">
        <result name="success">/jsp/Main.jsp</result>
    </action>
</package>
```

There are two actions here. The **chart** action is part of the **chart** package that extends **jfreechart-default**. This is the action that retrieves the chart. You can invoke this action by itself to quickly view the resulting chart.

The second action, **main**, displays a JSP that contains an **img** element whose source references the **chart** action. Note that both actions are contained in different packages. This has to be so because **jfreechart-default** does not extend **struts-default**, so only chart results are allowed under **jfreechart-default**.

The **GetChartAction** class is shown in Listing 25.2 and the **Main.jsp** page in Listing 25.3.

Listing 25.2: The GetChartAction class

```
package app25a;
import org.jfree.chart.JFreeChart;
```

```
import org.jfree.chart.axis.NumberAxis;
import org.jfree.chart.axis.ValueAxis;
import org.jfree.chart.plot.XYPlot;
import org.jfree.chart.renderer.xy.StandardXYItemRenderer;
import org.jfree.data.xy.XYSeries;
import org.jfree.data.xy.XYSeriesCollection;
import com.opensymphony.xwork2.ActionSupport;

public class GetChartAction extends ActionSupport {

    private JFreeChart chart;

    public String execute() throws Exception {
        ValueAxis xAxis = new NumberAxis("Input Increase");
        ValueAxis yAxis = new NumberAxis("Production");
        XYSeries xySeries = new XYSeries(new Integer(1));
        xySeries.add(0, 200);
        xySeries.add(1, 300);
        xySeries.add(2, 500);
        xySeries.add(3, 700);
        xySeries.add(4, 700);
        xySeries.add(5, 900);

        XYSeriesCollection xyDataset =
                new XYSeriesCollection(xySeries);

        // create XYPlot
        XYPlot xyPlot = new XYPlot(xyDataset, xAxis, yAxis,
                new StandardXYItemRenderer(
                        StandardXYItemRenderer.SHAPES_AND_LINES));
        chart = new JFreeChart(xyPlot);
        return SUCCESS;
    }

    public JFreeChart getChart() {
        return chart;
    }
}
```

Listing 25.3: The Main.jsp page

```
<%@ taglib prefix="s" uri="/struts-tags" %>
<html>
<head>
<style type="text/css">
img {
    float:right;
```

```
      margin:0 0 15px 20px;
      padding:15px;
      text-align:center;
}
</style>
</head>
<body>
<s:url action="chart" id="url"/>
<img src="<s:property value="url"/>"/>
<p>
XML is an open standard for data exchange as well as the

...

</p>
</body>
</html>
```

To test the plug-in, direct your browser to this URL.

```
http://localhost:8080/app25a/main.action
```

Figure 25.1 shows the result.

aThere are two things in the JFreeChart plug-in that I did not really like
and prompted me to write my own plug-in, the BrainySoftware JFreeChart
plug-in. The first is the fact that **jfreechart-default** does not extend **struts-
default**. The second is the fact that changing a chart size requires updating the
Struts configuration file. The exact size is often in the graphic designer's hand
and if he or she could resize the image without having to bother the
application administrator, it would be a much coveted feature.

Using the BrainySoftware JFreeChart Plugin

Like the standard JFreeChart plugin, The BrainySoftware JFreeChart plugin is
a free component that can be used in non-commercial and commercial
environments. Unlike the standard plug-in, however, the BrainySoftware
JFreeChart plug-in, which is included in the ZIP that contains the sample
applications for this book, extends **struts-default** and allows the graphic
designer to resize the chart without the help of a programmer.

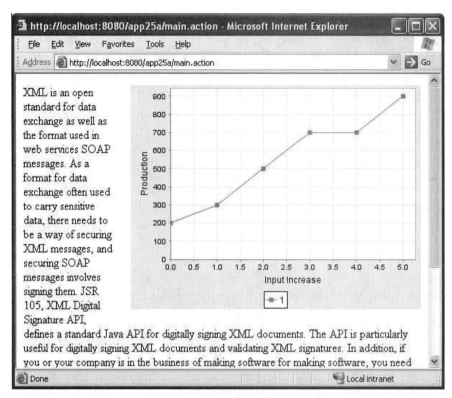

Figure 25.1: JFreeChart at work

Using it is not harder than the standard plug-in either, you just need to follow these steps.

1. Download the JFreeChart component and copy the **jfreechart-VERSION.jar** and **jcommon-VERSION.jar** files to the **WEB-INF/lib** directory.
2. Copy the brainyjfreechartplugin.jar file to the WEB-INF/lib directory.
3. Make sure that your Struts package **extends brainyjfreechart-default**.
4. Use **brainyjfreechart** as the result type.
5. Your action class must have a **chart** property that returns the **JFreeChart** object to be displayed. Optionally, you can have **chartWidth** and **chartHeight** properties to determine the chart size.

Application **app25b** shows an action that uses Brainy Software's JFreeChart plug-in. The action declarations are shown in Listing 25.4.

Listing 25.4: Action declarations for app25b

```xml
<package name="app25b" extends="brainyjfreechart-default">
    <action name="chart" class="app20b.GetBrainyChartAction">
        <result name="success" type="brainyjfreechart"/>
    </action>
    <action name="main">
        <result name="success" type="dispatcher" >
            /jsp/Main.jsp
        </result>
    </action>
</package>
```

The action class is given in Listing 25.5. This is similar to the one in Listing 25.2, however it has two additional properties, **chartWidth** and **chartHeight**.

Listing 25.5: The GetBrainyChartAction class

```java
package app25b;
import org.jfree.chart.JFreeChart;
import org.jfree.chart.axis.NumberAxis;
import org.jfree.chart.axis.ValueAxis;
import org.jfree.chart.plot.XYPlot;
import org.jfree.chart.renderer.xy.StandardXYItemRenderer;
import org.jfree.data.xy.XYSeries;
import org.jfree.data.xy.XYSeriesCollection;
import com.opensymphony.xwork2.ActionSupport;

public class GetBrainyChartAction extends ActionSupport {
    private JFreeChart chart;
    private int chartWidth = 250;
    private int chartHeight = 300;

    public String execute() {
        ValueAxis xAxis = new NumberAxis("Input Increase");
        ValueAxis yAxis = new NumberAxis("Production");
        XYSeries xySeries = new XYSeries(new Integer(1));

        xySeries.add(0, 200);
        xySeries.add(1, 300);
        xySeries.add(2, 500);
        xySeries.add(3, 700);
        xySeries.add(4, 700);
        xySeries.add(5, 900);

        XYSeriesCollection xyDataset =
                new XYSeriesCollection(xySeries);
```

```
    // create XYPlot
    XYPlot xyPlot = new XYPlot(xyDataset, xAxis, yAxis,
            new StandardXYItemRenderer(
                    StandardXYItemRenderer.LINES));
    chart = new JFreeChart(xyPlot);
    return SUCCESS;
}

// getters and setters not shown
}
```

Invoke this URL to test the application.

`http://localhost:8080/app25b/main.action`

Figure 25.2 shows the result.

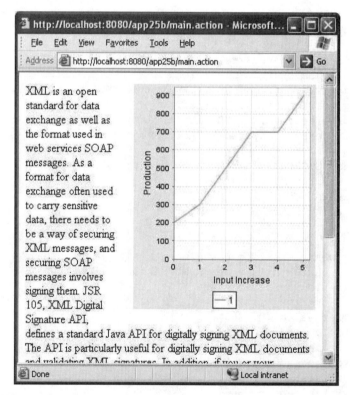

Figure 25.2: Using BrainySoftware JFreeChart plug-in

Summary

JFreeChart is a powerful open-source library for generating charts. To use it in Struts, you need a plug-in. At least two free JFreeChart plug-ins are available, the standard one that comes with Struts and the one downloadable from brainysoftware.com. This chapter showed how to use both.

Chapter 26
Zero Configuration

Struts configuration is easy, but it is possible not to have to configure at all. In other words, zero configuration. Instead of mapping actions and results in the **struts.xml** file, you annotate the action class. And if you're tired of annotating, you can use the CodeBehind plug-in to handle that for you.

> **Note**
> Appendix C, "Annotations" explains annotations.

This chapter explains zero configuration and the CodeBehind plug-in.

Conventions

Since you will not have a configuration file if you decide to go the zero configuration way, you will need to tell Struts how to find your action classes. You do this by telling Struts the Java packages of the action classes used in your application by including, in your **web.xml** file, an **actionPackages** initial parameter to the Struts filter dispatcher. Like this.

```
<filter>
    <filter-name>struts2</filter-name>
    <filter-class>
        org.apache.struts2.dispatcher.FilterDispatcher
    </filter-class>
    <init-param>
        <param-name>actionPackages</param-name>
        <param-value>app26a,com.example</param-value>
    </init-param>
</filter>
```

The value of the **actionPackages** parameter is a comma-delimited list of packages that Struts needs to scan for action classes. In the example above,

Struts will scan the **app26a** package and its sub-packages as well as the **com.example** package and its sub-packages.

An action class of a zero configuration application must either implement the **com.opensymphony.xwork2.Action** interface (or by extending **com.opensymphony.xwork2.ActionSupport**) or has an **Action** suffix on its name. For example, a POJO class named **CustomerAction** will comply. A child class of **ActionSupport** named **User** will also be acceptable.

Now, since without a **struts.xml** file you cannot give an action a name, you rely on Struts to do that. What name does Struts give your action? The action name will be the same as the name of the action class after the first letter of the class name is converted to lower case and its **Action** suffix, if any, is removed. Therefore, the action name for an action class named **EmployeeAction** will be **employee**, and you can invoke it using the URI **employee.action**.

Of course you must also take into account the namespace. If an action class is not a member of a package passed to the **actionPackages** parameter, but rather a member of its sub-package, the part of the subpackage name is not in the **actionPackages** parameter will be the namespace. For instance, if **com.example** is passed to the **actionPackages** parameter, the action class **com.example.action.CustomerAction** will be accessible through this URI:

```
/action/customer.action
```

Annotations

By following the conventions explained in the previous section, you can invoke action classes in your zero configuration application. But hold on, Struts does not know yet what results are associated with those action classes. This time you need to annotate, using the annotation types discussed in this section.

@Result

The **org.apache.struts2.config.Result** annotation type is used to define an action result. It has these elements, of which only **value** is required.

- **name**. The name of the result that corresponds to the return value of the action method.
- **params**. An array of **String**s used to pass parameters to the result.
- **type**. The class of the result type whose instance will handle the result.
- **value**. The value passed to the result.

For instance, the action class in Listing 26.1 is annotated **@Result**.

Listing 26.1: The Customer action class

```
package app26a;
import org.apache.struts2.config.Result;
import org.apache.struts2.dispatcher.ServletDispatcherResult;
import com.opensymphony.xwork2.ActionSupport;

@Result(name="success", value="/jsp/Customer.jsp",
        type=ServletDispatcherResult.class)
public class Customer extends ActionSupport {
    public String execute() {
        System.out.println("Help I'm being executed...");
        return SUCCESS;
    }
}
```

The annotation in Listing 26.1 indicates to Struts that if the action method returns "success," Struts must create an instance of **ServletDispatcherResult** and pass the instance "/jsp/Customer.jsp." The **ServletDispatcherResult** class is the underlying class for the Dispatcher result type. Practically this means the same as this.

```
<result name="success" type="dispatcher">/jsp/Customer.jsp</result>
```

You can use this URL to test it:

```
http://localhost:8080/app26a/customer.action
```

Note
When going zero configuration, you need to get familiar with the underlying classes for the bundled result types, not only their short names. You can look up the class names in Appendix A.

@Results

If an action method may return one of two values, say "success" or "input," you cannot use two **Result** annotations. Instead, use **@Results**. The syntax for this annotation type is as follows.

```
@Results({ @Result-1, @Result-2, … @Result-n })
```

For example, the **Supplier** action class in Listing 26.2 may return "success" or "error." It is annotated **@Results**.

Listing 26.2: The Supplier action class

```
package app26a;
import org.apache.struts2.config.Result;
import org.apache.struts2.config.Results;
import org.apache.struts2.dispatcher.ServletDispatcherResult;
import com.opensymphony.xwork2.ActionSupport;

@Results({
    @Result(name="success", value="/jsp/Customer.jsp",
            type=ServletDispatcherResult.class),
    @Result(name="error", value="/jsp/Error.jsp",
            type=ServletDispatcherResult.class)
})

public class Supplier extends ActionSupport {
    private String name;
    public String execute() {
        if (name == null || name.length() < 4) {
            return ERROR;
        } else {
            return SUCCESS;
        }
    }
    // getter and setter not shown
}
```

To test the class, use either one of the following URLs:

```
http://localhost:8080/app26a/supplier.action
http://localhost:8080/app26a/supplier.action?name=whatever
```

@Namespace

Use this annotation type to override the namespace convention. It has one element, **value**, which specifies the namespace for the annotated class.

For example, the **actionPackages** value of **app26a** is **app26a**. By convention, the namespace of the action class **app26a.admin.action.EditCustomer** will be **/admin/action**, and the class can be invoked using this URI: **/admin/action/editCustomer.action**. To override this, use the **Namespace** annotation type.

As an example, the **EditCustomer** class in Listing 26.3 is annotated **@Namespace**. Since the value of the annotation is "/," it can be invoked using this URI: **/editCustomer.action**.

Listing 26.3: The EditCustomer action class

```
package app26a.admin.action;
import org.apache.struts2.config.Namespace;
import org.apache.struts2.config.Result;
import org.apache.struts2.dispatcher.ServletDispatcherResult;
import com.opensymphony.xwork2.ActionSupport;

@Result(name="success", value="/jsp/Customer.jsp",
        type=ServletDispatcherResult.class)
@Namespace(value="/")
public class EditCustomer extends ActionSupport {
}
```

You can invoke the **editCustomer** action using this URL:

```
http://localhost:8080/app26a/editCustomer.action
```

Consequently, you can no longer use this URL to invoke the **editCustomer** action.

```
http://localhost:8080/app26a/admin/action/editCustomer.action
```

@ParentPackage

Use this annotation type to inherit an XWork package other than **struts-default**. For example, this annotation indicates that the action belongs to the **captcha-default** package:

```
@ParentPackage(value="struts-default")
```

The CodeBehind Plug-in

The CodeBehind plug-in does two things:

1. Provide mappings for actions with no action classes.
2. Find forward views for action classes without explicit **@Result** annotations.

To use this plug-in, you must first copy the **struts-codebehind-plugin-VERSION.jar** file to your **WEB-INF/lib** directory.

You still need to pass an **actionPackages** initial parameter in your **web.xml** file so that Struts can find default action classes.

For example, the **app26b** application shows how to use the CodeBehind plug-in. To the filter dispatcher, we pass an **actionPackages** initial parameter, as shown in Listing 26.4.

Listing 26.4: The filter declaration

```
<filter>
    <filter-name>struts2</filter-name>
    <filter-class>
        org.apache.struts2.dispatcher.FilterDispatcher
    </filter-class>
    <init-param>
        <param-name>actionPackages</param-name>
        <param-value>app26b</param-value>
    </init-param>
</filter>
```

The **Login** class in Listing 26.5 is an action class in **app26b**. By using the CodeBehind plug-in, the **Login** action will be able to forward to the correct JSP after the action is executed.

Listing 26.5: The Login action class

```
package app26b;
import com.opensymphony.xwork2.ActionSupport;

public class Login extends ActionSupport {
    private String userName;
    private String password;
    public String execute() {
        if (userName != null && password != null
```

```
            && userName.equals("don")
            && password.equals("secret")) {
        return SUCCESS;
    } else {
        return INPUT;
    }
}

// getters and setters not shown
}
```

The action method (**execute**) returns either "input" or "success." As such, the forward JSP will have to be either **login-input.jsp** or **login-success.jsp**. These JSPs are shows in Listings 26.6 and 26.7. Note that in Listing 26.6, because there's no explicit action declaration, you need to pass a URI and not an action name to the form's **action** attribute.

Listing 26.6: The login-input.jsp page

```
<%@ taglib prefix="s" uri="/struts-tags" %>
<html>
<head>
<title>Login</title>
<style type="text/css">@import url(css/main.css);</style>
</head>
<body>
<div id="global" style="width:400px">
    <h3>Enter your user name and password</h3>
    <s:form action="login.action">
        <s:textfield name="userName" label="User Name"/>
        <s:password name="password" label="Password"/>
        <s:submit value="Login"/>
    </s:form>
</div>
</body>
</html>
```

Listing 26.7: The login-success.jsp page

```
<html>
<head>
<title>CodeBehind</title>
</head>

<body>
You're logged in.
</body>
```

```
</html>
```

To test the application, direct your browser to this URL:

```
http://localhost:8080/app26b/login-input.action
```

The CodeBehind plug-in will kick in, invoke the **Login** action, and forward to the **login-input.jsp** page. The result is shown in Figure 26.1.

Figure 26.1: The login-input.jsp page

When you submit the form, the field values are sent to this URL:

```
http://localhost:8080/app26b/login.action
```

Summary

This chapter discussed the zero configuration feature in Struts that can match a URL with an action class. This feature does not match actions and results, however, and for the latter you need the CodeBehind plug-in.

Chapter 27
AJAX

The Struts Dojo plug-in bundles the Dojo Toolkit, an open source JavaScript framework, and provides custom tags to build AJAX components effortlessly. Thanks to this plug-in you can even use AJAX even if you know nothing about JavaScript. However, a solid command of JavaScript will help you tap the power of AJAX.

This chapter discusses the tags in the plug-in. To test the examples in this chapter, you have to be using Struts 2.1.0 or later. At the time of writing, version 2.1 has not been released and can be downloaded from here.

```
http://people.apache.org/builds/struts/2.1.0/
```

The Struts Dojo plug-in itself is not included in the **lib** directory of the Struts distribution and must be extracted from the Showcase application that comes with Struts. Unfortunately, the version of Dojo in this plug-in is 0.4, which is a much older version than what is available at the time of writing (version 1.01). Version 0.4 is very slow compared with its successors. The next release of the Struts Dojo plug-in is expected to bring Dojo 1.01 or later to the table.

Another unfortunate fact is that Dojo 1.0 or later is not backward compatible with version 0.4, which means any code you write that uses this plug-in may not work with a future version of the plug-in. Having said that, the plug-in is still great software that can help you write AJAX applications easily.

Note
Another popular JavaScript framework is Prototype (http://prototypejs.org/), which provides a set of JavaScript objects with a very small footprint, enabling fast download. In addition, Scriptaculous (http://script.aculo.us/) provides AJAX components that are based on Prototype.

AJAX Overview

AJAX is a name coined by Jesse James Garrett of Adaptive Path for two old technologies, JavaScript and XML. AJAX applications asynchronously connect to the server to collect more data that can be displayed in the current web page. As a result, new information can be shown without page refresh. Google was the first to popularize this strategy with their Gmail and Google Maps applications. However, Google was not the first to make full use of the **XMLHttpRequest** object, the engine that makes asynchronous connections possible. Microsoft added it to Internet Explorer 5 and seasoned developers discovered ways to reap its benefits. Soon afterwards Mozilla browsers also had their own version of this object. Prior to **XMLHttpRequest**, people used DHTML and HTML frames and iframes to update pages without refresh.

Despite advance in client-side technologies, writing JavaScript code, hence AJAX applications, is still intimidating. Even though IDEs are available for writing JavaScript code, programmers still have to overcome the biggest challenge in writing client-side applications: browser compatibility. It is a fact of life that every browser implements JavaScript slightly differently from each other. Even the same browser does not interpret JavaScript in the same way in different operating systems. As a result, you have to test your script in various operating systems using various browsers and write multiple versions of code that work in all browsers.

This is where a JavaScript framework like Dojo comes to rescue. With Dojo you only need to write and test once and let it worry about browser compatibility. Needless to say, using the Struts Dojo plug-in as your AJAX platform saves an awful lot of time.

Dojo's Event System

JavaScript is an event-based language, but managing events in a cross browser environment has proved a nightmare. Dojo comes to rescue by providing an identical way of working with events.

Dojo allows you to connect a JavaScript function with an event. As such, you can create an event handler that will get called when an event is triggered. The Dojo **connect** method links an event with a function. The **disconnect** method severs a connection. Dojo's **event** object is the normalized version of the JavaScript **event** object. Unlike the latter, which behaves slightly differently in different browsers and hence making developing cross browser applications very difficult, the former provide a uniform interface that works the same in all supported browsers. Using Dojo saves you time because you don't need to test and tweak your code to cater for a specific browser.

In addition to the normalized **event** object, Dojo supports a topic-based messaging system that enables anonymous event communication. Anonymous in the sense that you can connect elements in a web page that have no previous knowledge about each other. A topic is logical channel similar to an Internet mailing list. Anyone interested in a mailing list can subscribe to it to get notification every time a subscriber broadcasts a message. With a topic-based messaging system such as that in Dojo, a web object (a button, a link, a form, a div element) may subscribe to a topic and publish a topic. This means, an AJAX component can be programmed to do something upon the publication of a topic as well as publish a topic that may trigger other subscribers to do something.

To publish a topic, you use the **publish** method. Bear in mind that this is how you do it in Dojo 0.4, which may not work in newer versions of Dojo.

```
dojo.event.topic.publish(topicName, arguments)
```

The topic name can be anything. As long as the other parties know a topic name, they can subscribe to the topic.

In AJAX programming, you normally subscribe to a topic because you want something to be done upon a message publication to that topic. As such, when you subscribe to a topic, you also define what you need to do or what function to call. Here is the method to subscribe to a topic in Dojo. Again, this is Dojo 0.4 we're talking here.

```
Dojo.event.topic.subscribe(topicName, functionName)
```

The tags in the Struts Dojo plug-in make it even easier to work with topics. Most tags can subscribe and publish a topic without JavaScript code. For instance, the **a** tag has an **errorNotifyTopics** attribute you can use to list the topics to publish when the tag raises an error. The **div** tag has a **startTimerListenTopics** attribute to accept a list of topics that will cause the rendered div element to start its internal timer.

Topic-based messaging system will become clearer after you learn about the tags.

Using the Struts Dojo Plug-in

To use the tags in the plug-in, you must follow these steps.

1. Add this taglib directive to the top of your JSPs.

```
<%@ taglib prefix="sx" uri="/struts-dojo-tags" %>
```

2. Copy the Struts Dojo plug-in to your **WEB-INF/lib** directory. This plug-in is included in the lib directory of this book.
3. Write the **head** tag on each JSP.

Let's now look at the tags in the Struts Dojo plug-in.

The head Tag

The **head** tag renders JavaScript code that downloads Dojo files and configures Dojo. This tag must be added to every JSP that uses other Struts Dojo tags.

Table 27.1 shows the attributes of the **head** tag.

The **compressed** attribute, which is true by default, indicates whether or not the compressed version of Dojo files should be used. Using the compressed version saves loading time, but it is hard to read. In development mode you may want to set this attribute to false so that you can easily read the code rendered by the tags discussed in this chapter.

In development mode you should also set the **debug** attribute to true and the **cache** attribute to false. Turning on the **debug** attribute makes Dojo display warnings and error messages at the bottom of the page.

Here is how your head tag may look like in development mode.

```
<sx:head debug="true" cache="false" compressed="false" />
```

In production, however, it's likely you'll have this.

```
<sx:head/>
```

Name	Data Type	Default Value	Description
baseRelativePath	String	/struts/dojo	The path to the Dojo distribution folder
cache	boolean	true	Indicates if Dojo files should be cached by the browser.
compressed	boolean	true	Indicates whether or not the compressed version of Dojo files should be used.
debug	boolean	false	Indicates whether or not Dojo should be in debug mode.
extraLocales	String		Comma delimited list of locales to be used by Dojo.
locale	String		Overrides Dojo locale.
parseContent	boolean	false	Indicates whether or not to parse the whole document for widgets.

Table 27.1: head tag attributes

The div Tag

This tag renders an HTML div element that can load content dynamically. The rendered div element will also have an internal timer to reload its content at regular intervals. An ad rotator can be implemented using the div tag without programming.

The attributes for this tag are listed in Table 27.2.

Name	Data Type	Default Value	Description
afterNotifyTopics	String		Comma delimited topics to be published after the request, if the request is successful.
autoStart	boolean	true	Whether or not to start the timer automatically.
beforeNotifyTopics	String		Comma delimited topics to be published before the request.

closable	boolean	false	Whether or not to show a Close button when the div is inside a tabbed panel
delay	integer		The number of milliseconds that must elapse before the content is fetched
errorNotifyTopics	String		Comma delimited topics to be published after the request, if the request fails.
errorText	String		The text to be displayed if the request fails.
executeScripts	boolean	false	Indicates whether or not JavaScript code in the fetched content should be executed.
formFilter	String		The function to be used to filter the form fields.
formId	String		The identifier of the form whose fields will be passed as request parameters.
handler	String		The JavaScript function that will make the request.
highlightColor	String		The color to highlight the elements specified in the **targets** attribute.
highlightDuration	integer	2000	The duration in milliseconds the elements specified in the **targets** attribute will be highlighted. This attribute will only take effect if the **hightlightColor** attribute has a value.
href	String		The URL to call to fetch the content.
indicator	String		The identifier of the element that will be displayed while making the request.
javascriptTooltip	boolean	false	Indicates whether or not to use JavaScript to generate tooltips.
listenTopics	String		The topics that will trigger the remote call.

loadingText	String	Loading...	The text to display while content is being fetched.
notifyTopics	String		Comma delimited topics to be published before and after the request and upon an error occurring.
openTemplate	String		The template to use for opening the rendered HTML
parseContent	boolean	true	Whether or not to parse the returned content for widgets.
preload	boolean	true	Whether or not to load content when the page is loaded.
refreshOnShow	boolean	false	Whether or not to load content when the div becomes visible. This attribute takes effect only if the div is inside a tabbed panel.
separateScripts	boolean	true	Whether or not to run the script in a separate scope that is unique for each tag.
showErrorTransportText	boolean	true	Whether or not errors will be shown.
showLoadingText	boolean	false	Whether or not loading text will be shown on targets
startTimerListenTopics	String		Topics that will start the timer
stopTimerListenTopics	String		Topics that will stop the timer
transport	String	XMLHttp Transport	The transport for making the request
updateFreq	integer		The frequency (in milliseconds) of content update

Table 27.2: div tag attributes

The **div** tag also inherits the common attributes specified in Chapter 5, "Form Tags."

Three examples are given for this tag.

Example 1

The **Div1.jsp** page in Listing 27.1 uses a **div** tag that updates itself every three seconds. The **href** attribute is used to specify the server location that will return the content and the **updateFreq** attribute specifies the update frequency in milliseconds. The internal timer starts automatically because by default the value of the **autoStart** attribute is true.

Listing 27.1: The Div1.jsp page

```
<%@ taglib prefix="sx" uri="/struts-dojo-tags" %>
<html>
<head>
<title>Div</title>
<sx:head/>
</head>
<body>
<sx:div
        cssStyle="border:1px solid black;height:75px;width:100px"
        href="ServerTime.action"
        updateFreq="3000"
        highlightColor="#cecdee">
    Server time will be displayed here
</sx:div>
</body>
</html>
```

An interesting feature of this tag is the automatic highlight color that will highlight the div element and then fade. You can specify the highlight color using the **highlightColor** attribute.

Use this URL to test the **div** tag in Listing 27.1.

```
http://localhost:8080/app27a/Div1.action
```

Example 2

The **Div2.jsp** page in Listing 27.2 showcases a **div** tag whose **startTimerListenTopics** attribute is set to subscribe to a **startTimer** topic. Upon publication of this topic, the div's internal timer will start. A submit button is used to publish a **startTimer** topic.

Listing 27.2: The Div2.jsp page

```
<%@ taglib prefix="s" uri="/struts-tags" %>
<%@ taglib prefix="sx" uri="/struts-dojo-tags" %>
<html>
<head>
<title>Div</title>
<sx:head/>
</head>
<body>
<sx:div
        cssStyle="border:1px solid black;height:75px;width:100px"
        href="ServerTime.action"
        updateFreq="2000"
        autoStart="false"
        startTimerListenTopics="startTimer"
        highlightColor="#ddaaba">
    Server time will be displayed here
</sx:div>
<s:submit theme="simple" value="Start timer"
        onclick="dojo.event.topic.publish('startTimer')"
/>
</body>
</html>
```

To test this example, direct your browser here:

```
http://localhost:8080/app27a/Div2.action
```

Click the Start timer button to start the timer.

Example 3

This **div** tag in the **Div3.jsp** page in Listing 27.3 shows how you can use a div tag to publish a topic.

Listing 27.3: The Div3.jsp page

```
<%@ taglib prefix="s" uri="/struts-tags" %>
<%@ taglib prefix="sx" uri="/struts-dojo-tags" %>
<html>
<head>
<title>Div</title>
<sx:head/>
<script type="text/javascript">
var counter = 1;
```

```
dojo.event.topic.subscribe("updateCounter", function(event, widget){
    dojo.byId("counter").innerHTML =
        "The server has been hit " + counter++ + " times";
});
</script>
</head>
<body>
<sx:div
    cssStyle="border:1px solid black;height:75px;width:100px"
    href="ServerTime.action"
    updateFreq="2000"
    afterNotifyTopics="updateCounter"
    highlightColor="#ddaaba">
  Server time will be displayed here
</sx:div>
<div id="counter">
</div>
</body>
</html>
```

The **div** tag has its internal timer set to set off every two seconds. Every time it does, it publishes an **updateCounter** topic, which is assigned to its **afterNotifyTopics** attribute. The Dojo **subscribe** method is used to subscribe to the topic and run the specified function every time the **div** tag publishes the topic.

```
dojo.event.topic.subscribe("updateCounter", function(event, widget){
    dojo.byId("counter").innerHTML =
        "The server has been hit " + counter++ + " times";
});
```

The function associated with the **updateCounter** topic increments a counter and changes the content of a second div tag.

To test this example, direct your browser to this URL.

```
http://localhost:8080/app27a/Div3.action
```

The a Tag

The **a** tag renders an HTML anchor that, when clicked, makes an AJAX request. The **targets** attribute of the tag is used to specify elements, normally div elements, that will display the AJAX response. If nested within a form, this tag will submit the form when clicked. Table 27.3 lists the attributes of the **a** tag.

Name	Data Type	Default Value	Description
afterNotifyTopics	String		Comma delimited topics to be published after the request, if the request is successful.
ajaxAfterValidation	boolean	false	Indicates whether or not to make an asynchronous request if validation succeeds. This attribute will only take effect if the validate attribute is set to true.
beforeNotifyTopics	String		Comma delimited topics to be published before the request.
errorNotifyTopics	String		Comma delimited topics to be published after the request, if the request fails.
errorText	String		The text to be displayed if the request fails.
executeScripts	boolean	false	Indicates whether or not JavaScript code in the fetched content should be executed.
formFilter	String		The function to be used to filter the form fields.
formId	String		The identifier of the form whose fields will be passed as request parameters.
handler	String		The JavaScript function that will make the request.
highlightColor	String		The color to highlight the elements specified in the **targets** attribute.
highlightDuration	integer	2000	The duration in milliseconds the elements specified in the **targets** attribute will be highlighted. This attribute will only take effect if the **hightlightColor** attribute has a value.

href	String		The URL to call to fetch the content.
indicator	String		The identifier of the element that will be displayed while making the request.
javascriptTooltip	boolean	false	Indicates whether or not to use JavaScript to generate tooltips.
listenTopics	String		The topics that will trigger the remote call
loadingText	String	Loading...	The text to display while content is being fetched
notifyTopics	String		Comma delimited topics to be published before and after the request and upon an error occurring
openTemplate	String		The template to use for opening the rendered HTML
parseContent	boolean	true	Whether or not to parse the returned content for widgets.
separateScripts	boolean	true	Whether or not to run the script in a separate scope that is unique for each tag.
showErrorTransportText	boolean	true	Whether or not errors will be shown.
showLoadingText	boolean	false	Whether or not loading text will be shown on targets
targets	String		Comma delimited identifiers of the elements whose content will be updated
transport	String	XMLHttp Transport	The transport for making the request
validate	boolean	false	Whether or not AJAX validation should be performed

Table 27.3: a tag attributes

The **a** tag also inherits the common attributes specified in Chapter 5, "Form Tags."

For instance, the **A.jsp** page in Listing 27.4 uses an **a** tag to populate the div elements **div1** and **div2**.

Listing 27.4: The A.jsp page

```
<%@ taglib prefix="sx" uri="/struts-dojo-tags" %>
<html>
<head>
<title>A</title>
<sx:head/>
</head>
<body>
<sx:div id="div1"
    cssStyle="height:50px;width:200px;border:1px solid brown"/>
<sx:div id="div2"
    cssStyle="height:50px;width:200px;border:1px solid brown"/>
<sx:a href="ServerTime.action" targets="div1,div2">
    Update Time
</sx:a>
</body>
</html>
```

To test the tag, direct your browser to this location.

```
http://localhost:8080/app27a/A.action
```

The submit Tag

The **submit** tag renders a submit button that can submit a form asynchronously. There are three rendering types for this tag that you can choose by assigning a value to its **type** attribute. The three rendering types are:

- input. Renders **submit** as <input type="submit" …/>
- button. Renders **submit** as <button type="submit" …/>
- image. Renders **submit** as <input type="image" … />

Like the **a** tag, **submit** has a **targets** attribute to specify elements that will display the result of the form submit.

The **submit** tag attributes are listed in Table 27.4. In addition, the **submit** tag inherits the common attributes specified in Chapter 5, "Form Tags."

Name	Data Type	Default Value	Description
afterNotifyTopics	String		Comma delimited topics to be published after the request, if the request is successful.
ajaxAfterValidation	boolean	false	Indicates whether or not to make an asynchronous request if validation succeeds. This attribute will only take effect if the validate attribute is set to true.
beforeNotifyTopics	String		Comma delimited topics to be published before the request.
errorNotifyTopics	String		Comma delimited topics to be published after the request, if the request fails.
errorText	String		The text to be displayed if the request fails.
executeScripts	boolean	false	Indicates whether or not JavaScript code in the fetched content should be executed.
formFilter	String		The function to be used to filter the form fields.
formId	String		The identifier of the form whose fields will be passed as request parameters.
handler	String		The JavaScript function that will make the request.
highlightColor	String		The color to highlight the elements specified in the **targets** attribute.
highlightDuration	integer	2000	The duration in milliseconds the elements specified in the **targets** attribute will be highlighted. This attribute will only take effect if the **hightlightColor** attribute has a value.
href	String		The URL to call to fetch the content.

indicator	String		The identifier of the element that will be displayed while making the request.
javascriptTooltip	boolean	false	Indicates whether or not to use JavaScript to generate tooltips.
listenTopics	String		The topics that will trigger the remote call.
loadingText	String	Loading…	The text to display while content is being fetched.
method	String		The method attribute.
notifyTopics	String		Comma delimited topics to be published before and after the request and upon an error occurring.
parseContent	boolean	true	Whether or not to parse the returned content for widgets.
separateScripts	boolean	true	Whether or not to run the script in a separate scope that is unique for each tag.
showErrorTransportText	boolean	true	Whether or not errors will be shown.
showLoadingText	boolean	false	Whether or not loading text will be shown on targets
src	String		The image source for a submit button of type image.
targets	String		Comma delimited identifiers of the elements whose content will be updated
transport	String	XMLHttp Transport	The transport for making the request
type	String	input	The type of the submit button. Possible values are **input**, **image**, and **button**.
validate	boolean	false	Whether or not AJAX validation should be performed

Table 27.4: submit tag attributes

The **submit** tag can be nested within the form it submits or stand independently. This **submit** tag is nested within a form.

```
<s:div id="div1">
```

```
<s:form action="ServerTime.action">
    <s:submit  targets="div1"/>
</s:form>
</s:div>
```

And this is a **submit** tag outside the form it submits. In this case, you use the **formId** attribute to specify the form to submit.

```
<s:form id="loginForm" action="...">
    <s:textfield name="userName" label="User Name"/>
    <s:password name="password" label="Password"/>
</s:form>
<sx:submit formId="loginForm"/>
```

The bind Tag

The **bind** tag is used to attach an event with an event handler or to associate an object's event with a topic so that an element, even a non-AJAX component, can publish a topic.

The attributes that can appear inside a **bind** tag are presented in Table 27.5

Name	Data Type	Default Value	Description
afterNotifyTopics	String		Comma delimited topics to be published after the request, if the request is successful.
ajaxAfterValidation	boolean	false	Indicates whether or not to make an asynchronous request if validation succeeds. This attribute will only take effect if the validate attribute is set to true.
beforeNotifyTopics	String		Comma delimited topics to be published before the request.
errorNotifyTopics	String		Comma delimited topics to be published after the request, if the request fails.
errorText	String		The text to be displayed if the request fails.

events	String		Comma delimited event names to attach to
executeScripts	boolean	false	Indicates whether or not JavaScript code in the fetched content should be executed.
formFilter	String		The function to be used to filter the form fields.
formId	String		The identifier of the form whose fields will be passed as request parameters.
handler	String		The JavaScript function that will make the request.
highlightColor	String		The color to highlight the elements specified in the **targets** attribute.
highlightDuration	integer	2000	The duration in milliseconds the elements specified in the **targets** attribute will be highlighted. This attribute will only take effect if the **hightlightColor** attribute has a value.
href	String		The URL to call to fetch the content.
indicator	String		The identifier of the element that will be displayed while making the request.
listenTopics	String		The topics that will trigger the remote call.
loadingText	String	Loading…	The text to display while content is being fetched.
notifyTopics	String		Comma delimited topics to be published before and after the request and upon an error occurring.
separateScripts	boolean	true	Whether or not to run the script in a separate scope that is unique for each tag.
showErrorTransportText	boolean	true	Whether or not errors will be shown.

showLoadingText	boolean	false	Whether or not loading text will be shown on targets
sources	String		Comma delimited identifiers of the elements to attach to
targets	String		Comma delimited identifiers of the elements whose content will be updated
transport	String	XMLHttp Transport	The transport for making the request
validate	boolean	false	Whether or not AJAX validation should be performed

Table 27.5: bind tag attributes

The **bind** tag also inherits the common attributes specified in Chapter 5, "Form Tags."

As an example, the following **bind** tag attaches the **b1** submit button's **onclick** event with an AJAX call to **MyAction.action** and the response to the div element **div1**.

```
<sx:bind id="binder"
    href="MyAction.action"
    sources="b1"
    events="onclick"
    targets="div1" />

<s:submit id="b1" theme="simple" type="submit" />
```

The following **bind** tag causes the **onclick** event of the **b2** button to publish the **myTopic** topic.

```
<input id="b2" type="button">
<sx:bind
    id="binder"
    beforeNotifyTopics="myTopic"
    sources="b2"
    events="onclick"/>
```

The datetimepicker Tag

The **datetimepicker** tag renders either a date picker or a time picker. Figure 27.1 shows a date picker (on the left) and a time picker (on the right).

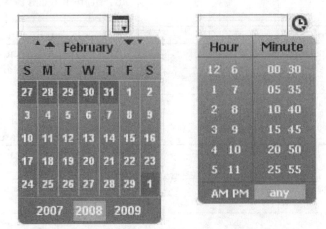

Figure 27.1: A date picker and a time picker

The list of attributes of the **datetimepicker** tag is given in Table 27.6.

Name	Data Type	Default Value	Description
adjustWeeks	boolean	false	Whether or not to adjust the number of rows in each month. If this attribute value is false, there are always six rows in each month.
dayWidth	String	narrow	Determines the day names in the header. Possible values are **narrow**, **abbr**, and **wide**.
displayFormat	String		The date and time pattern according to Unicode Technical Standard #35
displayWeeks	integer	6	The number of weeks to display
endDate	Date	2941-10-12	The last available date
formatLength	String	short	The formatting type for the display. Possible values are **short**, **medium**, **long**, and **full**.
javascriptTooltip	boolean	false	Indicates whether or not to use JavaScript to generate tooltips.

language	String		The language to use. The default language is the browser's default language.
startDate	Date	1492-10-12	The first available date
staticDisplay	boolean	false	Whether or not only the dates in the current month can be viewed and selected
toggleDuration	integer	100	The toggle duration in milliseconds
toggleType	String	plain	The toggle type for the dropdown. Possible values are **plain**, **wipe**, **explode**, and **fade**.
type	String	date	Whether this widget will be rendered as a date picker or a time picker. Allowed values are **date** and **time**.
valueNotifyTopics	String		Comma delimited topics that will be published when a value is selected.
weekStartsOn	integer	0	The first day of the week. 0 is Sunday and 6 is Saturday.

Table 27.6: datetimepicker tag attributes

The **datetimepicker** tag inherits the common specified in Chapter 5, "Form Tags."

The acceptable date and time patterns for the **displayFormat** attribute can be found here:

```
http://www.unicode.org/reports/tr35/tr35-4.html#Date_Format_Patterns
```

The **adjustWeeks** attribute plays an important role in the display. If the value of **adjustWeeks** is false, there are always six rows for each month. For example, in Figure 27.2 the picker on the left is displaying January 2008 and has its **adjustWeeks** attribute set to false. The one on the right, on the other hand, has its **adjustWeeks** attribute set to true and, as a result, the second week of February 2008 is not shown.

Figure 27.2: Different values of adjustWeeks

For instance, the following is an example of the **datetimepicker** tag.

```
<sx:datetimepicker
       adjustWeeks="true"
       displayFormat="MM/dd/yyyy"
       toggleType="explode" />
```

You can view the example by directing your browser to this URL.

```
http://localhost:8080/app27a/DateTimePicker.action
```

The tabbedpanel Tag

The **tabbedpanel** tag renders a tabbed panel like the one in Figure 27.3. It can contain as many panels as you want and each panel may be closable.

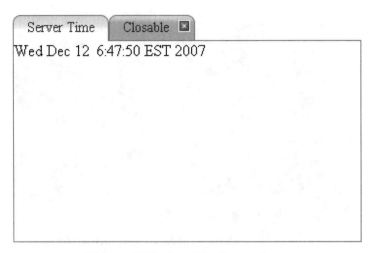

Figure 27.3: A tabbed panel

The attributes of the **tabbedpanel** tag are shown in Table 27.7.

Name	Data Type	Default Value	Description
afterNotifyTopics	String		Comma delimited topics to be published after the request, if the request is successful.
ajaxAfterValidation	boolean	false	Indicates whether or not to make an asynchronous request if validation succeeds. This attribute will only take effect if the validate attribute is set to true.
beforeNotifyTopics	String		Comma delimited topics to be published before the request.
errorNotifyTopics	String		Comma delimited topics to be published after the request, if the request fails.
errorText	String		The text to be displayed if the request fails.
executeScripts	boolean	false	Indicates whether or not JavaScript code in the fetched content should be executed.
formFilter	String		The function to be used to filter the form fields.

formId	String		The identifier of the form whose fields will be passed as request parameters.
handler	String		The JavaScript function that will make the request.
highlightColor	String		The color to highlight the elements specified in the **targets** attribute.
highlightDuration	integer	2000	The duration in milliseconds the elements specified in the **targets** attribute will be highlighted. This attribute will only take effect if the **hightlightColor** attribute has a value.
href	String		The URL to call to fetch the content.
indicator	String		The identifier of the element that will be displayed while making the request.
javascriptTooltip	boolean	false	Indicates whether or not to use JavaScript to generate tooltips.
listenTopics	String		The topics that will trigger the remote call.
loadingText	String	Loading…	The text to display while content is being fetched.
notifyTopics	String		Comma delimited topics to be published before and after the request and upon an error occurring.
parseContent	boolean	true	Whether or not to parse the returned content for widgets.
separateScripts	boolean	true	Whether or not to run the script in a separate scope that is unique for each tag.
showErrorTransportText	boolean	true	Whether or not errors will be shown.
showLoadingText	boolean	false	Whether or not loading text will be shown on targets

targets	String		Comma delimited identifiers of the elements whose content will be updated
transport	String	XMLHttp Transport	The transport for making the request
validate	boolean	false	Whether or not AJAX validation should be performed

Table 27.7: tabbedpanel tag attributes

The **tabbedpanel** tag also inherits the common attributes specified in Chapter 5, "Form Tags." In addition, the **id** attribute is mandatory for **tabbedpanel**.

For example, the following **tabbedpanel** tag contains two div elements as its panels.

```
<sx:tabbedpanel id="test">
    <sx:div label="Server Time" cssStyle="height:200px"
           href="ServerTime.action">
        Server Time
    </sx:div>
    <sx:div label="Closable" closable="true">
        This pane can be closed.
    </sx:div>
</sx:tabbedpanel>
```

To view the example in **app27a**, use this URL:

```
http://localhost:8080/app27a/TabbedPanel.action
```

The textarea Tag

The **textarea** tag renders a sophisticated text editor. Figure 27.4 shows the **textarea** tag used in a blog application.

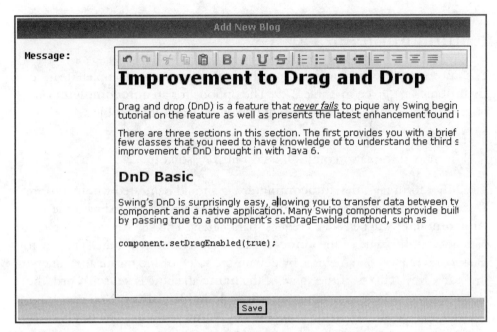

Figure 27.4: The textarea tag

In addition to the common attributes discussed in Chapter 5, "Form Tags," the **textarea** tag adds three more attributes, which are given in Table 27.8.

Name	Data Type	Default Value	Description
cols	integer		The cols attribute of the rendered textarea
rows	integer		The rows attribute of the rendered textarea
wrap	boolean	false	The wrap attribute of the rendered textarea

Table 27.8: textarea tag attributes

Test the example in **app27a** by directing your browser here:

```
http://localhost:8080/app27a/TextArea.action
```

The autocompleter Tag

The **autocompleter** tag renders a combo box with an auto-complete feature. Its attributes are given in Table 27.9. The options for an **autocompleter** can be assigned to its **list** attribute or sent dynamically as a JSON object.

Note
For more information on JSON, visit http://json.org.

Like other form tags, the **autocompleter** tag should be nested within a form. When the user submits the form, two key/value pairs associated with the **autocompleter** will be sent as request parameters. The key for the first request parameter is the value of the **autocompleter** tag's **name** attribute. The key for the second request parameter is by default the value of the **name** attribute plus the suffix **Key**. That is, if the value of the **name** attribute is **searchWord**, the key of the second request parameter will be **searchWordKey**. You can override the second key name using the **keyName** attribute. The **keyName** attribute is the one that should be mapped with an action property. Its value will be the value of the selected option.

The attributes for **autocompleter** are given in Table 27.9.

Name	Data Type	Default Value	Description
afterNotifyTopics	String		Comma delimited topics to be published after the request, if the request is successful.
autoComplete			
beforeNotifyTopics	String		Comma delimited topics to be published before the request.
dataFieldName	String	value in the name attribute	The name of the field in the returned JSON object that contains the data array
delay	integer	100	The delay in milliseconds before making the search
dropdownHeight	integer	120	The height of the dropdown in pixels
dropdownWidth	integer	the same as the textbox	The width of the dropdown in pixels

emptyOption	boolean	false	Whether or not to insert an empty option
errorNotifyTopics	String		Comma delimited topics to be published after the request, if the request fails.
forceValidOption	boolean	false	Whether or not only an included option can be selected
formFilter	String		The function to be used to filter the form fields.
formId	String		The identifier of the form whose fields will be passed as request parameters.
headerKey	String		The key for the first item in the list
headerValue	String		The value for the first item in the list
href	String		The URL to call to fetch the content.
iconPath	String		Path to the icon used for the dropdown
indicator	String		The identifier of the element that will be displayed while making the request.
javascriptTooltip	boolean	false	Indicates whether or not to use JavaScript to generate tooltips.
keyName	String		The property to which the selected key will be assigned.
list	String		An iterable source to populate from
listKey	String		The property of the object in the list that will supply the option values
listValue	String		The property of the object in the list that will supply the option labels
listenTopics	String		The topics that will trigger the remote call.
loadMinimumCount	integer	3	The minimum number of characters that must be entered to the textbox before options will be loaded

loadOnTextChange	boolean	true	Whether or not to reload options every time a character is entered to the texbox
maxlength	integer		Corresponds to the HTML maxlength attribute
notifyTopics	String		Comma delimited topics to be published before and after the request and upon an error occurring.
preload	boolean	true	Whether or not to reload options when the page loads
resultsLimit	integer	30	The maximum number of options. -1 indicates no limit.
searchType	String	startstring	Search type, possible values are **startstring**, **startword**, and **substring**.
showDownArrow	boolean	true	Whether or not to show the down arrow
transport	String	XMLHttp Transport	The transport for making the request
valueNotifyTopics	String		Comma delimited topics that will be published when a value is selected

Table 27.9: autocompleter tag attributes

The **autocompleter** tag also inherits the common specified in Chapter 5, "Form Tags."

Three examples illustrate the use of **autocompleter**. All examples use the **AutoCompleterSupport** class in Listing 27.5.

Listing 27.5: The AutoCompleterSupport class

```
package app27a;
import java.util.ArrayList;
import java.util.List;
import com.opensymphony.xwork2.ActionSupport;

public class AutoCompleterSupport extends ActionSupport {
    private static List<String> carMakes = new ArrayList<String>();
    private String carMakeKey;
    static {
        carMakes.add("Acura");
```

```
            carMakes.add("Audi");
            carMakes.add("BMW");
            carMakes.add("Chrysler");
            carMakes.add("Ford");
            carMakes.add("GM");
            carMakes.add("Honda");
            carMakes.add("Hyundai");
            carMakes.add("Infiniti");
            carMakes.add("Kia");
            carMakes.add("Lexus");
            carMakes.add("Toyota");
        }
    public List<String> getCarMakes() {
            return carMakes;
        }
    public String getCarMakeKey() {
            return carMakeKey;
        }
    public void setCarMakeKey(String carMakeKey) {
            this.carMakeKey = carMakeKey;
        }
}
```

There are two properties in the **AutoCompleterSupport** class, **carMakes** and **carMakeKey**. The **carMakes** property returns a list of car makes and is used to populate an **autocompleter**. The **carMakeKey** property is used to receive user selection.

Example 1

This example shows how you can populate an **autocompleter** by assigning a **List** to its **list** attribute. The JSP in Listing 27.6 shows the **autocompleter** tag.

Listing 27.6: The AutoCompleter1.jsp page

```
<%@ taglib prefix="s" uri="/struts-tags" %>
<%@ taglib prefix="sx" uri="/struts-dojo-tags" %>
<html>
<head>
<title>Auto Completer</title>
<sx:head/>
</head>
<body>
<s:form action="ShowSelection" theme="simple">
```

```
        <sx:autocompleter name="carMake" list="carMakes"/>
        <s:submit/>
</s:form>
</body>
</html>
```

You can test this example by directing your browser to this URL:

```
http://localhost:8080/app27a/AutoCompleter1.action
```

Figure 27.5 shows the **autocompleter** tag rendered.

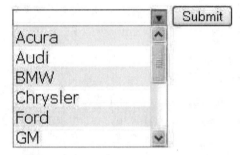

Figure 27.5: The car make list

When the containing form is submitted, the selected option will be sent as the request parameter **carMakeKey**.

Example 2

This example shows how to populate an **autocompleter** by assigning a JSON object. The location of the server that returns the object must be assigned to its href attribute and, for security reasons, it must be the same location as the origin of the page.

The **AutoCompleter2.jsp** page in Listing 27.7 shows the tag.

Listing 27.7: The AutoCompleter2.jsp page

```
<%@ taglib prefix="s" uri="/struts-tags" %>
<%@ taglib prefix="sx" uri="/struts-dojo-tags" %>
<html>
<head>
<title>Auto Completer</title>
<sx:head/>
```

```
</head>
<body>
<s:form action="ShowSelection" theme="simple">
    <sx:autocompleter name="carMake" href="CarMakesAsJSON1.action"/>
    <s:submit/>
</s:form>
</body>
</html>
```

Note that the **href** attribute of the **autocompleter** tag is assigned
CarMakesAsJSON1.action. This action forwards to the
CarMakesAsJSON1.jsp page in Listing 27.8 and sends a JSON object in the
following format:

```
[
    ['key-1','value-1'],
    ['key-2','value-2'],

    ...

    ['key-n','value-n']
]
```

Listing 27.8: CarMakesAsJSON1.jsp page

```
<%@ taglib prefix="s" uri="/struts-tags" %>
[
<s:iterator value="carMakes" status="status">
        ['<s:property/>','<s:property/>']
        <s:if test="!#status.last">,</s:if>
</s:iterator>
]
```

Test this example by directing your browser here.

```
http://localhost:8080/app27a/AutoCompleter2.action
```

Example 3

This example is similar to Example 2 and the JSP is shown in Listing 27.9.

Listing 27.9: The AutoCompleter3.jsp page

```
<%@ taglib prefix="s" uri="/struts-tags" %>
<%@ taglib prefix="sx" uri="/struts-dojo-tags" %>
<html>
<head>
```

```
<title>Auto Completer</title>
<sx:head/>
</head>
<body>
<s:form action="ShowSelection" theme="simple">
    <sx:autocompleter
      name="carMake"
      dataFieldName="make"
      href="CarMakesAsJSON2.action"/>
    <s:submit/>
</s:form>
</body>
</html>
```

The difference between this one and Example 2 is the format of the JSON object. For this example, the JSON object contains a property (**make**) that contains the list of options to display. The format of the JSON object is as follows.

```
{
    "make" : {
        'key-1':'value-1',
        'key-2':'value-2',

        ...

        'key-n':'value-n'
    }
}
```

You use the **dataFieldName** attribute to tell the **autocompleter** the name of the JSON object's property that contains the options.

Listing 27.10 shows the JSP that formats the options as a JSON object.

Listing 27.10: CarMakesAsJSON2.jsp page

```
<%@ taglib prefix="s" uri="/struts-tags" %>
{
    "make" : {
        <s:iterator value="carMakes" status="status">
            '<s:property/>':'<s:property/>'
            <s:if test="!#status.last">,</s:if>
        </s:iterator>
    }
}
```

To test this example, direct your browser to this URL.

```
http://localhost:8080/app27a/AutoCompleter3.action
```

The tree and treenode Tags

The **tree** tag renders a Dojo tree. It may contain **treenode** tags or it can obtain children dynamically. The attributes of the **tree** tag are given in Table 27.10 and those of the **treenode** tag in Table 27.11.

Name	Data Type	Default Value	Description
blankIconSrc	String		The source for the blank icon
childCollectionProperty	String		The name of the property that returns a collection of child nodes
collapsedNotifyTopics	String		Comma separated topics to be published when a node is collapsed
errorNotifyTopics	String		Comma delimited topics to be published after the request, if the request fails.
expandIconSrcMinus	String		The source for the expand icon
expandIconSrcPlus	String		The source for the expand icon
expandedNotifyTopics	String		Comma delimited topics to be published when a node is expanded
gridIconSrcC	String		Image source for under child item child icons
gridIconSrcL	String		Image source for the last child grid
gridIconSrcP	String		Image source for under parent item child icons
gridIconSrcV	String		Image source for vertical line
gridIconSrcX	String		Image source for grid for sole root item
gridIconSrcY	String		Image source for grid for last root item
href	String		The URL to call to fetch the content.
iconHeight	String	18px	The icon height
iconWidth	String	19px	The icon width
javascriptTooltip	boolean	false	Indicates whether or not to use JavaScript to generate tooltips.

nodeIdProperty			The name of the property whose value is to be used as the node id
nodeTitleProperty			The name of the property whose value is to be used as the node title
openTemplate	String		The template to use for opening the rendered HTML
rootNode	String		The name of the property whose value is to be used as the root
selectedNotifyTopics	String		Comma delimited topics to be published when a node is selected. An object with a property named **node** will be passed to the subscribers.
showGrid	boolean	true	Whether or not to show the grid
showRootGrid	boolean	true	The showRootGrid property
toggle	String	fade	The toggle property. Possible values are **fade** or **explode**.
toggleDuration	integer	150	Toggle duration in milliseconds

Table 27.10: tree tag attributes

The **tree** tag also inherits the common attributes specified in Chapter 5, "Form Tags."

Name	Data Type	Default Value	Description
javascriptTooltip	boolean	false	Indicates whether or not to use JavaScript to generate tooltips.
openTemplate	String		The template to use for opening the rendered HTML

Table 27.11: treenode tag attributes

Example 1

This example shows how to build a tree statically, by adding all nodes to the page. This is a simple example that is pretty much self-explanatory. The **Tree1.jsp** page in Listing 27.11 shows the **tree** and **treenode** tags used for the tree.

Listing 27.11: The Tree1.jsp page

```
<%@ taglib prefix="sx" uri="/struts-dojo-tags" %>
<html>
<head>
<title>Tree</title>
<sx:head debug="true"/>
</head>
<body>
<sx:tree id="root" label="Root">
   <sx:treenode id="F1" label="F1" />
   <sx:treenode id="F2" label="F2">
       <sx:treenode id="F2a" label="F2a" />
       <sx:treenode id="F2b" label="F2b" />
   </sx:treenode>
   <sx:treenode id="F3" label="F3" />
</sx:tree>
</body>
</html>
```

To test the example, direct your browser to this URL.

```
http://localhost:8080/app27a/Tree1.action
```

You'll see the tree like the one in Figure 27.6.

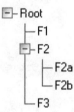

Figure 27.6: A static tree

Example 2

This example shows how you can construct a tree dynamically. At minimum, the **tree** tag must have the following attributes: **rootNode**, **nodeTitleProperty**, **nodeIdProperty**, **childCollectionProperty**. In addition, you must also create a model object to back up your view.

The **Tree2** action, the action for this example, is associated with the **TreeSupport** action class in Listing 27.12. The class provides the **rootNode** property that maps to the **rootNode** attribute of the **tree** tag.

Listing 27.12: TreeSupport action class

```
package app27a;
import com.opensymphony.xwork2.ActionSupport;
public class TreeSupport extends ActionSupport {
    public Node getRootNode() {
        return new Node("root", "ROOT");
    }
}
```

In this example, a tree node is represented by a Node object. The Node class is shown in Listing 27.13. It is a simple JavaBean class with three properties, **id**, **title**, and **children**. The children property returns the children for the tree node. A static counter is used so that it does not loop indefinitely.

Listing 27.13: The Node class

```
package app27a;
import java.util.ArrayList;
import java.util.List;
public class Node {
    private String id;
    private String title;
    public Node() {
    }
    public Node(String id, String title) {
        this.id = id;
        this.title = title;
    }
    // getters and setters not shown

    public static int counter = 1;
    public List getChildren() {
        List<Node> children = new ArrayList();
        if (counter < 5) {
            Node child = new Node("node" + counter,
                    "Generation " + counter);
            children.add(child);
            counter++;
        }
        return children;
    }
}
```

```
}
```

The **Tree2.jsp** in Listing 27.14 shows the JSP with a **tree** tag used to construct a tree dynamically. The **tree** tag also has its **selectedNotifyTopics** assigned a **nodeSelected** topic to indicate to Dojo that selecting a node must publish the topic. A JavaScript function subscribes to the topic.

Listing 27.14: The Tree2.jsp page

```jsp
<%@ taglib prefix="sx" uri="/struts-dojo-tags" %>
<html>
<head>
<title>Tree</title>
<sx:head debug="true"/>
<script type="text/javascript">
dojo.event.topic.subscribe("nodeSelected", function(source) {
    var selectedNode = source.node;
    alert("You selected node " + selectedNode.title);
});
</script>
</head>
<body>
<sx:tree rootNode="rootNode"
        nodeTitleProperty="title"
        nodeIdProperty="id"
        childCollectionProperty="children"
        selectedNotifyTopics="nodeSelected"
    >
</sx:tree>
</body>
</html>
```

The JavaScript function in Tree2.jsp will be executed every time a node is selected. It will receive a JavaScript object that has a node property. In the example, the function simply prints the node title.

To test the example, direct your browser here.

```
http://localhost:8080/app27a/Tree2.action
```

The constructed tree is shown in Figure 27.7. Click a node and you'll see an alert box displaying the node title.

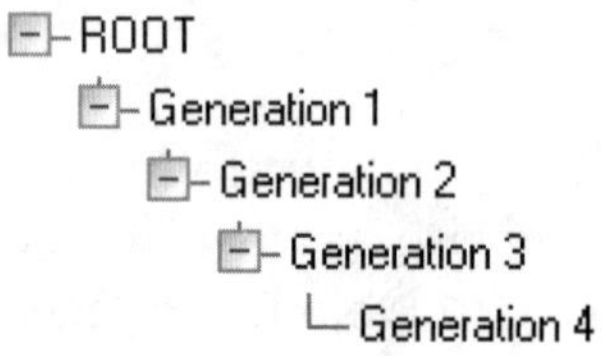

```
⊟- ROOT
   ⊟- Generation 1
      ⊟- Generation 2
         ⊟- Generation 3
            └─ Generation 4
```

Figure 27.7: A dynamic tree

Summary

Struts comes with a plug-in that provides custom tags to construct AJAX components. This plug-in, the Struts Dojo plug-in, is part of Struts 2.1 and later and is based on Dojo 0.4. This chapter showed how you can use the tags.

Appendix A
Struts Configuration

The two main configuration files in a Struts application are the **struts.xml** and the **struts.properties** files. The former registers interceptors and result types as well as maps action with action classes and results. The latter specifies other aspects of the application, such as the default theme and whether or not the application is in development mode. This appendix is a complete guide to writing the two configuration files.

The struts.xml File

A **struts.xml** file always contains this **DOCTYPE** element, which indicates that it complies with the type definitions specified in the **struts-2.0.dtd** file.

```
<!DOCTYPE struts PUBLIC
    "-//Apache Software Foundation//DTD Struts Configuration 2.0//EN"
    "http://struts.apache.org/dtds/struts-2.0.dtd">
```

The root element of a **struts.xml** file is **struts**. This section explains elements that may appear under the **struts** element, either directly or indirectly. The following elements can be direct sub-elements of **<struts>**.

- package
- include
- bean
- constant

The action Element

An **action** element is nested within a **package** element and represents an action. Its attributes are listed in Table A.1. Note that the name attribute is required.

Attribute	Description
name*	The action name.
class	The action class associated with this action.
method	The action method.
converter	The converter for this action.

Table A.1: action element attributes

An action may or may not specify an action class. Therefore, an **action** element may be as simple as this.

```
<action name="MyAction">
```

An action that does not specify an action class will be given an instance of the default action class.

If an action has a non-default action class, however, you must specify the fully class name using the **class** attribute. In addition, you must also specify the name of the action method, which is the method in the action class that will be executed when the action is invoked. Here is an example.

```
<action name="Address_save" class="app.Address" method="save">
```

If the **class** attribute is present but the **method** attribute is not, **execute** is assumed for the method name. In other words, the following **action** elements mean the same thing.

```
<action name="Employee_save" class="app.Employee" method="execute">
```

```
<action name="Employee_save" class="app.Employee">
```

The bean Element

Use this element to instruct Struts either to create a bean or have a bean's static methods available for use by the application. The attributes that may appear in this element are listed in Table A.2. Only **class**, indicated by an asterisk, is required.

Attribute	Description
class*	The Java class to be instantiated or whose static methods to be made available.
type	The primary interface the Java class implements.
name	A unique name for referring to this bean.
scope	The bean scope. Allowable values are **default, singleton, request, session**, and **thread**.
static	Indicates whether or not to inject static methods.
optional	Indicates whether or not the bean is optional.

Table A.2: bean element attributes

The following is an example of **<bean>**.

```
<bean name="uniqueBean" type="MyInterface" class="MyBeanClass"/>
```

The constant Element

The **constant** element is used to override a value in the **default.properties** file. By using a constant element, you may not need to create a **struts.properties** file. The attributes for this element are given in Table A.3. Both the **name** and **value** attributes are required.

Attribute	Description
name*	The name of the constant.
value*	The value of the constant.

Table A.3: constant element attributes

For example, the **struts.devMode** setting determines whether or not the Struts application is in development mode. By default, the value is **false**, meaning the application is not in development mode. The following **constant** element sets **struts.devMode** to **true**.

```
<constant name="struts.devMode" value="true"/>
```

The default-action-ref Element

This element must appear under a **package** element and specifies the default action that will be invoked if no matching for a URI is found for that package. It has a **name** attribute that specifies the default action. For example, this

default-action-ref element indicates that the **Main** action should be invoked for any URI with no matching action.

```
<default-action-ref name="Main"/>
```

The default-interceptor-ref Element

This element must appear under a package element and specifies the default interceptor or interceptor stack to be used for an action in that package that does not specify any interceptor. The name attribute is used to specify an interceptor or interceptor stack. For example, the **struts-default** package in the **struts-default.xml** file defines the following **default-interceptor-ref** element.

```
<default-interceptor-ref name="defaultStack"/>
```

The exception-mapping Element

An **exception-mapping** element must appear under an **action** element or the **global-exception-mappings** element. It allows you to catch any exception you don't catch in the action class associated with the action. The attributes of the exception-mapping element are shown in Table A.4.

Attribute	Description
name	The name for this mapping.
exception*	Specifies the exception type to be caught.
result*	Specifies a result that will be executed if an exception is caught. The result may be in the same action or in the global-results element.

Table A.4: exception-mapping element attributes

You can nest one or more **exception-mapping** elements under your action declaration. For example, the following **exception-mapping** element catches all exceptions thrown by the **User_save** action and executes the **error** result.

```
<action name="User_save" class="...">
    <exception-mapping exception="java.lang.Exception"
            result="error"/>
    <result name="error">/jsp/Error.jsp</result>
    <result>/jsp/Thanks.jsp</result>
</action>
```

The global-exception-mappings Element

A **global-exception-mappings** element must appear under a **package** element and allows you to declare **exception-mappings** elements to catch exceptions not caught in an action class or by using a class-level **exception-mapping** element. Any **exception-mapping** declared under the **global-exception-mappings** element must refer to a result in the **global-results** element. Here is an example of **global-exception-mappings**.

```
<global-results>
    <result name="error">/jsp/Error.jsp</result>
    <result name="sqlError">/jsp/SQLError.jsp</result>
</global-results>
<global-exception-mappings>
    <exception-mapping exception="java.sql.SQLException"
            result="sqlError"/>
    <exception-mapping exception="java.lang.Exception"
            result="error"/>
</global-exception-mappings>
```

The Exception interceptor handles all exceptions caught. For each exception caught, the interceptor adds these two objects to the Value Stack.

- **exception**, that represents the **Exception** object thrown
- **exceptionStack**, that contains the value from the stack trace

See Chapter 3, "Actions and Results" to learn how to handle these objects.

The global-results Element

A **global-results** element must appear under a **package** element and specifies global results that will be executed if an action cannot find a result locally. For example, the following **global-results** element specifies two result elements.

```
<global-results>
    <result name="error">/jsp/Error.jsp</result>
    <result name="sqlError">/jsp/SQLError.jsp</result>
</global-results>
```

The include Element

A large application may have many packages. In order to make the **struts.xml** file easier to manage for a large application, you can divide it into smaller files and use **include** elements to reference the files. Each file would ideally include a package or related packages and is referred to by using the **include** element's **file** attribute. An include element must appear directly under **<struts>**.

For example, the following are examples of **include** elements.

```
<struts>
    <include file="module-1.xml" />
    <include file="module-2.xml" />
    ...
    <include file="module-n.xml" />
</struts>
```

Each **module.xml** file would have the same DOCTYPE element and a **struts** root element. Here is an example:

```
<?xml version="1.0" encoding="UTF-8"?>
<!DOCTYPE struts PUBLIC
    "-//Apache Software Foundation//DTD Struts Configuration 2.0//EN"
    "http://struts.apache.org/dtds/struts-2.0.dtd">

<!-- file module-n.xml -->
<struts>
    <package name="test" extends="struts-default">
        <action name="Test1" class="test.Test1Action">
            <result>/jsp/Result1.jsp</result>
        </action>
        <action name="Test2" class="test.Test2Action">
            <result>/ajax/Result2.jsp</result>
        </action>
    </package>
</struts>
```

The interceptor Element

The **interceptor** element must appear under an **interceptors** element. An **interceptor** element registers an interceptor for the package under which the **interceptors** element is declared. The attributes for this element are given in Table A.5. Both attributes are required.

Attribute	Description
name*	The name to refer to the interceptor.
class*	The Java class for this interceptor.

Table A.5: interceptor element attributes

For instance, the following interceptor element registers the File Upload interceptor.

```
<interceptor name="fileUpload"
      class="org.apache.struts.interceptor.FileUploadInterceptor"/>
```

The interceptor-ref Element

This element is used to reference a registered interceptor and can appear either under an **interceptor-stack** element or an **action** element. If it appears under an **interceptor-stack** element, the **interceptor-ref** element specifies an interceptor that will become part of the interceptor stack. If it appears under an **action** element, it specifies an interceptor that will be used to process the action.

You use its **name** attribute to refer to a registered interceptor. For instance, the following configuration registers four interceptors and applies them to the **Product_save** action.

```
<package name="main" extends="struts-default">
    <interceptors>
        <interceptor name="alias" class="..."/>
        <interceptor name="i18n" class="..."/>
        <interceptor name="validation" class="..."/>
        <interceptor name="logger" class="..."/>
    </interceptors>

    <action name="Product_save" class="...">
        <interceptor-ref name="alias"/>
        <interceptor-ref name="i18n"/>
        <interceptor-ref name="validation"/>
        <interceptor-ref name="logger"/>
        <result name="input">/jsp/Product.jsp</result>
        <result>/jsp/ProductDetails.jsp</result>
    </action>
</package>
```

The interceptor-stack Element

With most Struts application having multiple **action** elements, repeating the list of interceptors for each action can be a daunting task. In order to alleviate this problem, Struts allows you to create interceptor stacks that group interceptors. Instead of referencing interceptors from within each **action** element, you can reference the interceptor stack instead.

For instance, six interceptors are often used in the following orders: **exception**, **servletConfig**, **prepare**, **checkbox**, **params**, and **conversionError**. Rather than referencing them again and again in your action declarations, you can create an interceptor stack like this:

```
<interceptor-stack name="basicStack">
    <interceptor-ref name="exception"/>
    <interceptor-ref name="servlet-config"/>
    <interceptor-ref name="prepare"/>
    <interceptor-ref name="checkbox"/>
    <interceptor-ref name="params"/>
    <interceptor-ref name="conversionError"/>
</interceptor-stack>
```

To use these interceptors, you just need to reference the stack:

```
<action name="..." class="...">
    <interceptor-ref name="basicStack"/>
    <result name="input">/jsp/Product.jsp</result>
    <result>/jsp/ProductDetails.jsp</result>
</action>
```

The interceptors Element

An **interceptors** element must appear directly under a **package** element and registers interceptors for that package. For example, the following **interceptors** element registers two interceptors, **validation** and **logger**.

```
<package name="main" extends="struts-default">
    <interceptors>
        <interceptor name="validation" class="..."/>
        <interceptor name="logger" class="..."/>
    </interceptors>
</package>
```

The package Element

For the sake of modularity, Struts actions are grouped into packages, which can be thought of as modules. A **struts.xml** file can have one or many **package** elements. The attributes for this element are given in Table A6.

Attribute	Description
name*	The package name that must be unique throughout the **struts.xml** file.
extends	The parent package extended by this package.
namespace	The namespace for this package.
abstract	Indicates whether or not this is an abstract package.

Table A.6: package element attributes

A **package** element must specify a **name** attribute and its value must be unique throughout the **struts.xml** file. It may also specify a **namespace** attribute. If **namespace** is not present, the default value "/" will be assumed. If the **namespace** attribute has a non-default value, the namespace must be added to the URI that invokes the actions in the package. For example, the URI for invoking an action in a package with a default namespace is this:

```
/context/actionName.action
```

To invoke an action in a package with a non-default namespace, you need this URI:

```
/context/namespace/actionName.action
```

A **package** element almost always extends the **struts-default** package defined in **struts-default.xml**. The latter is the default configuration file included in the Struts core JAR and defines the standard interceptors and result types. A package that extends **struts-default** can use the interceptors and result types without re-registering them. The content of the **struts-default.xml** file is given in the next section.

The param Element

The **param** element can be nested within another element such as **action**, **result-type**, and **interceptor** to pass a value to the enclosing object. The **param** element has a **name** attribute that specifies the name of the parameter. The format is as follows:

```
<param name="property">value</param>
```

Used within an **action** element, **param** can be used to set an action property. For example, the following **param** element sets the **siteId** property of the action.

```
<action name="customer" class="...">
    <param name="siteId">california01</param>
</action>
```

And the following **param** element sets the **excludeMethod** of the validation **interceptor-ref**:

```
<interceptor-ref name="validation">
    <param name="excludeMethods">input,back,cancel</param>
</interceptor-ref>
```

The result Element

A **result** element may appear under an **action** element or a **global-results** element. It specifies a result for an action.

A **result** element corresponds to the return value of an action method. Because an action method may return different values for different situations, an **action** element may have several **result** elements, each of which corresponds to a possible return value of the action method. This is to say, if a method may return "success" and "input," you must have two **result** elements. The attributes for this element are listed in Table A.7.

Attribute	Description
name	The result name, associated with the action method's return value.
type	The registered result type associated with this result.

Table A.7: result element attributes

For instance, the following **action** element contains two **result** elements.

```
<action name="Product_save" class="app.Product" method="save">
    <result name="success" type="dispatcher">
        /jsp/Confirm.jsp
    </result>
    <result name="input" type="dispatcher">
        /jsp/Product.jsp
    </result>
```

```
</action>
```

The result-type Element

This element registers a result type for a package and must appear directly under a **result-types** element. The attributes for this element are given in Table A.8.

Attribute	Description
name	The name to refer to this result type.
class	The Java class for this result type.
default	Specifies whether or not this is the default result type for the package.

Table A.8: result-type element attributes

For instance, these two **result-type** elements register the Dispatcher and FreeMarket result types in the **struts-default** package. Note that the **default** attribute of the first **result-type** element is set to true.

```
<result-type name="dispatcher" default="true" class="org.apache.
       ➥struts2.dispatcher.ServletDispatcherResult"/>
<result-type name="freemarker" class="org.apache.struts2.views.
       ➥freemarker.FreemarkerResult"/>
```

The result-types Element

This element groups **result-type** elements and must appear directly under a **package** element. For example, this result-types element groups three result types.

```
<result-types>
    <result-type name="chain" class="..."/>
    <result-type name="dispatcher" class="..." default="true"/>
    <result-type name="freemarker" class="..."/>
</result-types>
```

The struts-default.xml File

The **struts-default.xml** file is the default configuration file included in the Struts core JAR and defines the standard interceptors and result types. A package that extends **struts-default** can use the interceptors and result types without re-registering them. This file is shown in Listing A.1.

Listing A.1: The struts-default.xml file

```
<?xml version="1.0" encoding="UTF-8" ?>
<!DOCTYPE struts PUBLIC
  "-//Apache Software Foundation//DTD Struts Configuration 2.0//EN"
  "http://struts.apache.org/dtds/struts-2.0.dtd">

<struts>
    <package name="struts-default">
        <result-types>
            <result-type name="chain" class="com.opensymphony.
                xwork2.ActionChainResult"/>
            <result-type name="dispatcher" class="org.apache.
                struts2.dispatcher.ServletDispatcherResult"
                default="true"/>
            <result-type name="freemarker" class="org.apache.
                struts2.views.freemarker.FreemarkerResult"/>
            <result-type name="httpheader" class="org.apache.
                struts2.dispatcher.HttpHeaderResult"/>
            <result-type name="redirect" class="org.apache.struts2.
                dispatcher.ServletRedirectResult"/>
            <result-type name="redirect-action" class="org.apache.
                struts2.dispatcher.ServletActionRedirectResult"/>
            <result-type name="stream" class="org.apache.struts2.
                dispatcher.StreamResult"/>
            <result-type name="velocity" class="org.apache.struts2.
                dispatcher.VelocityResult"/>
            <result-type name="xslt" class="org.apache.struts2.
                views.xslt.XSLTResult"/>
            <result-type name="plaintext" class="org.apache.struts2.
                dispatcher.PlainTextResult"/>
        </result-types>

        <interceptors>
            <interceptor name="alias" class="com.opensymphony.
                xwork2.interceptor.AliasInterceptor"/>
            <interceptor name="autowiring" class="com.opensymphony.
```

```
➡xwork2.spring.interceptor.
➡ActionAutowiringInterceptor"/>
<interceptor name="chain" class="com.opensymphony.
➡xwork2.interceptor.ChainingInterceptor"/>
<interceptor name="conversionError" class="org.apache.
➡struts2.interceptor.
➡StrutsConversionErrorInterceptor"/>
<interceptor name="createSession" class="org.apache.
➡struts2.interceptor.CreateSessionInterceptor"/>
<interceptor name="debugging" class="org.apache.struts2.
➡interceptor.debugging.DebuggingInterceptor"/>
<interceptor name="external-ref" class="com.
➡opensymphony.xwork2.interceptor.
➡ExternalReferencesInterceptor"/>
<interceptor name="execAndWait" class="org.apache.
➡struts2.interceptor.ExecuteAndWaitInterceptor"/>
<interceptor name="exception" class="com.opensymphony.
➡xwork2.interceptor.ExceptionMappingInterceptor"/>
<interceptor name="fileUpload" class="org.apache.
➡struts2.interceptor.FileUploadInterceptor"/>
<interceptor name="i18n" class="com.opensymphony.xwork2.
➡interceptor.I18nInterceptor"/>
<interceptor name="logger" class="com.opensymphony.
➡xwork2.interceptor.LoggingInterceptor"/>
<interceptor name="model-driven" class="com.
➡opensymphony.xwork2.interceptor.
➡ModelDrivenInterceptor"/>
<interceptor name="scoped-model-driven" class="com.
➡opensymphony.xwork2.interceptor.
➡ScopedModelDrivenInterceptor"/>
<interceptor name="params" class="com.opensymphony.
➡xwork2.interceptor.ParametersInterceptor"/>
<interceptor name="prepare" class="com.opensymphony.
➡xwork2.interceptor.PrepareInterceptor"/>
<interceptor name="static-params" class="com.
➡opensymphony.xwork2.interceptor.
➡StaticParametersInterceptor"/>
<interceptor name="scope" class="org.apache.struts2.
➡interceptor.ScopeInterceptor"/>
<interceptor name="servlet-config" class="org.apache.
➡struts2.interceptor.ServletConfigInterceptor"/>
<interceptor name="sessionAutowiring" class="org.apache.
➡struts2.spring.interceptor.
➡SessionContextAutowiringInterceptor"/>
<interceptor name="timer" class="com.opensymphony.
➡xwork2.interceptor.TimerInterceptor"/>
```

```
<interceptor name="token" class="org.apache.struts2.
   ➡interceptor.TokenInterceptor"/>
<interceptor name="token-session" class="org.apache.
   ➡struts2.interceptor.
   ➡TokenSessionStoreInterceptor"/>
<interceptor name="validation" class="com.opensymphony.
   ➡xwork2.validator.ValidationInterceptor"/>
<interceptor name="workflow" class="com.opensymphony.
   ➡xwork2.interceptor.DefaultWorkflowInterceptor"/>
<interceptor name="store" class="org.apache.struts2.
   ➡interceptor.MessageStoreInterceptor"/>
<interceptor name="checkbox" class="org.apache.struts2.
   ➡interceptor.CheckboxInterceptor"/>
<interceptor name="profiling" class="org.apache.struts2.
   ➡interceptor.ProfilingActivationInterceptor"/>

<!-- Basic stack -->
<interceptor-stack name="basicStack">
    <interceptor-ref name="exception"/>
    <interceptor-ref name="servlet-config"/>
    <interceptor-ref name="prepare"/>
    <interceptor-ref name="checkbox"/>
    <interceptor-ref name="params"/>
    <interceptor-ref name="conversionError"/>
</interceptor-stack>

<!-- Sample validation and workflow stack -->
<interceptor-stack name="validationWorkflowStack">
    <interceptor-ref name="basicStack"/>
    <interceptor-ref name="validation"/>
    <interceptor-ref name="workflow"/>
</interceptor-stack>

<!-- Sample file upload stack -->
<interceptor-stack name="fileUploadStack">
    <interceptor-ref name="fileUpload"/>
    <interceptor-ref name="basicStack"/>
</interceptor-stack>

<!-- Sample model-driven stack  -->
<interceptor-stack name="modelDrivenStack">
    <interceptor-ref name="model-driven"/>
    <interceptor-ref name="basicStack"/>
</interceptor-stack>

<!-- Sample action chaining stack -->
```

```
<interceptor-stack name="chainStack">
    <interceptor-ref name="chain"/>
    <interceptor-ref name="basicStack"/>
</interceptor-stack>

<!-- Sample i18n stack -->
<interceptor-stack name="i18nStack">
    <interceptor-ref name="i18n"/>
    <interceptor-ref name="basicStack"/>
</interceptor-stack>

<!-- An example of the params-prepare-params trick. This
    stack is exactly the same as the defaultStack,
    except that it \includes one extra interceptor
    before the prepare interceptor: the params
    interceptor.

    This is useful for when you wish to apply
    parameters directly to an object that you wish to
    load externally (such as a DAO or database or
    service layer), but can't load that object until at
    least the ID parameter has been loaded. By loading
    the parameters twice, you can retrieve the object
    in the prepare() method, allowing the second params
    interceptor to apply the values on the object. -->
<interceptor-stack name="paramsPrepareParamsStack">
    <interceptor-ref name="exception"/>
    <interceptor-ref name="alias"/>
    <interceptor-ref name="params"/>
    <interceptor-ref name="servlet-config"/>
    <interceptor-ref name="prepare"/>
    <interceptor-ref name="i18n"/>
    <interceptor-ref name="chain"/>
    <interceptor-ref name="model-driven"/>
    <interceptor-ref name="fileUpload"/>
    <interceptor-ref name="checkbox"/>
    <interceptor-ref name="static-params"/>
    <interceptor-ref name="params"/>
    <interceptor-ref name="conversionError"/>
    <interceptor-ref name="validation">
        <param name="excludeMethods">
            input,back,cancel
        </param>
    </interceptor-ref>
    <interceptor-ref name="workflow">
        <param name="excludeMethods">
```

```
                    input,back,cancel
                </param>
            </interceptor-ref>
        </interceptor-stack>

        <!-- A complete stack with all the common interceptors
             in place.
             Generally, this stack should be the one you use,
             though it may do more than you need. Also, the
             ordering can be switched around (ex: if you wish to
             have your servlet-related objects applied before
             prepare() is called, you'd need to move servlet-
             config interceptor up.

             This stack also excludes from the normal validation
             and workflow the method names input, back, and
             cancel. These typically are associated with
             requests that should not be validated. -->
        <interceptor-stack name="defaultStack">
            <interceptor-ref name="exception"/>
            <interceptor-ref name="alias"/>
            <interceptor-ref name="servlet-config"/>
            <interceptor-ref name="prepare"/>
            <interceptor-ref name="i18n"/>
            <interceptor-ref name="chain"/>
            <interceptor-ref name="debugging"/>
            <interceptor-ref name="profiling"/>
            <interceptor-ref name="scoped-model-driven"/>
            <interceptor-ref name="model-driven"/>
            <interceptor-ref name="fileUpload"/>
            <interceptor-ref name="checkbox"/>
            <interceptor-ref name="static-params"/>
            <interceptor-ref name="params"/>
            <interceptor-ref name="conversionError"/>
            <interceptor-ref name="validation">
                <param name="excludeMethods">
                    input,back,cancel,browse
                </param>
            </interceptor-ref>
            <interceptor-ref name="workflow">
                <param name="excludeMethods">
                    input,back,cancel,browse
                </param>
            </interceptor-ref>
        </interceptor-stack>
```

```
<!-- The completeStack is here for backwards
     compatibility for applications that still refer to
     the defaultStack by the old name -->
<interceptor-stack name="completeStack">
    <interceptor-ref name="defaultStack"/>
</interceptor-stack>

<!-- Sample execute and wait stack.
     Note: execAndWait should always be the *last*
     interceptor. -->
<interceptor-stack name="executeAndWaitStack">
    <interceptor-ref name="execAndWait">
        <param name="excludeMethods">
            input,back,cancel
        </param>
    </interceptor-ref>
    <interceptor-ref name="defaultStack"/>
    <interceptor-ref name="execAndWait">
        <param name="excludeMethods">
            input,back,cancel
        </param>
    </interceptor-ref>
</interceptor-stack>
</interceptors>

<default-interceptor-ref name="defaultStack"/>
</package>
</struts>
```

The struts.properties File

You may have a **struts.properties** file in the WEB-INF/classes file to override configuration settings defined in the **default.properties** file.

The keys and default values, if any, are explained below.

```
struts.i18n.encoding = UTF-8
```
Struts default encoding.

```
struts.objectFactory
```
The default object factory. The value must be a subclass of **com.opensymphony.xwork2.ObjectFactory**. A short-hand notation, such as **spring** that represents **SpringObjectFactory**, is supported.

`struts.objectFactory.spring.autoWire = name`
> The auto-wiring logic when using the **SpringObjectFactory**. Valid values are **name** (the default), **type**, **auto**, and **constructor**.

`struts.objectFactory.spring.useClassCache = true`
> Indicates to the Struts-Spring integration module if Class instances should be cached.

`struts.objectTypeDeterminer`
> Specifies the object type determiner. The value must be an implementation of **com.opensymphony.xwork2.util.ObjectTypeDeterminer**. Shorthand notations such as tiger or notiger are supported.

`struts.multipart.parser=jakarta`
> Specifies the parser to handle multipart/form-data requests in file upload.

`struts.multipart.saveDir`
> The default save directory for file upload. The default value is the directory indicated by **javax.servlet.context.tempdir**.

`struts.multipart.maxSize = 2097152`
> The maximum size for uploaded files.

`struts.custom.properties`
> The list of custom properties files that must be loaded.

`struts.mapper.class`
> The action mapper to handle how request URLs are mapped to and from actions. The default value is **org.apache.struts2.dispatcher.mapper.DefaultActionMapper**.

`struts.action.extension = action`
> A comma separated list of action extensions.

`struts.serve.static = true`
> Indicates whether or not Struts should serve static content from inside its JAR. A value of false indicates that the static content must be available at **<contextPath>/struts**.

`struts.serve.static.browserCache = true`
> Indicates if the filter dispatcher should write out headers for static contents that will be cached by web browsers. A value of true is suitable for development mode. This key will be ignored if struts.serve.static is false.

`struts.enable.DynamicMethodInvocation = true`
> Indicates if dynamic method invocation is enabled. The default value is true, but for security reasons its value should be false. Dynamic method invocation is discussed in Chapter 2.

`struts.enable.SlashesInActionNames = false`
> Indicates if slashes are allowed in action names.

`struts.tag.altSyntax = true`
> Indicates if the alternative expression evaluation syntax that requires %{ ... } is allowed.

`struts.devMode = false`
> Indicates if development mode should be enabled. When the value is true, Struts will reload the application struts.xml file, validation files, and resource bundles on every request, which means you do not need to reload the application if any of these files changes. In addition, a value of true will raise the level of debug or ignorable problems to errors. For example, in development mode a form field with no matching action property will throw an exception. In production mode, it will be ignored.

`struts.ui.theme = xhtml`
> The default theme.

`struts.ui.templateDir = template`
> The default location for templates.

`struts.ui.templateSuffix = ftl`
> The default template type. Other values in addition to ftl (FreeMarker) are vm (Velocity) and jsp (JSP).

`struts.configuration.xml.reload=false`
> Indicates if struts.xml should be reloaded if it has been changed.

`struts.velocity.configfile = velocity.properties`
> The default Velocity configuration file.

`struts.velocity.contexts`
> A comma separated list of VelocityContext class names to chain to the StrutsVelocityContext.

`struts.velocity.toolboxlocation`
> The location of the Velocity toolbox.

`struts.url.http.port = 80`
> The HTTP port number to be used when building URLs.

Appendix A: Struts Configuration

`struts.url.https.port = 443`
>   The HTTPS port number to be used when building URLs.

`struts.custom.i18n.resources`
>   The load custom default resource bundles.

`struts.dispatcher.parametersWorkaround = false`
>   Indicates if workaround for applications that don't handle
>   HttpServletRequest.getParameterMap() should be enabled.

`struts.freemarker.manager.classname`
>   The FreeMarker Manager class to be used. It must be a child of
>   org.apache.struts2.views.freemarker.FreemarkerManager.

`struts.xslt.nocache = false`
>   Specifies if the XSLTResult class should use stylesheet caching.

`struts.configuration.files = struts-default.xml,struts-`
`➡plugin.xml,struts.xml`
>   The list of configuration files that should be loaded automatically.

`struts.mapper.alwaysSelectFullNamespace=false`

>   Indicates if Struts should select the namespace to be everything before
>   the last slash.

Appendix B
The JSP Expression Language

OGNL is the expression language used with the Struts custom tags. However, there are cases whereby the JSP Expression Language (EL) can help. For example, the JSP EL provides shorter syntax for printing a model object than what the **property** tag and OGNL offer. With the JSP EL, instead of this

```
<s:property value="serverValue"/>
```

You can simply write this.

```
${serverValue}
```

In addition, there's no easy way to use Struts custom tags to print a request header. With EL, it's easy. For instance, the following EL expression prints the value of the **host** header:

```
${header.host}
```

This appendix is a tutorial on the JSP EL.

The Expression Language Syntax

One of the most important features in JSP 2.0 is the expression language (EL). Inspired by both the ECMAScript and the XPath expression languages, the EL is designed to make it possible and easy to author script-free JSPs, that is, pages that do not use JSP declarations, expressions, and scriptlets.

The EL that was adopted into JSP 2.0 first appeared in the JSP Standard Tag Library (JSTL) 1.0 specification. JSP 1.2 programmers could use the language by importing the standard libraries into their applications. JSP 2.0 developers can use the EL without JSTL. However, JSTL also provides other libraries useful for JSP page authoring.

An EL expression starts with **${** and ends with **}**. The construct of an EL expression is as follows:

```
${expression}
```

For example, to write the expression **x+y**, you use the following construct:

```
${x+y}
```

It is also common to concatenate two expressions. A sequence of expressions will be evaluated from left to right, coerced to **String**s, and concatenated. If **a+b** equals **8** and **c+d** equals **10**, the following two expressions produce **810**:

```
${a+b}${c+d}
```

And **${a+b}some$c+d}** results in **8some10text**.

If an EL expression is used in an attribute value of a custom tag, the expression will be evaluated and the resulting string coerced to the attribute's expected type:

```
<my:tag someAttribute="${expression}"/>
```

The **${** sequence of characters denotes the beginning of an EL expression. If you want to send the literal **${** instead, you need to escape the first character: **\${**.

Reserved Words

The following words are reserved and must not be used as identifiers:

and	**eq**	**gt**	**true**	**instanceof**
or	**ne**	**le**	**false**	**empty**
not	**lt**	**ge**	**null**	**div**	**mod**

The [ ] and . Operators

The return type of an EL expression can be any type. If an EL expression results in an object that has a property, you can use the **[]** or **.** operators to access the property. The **[]** and **.** operators function similarly; **[]** is a more generalized form, but **.** provides a nice shortcut.

To access a scoped object's property, you use one of the following forms:

```
${object["propertyName"]}
${object.propertyName}
```

However, you can only use the first form (using the **[]** operator] if *propertyName* is not a valid Java variable name.

For instance, the following two EL expressions can be used to access the HTTP header **host** in the implicit object header.

```
${header["host"]}
${header.host}
```

However, to access the **accept-language** header, you can only use the **[]** operator because **accept-language** is not a legal Java variable name. Using the **.** operator to access it will throw an exception.

If an object's property happens to return another object that in turn has a property, you can use either **[]** or **.** to access the property of the second object. For example, the **pageContext** implicit object represents the **PageContext** object of the current JSP. It has the **request** property, which represents the **HttpServletRequest** object. The **HttpServletRequest** object has the **servletPath** property. The following expressions are equivalent and result in the value of the **servletPath** property of the **HttpServletRequest** object in **pageContext**:

```
${pageContext["request"]["servletPath"]}
${pageContext.request["servletPath"]}
${pageContext.request.servletPath}
${pageContext["request"].servletPath}
```

The Evaluation Rule

An EL expression is evaluated from left to right. For an expression of the form *expr-a[expr-b]*, here is how the EL expression is evaluated:

1. Evaluate *expr-a* to get *value-a*.
2. If *value-a* is **null**, return **null**.
3. Evaluate *expr-b* to get *value-b*.
4. If *value-b* is **null**, return **null**.
5. If the type of *value-a* is **java.util.Map**, check whether *value-b* is a key in the **Map**. If it is, return *value-a*.**get(***value-b***)**. If it is not, return **null**.

6. If the type of *value-a* is **java.util.List** or if it is an array, do the following:

   a. Coerce *value-b* to **int**. If coercion fails, throw an exception.

   b. If *value-a*.**get**(*value-b*) throws an **IndexOutOfBoundsException** or if Array.get(*value-a*, *value-b*) throws an ArrayIndexOutOfBoundsException, return null.

Otherwise, return *value-a*.**get**(*value-b*) if *value-a* is a **List**, or return **Array.get**(*value-a*, *value-b*) if *value-a* is an array.

7. If *value-a* is not a **Map**, a **List**, or an array, *value-a* must be a JavaBean. In this case, coerce *value-b* to **String**. If *value-b* is a readable property of *value-a*, call the getter of the property and return the value from the getter method. If the getter method throws an exception, the expression is invalid. Otherwise, the expression is invalid.

Accessing JavaBeans

You can use either the **.** operator or the **[]** operator to access a bean's property. Here are the constructs:

```
${beanName["propertyName"]}
${beanName.propertyName}
```

For example, to access the property called **secret** on a bean named **myBean**, you use the following expression:

```
${myBean.secret}
```

If the property is an object that in turn has a property, you can access the property of the second object too, again using the **.** or **[]** operator. Or, if the property is a **Map**, a **List**, or an array, you can use the same rule explained in the preceding section to access the **Map**'s values or the members of the **List** or the element of the array.

EL Implicit Objects

From a JSP, you can use JSP scripts to access JSP implicit objects. However, from a script-free JSP page, it is impossible to access these implicit objects. The EL allows you to access various objects by providing a set of its own implicit objects. The EL implicit objects are listed in Table B.1.

Object	Description
pageContext	The **javax.servlet.jsp.PageContext** object for the current JSP.
initParam	A **Map** containing all context initialization parameters with the parameter names as the keys.
param	A **Map** containing all request parameters with the parameters names as the keys. The value for each key is the first parameter value of the specified name. Therefore, if there are two request parameters with the same name, only the first can be retrieved using the **param** object. For accessing all parameter values that share the same name, use the **params** object instead.
paramValues	A **Map** containing all request parameters with the parameter names as the keys. The value for each key is an array of strings containing all the values for the specified parameter name. If the parameter has only one value, it still returns an array having one element.
header	A **Map** containing the request headers with the header names as the keys. The value for each key is the first header of the specified header name. In other words, if a header has more than one value, only the first value is returned. To obtain multi-value headers, use the **headerValues** object instead.
headerValues	A **Map** containing all request headers with the header names as the keys. The value for each key is an array of strings containing all the values for the specified header name. If the header has only one value, it returns a one-element array.
cookie	A **Map** containing all **Cookie** objects in the current request object. The cookies' names are the **Map**'s keys, and each key is mapped to a **Cookie** object.
applicationScope	A **Map** that contains all attributes in the **ServletContext** object with the attribute names as the keys.
sessionScope	A **Map** that contains all the attributes in the **HttpSession** object in which the attribute names are the keys.
requestScope	A **Map** that contains all the attributes in the current **HttpServletRequest** object with the attribute names as the keys.
pageScope	A **Map** that contains all attributes with the page scope. The attributes' names are the keys of the **Map**.

Table B.1: The EL Implicit Objects

Each of the implicit objects is given in the following subsections.

pageContext

The **pageContext** object represents the current JSP's **javax.servlet.jsp.PageContext** object. It contains all the other JSP implicit objects. These implicit objects are given in Table B.2.

Object	Type From the EL
request	javax.servlet.http.HttpServletRequest
response	javax.servlet.http.HttpServletResponse
out	javax.servlet.jsp.JspWriter
session	javax.servlet.http.HttpSession
application	javax.servlet.ServletContext
config	javax.servlet.ServletConfig
pageContext	javax.servlet.jsp.PageContext
page	javax.servlet.jsp.HttpJspPage
exception	java.lang.Throwable

Table B.2: JSP Implicit Objects

For example, you can obtain the current **ServletRequest** object using one of the following expressions:

```
${pageContext.request}
${pageContext["request"]}
```

And, the request method can be obtained using one of the following expressions:

```
${pageContext["request"]["method"]}
${pageContext["request"].method}
${pageContext.request["method"]}
${pageContext.request.method}
```

Request parameters are accessed more frequently than other implicit objects; therefore, two implicit objects, **param** and **paramValues**, are provided. The param and paramValues implicit objects are discussed in the sections "param" and "paramValues."

initParam

The **initParam** implicit object is used to retrieve the value of a context parameter. For example, to access the context parameter named password, you use the following expression:

```
${initParam.password}
```

or

```
${initParam["password"]
```

param

The **param** implicit object is used to retrieve a request parameter. This object represents a **Map** containing all the request parameters. For example, to retrieve the parameter called **userName**, use one of the following:

```
${param.userName}
${param["userName"]}
```

paramValues

You use the **paramValues** implicit object to retrieve the values of a request parameter. This object represents a **Map** containing all request parameters with the parameters' names as the keys. The value for each key is an array of strings containing all the values for the specified parameter name. If the parameter has only one value, it still returns an array having one element. For example, to obtain the first and second values of the **selectedOptions** parameter, you use the following expressions:

```
${paramValues.selectedOptions[0]}
${paramValues.selectedOptions[1]}
```

header

The **header** implicit object represents a **Map** that contains all request headers. To retrieve a header value, you use the header name as the key. For example, to retrieve the value of the **accept-language** header, use the following expression:

```
${header["accept-language"]}
```

If the header name is a valid Java variable name, such as **connection**, you can also use the . operator:

```
${header.connection}
```

headerValues

The **headerValues** implicit object represents a **Map** containing all request headers with the header names as the keys. Unlike **header**, however, the **Map** returned by the **headerValues** implicit object returns an array of strings. For example, to obtain the first value of the **accept-language** header, use this expression:

```
${headerValues["accept-language"][0]}
```

cookie

You use the **cookie** implicit object to retrieve a cookie. This object represents a **Map** containing all cookies in the current **HttpServletRequest** object. For example, to retrieve the value of a cookie called **jsessionid**, use the following expression:

```
${cookie.jsessionid.value}
```

To obtain the path value of the **jsessionid** cookie, use this:

```
${cookie.jsessionid.path}
```

applicationScope, sessionScope, requestScope, and pageScope

You use the **applicationScope** implicit object to obtain the value of an application-scoped variable. For example, if you have an application-scoped variable called **myVar**, you use this expression to access the attribute:

```
${applicationScope.myVar}
```

The **sessionScope**, **requestScope**, and **pageScope** implicit objects are similar to **applicationScope**. However, the scopes are session, request, and page, respectively.

Using Other EL Operators

In addition to the **.** and **[]** operators, the EL also provides several other operators: arithmetic operators, relational operators, logical operators, the conditional operator, and the **empty** operator. Using these operators, you can perform various operations. However, because the aim of the EL is to facilitate the authoring of script-free JSPs, these EL operators are of limited use, except for the conditional operator.

The EL operators are given in the following subsections.

Arithmetic Operators

There are five arithmetic operators:

- Addition (**+**)
- Subtraction (**-**)
- Multiplication (*****)
- Division (**/** and **div**)
- Remainder/modulo (**%** and **mod**)

The division and remainder operators have two forms, to be consistent with XPath and ECMAScript.

Note that an EL expression is evaluated from the highest to the lowest precedence, and then from left to right. The following are the arithmetic operators in the decreasing lower precedence:

```
* / div % mod
+ -
```

This means that *****, **/**, **div**, **%**, and **mod** operators have the same level of precedence, and **+** has the same precedence as **-** , but lower than the first group. Therefore, the expression

```
${1+2*3}
```

results in 7 and not 6.

Relational Operators

The following is the list of relational operators:

- equality (== and **eq**)
- non-equality (!= and **ne**)
- greater than (> and **gt**)
- greater than or equal to (>= and **ge**)
- less than (< and **lt**)
- less than or equal to (<= and **le**)

For instance, the expression **${3==4}** returns **false**, and **${"b"<"d"}** returns **true**.

Logical Operators

Here is the list of logical operators:

- AND (**&&** and **and**)
- OR (**||** and **or**)
- NOT (**!** and **not**)

The Conditional Operator

The EL conditional operator has the following syntax:

```
${statement? A:B}
```

If *statement* evaluates to **true**, the output of the expression is *A*. Otherwise, the output is *B*.

For example, you can use the following EL expression to test whether the **HttpSession** object contains the attribute called **loggedIn**. If the attribute is found, the string "You have logged in" is displayed. Otherwise, "You have not logged in" is displayed.

```
${(sessionScope.loggedIn==null)? "You have not logged in" :
  "You have logged in"}
```

The empty Operator

The **empty** operator is used to examine whether a value is **null** or empty. The following is an example of the use of the **empty** operator:

```
${empty X}
```

If *X* is **null** or if *X* is a zero-length string, the expression returns **true**. It also returns **true** if *X* is an empty **Map**, an empty array, or an empty collection. Otherwise, it returns **false**.

Configuring the EL in JSP 2.0 and Later Versions

With the EL, JavaBeans, and custom tags, it is now possible to write script-free JSPs. JSP 2.0 even provides a setting to disable scripting in all JSPs. Software architects can now enforce the writing of script-free JSPs.

On the other hand, in some circumstances you'll probably want to disable the EL in your applications. For example, you'll want to do so if you are using a JSP 2.0-compliant container but are not ready yet to upgrade to JSP 2.0. In this case, you can disable the evaluation of EL expressions.

This section discusses how to enforce script-free JSPs and how to disable the EL in JSP 2.0.

Achieving Script-Free JSPs

To disable scripting elements in JSPs, you use the **jsp-property-group** element with two subelements: **url-pattern** and **scripting-invalid**. The **url-pattern** element defines the URL pattern to which scripting disablement will apply. Here is how you disable scripting in all JSPs in an application:

```
<jsp-config>
  <jsp-property-group>
    <url-pattern>*.jsp</url-pattern>
    <scripting-invalid>true</scripting-invalid>
  </jsp-property-group>
```

```
</jsp-config>
```

Note

There can be only one **jsp-config** element in the deployment descriptor. If you have specified a **jsp-property-group** for deactivating the EL, you must write your **jsp-property-group** for disabling scripting under the same **jsp-config** element.

Deactivating the EL Evaluation

In some circumstances, such as when you need to deploy JSP 1.2 applications in a JSP 2.0 container, you may want to deactivate EL evaluation in a JSP. When you do so, an occurrence of the EL construct will not be evaluated as an EL expression. There are two ways to deactivate EL evaluation in a JSP.

First, you can set the **isELIgnored** attribute of the **page** directive to **true**, such as in the following:

```
<%@ page isELIgnored="true" %>
```

The default value of the **isELIgnored** attribute is **false**. Using the **isELIgnored** attribute is recommended if you want to deactivate EL evaluation in one or a few JSPs.

Second, you can use the **jsp-property-group** element in the deployment descriptor. The **jsp-property-group** element is a subelement of the **jsp-config** element. You use **jsp-property-group** to apply certain settings to a set of JSPs in the application.

To use the **jsp-property-group** element to deactivate the EL evaluation, you must have two subelements: **url-pattern** and **el-ignored**. The **url-pattern** element specifies the URL pattern to which the EL deactivation will apply. The **el-ignored** element must be set to **true**.

As an example, here is how you deactivate the EL evaluation in a JSP named **noEl.jsp**.

```
<jsp-config>
    <jsp-property-group>
        <url-pattern>/noEl.jsp</url-pattern>
        <el-ignored>true</el-ignored>
    </jsp-property-group>
</jsp-config>
```

You can also deactivate the EL evaluation in all the JSPs in an application by assigning ***.jsp** to the **url-pattern** element, as in the following:

```
<jsp-config>
    <jsp-property-group>
        <url-pattern>*.jsp</url-pattern>
        <el-ignored>true</el-ignored>
    </jsp-property-group>
</jsp-config>
```

The EL evaluation in a JSP will be deactivated if either the **isELIgnored** attribute of its **page** directive is set to **true** or its URL matches the pattern in the **jsp-property-group** element whose **el-ignored** subelement is set to **true**. For example, if you set the **page** directive's **isELIgnored** attribute of a JSP to **false** but its URL matches the pattern of JSPs whose EL evaluation must be deactivated in the deployment descriptor, the EL evaluation of that page will be deactivated.

In addition, if you use a deployment descriptor that is compliant to Servlet 2.3 or earlier, the EL evaluation is already disabled by default, even though you are using a JSP 2.0 container.

Summary

The EL is one of the most important features in JSP 2.0. It can help you write shorter and more effective JSPs, as well as helping you author script-free pages. In this chapter you have seen how to use the EL to access JavaBeans and implicit objects. Additionally, you have seen how to use EL operators. In the last section of this chapter, you learned how to use the application settings related to the EL in JSP 2.0 and later versions.

Appendix C
Annotations

A new feature in Java 5, annotations are notes in Java programs to instruct the Java compiler to do something. You can annotate any program elements, including Java packages, classes, constructors, fields, methods, parameters, and local variables. Java annotations are defined in JSR 175 (http://www.jcp.org/en/jsr/detail?id=175). Java 5 provided three standard annotations and four standard meta-annotations. Java 6 added dozens of others.

This appendix is for you if you are new to annotations. It tells you everything you need to know about annotations and annotation types. It starts with an overview of annotations, and then teaches you how to use the standard annotations in Java 5 and Java 6. It concludes with a discussion of custom annotations.

An Overview of Annotations

Annotations are notes for the Java compiler. When you annotate a program element in a source file, you add notes to the Java program elements in that source file. You can annotate Java packages, types (classes, interfaces, enumerated types), constructors, methods, fields, parameters, and local variables. For example, you can annotate a Java class so that any warnings that the **javac** program would otherwise issue be suppressed. Or, you can annotate a method that you want to override to get the compiler to verify that you are really overriding the method, not overloading it. Additionally, you can annotate a Java class with the name of the developer. In a large project, annotating every Java class can be useful for the project manager or architect to measure the productivity of the developers. For example, if all classes are annotated this way, it is easy to find out who is the most or the least productive programmer.

The Java compiler can be instructed to interpret annotations and discard them (so those annotations only live in source files) or include them in resulting Java classes. Those that are included in Java classes may be ignored by the Java virtual machine, or they may be loaded into the virtual machine. The latter type is called runtime-visible and you can use reflection to inquire about them.

Annotations and Annotation Types

When studying annotations, you will come across these two terms very often: annotations and annotation types. To understand their meanings, it is useful to first bear in mind that an annotation type is a special interface type. An annotation is an instance of an annotation type. Just like an interface, an annotation type has a name and members. The information contained in an annotation takes the form of key/value pairs. There can be zero or multiple pairs and each key has a specific type. It can be a **String**, **int**, or other Java types. Annotation types with no key/value pairs are called marker annotation types. Those with one key/value pair are often referred to single-value annotation types.

There are three annotation types in Java 5: **Deprecated**, **Override**, and **SuppressWarnings**. They are part of the **java.lang** package and you will learn to use them in the section "Built-in Annotations." On top of that, there are four other annotation types that are part of the **java.lang.annotation** package: **Documented**, **Inherited**, **Retention**, and **Target**. These four annotation types are used to annotate annotations, and you will learn about them in the section "Custom Annotation Types" later in this chapter. Java 6 adds many annotations of its own.

Annotation Syntax

In your code, you use an annotation differently from using an ordinary interface. You declare an annotation type by using this syntax.

```
@AnnotationType
```

or

```
@AnnotationType(elementValuePairs)
```

The first syntax is for marker annotation types and the second for single-value and multi-value types. It is legal to put white spaces between the at sign (@) and annotation type, but this is not recommended.

For example, here is how you use the marker annotation type **Deprecated**:

```
@Deprecated
```

And, this is how you use the second element for multi-value annotation type Author:

```
@Author(firstName="Ted",lastName="Diong")
```

There is an exception to this rule. If an annotation type has a single key/value pair and the name of the key is **value**, then you can omit the key from the bracket. Therefore, if the fictitious annotation type **Stage** has a single key named **value**, you can write

```
@Stage(value=1)
```

or

```
@Stage(1)
```

The Annotation Interface

Know that an annotation type is a Java interface. All annotation types are subinterfaces of the **java.lang.annotation.Annotation** interface. It has one method, **annotationType**, that returns an **java.lang.Class** object.

```
java.lang.Class<? extends Annotation> annotationType()
```

In addition, any implementation of **Annotation** will override the **equals**, **hashCode**, and **toString** methods from the **java.lang.Object** class. Here are their default implementations.

```
public boolean equals(Object object)
```
> Returns **true** if *object* is an instance of the same annotation type as this one and all members of *object* are equal to the corresponding members of this annotation.

```
public int hashCode()
```
> Returns the hash code of this annotation, which is the sum of the hash codes of its members

```
public String toString()
```
Returns a string representation of this annotation, which typically lists all the key/value pairs of this annotation.

You will use this class when learning custom annotation types later in this chapter.

Standard Annotations

Java 5 comes with three built-in annotations, all of which are in the **java.lang** package: **Override**, **Deprecated**, and **SuppressWarnings**. They are discussed in this section.

Override

Override is a marker annotation type that can be applied to a method to indicate to the compiler that the method overrides a method in a superclass. This annotation type guards the programmer against making a mistake when overriding a method.

For example, consider this class **Parent**:

```
class Parent {
    public float calculate(float a, float b) {
        return a * b;
    }
}
```

Suppose, you want to extend **Parent** and override its **calculate** method. Here is a subclass of **Parent**:

```
public class Child extends Parent {
    public int calculate(int a, int b) {
        return (a + 1) * b;
    }
}
```

The **Child** class compiles. However, the **calculate** method in **Child** does not override the method in **Parent** because it has a different signature, namely it returns and accepts **int**s instead of **float**s. In this example, a programming mistake like this is easy to spot because you can see both the **Parent** and

Child classes. However, you are not always this lucky. Sometimes the parent class is buried somewhere in another package. This seemingly trivial error could be fatal because when a client class calls the **calculate** method on an **Child** object and passes two floats, the method in the **Parent** class will be invoked and a wrong result will be returned.

Using the **Override** annotation type will prevent this kind of mistake. Whenever you want to override a method, declare the **Override** annotation type before the method:

```
public class Child extends Parent {
    @Override
    public int calculate(int a, int b) {
        return (a + 1) * b;
    }
}
```

This time, the compiler will generate a compile error and you'll be notified that the **calculate** method in **Child** is not overriding the method in the parent class.

It is clear that **@Override** is useful to make sure programmers override a method when they intend to override it, and not overload it.

Deprecated

Deprecated is a marker annotation type that can be applied to a method or a type (class/interface) to indicate that the method or type is deprecated. A deprecated method or type is marked so by the programmer to warn the users of his code that they should not use or override the method or use or extend the type. The reason why a method or a type is marked deprecated is usually because there is a better method or type and the method or type is retained in the current software version for backward compatibility.

For example, the **DeprecatedTest** class in Listing C.1 uses the **Deprecated** annotation type.

Listing C.1: Deprecating a method

```
public class DeprecatedTest {
    @Deprecated
    public void serve() {
    }
```

```
}
```

If you use or override a deprecated method, you will get a warning at compile time. For example, Listing C.2 shows the **DeprecatedTest2** class that uses the **serve** method in **DeprecatedTest**.

Listing C.2: Using a deprecated method

```
public class DeprecatedTest2 {
    public static void main(String[] args) {
        DeprecatedTest test = new DeprecatedTest();
        test.serve();
    }
}
```

Compiling **DeprecatedTest2** generates this warning:

```
Note: DeprecatedTest2.java uses or overrides a deprecated API.
Note: Recompile with -Xlint:deprecation for details.
```

On top of that, you can use **@Deprecated** to mark a class or an interface, as shown in Listing C.3.

Listing C.3: Marking a class deprecated

```
@Deprecated
public class DeprecatedTest3 {
    public void serve() {
    }
}
```

SuppressWarnings

SuppressWarnings is used, as you must have guessed, to suppress compiler warnings. You can apply **@SuppressWarnings** to types, constructors, methods, fields, parameters, and local variables.

You use it by passing a **String** array that contains warnings that need to be suppressed. Its syntax is as follows.

```
@SuppressWarnings(value={string-1, ..., string-n})
```

where *string-1* to *string-n* indicate the set of warnings to be suppressed. Duplicate and unrecognized warnings will be ignored.

The following are valid parameters to **@SuppressWarnings**:

- **unchecked**. Give more detail for unchecked conversion warnings that are mandated by the Java Language Specification.
- **path**. Warn about nonexistent path (classpath, sourcepath, etc) directories.
- **serial**. Warn about missing serialVersionUID definitions on serializable classes.
- **finally**. Warn about finally clauses that cannot complete normally.
- **fallthrough**. Check switch blocks for fall-through cases, namely cases, other than the last case in the block, whose code does not include a **break** statement, allowing code execution to "fall through" from that case to the next case. As an example, the code following the case 2 label in this **switch** block does not contain a **break** statement:

```
switch (i) {
case 1:
    System.out.println("1");
    break;
case 2:
    System.out.println("2");
    //  falling through
case 3:
    System.out.println("3");
}
```

As an example, the **SuppressWarningsTest** class in Listing C.4 uses the **SuppressWarnings** annotation type to prevent the compiler from issuing unchecked and fallthrough warnings.

Listing C.4 Using @SuppressWarnings

```
import java.io.File;
import java.io.Serializable;
import java.util.ArrayList;

@SuppressWarnings(value={"unchecked","serial"})
public class SuppressWarningsTest implements Serializable {
    public void openFile() {
        ArrayList a = new ArrayList();
        File file = new File("X:/java/doc.txt");
    }
}
```

Standard Meta-Annotations

Meta annotations are annotations that are applied to annotations. There are four meta-annotation types that come standard with Java 5 that are used to annotate annotations; they are **Documented, Inherited, Retention**, and **Target**. All the four are part of the **java.lang.annotation** package. This section discusses these annotation types.

Documented

Documented is a marker annotation type used to annotate the declaration of an annotation type so that instances of the annotation type will be included in the documentation generated using Javadoc or similar tools.

For example, the **Override** annotation type is not annotated using **Documented**. As a result, if you use Javadoc to generate a class whose method is annotated **@Override**, you will not see any trace of **@Override** in the resulting document.

For instance, Listing C.5 shows the **OverrideTest2** class that uses **@Override** to annotate the **toString** method.

Listing C.5: The OverrideTest2 class

```
public class OverrideTest2 {
    @Override
    public String toString() {
        return "OverrideTest2";
    }
}
```

On the other hand, the **Deprecated** annotation type is annotated **@Documented**. Recall that the **serve** method in the **DeprecatedTest** class in Listing C.2 is annotated **@Deprecated**. Now, if you use **Javadoc** to generate the documentation for **OverrideTest2**, the details of the **serve** method in the documentation will also include **@Deprecated**, like this:

```
serve
@Deprecated
public void serve()
```

Inherited

You use **Inherited** to annotate an annotation type so that any instance of the annotation type will be inherited. If you annotate a class using an inherited annotation type, the annotation will be inherited by any subclass of the annotated class. If the user queries the annotation type on a class declaration, and the class declaration has no annotation of this type, then the class's parent class will automatically be queried for the annotation type. This process will be repeated until an annotation of this type is found or the root class is reached.

Check out the section "Custom Annotation Types" on how to query an annotation type.

Retention

@Retention indicates how long annotations whose annotated types are annotated @Retention are to be retained. The value of **@Retention** can be one of the members of the **java.lang.annotation.RetentionPolicy** enum:

- **SOURCE**. Annotations are to be discarded by the Java compiler.
- **CLASS**. Annotations are to be recorded in the class file but not be retained by the JVM. This is the default value.
- **RUNTIME**. Annotations are to be retained by the JVM so you can query them using reflection.

For example, the declaration of the **SuppressWarnings** annotation type is annotated **@Retention** with the value of **SOURCE**.

```
@Retention(value=SOURCE)
public @interface SuppressWarnings
```

Target

Target indicates which program element(s) can be annotated using instances of the annotated annotation type. The value of **Target** is one of the members of the **java.lang.annotation.ElementType** enum:

- **ANNOTATION_TYPE**. The annotated annotation type can be used to annotate annotation type declaration.

- **CONSTRUCTOR**. The annotated annotation type can be used to annotate constructor declaration.
- **FIELD**. The annotated annotation type can be used to annotate field declaration.
- **LOCAL_VARIABLE**. The annotated annotation type can be used to annotate local variable declaration.
- **METHOD**. The annotated annotation type can be used to annotate method declaration.
- **PACKAGE**. The annotated annotation type can be used to annotate package declarations.
- **PARAMETER**. The annotated annotation type can be used to annotate parameter declarations.
- **TYPE**. The annotated annotation type can be used to annotate type declarations.

As an example, the **Override** annotation type declaration is annotated the following **Target** annotation, making **Override** can only be applied to method declarations.

```
@Target(value=METHOD)
```

You can have multiple values in the **Target** annotation. For example, this is from the declaration of **SuppressWarnings**:

```
@Target(value={TYPE,FIELD, METHOD, PARAMETER,CONSTRUCTOR,
LOCAL_VARIABLE})
```

Custom Annotation Types

An annotation type is a Java interface, except that you must add an at sign before the **interface** keyword when declaring it.

```
public @interface CustomAnnotation {
}
```

By default, all annotation types implicitly or explicitly extend the **java.lang.annotation.Annotation** interface. In addition, even though you can extend an annotation type, its subtype is not treated as an annotation type.

A Custom Annotation Type

As an example, Listing C.6 shows a custom annotation type called **Author**.

Listing C.6: The Author annotation type

```
import java.lang.annotation.Documented;
import java.lang.annotation.Retention;
import java.lang.annotation.RetentionPolicy;

@Documented
@Retention(RetentionPolicy.RUNTIME)
public @interface Author {
    String firstName();
    String lastName();
    boolean internalEmployee();
}
```

Using the Custom Annotation Type

The **Author** annotation type is like any other Java type. Once you import it into a class or an interface, you can use it simply by writing

```
@Author(firstName="firstName",lastName="lastName",
internalEmployee=true|false)
```

For example, the **Test1** class in Listing C.7 is annotated **Author**.

Listing C.7: A class annotated Author

```
@Author(firstName="John",lastName="Guddell",internalEmployee=true)
public class Test1 {
}
```

Is that it? Yes, that's it. Very simple, isn't it?

The next subsection "Using Reflection to Query Annotations" shows how the **Author** annotations can be of good use.

Using Reflection to Query Annotations

In Java 5, the **java.lang.Class** has a few methods related to annotations.

```
public <A extends java.lang.annotation.Annotation> A getAnnotation
    (Class<A> annotationClass)
```

Returns this element's annotation for the specified annotation type, if present. Otherwise, returns **null**.

```
public java.lang.annotation.Annotation[] getAnnotations()
```
Returns all annotations present on this class.

```
public boolean isAnnotation()
```
Returns **true** if this class is an annotation type.

```
public boolean isAnnotationPresent(Class<? extends
        java.lang.annotation.Annotation> annotationClass)
```
Indicates whether an annotation for the specified type is present on this class

The **com.brainysoftware.jdk5.app18.custom** package includes three test classes, **Test1**, **Test2**, and **Test3**, that are annotated Author. Listing C.8 shows a test class that employs reflection to query the test classes.

Listing C.8: Using reflection to query annotations

```
public class CustomAnnotationTest {
    public static void printClassInfo(Class c) {
        System.out.print(c.getName() + ". ");
        Author author = (Author) c.getAnnotation(Author.class);
        if (author != null) {
            System.out.println("Author:" + author.firstName()
                    + " " + author.lastName());
        } else {
            System.out.println("Author unknown");
        }
    }
    public static void main(String[] args) {
        CustomAnnotationTest.printClassInfo(Test1.class);
        CustomAnnotationTest.printClassInfo(Test2.class);
        CustomAnnotationTest.printClassInfo(Test3.class);
        CustomAnnotationTest.printClassInfo(
                CustomAnnotationTest.class);
    }
}
```

When run, you will see the following message in your console:

```
Test1. Author:John Guddell
Test2. Author:John Guddell
Test3. Author:Lesley Nielsen
CustomAnnotationTest. Author unknown
```

Index